Mastering Tort Law

CAROLINA ACADEMIC PRESS MASTERING SERIES
RUSSELL WEAVER, SERIES EDITOR

Mastering Administrative Law
William R. Andersen

Mastering Adoption Law and Policy
Cynthia Hawkins DeBose

Mastering Alternative Dispute Resolution
Kelly M. Feeley, James A. Sheehan

Mastering American Indian Law
Angelique Wambdi EagleWoman, Stacy L. Leeds

Mastering Appellate Advocacy and Process, Revised Printing
Donna C. Looper, George W. Kuney

Mastering Art Law
Herbert Lazerow

Mastering Bankruptcy
George W. Kuney

Mastering Civil Procedure, Second Edition
David Charles Hricik

Mastering Constitutional Law, Second Edition
John C. Knechtle, Christopher J. Roederer

Mastering Contract Law
Irma S. Russell, Barbara K. Bucholtz

Mastering Corporate Tax
Reginald Mombrun, Gail Levin Richmond, Felicia Branch

Mastering Corporations and Other Business Entities, Second Edition
Lee Harris

Mastering Criminal Law, Second Edition
Ellen S. Podgor, Peter J. Henning, Neil P. Cohen

Mastering Criminal Procedure, Volume 1:
The Investigative Stage, Second Edition
Peter J. Henning, Andrew Taslitz, Margaret L. Paris, Cynthia E. Jones, Ellen S. Podgor

Mastering Criminal Procedure, Volume 2:
The Adjudicatory Stage, Second Edition
Peter J. Henning, Andrew Taslitz, Margaret L. Paris, Cynthia E. Jones, Ellen S. Podgor

Mastering Elder Law, Second Edition
Ralph C. Brashier

Mastering Tort Law

Second Edition

Russell L. Weaver

PROFESSOR OF LAW & DISTINGUISHED UNIVERSITY SCHOLAR
UNIVERSITY OF LOUISVILLE, LOUIS D. BRANDEIS SCHOOL OF LAW

Edward C. Martin

PROFESSOR OF LAW
SAMFORD UNIVERSITY, CUMBERLAND SCHOOL OF LAW

Andrew R. Klein

PAUL E. BEAM PROFESSOR OF LAW &
CHIEF OF STAFF FOR THE OFFICE OF THE CHANCELLOR
INDIANA UNIVERSITY SCHOOL OF LAW — INDIANAPOLIS

Paul J. Zwier, II

PROFESSOR OF LAW
EMORY UNIVERSITY SCHOOL OF LAW

John H. Bauman

PROFESSOR OF LAW
SOUTH TEXAS COLLEGE OF LAW

CAROLINA ACADEMIC PRESS
Durham, North Carolina

Library of Congress Cataloging-in-Publication Data

Names: Weaver, Russell L., 1952- author.
Title: Mastering tort law / Russell L. Weaver [and four others].
Description: Second Edition. | Durham, North Carolina : Carolina Academic
   Press, [2016] | Series: Mastering series | Includes bibliographical
   references and index.
Identifiers: LCCN 2016027275 | ISBN 9781611634419 (alk. paper)
Subjects: LCSH: Torts--United States. | Liability (Law)--United States. |
   Damages--United States.
Classification: LCC KF1250 .M328 2016 | DDC 346.7303--dc23
LC record available at https://lccn.loc.gov/2016027275

Carolina Academic Press, LLC
700 Kent Street
Durham, North Carolina 27701
Telephone (919) 489-7486
Fax (919) 493-5668
www.cap-press.com

Printed in the United States of America

To Ben, Kate and Laurence, with love,
RLW

*To Susan with love, and to all of my current and former Torts students
who have made teaching this subject such a joy!*
ECM

To Diane, Timothy & Jason,
ARK

To my Torts students, and to Marlene with Love.
PJZ

To Kathee, and to Mary, Hannah and Clare,
JHB

Contents

Table of Cases

Table of Restatement References

Series Editor's Foreword

The Carolina Academic Press Mastering Series is designed to provide you with a tool that will enable you to easily and efficiently "master" the substance and content of law school courses. Throughout the series, the focus is on quality writing that makes legal concepts understandable. As a result, the series is designed to be easy to read and is not unduly cluttered with footnotes or cites to secondary sources.

In order to facilitate student mastery of topics, the Mastering Series includes a number of pedagogical features designed to improve learning and retention. At the beginning of each chapter, you will find a "Roadmap" that tells you about the chapter and provides you with a sense of the material that you will cover. A "Checkpoint" at the end of each chapter encourages you to stop and review the key concepts, reiterating what you have learned. Throughout the book, key terms are explained and emphasized. Finally, a "Master Checklist" at the end of each book reinforces what you have learned and helps you identify any areas that need review or further study.

We hope that you will enjoy studying with, and learning from, the Mastering Series.

Russell L. Weaver
Professor of Law & Distinguished University Scholar
University of Louisville, Louis D. Brandeis School of Law

Mastering Tort Law

Chapter 1

Introduction

Tort law has ancient roots in the common law as a system for providing compensation for those who suffer injury as the result of the wrongful conduct of another. These ancient roots have grown a bewildering tangle of modern branches, as the law has broadened its view of what constitutes both "wrongful" conduct and compensable injury. This second edition continues our effort to provide the student with a useful survey of the variety of tort claims normally studied in a first year torts course, and to explain clearly the legal doctrines applicable to each.

Tort law's origins connect it with criminal law, and indeed some of the same terms, such as "assault" and "battery," are still used in both tort law, as well as criminal law, today. The student should understand, however, that tort law has a different view of the significance of wrongful conduct than criminal law. While criminal law is often concerned with conduct that is morally wrong and seeks to punish it, tort law considers a wrong to involve the violation of the rights of another under circumstances that justify providing a remedy, usually monetary damages, to the injured party. For this reason, it is useful to consider the specific rights that tort law protects. These include rights in personal security and freedom from unwanted bodily injury, as well as rights to reputation, privacy, and emotional tranquility. They also include certain economic rights and rights in property. These rights can be violated not only by conduct that is intended to cause harm, but also conduct that is merely negligent, or that is wrongful merely because it inflicted injury.

This description should suggest the enormous scope of modern tort law and how difficult it can be to cover such a wide field in a single volume. The task can be made manageable, however, if the student understands how the general classifications of tort liability are usually laid out. Thus, this book begins by considering in turn the three basic types of conduct that can give rise to tort liability and the defenses that defendants can assert to avoid such liability. First is conduct that is intended by the actor to invade the rights of another, typically giving rise to an intentional tort. Second is conduct that falls below what the law considers to be a minimal standard of care, that is, negligent conduct. Finally, there is conduct that leads to liability simply because it causes harm, giving rise to what is referred to as strict liability. Additionally, there are some other important doctrines that govern how responsibility is allocated among multiple tortfeasors. Many torts courses will consider no more than these basic doctrines, which are most prominent in the familiar setting of harms (especially accidental harms) involving personal injury and damage to property.

The concluding chapters of this book also cover many additional areas of tort law that are often included in longer torts courses, including nuisance, defamation, privacy, as well as economic torts such as misrepresentation and unfair competition. This book, therefore, offers students a broad and understandable coverage of the basic framework of tort law today.

Chapter 2

Intentional Interference with Person or Property

Roadmap

- Understand the different bases of liability.
- Learn the definition of "intent."
- Distinguish between the application of intent for average adults and its application to children and others of diminished capacity.
- Be able to apply the "transferred intent" principle.
- Learn the individual elements of the intentional torts, including assault, battery, false imprisonment, intentional infliction of emotional distress, trespass to land, trespass to chattels, and conversion.

There are three bases (or categories) of liability in tort law: intent, negligence, and strict liability. This chapter will discuss the intentional torts. In subsequent chapters, we will examine negligence and strict liability. After we have examined all three categories of tort liability, we will also examine a few specialized topics such as nuisance, misrepresentation, defamation, and products liability, among others. Those additional topics do not involve new bases of liability; instead, they rely upon one (or more) of the three bases of liability. Nuisance and misrepresentation, for example, may be based on intent, negligence or strict liability. Defamation was once a strict liability tort, but now public figures must prove something like intent.

For purposes of comparison, it can be said that every area of law focuses primarily upon at least one of the three bases of liability: intent, negligence, or strict liability. Contract law, for example, is primarily a strict liability area. Criminal law requires intent for most crimes, although there are some negligent crimes, and even a few strict liability crimes, such as overtime parking. However, tort law is somewhat unique in that many of the specialized areas of tort law actually involve distinctly different tort causes of action, each with different requirements, depending upon whether the individual claim is based upon intent, negligence, or strict liability.

Since intent, negligence and strict liability are the only bases of liability, they are the building blocks for understanding all of tort law. Therefore, it is necessary to obtain a clear understanding of those bases of liability in order to understand torts. For this reason, it is appropriate to spend some time discussing the basic definitions and concepts of each of the three bases of liability. In this chapter we will begin by exploring the meaning of the word "intent."

I. Basic Definition

In tort law, the term "intent" assumes that an individual knows (i.e., understands) the consequences of his or her actions, and engages in conduct knowing that certain consequences will result. At this point in our discussion, in order to help illustrate how the concept of intent works, we will focus on the tort of "battery." For a battery, the defendant must have acted to bring about a harmful or offensive touching of another. The mere touching of another is not enough. That harmful or offensive touching must have been done with the necessary intent. Later in the chapter, we will examine other intentional torts.

In order for a battery to occur, the defendant must have acted "knowing" that the harmful or offensive touching would occur. This knowing is the critical difference between intentional torts, negligent torts, or no liability at all. For example, suppose that the defendant is at a rifle range practicing shooting a rifle. If the defendant sees another person at the range, aims the rifle at that person, and fires the rifle at that other person, the necessary intent is clearly met. The shooter *knows* that the bullet might strike the other person when the gun is pointed directly at that person and the trigger is pulled. If the bullet does subsequently strike the other person (thereby causing harm or at least offense), then there is a battery. The defendant has engaged in a purposeful act (whatever the shooter's personal motive in doing so may have been), and in such situations the defendant is said to have possessed the requisite intent for a battery. When that intent is also accompanied by the resulting harmful or offensive touching of the victim, then all of the requisite elements for the tort of "battery" have been established.

However, if we change the facts, our legal analysis may also change somewhat, along with the outcome of that analysis. For example, suppose that the defendant is simply shooting targets at a rifle range. Other shooters on the range go down the range to check targets. The defendant shooter does not watch what is going on but just continues shooting. While the other shooters are checking their targets, one of the bullets from the defendant's rifle ricochets off the target stand and hits one of the other people. In this situation, just as in the previous example, there clearly is a harmful or offensive touching because a bullet has hit one of the other shooters. The existence of this consequence alone, however, is not enough, by itself, to conclude that an intentional tort has been committed. There must also be intent. Here, while the defendant intended to pull the trigger (a volitional act), and therefore the defendant had the purpose to fire the gun (just as in the previous example), this "simple" form of intent may be insufficient to support a claim for battery. The defendant must also have had the purpose of shooting the victim, or at least the defendant must have had knowledge that such consequences were likely. That element is missing here.

As these two examples illustrate, proving that a defendant has acted with the requisite intent to support an intentional tort action can be quite challenging, depending upon the particular type of intent involved, as well as the specific intentional tort claim that is asserted. We will discuss the requisite type(s) of intent necessary for different intentional tort claims later in this chapter, but for now let's continue with our "battery" example. Sometimes, a finding of intent can be based upon the defendant's actual admission. For example, suppose that in the first situation (where the shooter pointed the gun and shot it directly at the victim), the shooter also simultaneously made the following statements: "I hate Victim. I'm going to shoot that dirty rotten scoundrel." Based on the shooter's own admissions, plus the fact that the defendant pointed the gun and fired it directly at the victim, a jury can easily conclude that the shooter "intended" to shoot the victim. This type of intent, sometimes referred to as "actual intent," can always be used to prove the requisite intent for a "battery," as well as most any other intentional tort.

In some instances, however, the jury may be allowed to "infer" (or "imply") the existence of intent, even though the plaintiff may be unable to prove that the defendant acted with any "actual intent" to commit a battery. For example, if the shooter appears to be aiming directly at the victim when discharging the gun, a reasonable jury might infer that the shooter intended to shoot the victim, even though that may not have been the shooter's "actual" intent. This type of intent is known as "implied intent," and in certain situations it may also be used to prove the requisite intent for the tort of "battery." On the other hand, as in the second situation presented, *supra*, where the defendant is simply inattentive, and the bullet ricochets off of a target and strikes the victim, a jury might (or might not) be willing to infer that the defendant "impliedly intended" to hit the victim. The facts in that scenario suggest that the shooter did not act with the purpose of bringing about the harmful or offensive touching of the bullet to the victim (i.e., "specific" intent), or that the shooter was even aware of the victim's presence near the target area. The plaintiff will, of course, allege that the defendant still knew that these consequences were substantially certain to occur (perhaps relying upon evidence as to the number and location of other shooters in the vicinity of the target area). If the jury believes the plaintiff's evidence, then plaintiff can still win the case for the intentional tort of "battery." If, however, the jury does not believe such proof, then the plaintiff will have to offer other additional evidence to establish "implied" intent, or else prove some other type of intent altogether.

Intent, as noted above, is only one of the bases of liability that can give rise to a claim. Negligence would be another possible claim in this second hypothetical, *supra*. While intent involves actions designed to purposely cause a result, or acting with knowledge that certain consequences will result, negligence involves the act of creating an unreasonable risk that injury will occur. In the second scenario discussed, *supra*, even though the shooter may not be liable for the intentional tort of "battery," (s)he was probably at least negligent. Firing a rifle is a dangerous activity, and a reasonable person likely would be careful and watch for others before firing at a rifle range when other persons might be present near the target area. Given that the shooter in our example failed to watch out for others, (s)he has created an unreasonable risk to others. As a result, the defendant was probably at least negligent, even if liability for the tort of "battery" cannot otherwise be established. (We will discuss the tort of "negligence" at length in Chapter 4, *infra*, but that tort is mentioned here merely to illustrate how it differs from the intentional tort of "battery.") In short, there is a difference between intent and negligence. Intent is acting for the purpose of bringing about a particular consequence or acting with knowledge that certain consequences are substantially certain to occur. Negligence is the creation of an unreasonable risk that an injury will occur.

One additional hypothetical needs to be considered in order to fully understand the basic elements of intent. Assume that the shooter is again at the rifle range, but is being very careful. The shooter checks the range and makes sure that no one is on the target range. Unknown to the shooter, however, there is another person who likes to sneak around the range in order to watch others shoot. This person goes behind the targets and hides in a place where he cannot be seen. While he is hiding there, our shooter fires a shot that misses the target and hits him. In this situation, the victim is unlikely to recover at all. First, the shooter did not act with the purpose of causing the harmful or offensive touching (i.e., the shooter had no "actual" or "specific" intent), and there are no facts showing that the shooter knew the touching would occur to a substantial certainty (i.e., the shooter had no "implied" intent). There likely would be, therefore, no intentional tort claim. Moreover, the victim is also unlikely to prevail on a negligence claim either, because the facts indicate that the shooter used all reasonable care while shooting the rifle. As a result, although a harmful or offensive touching occurred, there likely would be no successful tort claim against the shooter. There was no intent (so there would not be any intentional tort liability) and there was no negligence. (It was noted earlier that there is a third basis of liability for strict liability. That basis will be discussed later in this book. However, to avoid unnecessary confusion please accept for now that the above hypothetical would not give rise to a claim for strict liability.) There are several computer lessons on the basic topic of intent. *See* Intent One: The Use of Intent in Tort (CALI); Intent Two: Computer-Aided Intent Questions (CALI).

A. Intent and Motive Distinguished

One particular issue in the definition of intent requires additional discussion: the distinction between intent and an evil (or bad) state of mind that is often referred to as motive. Intent is a neutral concept that merely seeks to show that the defendant had the purpose of causing a particular result, or that the defendant committed acts knowing that certain consequences would likely occur. Motive, by contrast, focuses on the individual defendant's personal reasons or motivations for engaging in particular acts. These very different legal concepts also represent a significant distinction between intentional torts (which focus primarily upon the concept of "intent") and criminal law (which focuses primarily upon the concept of "motive.") Consider the previous example of the shooter who fires a rifle with the intent to hit another person. Intending to hit another with a bullet is clearly a sufficient intent for a battery (i.e., "specific" intent if not also "actual" intent). An evil or otherwise unlawful motive is not required for the tort of "battery," even though it may have been present in this case. However, proof of such a motive would still be required in order to convict the defendant for the crime of "battery."

The difficulty in distinguishing between the concepts of intent and motive in a typical tort case is more likely to be important when one person pulls a prank or practical joke on another. Even though the defendant may claim that (s)he did not possess an evil motive, and argue that (s)he "did not intend to harm the plaintiff," the fact that the defendant did intend the prank itself provides sufficient evidence of the requisite intent to support an action for intentional tort.

Consider an actual hypothetical situation where an individual wishes to commit a simple "prank" by pulling a chair out from under someone else just as that person is about to sit down. The usual intended result is that the victim of the joke lands on the floor and is embarrassed and everyone laughs. The victim of such a prank often simply responds by plotting a different prank to seek revenge against the jokester. If, however, the victim decided to sue the prankster in tort instead, the defendant's typical response would be that: "I did not intend to harm the plaintiff. I only meant my prank to be a joke and to be funny." This response, although an accurate statement of the defendant's motive, is legally insufficient as a response to the plaintiff's intentional tort claim. The legal definition of intent merely asks whether the defendant knew that the consequences were substantially certain to occur. Here, the defendant almost certainly knew that there was going to be contact between the plaintiff and the floor. In fact, the defendant purposefully "intended" this very contact to occur in order for the joke to be funny. That intent (i.e., "specific" intent) would be a sufficient basis for establishing an intentional tort. It is not necessary for the plaintiff to also prove that defendant had an evil motive. It is only necessary that the defendant know that the consequences that give rise to the alleged intentional tort were substantially certain to occur. Thus, as this example illustrates, many practical joke situations also give rise to at least potential intentional tort claims. *See also Garratt v. Dailey*, 279 P. 2d 1091 (Wash. 1955).

So, why do people usually not sue for such conduct, instead of merely retaliating with their own additional pranks against the practical joker? The answer is one of practicality. Most intentional torts do not require actual physical injury or harm to the victim in order to bring the action. However, the damages that can be recovered in the tort action are nevertheless still based on the severity of the injury suffered. Fortunately, with most practical jokes and pranks the plaintiff does not suffer any significant actual injury (apart from perhaps embarrassment); therefore, even if the plaintiff prevailed in a tort claim against the defendant, the plaintiff would not be able to recover a substantial judgment for the embarrassing joke. Moreover, most plaintiffs' lawyers would not be willing to take a case that did not offer at least a chance for a large damage recovery. In addition, most plaintiffs would not want to pay substantial legal fees in order to bring an action that would generate only a small award. As a result, the distinction between intent and motive does not arise on a regular basis.

B. Children and the Mentally Challenged

Children and defendants with less than full adult mental capacity present certain unique difficulties in regard to intentional torts. Some have argued that, since at least some state of mind requirement is necessary even for intent, children and those other persons with reduced mental capacity might not be liable for intentional torts. That, however, is not a definitive rule. As explained in the preceding discussion, *supra*, intentional torts only require that the defendant act for the purpose of causing a particular consequence or at least with knowledge that such consequences are substantially certain to occur. Since the victim of an intentional tort does not have to prove that the defendant acted with an evil motive in order to prevail, sometimes even children and others with reduced mental capacity can be shown to possess a minimally sufficient intent to satisfy the legal requirements for an intentional tort.

Consider the following example: a child throws a ball at another child, intending to strike the other child. The child may have thrown the ball to be funny or because the child wishes to retaliate for some perceived insult or harm, or for any number of other reasons. In intentional torts (unlike in criminal law) the child's personal motive in throwing the ball is completely irrelevant. If the ball strikes the other child and causes a harmful or offensive touching of that other child, the child who threw the ball can be held liable for the intentional tort of "battery," provided that the (s)he is shown to have acted with the required intent (i.e., with a volitional purpose to throw the ball and to cause it to strike the other child, for whatever reason). The fact that the child may have been motivated to throw the ball just to be funny, or in retaliation for some other wrong, is not a defense. The issue is simply whether the child intended to bring about the harmful or offensive touching by throwing the ball.

Of course, in order to commit an intentional tort, the child must not only have been capable of forming the required intent, (s)he must also have actually formed it. The simple fact that a child throws a ball and hits another child does not necessarily mean that the child who threw the ball actually intended to cause a harmful or offensive touching by such an action. Instead, that child merely may have intended for the other child to catch the ball. However, due to a lack of skill by either the throwing child or the catching child, the catching child may have been hit instead of simply catching the ball as intended. In such a situation, the throwing child may (or may not) have committed an intentional tort, depending upon the circumstances, as well as what the throwing child knew or understood as to the consequences that were substantially certain to occur from his or her mere act of throwing the ball at the other child. Whether this act would be negligent (as opposed to a battery) will be discussed in the Chapter 4, *infra*, on negligence.

As in the case of children, adults with reduced mental capacity can also be held liable for their intentional torts. Imagine, for example, that an adult with a mental illness believes that a nurse or aide is trying to harm the mentally ill adult as the nurse approaches to administer some medication. The mentally ill adult responds in defense by striking and injuring the nurse. The adult's action may constitute the intentional tort of "battery" if the mentally ill adult acted for the purpose of bringing about a harmful or offensive touching. The mere fact that the mentally ill adult believed that the nurse was an attacker does not necessarily defeat the tort, as long as the mentally ill adult was at least capable of understanding the purpose of his or her actions.

It should be noted with respect to both children and mentally challenged adults that the law of torts differs significantly from the criminal law in several important respects. For example, the criminal law recognizes a special defense for insanity, whereas tort law does not. If the insane person (or child) has sufficient mental capacity to act for the purpose of bringing about the desired consequences or if the insane person (or child) knows that such consequences are substantially certain to occur as a result of the allegedly tortious actions, then the required intent for an intentional tort is established.

Additionally, there is no absolute minimum age, below which children are presumptively incapable of formulating the requisite intent for an intentional tort. Each case must be determined on the basis of its own facts and circumstances. As long as it otherwise can be proven that a child has at least sufficient mental capacity to form the necessary intent, then liability for intentional torts can be imposed, regardless of the child's age. Thus, liability for the tort of "battery" has been imposed upon children even as young a few years old. Of course, at some point, infants and very young children are simply too young to form even the most basic type of intent of acting with the purpose of bringing about the desired consequences or of knowing that such consequences are substantially certain to occur as a result of their actions. Just as with mentally challenged adults who cannot form this most basic kind of intent, in cases involving such infants and very young children intentional tort liability cannot be established.

C. Transferred Intent

Sometimes questions arise in intentional tort situations as to whether the defendant possessed the required intent to commit the tort in question when an intended tort actually brings about an unintended tort, or when the defendant intends to commit a tort against one person but ultimately accomplishes that same tort against an unintended victim. For example, suppose that defendant throws a stick at a group of boys, intending only to frighten them (i.e., an assault). The stick misses the group of boys, but hits another child that the defendant did not see (i.e., a battery). Using only the rules of intentional torts that we have already discussed, the child who was hit with the stick would not be able to recover for an intentional tort, since the defendant did not have the purpose of hitting that child with the stick, and did not know that the child was substantially certain to be struck by the stick that was thrown.

The doctrine of "transferred intent" is important in resolving such situations. Although something of a legal fiction that was invented by early common law courts primarily to address these very types of situations, it was limited in its application only to the original common law writ of trespass torts which included: assault, battery, false imprisonment, trespass to land, and trespass to chattels. Under this doctrine, when the defendant intends to accomplish one of the intentional torts that was included within the original writ of trespass (i.e., an assault, battery, false imprisonment, trespass to land, or trespass to chattels), and nevertheless actually accomplishes a different one of those same trespass writ intentional torts, then the requisite intent will transfer from the intended tort to the tort actually committed. In the hypothetical referred to in the previous paragraph, transferred intent principles might apply to establish the defendant's requisite intent for the tort of "battery" against the child who was actually struck by the stick, even though the defendant child who threw the stick did not intend a battery upon that child. The defendant merely intended to frighten the group of boys and therefore intended to commit an assault upon them. However, the defendant actually hit another, unseen, child, which would have been a battery as to that child except that the defendant did not have any intent to commit such a tort. Using the doctrine of "transferred intent," the intent from the assault (actually intended by the defendant) may be transferred to the accomplished battery against the defendant's unintended victim.

It is important to reiterate that "transferred intent" at early common law and even still today *only* applies when intent is being transferred from and to one of the original five common law trespass writ torts of assault, battery, false imprisonment, trespass to land, or trespass to chattels. Although there are other intentional torts and, of course, other torts in general, the doctrine of "transferred intent" will not work with any other intentional torts.

II. Interference with the Person

A. Assault

Assault is one of the original common law writ of trespass intentional torts, and therefore it requires proof of intent. For this tort, the plaintiff must prove that the defendant intended to cause the *apprehension* of an immediate harmful or offensive touching. (Keep in mind, just as with the tort of "battery," that intent means that the defendant acted for the purpose of bringing about such apprehension or knew that such a consequence was substantially certain to occur.) The specific elements of this tort require the plaintiff to prove:

(1) intent;
(2) apprehension of immediate bodily contact by the plaintiff; and
(3) some overt act on the part of the defendant; and
(4) the present ability of the defendant to carry out that immediate bodily contact.

A successful action for assault requires proof of each of these elements.

The requirement of intent is what separates the tort of assault from other possible tort claims. Imagine, for example, that a pedestrian is crossing the street and is almost struck by an automobile. Unless the plaintiff could prove that the driver intended to hit the pedestrian or, at least, intended to cause the pedestrian the apprehension of being struck, there is no assault. It is more likely that the driver of the automobile was merely negligent. As a result, a suit for such injuries would have to be based in negligence rather than for the intentional tort of assault.

The requirement of "apprehension of immediate bodily contact" differentiates the tort of assault from the tort of "battery." Whereas battery requires an actual harmful or offensive *touching* of the plaintiff's person, the tort of assault requires only an *apprehension* of such a touching. This apprehension may occur when a defendant throws a rock at the plaintiff and the plaintiff manages to duck just before it narrowly misses the plaintiff. In such a scenario, there can be no battery, since the rock missed, but there is still the tort of "assault." Similarly, if the rock subsequently strikes the plaintiff (causing a harmful or offensive contact), despite the plaintiff's efforts of attempting to duck away from it, the defendant has now committed an assault, in addition also to the tort of battery as well.

The requirement of "apprehension" is not the same as "fear." Instead, it is more akin to the concept of "awareness." Thus, to be "apprehensive" of an imminent battery the plaintiff does not have to actually be "afraid" of a harmful or offensive touching. It is only necessary that the plaintiff anticipate that the defendant is about to make such a contact. Imagine, for example, that a famous boxer is enjoying an evening out with friends. A smaller, non-athletic person approaches the boxer and threatens to strike him with his or her fist. The smaller person may even swing a fist at the face of the boxer and try to hit the boxer. The boxer is likely not afraid of the other person at all. Nevertheless, an assault has still occurred. Even though the boxer was not in fear of being struck by the other person, the boxer was certainly still apprehensive that the other person was attempting to make a physical contact with him that, even if not harmful, was at least offensive under these circumstances.

The tort of "assault" also requires that there be some overt act on the part of the defendant. Usually, this requires some movement or conduct in addition to mere words of threat. This element appears to have its origin in the early common law. When the law was developing, available weapons involved sticks, stones and swords. In order to carry out a threatened battery, the defendant had to begin the process by picking up something like a stone or stick, or drawing a sword or knife. The requirement of an overt act was inserted in the law as a way of ensuring that the threat was *imminent*. Imagine, for example, an attacker of several hundred years ago saying that (s)he was going to strike the plaintiff with a stone. If the defendant had no stone in his or her hand, there was not much of a threat of an imminent battery. That threat would only develop when the defendant acted by actually picking up stones. However, if a defendant threatens to shoot the plaintiff with a gun, and points it directly at him or her, such an overt act may be sufficient by itself, regardless whether the gun was in fact loaded or otherwise actually capable of firing a bullet at the plaintiff. The overt act of pointing the gun at the plaintiff and threatening to shoot it is sufficient to create at least an "apprehension" by the plaintiff that the defendant intended to commit a battery as threatened by the overt act itself.

The final element of assault is that there must be proof of an immediate present ability to carry out the threat. In some ways, this element illustrates the need for an overt act. A defendant who threatens to strike the plaintiff with a stone, but who has no stone and makes no overt effort to get one, does not appear to have the present ability to carry out that threat. Thus, there would be no assault because the threatened battery was not imminent or otherwise immediate. By the time that the defendant went off somewhere to get a stone (in which to carry out the threat) and then returned to the scene of the threat, the plaintiff has plenty of time to leave the scene and thus avoid the previously threatened battery.

The present ability to carry out the threat is to be measured from the eyes of the plaintiff. If, for example, the defendant is holding a gun and threatening to shoot the plaintiff, there is a present threat. Even if the gun is not loaded, so that defendant can claim that there is no actual present threat, there would still be an assault if the gun appears to present an immediate threat to the plaintiff who is looking at it and listening to the threat. Since there is no way for the plaintiff to know whether the gun is loaded or unloaded, the plaintiff will understandably be apprehensive about a possible imminent battery if the gun is loaded and it is discharged.

Likewise, the threat itself must be a present, imminent threat. If, for example, the defendant makes a future threat or a conditional threat, then no assault exists. The law assumes that by making a future or conditional threat, the defendant is informing the plaintiff that the threat will not be carried out immediately, if at all. Such conditional or future threats are easy to imagine. The defendant could say, for example, "I'll hit you tomorrow," or "If you weren't so old I would hit you." The first is a future threat and the second is a conditional threat. Neither would be actionable as an assault.

The tort of assault is frequently linked to the tort of battery. For example, it is common to say that someone committed an assault and a battery. However, both of these torts represent two separate and distinct causes of action. It is possible to have an assault without a battery or a battery without an assault. It is also possible, of course, to have both an assault and a battery in the same case. At the end of the next section on battery, the relationship between the two torts will be discussed in further detail. (*See* section II.B., *infra*).

Since the torts of assault and battery are of ancient origin, they have parallels in the criminal law. As such, they carry names that are the same as the crimes of assault and battery. After all of the intervening years, however, the elements of the torts and crimes are different. For a computer lesson on assault, *see* Assault (CALI).

B. Battery

The tort of battery is another of the original common law trespass writ intentional torts. As noted above, it is similar in some ways to assault, but as with every tort cause of action there are also certain unique requirements that the plaintiff must prove to establish liability. Specifically, the tort of "battery" requires the plaintiff to prove:

(1) intent;
(2) harmful or offensive contact with; and,
(3) the plaintiff's person.

The first element of battery is, in fact, the same as the first element of assault: intent. To establish the requisite intent for the tort of "battery," the plaintiff must prove that the defendant acted intentionally to bring about a harmful or offensive *touching* of another person. As with assault, the absence of the requisite intent will defeat the tort of "battery." Likewise, as with all of the common law trespass writ intentional torts, there are several different ways in which the requisite intent for a battery can be established, each of which previously has been discussed in section I. of this chapter, *supra*.

The second element of battery is that the defendant must actually complete the harmful or offensive touching of the plaintiff's person. This is the element that uniquely distinguishes battery from assault. Whereas assault involves merely the *apprehension* of a touching, a battery requires the actual completion of that touching. For example, where the defendant intends to punch the plaintiff in the nose and subsequently does punch the plaintiff in the nose, there is a battery. However, if the defendant stops just short of actually striking the plaintiff's nose, then there is no battery. Of course, there may still be an assault, provided that the plaintiff can prove that (s)he was apprehensive about being punched in the nose as a result of the defendant's actions.

Nevertheless, some personal touchings are so commonplace in society that they simply do not give rise to a claim for the tort of "battery." Imagine, for example, that the plaintiff is walking across a university campus when the defendant comes up behind the plaintiff. The defendant lightly taps the plaintiff on the shoulder and politely asks, "Excuse me, but do you know what time it is?" It appears that the defendant certainly intended to touch the plaintiff's physical person and did, in fact, touch the plaintiff. Although the plaintiff may even claim that (s)he was frightened by the sudden and unexpected "touching" by a stranger, or perhaps offended by it, most courts simply would not allow this type of claim, at least where the plaintiff was otherwise unharmed by the contact. There are several explanations for denying relief in such situations. One is that this type of touching is simply neither harmful nor offensive, and thus, an essential element of the tort has not been established. A second explanation is based upon the doctrine of implied consent, where courts have noted that, in a crowded world, there is some inevitable harmless bumping and inadvertent physical "touchings" that simply cannot reasonably be considered as offensive. By walking around in the world today, people impliedly consent to such harmless touches and bumping.

Many tort cases today involve automobile actions. When two automobiles collide, a harmful or offensive touching often occurs. However, drivers of automobiles rarely intend to cause these touchings. Instead, automobiles usually run together unintentionally because someone is failing to use reasonable care. Such a set of circumstances may create a negligence claim for relief, but it will not be a battery.

Again, it is important to remember the distinction between intent and motive. The mere fact of a casual, inadvertent touching such as the one in the previous example, *supra*, involving the light tap on the plaintiff's shoulder does not defeat a claim for the tort of battery simply because the defendant had no evil motive. As with other intentional torts, the motive is not important. The issue is merely one of intent. Imagine that a person has been injured and is found lying on the side of the road by the defendant who stops and says: "I am a doctor, let me treat you." The injured person then says, "Don't touch me. I've already called my regular doctor and she is on the way." Nevertheless, the defendant goes ahead and begins to administer first aid. This first aid requires some touching. The defendant's conduct in this situation would constitute a battery. Even though the defendant wanted to do a good deed, the touching likely would be viewed as "offensive" under these circumstances, even if not harmful. Even if the defendant's first aid was successful, the absence of consent by the plaintiff establishes liability for the tort of battery. This example also illustrates the reason that medical professionals are required to get consent before performing medical treatment. Since medical treatment sometimes can be harmful or at least offensive, it is a battery if done in the absence of consent by the patient. Moreover, even if the treatment is otherwise effective, it is still a battery if performed without the patent's consent. There are several computer lessons on battery. *See* Battery Basics (CALI); Battery Puzzlers (CALI).

C. False Imprisonment

False imprisonment, sometimes called false arrest, is another one of the original common law writ of trespass intentional torts. The first element of this tort is similar to the other trespass writ intentional torts: intent. For this tort, the plaintiff must prove that the defendant had the intent to confine the plaintiff. Thus, just as with the other trespass writ intentional torts, the requisite intent is articulated with specific reference to the other requirements for a false imprisonment. Specifically, the tort of false imprisonment requires the plaintiff to prove:

(1) intent (to confine the plaintiff);
(2) confinement within boundaries;
(3) the confinement must be physical;

(4) the plaintiff must have knowledge of the confinement or be harmed by it; and,

(5) absence of legal authority for the confinement.

Each of these elements will be discussed individually.

By intent, of course, false imprisonment requires the defendant either to act for the purpose of bringing about the confinement or to act with knowledge that the confinement was substantially certain to occur. It is also possible, of course, that a defendant could negligently or carelessly confine someone. For example, a night guard might be locking up a building at night and not do a good job of making sure that no one was left inside the building. As a result, the guard might carelessly lock the building while leaving someone inside. Although the guard intended to lock the building, the guard probably would not have had the necessary intent for false imprisonment, since the guard did not know that anyone was left inside the building. Thus, plaintiff would likely not recover for the intentional tort of "false imprisonment" under these circumstances. The plaintiff could, however, bring a negligence action. However, in order to recover in negligence, plaintiff must prove that (s)he suffered actual harm. By contrast, in a claim for the intentional tort of false imprisonment, proof of actual harm is not necessary as long as the plaintiff is at least aware of the confinement.

The element of confinement actually requires that the plaintiff must be confined within boundaries that have been fixed or otherwise controlled by the defendant. Thus, to satisfy this requirement for the tort of false imprisonment, there must be something more than merely some interference with the plaintiff's freedom of movement; the plaintiff must actually be physically confined. Imagine, for example, that the plaintiff has a valid ticket for a concert. The plaintiff shows up at the front door and is denied entry to the concert. The plaintiff may still go anywhere that (s)he wants to, except enter the concert. That would not give rise to a claim for false imprisonment because the plaintiff is not confined. The plaintiff may have a claim for breach of contract, but not for false imprisonment.

The boundaries that make up the confinement may be large. For example, the plaintiff may be forced to stay within a large room or a large building. As long as the plaintiff is prevented from leaving the enclosed space, that constitutes a sufficient confinement. Of course, the size of a confinement could eventually get so large as to defeat a realistic claim for false imprisonment. Thus, telling the plaintiff to remain on planet earth certainly would not give rise to a claim for false imprisonment.

The confining space may even be one that is in motion. Imagine that the plaintiff is forced to get into an automobile and is then driven around the city. The confinement within the automobile is a false imprisonment even though the car is moving.

The confinement also must be adequate to prevent reasonable escape. If the plaintiff has a means of reasonable escape from the confinement, then there is no false imprisonment. If, for example, a plaintiff is told to stay in a room, but the door to the room is open so that the plaintiff may leave, that would defeat a false imprisonment claim. Of course, if there is a reasonable means of escape (such as a hidden doorway) but the plaintiff is unaware of it, then there is still a confinement.

The confinement that is at issue in the false imprisonment must also be one that is enforced by some physical restraint. Chaining a person to a chair or locking the person in a small room would obviously be sufficient. In addition, holding the plaintiff at "gun point" or under some other physical threat would constitute a sufficient physical restraint. However, a merely moral or ethical threat for the plaintiff to remain in place is not sufficient for false imprisonment. Imagine, for example, that the plaintiff is suspected of shoplifting in a department store. A store clerk approaches the plaintiff and says, "I think you have stolen something. Unless you stay here and let me search your bags, I will always believe you are a thief." If the plaintiff stays and allows the search merely because of some moral compulsion to "clear his or her good name," that would not give rise to a claim for false imprisonment. The plaintiff would be staying merely because of the fear of being thought a thief, and not because of any actual physical threat to remain confined. There are many false imprisonment claims where the primary issue requires the jury to determine whether the threat for the plaintiff to remain confined was physical or merely moral. The plaintiff must prove to the jury that the confinement was caused by the physical restraint of the plaintiff.

The next element is that the plaintiff must prove that the plaintiff either knew of the confinement or was otherwise harmed by it. This element also presents an interesting issue regarding consent. Although a person may be confined within boundaries, there is no false imprisonment claim if that person consents to the imprisonment. Imagine, for example, a law student who enters a classroom at 9:00 a.m. for a 50-minute class. The student may feel imprisoned, but that student has consented to be there, so there can be no "awareness" of confinement. The student may also believe that (s)he has a reasonable means of escape if (s)he decides at any time during the class to get up and leave the room. Once again, in such a situation, the student is not "aware" of any confinement. However, suppose that unknown to the student the faculty member locked the door when (s)he entered at 9:01 a.m. Since the door has been locked, the student is, in fact, confined and unable to leave the room. Between 9:01 and 9:50, there is probably no claim for false imprisonment, since the student is unaware that there is a confinement and the student is not harmed by it.

To continue the law student example, imagine some additional facts. Suppose that the student gets up at 9:20 a.m., tries to leave the room, and now discovers that the door is locked. Is this not sufficient to support the student's claim for false imprisonment? The student is certainly confined within boundaries by the physical restraint of a lock controlled by the professor. Furthermore, the student is also now aware that (s)he is confined, so no additional harm would be necessary to support a claim for false imprisonment. The only remaining question is whether the student's initial consent to attend the entire 50-minute class negates any claim of confinement occurring within the entire scheduled class period. Ultimately, this may be a question to be resolved by the jury as to whether a "confinement" existed or whether the student, by getting up in an attempt to leave during the class sufficiently expressed the intent to revoke his or her prior consent. Likewise, if the building suddenly caught on fire at 9:30 a.m., and the fire injured the student since (s)he could not escape from the locked classroom, there would be a claim for false imprisonment, even though the student originally had consented to remain in the class during the entire period. The circumstances of the sudden fire altered the conditions under which the student had originally given consent to remain inside the classroom. The student is now confined within the physical space of a locked room, for which (s)he no longer has consented, and now (s)he has also been physically harmed by that confinement. Finally, suppose that there is no fire and that all of the students remain in the classroom (either unlocked or otherwise unaware that it was locked) until 9:50 a.m. At that point the professor announces that the door is locked and that no one can leave the room. Beginning from that moment (i.e., 9:50 a.m.) the students are now confined in a locked room, and they are also aware of the confinement. Their awareness of the confinement after the scheduled class time also helps to show that they all now wish to leave the room. Even though the students may have initially consented to remain in the classroom during the entire class period, such consent is no longer valid after class is over.

Notice from the examples, *supra*, that the actual length of the confinement is not relevant in determining whether or not a "confinement" exists. Any confinement of any length of time, no matter how brief, is sufficient to establish the requirement of a "confinement" for purposes of imposing liability for the tort of false imprisonment, just as long as the plaintiff is aware of the confinement or is otherwise harmed by that confinement. Of course, the length of time in which the plaintiff is confined without sustaining any actual physical harm may still be quite relevant in determining how much damages the plaintiff may receive in an action for false imprisonment.

One final aspect of false imprisonment involves the defendant's legal authority for the confinement. In some jurisdictions, the absence of legal authority for the confinement is listed as one of the requirements of the plaintiff's *prima facie* cause of action for false imprisonment. However, in other jurisdictions, the existence of a proper legal authority for the confinement is a matter for the defendant to plead and prove in defense of the plaintiff's claim for false imprisonment. Many of the details for determining when one person has legal authority to make an arrest or to confine another person are covered in criminal law and criminal procedure. Those issues arise most often in cases where a law enforcement officer has made an arrest and the person arrested is contesting that arrest. Clearly, if the law enforcement officer had the authority to make the arrest, there is no claim for false imprisonment. Typical examples of when a law enforcement officer has the authority to make an arrest involve situations where that officer has a lawful warrant for the arrest or when the officer actually observes a crime being committed.

However, sometimes persons other than law enforcement officers may also confine people. One obvious example is when a parent tells a 12-year-old son or daughter that they are confined to their room for the evening and forced to do homework. The child may believe that such a confinement is unfair, but it will not give rise to a claim for false imprisonment. The parent has the right to control the child.

Members of the public may also, at times, make what are called "citizens' arrests." In a citizens' arrest, an individual who is not a law enforcement officer observes a crime being committed and takes the offender into custody. These situations do not occur very often and they usually result in litigation over whether the arrest was made with proper legal authority.

One additional point must be considered in light of the discussion of imprisonment with authority. Even in situations where people are held in custody under proper legal authority, false imprisonment claims can sometimes still be asserted if the confinement continues beyond the period of the lawful custodial authority. For example, people held in jails and prisons as the result of appropriate legal procedures do not have claims for false imprisonment. However, once the authority for holding the person is over, that person must be released, and the failure to release the person will result in a false imprisonment claim. Imagine, for example, that a person is being held in the county jail awaiting trial. After the trial, the person is found not guilty, but the sheriff refuses to release the former prisoner or otherwise unlawfully delays his or her release. There would be no false imprisonment claim for the period between the arrest and the trial, but there would be a claim for the period between the not guilty verdict and the prisoner's ultimate release. For a computer lesson on False Imprisonment, *see* False Imprisonment (CALI).

D. Intentional Infliction of Emotional Distress

The tort of intentional infliction of emotional distress is of fairly recent origin. It was never a part of the original common law writ torts. In fact, this tort was first adopted by the state of California in the 1950s, and since that time it has been slowly recognized throughout the United States. Many jurisdictions that recognize this tort now refer to it by the name used in the Restatement of Torts: "outrageous conduct." Specifically, as noted by the Restatement, the tort of intentional infliction of emotional distress (IIED) requires the plaintiff to prove:

(1) intent (to cause emotional distress);
(2) extreme or reckless conduct that is "outrageous"; and,
(3) severe emotional distress by the plaintiff.

Each of those elements will be discussed individually below.

The element of intent (or recklessness) is similar to the other intentional torts insofar as the plaintiff must prove that the defendant acted for the purpose of bringing about the emotional distress or acted with knowledge that it was substantially certain to follow. However, a somewhat unique issue that seems to recur with the intent element for this tort is the need for some proof that the defendant acted specifically for the purpose of causing the emotional harm to the plaintiff. In some cases, for example, where a defendant has beaten or otherwise harmed one individual, a different person (often a close family member) upon learning of the beating suffers emotional distress because of the news. When this other family member sues to recover damages for his or her own separate emotional harm, most courts have found that there is no intent for this tort. The defendant did not act for the purpose of causing emotional harm to this particular plaintiff. And, unless the defendant had some special knowledge of circumstances from which severe emotional distress to this other family member otherwise could have been anticipated, there is no legal basis for implying knowledge that such emotional harm was substantially certain to follow.

Initially, it may seem that this would be an appropriate case for "transferred intent." Since the defendant clearly intended to batter the victim, and subsequently inflicted emotional distress upon another person, there may be some desire to transfer the requisite intent. However, a review of the doctrine of "transferred intent" reveals why this will not work. "Transferred intent" only allows the intent to be transferred when the defendant intends one of the five torts derived from the original common law trespass writ (i.e., assault, battery, false imprisonment, trespass to land, and trespass to chattels) and subsequently accomplishes one of those same five trespass writ torts. Intentional infliction of emotional distress is not one of those five trespass writ torts, and therefore "transferred intent" cannot be used with that tort. *See* section I.C., *supra.*

There are, of course, certain situations in which special knowledge of the existence of severe emotional harm sufficient to support this tort may still be implied. Imagine, for example, that an adult comes to the plaintiffs' home to watch their young children while the parents go out for the evening. If the adult intentionally abuses the children while the parents are away, and the parents suffer emotional harm upon learning of the abuse, an intentional infliction of emotional distress claim is at least possible, since it is likely that the parents can prove that the abuser knew that they were substantially certain to suffer emotional harm when they learned of the abuse.

The second element of this tort requires that the defendant's conduct must be extreme and outrageous. Courts do not allow recovery for every insult. Instead, the defendant's conduct must be so extreme and outrageous as to exceed the bounds of conduct permitted by a civilized society. There is an assumption, just as with slight, inadvertent touchings in the context of the tort of battery, that people must deal with a certain amount of rude and offensive conduct when living in a crowded world. Therefore, the typical types of conduct that lead to successful claims for this tort are those where a defendant has abused his or her authority over another person, or where the defendant has intentionally abused some known weakness or infirmity on the part of the plaintiff. Frequently, successful cases for the tort of "intentional infliction of emotional distress" also involve continuous or repeated patterns of abuse, rather than mere isolated instances.

The third element of this tort requires proof that the plaintiff suffered *severe* emotional harm. There is generally no requirement of an actual physical manifestation of the distress, but plaintiffs' lawyers know that such physical evidence, if available, can help sway the judge and jury that the plaintiff's injury is legitimate and not feigned. A plaintiff who testifies that (s)he was merely "made nervous" by the defendant's misconduct will probably be unsuccessful. However, a plaintiff who can point to specific medical problems and recurring medical treatment caused by extreme emotional distress will be more likely to recover. Of course, it is important to keep in mind that this is a matter of practical proof and not an element of the tort itself. The element simply requires proof of severe emotional harm. The practical proof problem is that it is easier to prove severe emotional harm if the plaintiff also has suffered some physical result.

With the adoption of this tort by many jurisdictions since the 1950s, plaintiffs' lawyers, law professors, and law students have seen it as a way to seek recovery for those plaintiffs who might not be able to prove the existence of another intentional tort claim. However, courts have been reluctant to use the tort merely as a fill in tort when the plaintiff is simply unable to prove one of the other intentional torts. Although many jurisdictions have adopted this tort, plaintiffs are not always successful in establishing it. For a computer lesson on the topic, *see* Intentional Infliction of Mental Distress (CALI).

III. Interference with Property

The previously discussed intentional torts in this chapter have dealt with interference with some aspect of the bodily integrity of individuals (either physically or at least emotionally). Assault, battery, false imprisonment, and intentional infliction of emotional distress all concerned the infliction of some type of harm to the plaintiff's person. Intentional torts, however, also protect individuals from the infliction of harm to their property. The following materials discuss those intentional torts.

Initially, it is necessary to distinguish between two types of property: real and personal property. There are also other forms of property that include, among others, intellectual property and intangible property. However, the traditional categories of intentional torts normally do not affect those properties, so they will not be discussed here. *See* Chapter 22, *infra*, Business Torts, for a discussion of a few other tort causes of action that may be applicable to some of these other kinds of property.

Real property is generally considered to be land and things permanently attached to the land. The land itself, as well as growing trees, growing crops, and minerals in the soil would all be part of the realty. Houses and other buildings that are permanently attached to the land are also considered part of the realty. By contrast to real property, personal property (also called chattels) consists of things that are not attached to the land, including almost all other physical items. Examples of chattels include automobiles, clothes, smartphones, laptop computers, and other personal items. Occasionally, some interesting problems can arise as to whether something is permanently attached to the land (and therefore considered a "fixture" and, as such, part of the land itself), or whether it is not. Thus, questions can arise as to whether things like refrigerators and stoves inside a house are actually part of the realty, since they can be removed from the land fairly easily.

In discussing property torts, it is important to carefully distinguish between land and chattels. There are two different torts: the tort of trespass to land and the tort of trespass to chattels. For this reason, it is important to use the correct terms in discussing these two different torts. If, for example, someone merely referred to "trespass to property," it is unclear which of these two specific torts was intended. Therefore, it is important always to be specific and refer to either trespass *to land* or trespass to *chattels.*

A. Trespass to Land

The first property based intentional tort is trespass to land. Also recognized as one of the original common law trespass writ torts, the specific writ was called trespass *quare clausem fregit.* This roughly translates as "a trespass because he broke the close." At common law, the trespass was committed when someone simply entered upon the land of another. Originally, if the person entered with consent, but overstayed the invitation, there was no trespass. However, this tort now extends to either the situation when someone enters on the land of another, or when (s)he wrongfully stays or remains on the land of another. The modern two elements of this tort may be simply stated as:

(1) intent (to be on the land); and
(2) being on the land of another.

The intent to be on the land merely requires the defendant to intend to be where (s)he is physically located. It does not require a specific intent to trespass. Imagine, for example, that a defendant is walking in a pasture believing in good faith that the area where the defendant is walking is part of the defendant's own farm. It is sufficient for the intent element of trespass to land for the plaintiff to prove that in fact the defendant is physically standing on the plaintiff's land. This is a trespass to land. The plaintiff does not have to prove that the defendant actually knew that (s)he was on the plaintiff's land. The plaintiff need only prove that the defendant intended to be on the land where (s)he in fact was situated at the time of the alleged tort.

Questions sometimes arise regarding the minimum intent required for this tort. Suppose, for example, that the defendant is driving an automobile along a street, loses control of the car and negligently runs off the road and into the plaintiff's yard. In this situation, the plaintiff must choose between the intentional tort of "trespass to land" and the separate tort of "negligence." Clearly, the car entered onto the plaintiff's land. However, the defendant did not intend for the automobile to be in the yard, but instead intended for it to be on the street. The car was in the yard only because of the defendant's negligence. In such a situation, the owner of the yard would likely sue the defendant for the negligent damage to the yard, instead of the intentional tort of trespass to land.

Even if not negligent or intentional, it is sometimes possible for the defendant to be on the land of another through mere innocence. Imagine, for example, that the defendant was kidnapped, tied up and blindfolded, and then placed on the plaintiff's land. Again, the defendant did not possess the intent to be there, nor did the defendant enter onto the land by virtue of any volitional act of his or her own. Moreover, the defendant would not have been there negligently. Therefore, the plaintiff landowner would not have an intentional tort claim against the defendant, nor would there be a negligence claim. However, under this set of facts the plaintiff still would have an intentional tort claim against the kidnappers for their trespass upon the land, since the kidnappers did intentionally enter onto the land in order to place their kidnapping victim on the land.

The next element requires that the plaintiff prove that the defendant was *on* the land *of another*. Ordinarily, this element is met whenever the defendant is physically present on the surface of another person's land. Walking upon the land or driving a vehicle on it, even if only briefly, are certainly sufficient to satisfy this requirement. However, certain additional issues sometimes also arise in regard to this element. A trespass to land can also occur when the defendant interferes with the rights of the possessor of the land in regard to the air above the surface, as well as the soil below the surface. At common law, it was assumed that the person who possessed the surface also possessed the land upward to the "very heavens" and downward to the "center of the earth."

Possessing the "land" upward to the "very heavens" worked very well in ancient times, but it did not work when people began to travel by air. At common law, shooting a gun or an arrow over the land of another would be a trespass to land. In fact, such conduct would involve a trespass to land even today. However, as air travel began, this same scenario became more problematic. If the person with rights to the surface continued to control the land all the way to the heavens, then every air flight would create hundreds, if not thousands, of trespasses to land. Each property owner whose land was passed over would have a claim. Obviously, that is impractical today, and it is certainly not the law. Instead, the law began to reduce the amount of air space that the possessor of the surface could control for purposes of asserting this tort. The law now generally assumes that the possessor of land has control only over that air space that is within the reasonable use of that possessor. Above that space, air flights are permissible in what is now considered to be the public area.

The ancient idea, that a landowner also controlled land to the center of the earth, involves somewhat different problems. Mining of minerals is an ancient industry that continues today. Owners of land may divide their ownership rights into many different parts. An owner may lease the surface of farmland to a tenant farmer to grow crops. That same owner may sell mineral rights under that land to a mining company. In some areas of the country, the value of the minerals below the surface of the land is more important then the value of the surface rights. Controlling possession of the land beneath the surface continues to be a part of the law of trespass. If a defendant mines underground and enters into an area to which the defendant does not have rights, then the plaintiff will have a claim for trespass to land.

Throughout this discussion, it has been noted that the plaintiff is ordinarily the one with the right to *possession* of the land. Indeed, trespass to land is a cause of action that is designed to protect the right of possession. However, it must be kept in mind that the person with the right of possession may not always be the person who actually owns the land. A landowner may lease the property to another so that the other person may farm or live on the land. The person who is currently leasing the property has the right of possession. If a third party were to trespass on the land, the person with the right of possession would have the claim for trespass.

B. Trespass to Chattels

Trespass to chattels was called trespass *de bonis asportatis* at common law. Roughly translated, this was a trespass for "carrying away the goods." Historically, this was also one of the original trespass writ torts, and it focused primarily upon the interference with or intermeddling with the chattel of another. Modern definitions of the tort of "trespass to chattels" continue to allow recovery for *interference* with personal property, but do so mostly with respect to those interferences that cause less than total loss of the personal property. Specifically, the tort of trespass to chattels requires the plaintiff to prove:

(1) intent (to interfere or to intermeddle with);
(2) chattel of another; and,
(3) non-trivial harm that is less than the chattel's full market value.

The first element requires that the defendant intend to interfere with the chattel. As with most other intentional torts, the plaintiff must prove that the defendant acted for the purpose of dispossessing or intermeddling with the chattel, or acted with knowledge that such was substantially certain to follow. Damage to a chattel that is not the result of this intent may give rise to a negligence claim, but ordinarily there will not be a trespass to chattels. A good example of this distinction can be illustrated by a typical traffic accident. Most traffic accidents result in some damage to personal property, including automobiles involved in the accident. However, such actions are usually brought as negligence claims, where the defendant is alleged to have been negligent in causing the accident, because there is usually no intent to interfere with the other vehicle.

The next element of the tort is that the plaintiff must prove that there was some non-trivial damage to the chattel. This means that something more is necessary than a merely inadvertent or trivial interference with a chattel that causes no harm. Typically, this damage requirement may occur in one of three ways: 1) the defendant may cause some actual harm to the chattel; 2) the defendant may use the chattel (thereby depriving the possessor of its use) but without actually harming it; or 3) the defendant may cause some change in the chattel that results in some further injury to the plaintiff. Notice that each of these possibilities reflects some less-than-total destruction of the chattel. Where a total destruction of the chattel occurs, the more appropriate claim is typically based upon a different intentional tort, known as the tort of "conversion," which is discussed in the next section, *infra*. For a computer lesson on the tort of trespass to chattels, *see* Trespass to Chattels (CALI).

C. Conversion

The tort of conversion is another intentional tort that protects against an intentional interference with a chattel. Among most courts today, the difference between the torts of "trespass to chattels" and "conversion" relates primarily to the extent of harm to the chattel. Whereas trespass to chattels involves something less than the total destruction of the chattel, conversion allows recovery of the full value of the chattel.

The tort of conversion may be described as an intentional exercise of dominion over the chattel to the exclusion of the rights of the true owner. Specifically, the tort of conversion requires the plaintiff to prove:

(1) intent (to exercise dominion and control over a chattel);
(2) chattel of another; and,
(3) total destruction of the chattel or serious interference with the plaintiff's right of control.

The requisite intent for this tort requires the defendant to act for the purpose of exercising dominion and control over the chattel or to act with knowledge that such was substantially certain to follow. Typically, a conversion may be accomplished in one of two ways: 1) the defendant (while merely trespassing to a chattel) may actually destroy the chattel (thereby effectively permanently preventing the plaintiff from his or her continued exercise of dominion and control over it); or 2) the defendant purposefully may take the chattel and claim it as his or her own (i.e., steal it). Either of these actions effectively deprives the plaintiff of the chattel's dominion and control, thus requiring the defendant to pay the full value of the chattel. For a computer lesson on the tort of conversion, *see* Conversion (CALI).

Checkpoints

- Intent, negligence and strict liability are the three bases of liability.

- Intent is proven by showing that the defendant acted for the purpose of bringing about the consequences or acted with knowledge that the consequences were substantially certain to occur.

- Children and others of diminished capacity are not automatically exempt from intentional torts. The question is whether such defendants had sufficient mental capacity to form the requisite intent.

- "Transferred intent" operates where a defendant intended one of the five intentional torts in the original writ of trespass and accomplishes one of those same five intentional torts in the original writ of trespass. The law will allow the intent to transfer from the tort intended to the tort accomplished. The five original writ of trespass torts are assault, battery, false imprisonment, trespass to land, and trespass to chattels.

- The elements of assault are:

  - intent to bring about a harmful or offensive touching or the apprehension of that touching;

  - apprehension of immediate bodily contact;

  - some overt act on the part of the defendant; and

  - the present ability of the defendant to carry out that immediate bodily contact.

- The elements of battery are:

  - intent to bring about a harmful or offensive touching or the apprehension of that touching; and

  - a harmful or offensive touching.

- The elements of false imprisonment are:
  - intent to bring about a confinement;
  - confinement within boundaries;
  - physical confinement;
  - knowledge on the part of the plaintiff of the confinement or harm to the plaintiff by the confinement; and
  - no legal authority for the confinement.
- The elements of intentional infliction of emotional distress are:
  - intent or reckless conduct;
  - extreme and outrageous behavior by the defendant; and
  - severe emotional distress.
- The elements of trespass to land are:
  - intent to be on the land; and
  - being on the land of another.
- The elements of trespass to chattels are:
  - intent to interfere or to intermeddle with a chattel; and
  - harm to the chattel that is less than full market value.
- The elements of conversion are:
  - intent to exercise dominion and control over a chattel; and
  - harm or interference that causes total destruction of the chattel or an exercise of dominion over the chattel to the exclusion of the rights of the true owner.

Chapter 3

Defenses to Intentional Torts

Roadmap

- Understand the individual elements of the defenses to intentional torts, including consent, self-defense, defense of others, defense of property, and necessity.
- Distinguish between express and implied consent.
- Recognize the special problems created by medical consent cases in distinguishing between the tort of "battery" and the negligence concept of "informed consent."
- Learn how to create a personalized study outline, using the law of "consent" as an example.
- Distinguish between the two different types of necessity: public necessity and private necessity.

The ability to think precisely is one key skill of being a lawyer. In other words, a lawyer must read cases closely to insure that (s)he understands the way the court is defining a *prima facie* case or defense, and then look for extensions, exceptions, modifications, or deletions in the way the court uses these definitions to predict what a court might do in the next case. Therefore, the language of the common law is the starting point of the teaching and study of tort law. In this chapter we will examine the defenses the common law recognizes with respect to intentional torts. They are consent, defense of self, defense of others, defense of property, and defense of necessity. Note that contributory negligence and assumption of risk are not listed as common law defenses to intentional torts. Instead, they are traditionally recognized as defenses to the tort of negligence that we will study in Chapter 4, *infra*. Unless your jurisdiction has a comparative fault statute that allows the jury to take into account comparative fault in intentional torts, these negligence defenses are inapplicable in traditional common law intentional tort jurisdictions.

This can have major consequences for the plaintiff's choice of action (s)he brings against a defendant. For example, in cancer caused from smoking tobacco cases, lack of informed consent in medical malpractice cases, or for injuries caused by allegedly defective pharmaceuticals, if the plaintiff sues for battery, misrepresentation, or fraud (all of which are intentional tort causes of action) the plaintiff's own contributory negligence or assumption of risk will not be a defense to any of these causes of action. The plaintiff's behavior will not defeat these causes of action unless it can be said to rise to the level of consent. What, then, is the definition of consent and how do common law courts process this decision?

I. Consent

Most torts casebooks start with the defense of consent because it was initially not clear at common law whether the *lack* of consent (unlawfulness) was part of the plaintiff's *prima facie* case, and therefore the plaintiff's burden to show, or whether it was a defense that had to be proven by the defendant. As it has now evolved, consent is a classic defense, meaning that once the plaintiff establishes that an intentional tort has occurred, the question of whether the plaintiff consented to that invasion is for the defendant to prove. This can have a major effect on the outcome of a case, as we will soon see.

The Restatement (Second) of Torts § 892 defines consent as follows: "Consent is willingness in fact for conduct to occur. It may be manifested by action or inaction and need not be communicated to the actor."

A. Express Consent

Express consent is the easiest type of consent to prove, as it is conveyed in words or gestures. If a person signs a consent form before a medical procedure, the question of consent focuses upon the meaning of the specific language found in the consent form. The person signing the form tests the language to determine whether there has been full disclosure of the risks involved and whether the language is clear and understandable. These cases treat the consent form like a question of contract interpretation, and any ambiguity in the contract is interpreted against the contract drafter. It should be noted that express consent forms are sometimes confused with express waivers. While both types of forms are somewhat similar insofar as they are both contractual in nature, express consent forms expressly manifest the parties' consent or agreement with respect to certain specific actions (e.g., to submit to a particular surgical procedure, or to participate in a contact sport activity), whereas waivers actually release one party from tort *liability* altogether with respect to certain tort causes of action brought by the other party. While both types of forms may be asserted as bars to specific causes of action, consent is only applicable with respect to intentional tort actions as discussed in the preceding section, *supra*, whereas waivers may also be used to bar liability for negligence.

The tendency in express consent forms is for the defendant to define the types of behavior and harm very broadly to cover his or her actions. There is also a temptation to be a bit vague, so as to not scare the plaintiff away from engaging in the behavior to which consent has been given. The combination of breadth and ambiguity can raise the possibility for the plaintiff to argue that the defendant has tried to gain the patient's consent for illegality, or for crimes. Plaintiffs might even choose to strike the offending language in the consent form and then still go ahead with the proposed procedure, or to allow their child to engage in school sports, or to go on a trip. If these consent form contracts are for illegal acts, or if they are coerced, or if they are found to be "adhesion contracts," the consent contracts may be void against public policy, just as with any contract.

As a result, in some cases the consent may be invalid, even when explicitly given. This is true whether a consent form is involved or not. For example, tort liability may follow the defendant in a statutory rape case, or for inducing a person to engage in a boxing match that is not licensed, even where the fact of the consent is undisputed.

In addition, consent cannot be gained from a minor, unless it involves a situation of a medical emergency and the parent can be said to impliedly consent to the life saving operation. Also, living wills and advance health care directives may limit a medical professional's ability to provide medical care in end-of-life situations. If medical care is provided against the wishes of the patient it can constitute a battery.

B. Implied Consent

Since consent can also arise from conduct, the defendant sometimes can defend on a theory of implied consent even where no express consent has been given. For example, in a famous case, *O'Brien v. Cunard Steamship Co.*, 28 N.E. 266 (Mass. 1891), the plaintiff silently extended her arm toward a doctor to receive a smallpox vaccination required for her entry into the United States. The plaintiff's behavior communicated to the doctor that she consented.

In "date rape" cases, defendants may try to defend claims for the tort of battery by saying that although the plaintiff said "no," the plaintiff's conduct indicated that (s)he did not really mean "no." In these cases, just as in criminal rape cases, the defendant may attempt to prove that by dress, or other words, or conduct, the defendant was reasonable in believing the sexual conduct was consented to. The burden of proof, however, in these civil cases, is on the defendant, and with evidence of prior sexual conduct by the plaintiff excluded from evidence under rape shield laws, (*see* FRE 412, unless to show motive, common scheme, or plan, and then only if the probative value substantially outweighs the danger of harm to the victim, or unless the victim has put her reputation forward as evidence she did not consent), the defendant's burden to show consent may be difficult to meet.

Another type of case that raises implied consent issues involves parents who try to "rescue" a child from a cult. For example, in *Peterson v. Sorlien*, 299 N.W.2d 123 (Minn. 1980), the plaintiff joined a religious cult and was later abducted by her parents for 16 days in an attempt to "deprogram" her from the cult's influence. For the first 3 days, she resisted all attempts at the deprogramming, plugging her ears, crying, and at one point screaming hysterically and flailing at her father. However, for the next 13 days the plaintiff behaved normally toward her parents, and took many public excursions with them during which she had opportunities to alert authorities that she was being abducted, including: attending a softball game where she was observed by two police officers; passing thru airport security while flying; and being interviewed by an FBI agent seeking assurances of her safety. At no time did the plaintiff alert authorities or claim that she was being held against her will. As such, the court held that, given the relationship of parent and child, the involvement of the "cult," and the fact that the plaintiff at least "at some juncture" assented to the imprisonment, there was no liability for false imprisonment.

In *Eilers v. Coy*, 582 F. Supp. 1093, 1097 (1984), however, the court distinguished *Peterson*. In *Eilers*, the court held that there was an actual confinement and no means of escape. There, the parents had tried to claim acquiescence by the fourth day, relying upon *Peterson*. However, the court found that the defendants' son had only "pretended" to acquiesce. The result seems to be that parents are justified in kidnapping back their daughters, but not their sons.

C. Medical Consent Cases: Battery vs. "Informed Consent"

When a doctor operates without getting a valid consent from a patient, the patient potentially can bring a case for both battery and negligence, depending on the statute of limitations. Usually, the battery cause of action must be brought one year from the time the patient learns of the harm. In the case of negligence, the plaintiff has two years from discovery of the injury to bring the case.

In battery cases the question is simply whether the doctor has obtained *any* consent whatsoever from the patient. By contrast, in negligence (also known as "informed consent") cases the patient has given at least *some* consent to the procedure in question. In these cases two separate issues are presented: 1) whether the doctor has a duty to inform the patient of the particular risk of injury from the surgical procedure and whether the doctor reasonably informed the patient of that risk, and 2) whether, had the patient been informed of the risk (s)he would not have had the procedure, (i.e., causation). The duty to inform is spelled out in *Canterbury v. Spence*, 464 F.2d 772 (D.C. Cir. 1972). It is an objective test described as the duty to inform the patient of all material risks. Material risks are those that a reasonable patient in the patient's position would likely attach significance to in deciding whether or not to forgo the proposed therapy. Expert testimony is often required to establish the breach of this duty. As broad as that duty may appear to be, the doctor is protected in that the patient must also show that a *reasonable* patient would not have had the operation if the patient knew of those risks of injury.

Again, remember that in the case of an emergency, consent sometimes can be implied. In the case of a minor who has a religious objection, this presents dilemmas between principles of autonomy and beneficence. At times, courts may even require the hospital to seek a legal guardian to act on behalf of a youthful patient in order to override a parent's religious objections to a blood transfusion or other life-saving surgical procedure. Otherwise, the doctor may be liable for battery.

D. Sporting Events

In the world of pickup sports played by both neophytes as well as serious athletes, the questions of battery and the defense of consent are also fairly common issues in court. Is it battery for one soccer player to kick the goalie in the head while trying to score a goal, or for a hockey player to "high stick" an opponent while skating in a hockey game, or for a football defender to push down an offensive player and step on his or her hand while trying to intercept a pass in a game of pickup touch football?

The question in these cases is often framed as one of implied consent: whether the plaintiff "knew or should have known" of the risk of physical injury from playing such a hard and vigorous sport. What happens if the uninitiated participant doesn't know of the risk? What if the plaintiff consented, but only after first warning the defendant not to play rough? What if the defendant agreed not to play rough, but then got carried away in the heat of the moment? These cases are often resolved in favor of the defendants because the court finds implied consent on the part of the plaintiff.

In professional sporting activities, intentional violations of the rules of the game can also raise questions of battery and assault, especially when the career of the injured athlete has been jeopardized. Most courts require the plaintiff at least to show that the defendant acted recklessly. Proof of negligence will not suffice. *Nabonzy v. Barnhill*, 334 N.E.2d 258 (Ill. App. Ct. 1975). *Cf. Landrum v. Gonzalez*, 629 N.E.2d 710, 715 (Ill. App. Ct. 1st Dist. 1994) which appears to be limited to "contact" sports.

E. Summary Outline of Consent

To provide an example to students who may wish to create their own personalized torts study outlines, here is what a "Summary Outline" of the preceding materials on the defense of "consent" might actually look like. This can be used as a starting point from which to develop a more detailed study outline.

   I. Consent may be conveyed
     1. Expressly
       A. By words or
       B. Gestures
     2. Impliedly
       A. By any action or inaction that reasonably conveys consent (This relies on the objective manifestation of the action or inaction)
       B. By law
       C. By Custom
          Custom and use argument can be made for consent
       D. Inaction
          Inaction or silence can manifest consent
  II. Consent is invalidated by
     1. Incapacity
       A. Exception—Consent is implied as a matter of law if all of the following exist:
          i. Incapacity
          ii. An emergency situation
          iii. The lack of consent is not indicated
          iv. A reasonable person would consent under the circumstances
     2. Action Beyond the Scope of Consent
     3. Fraud
     4. Duress
     5. Illegality
 III. The defense of consent is not available in negligence cases.

II. Self-Defense

The second defense identified by most torts texts is that of self-defense. This defense is important for understanding when a person is privileged to use deadly force in defense of self, but it is also important to illustrate the tort law's first use of the qualifier, *reasonable*, to define the limitation on both the force itself as well as how much of that force can be used.

RESTATEMENT (SECOND) OF TORTS § 65 (1965) is peppered with the word reasonable:

(1) Subject to the statement in Subsection (3), an actor is privileged to defend himself against another by force intended or likely to cause death or serious bodily harm, when he *reasonably* believes that
  (a) the other is about to inflict upon him an intentional contact or other bodily harm, and that
  (b) he is thereby put in peril of death or serious bodily harm or ravishment, which can safely be prevented only by the immediate use of such force.

(2) The privilege stated in Subsection (1) exists although the actor correctly or *reasonably* believes that he can safely avoid the necessity of so defending himself by
  (a) retreating if he is attacked within his dwelling place, which is not also the dwelling place of the other, or
  (b) permitting the other to intrude upon or dispossess him of his dwelling place, or
  (c) abandoning an attempt to effect a lawful arrest.

(3) The privilege stated in Subsection (1) does not exist if the actor correctly or *reasonably* believes that he can with complete safety avoid the necessity of so defending himself by
  (a) retreating if attacked in any place other than his dwelling place, or in a place which is also the dwelling of the other, or
  (b) relinquishing the exercise of any right or privilege other than his privilege to prevent intrusion upon or dispossession of his dwelling place or to effect a lawful arrest. (*Emphasis supplied*).

So, in *Roberts v. American Employers Insurance Company* 221 So. 2d 550 (La. Ct. App. 1969), a drunken plaintiff was shot as he reached for an arresting officer's gun while resisting an arrest. The plaintiff was larger than the officer, had a criminal record that the officer knew about, had been drinking, cursed at the officer during his arrest, and was clearly the aggressor in the confrontation. All of this contributed to the officer's reasonable belief that he was going to be attacked and that he had to use the gun to defend himself. On the other hand, the evidence also showed that the plaintiff was unarmed, and handcuffed, and was shot in the jaw. Therefore, there was also reason to think that the officer was unreasonable in his belief that he would be attacked and unreasonable as to where he had aimed the gun. Cases like these present especially nice torts exam questions, because arguments easily can be made both for and against the use of force, as well as whether it was excessive, testing the students' ability to think comprehensively and objectively and to argue both sides. The famous Trayvon Martin case, (where a neighborhood vigilante confronted a black high school student, dressed in a "hoodie," and later killed him, claiming self-defense after the two became engaged in an altercation), is a prime example of how these policies can get even further complicated by issues of race, and various state "stand-your-ground" statutes.

Akin to the defense of self is the defense of others. This topic can often involve a close reading of rules regarding whether the use of force is necessary for the defense of another person, and, if so, how much force. Additionally, in defense of others cases, an important question is whether the defense is even applicable at all when the defendant acts in defense of another person who is reasonably, although mistakenly, believed to have been in peril. Such a situation pits two competing tort policies against each other: the policy of compensating the innocent from injury, versus that of finding no blameworthiness in the actor's reasonable belief that force was necessary.

III. Defense of Property

Looking at the defenses from a perspective of how much force can be used to defend the particular interest, the defense of property, no matter how valuable, is a defense where only a lesser amount of force is allowed. So, where a defendant uses force to defend his or her property, it is important to consider whether the defendant can also claim self defense (*see* section II., *supra*) as a justification for his or her actions, as well as the amount or type of force used, since each of these additional factors will be relevant in determining if the defense of property defense ultimately will be successful. RESTATEMENT (SECOND) OF TORTS §77 (1965). For example, in the famous case of *Bird v. Holbrook*, 4 Bing. 628, 130 Eng. Rep. 911, a property owner who set a spring gun to protect his flowers in his garden was held liable for injuries both because the property interest was not sufficiently important, and because the amount of force that was used was deemed excessive. This is true although the property owner may have been able to use the same force (i.e., shoot the trespasser in the leg) in self defense because the trespass occurred after sundown (i.e., such a trespass may have also constituted a common law burglary). *Bird v. Holbrook* is also of note because it says in justification of its holding that property is never more valuable than life, according to the laws of Christianity, and so makes explicit a connection between religion and the English common law.

A more modern example of the spring gun defense is found in *Katko v. Briney*, 183 N.W.2d 657 (Iowa 1971). There, a property owner who set a spring gun was again found liable for the injuries sustained by the trespasser. The property this time was a boarded up farmhouse with no trespassing signs. The trespasser was an antique bottle collector who opened the door to search inside an upstairs bedroom where the spring gun was set. The case is also remarkable because of the community's reaction: a collection was taken up to pay the defendant's judgment. Nevertheless, the law seems to be at odds with that community's sensibilities of moral responsibility for harm done by a spring gun. Sometimes, the setting alone can make a big difference in the outcome of the case. Thus, whether the spring gun is set in the defendant's summer home property or a cabin in Alaska may determine if the plaintiff can recover for injuries from such a device. The rationale appears to tie the use of deadly force in protection of property to the necessity and actuality for self-defense. A recent example of a case that explores whether deadly force is justified in the defense of one's self, home, and loved ones is the case of Oscar Pistorius, the South African Olympian, who claimed that he shot his 9 mm pistol 4 times through his closed toilet door to kill an intruder, only to find out that he had actually killed his live-in girlfriend.

A. Fresh Pursuit

Some torts courses devote a good deal of time on self-help remedies in defense of personal property and how tort rules, developed in personal property cases, affected later developments in landlord tenant law and the law of commercial sales. While individuals can use reasonable force to prevent a taking of their property that is occurring in their presence or has just occurred (i.e., request the taker to stop and then use non-excessive force to prohibit the taking), commercial businesses that experience repeated takings may not be able to use the same methods to prevent these types of takings. *See* UCC § 9-503 (3d ed. 1999). For example, while it is permissible to detain someone the business has probable cause to believe is a shoplifter, the use of public confrontations that merely accuse someone of theft is generally prohibited, since these types of detention can turn quickly into claims for false imprisonment and defamation. To avoid such claims, shopkeepers have generally preferred the use of more direct methods of proving theft, such as by installing security cameras and placing security tags on merchandise.

In addition, there are other tort cases dealing with forcible entry and "self-help" where a landlord attempts to get payment of rent from a delinquent tenant. While (s)he cannot threaten the tenant with a gun, can a landlord change the locks and constructively evict the tenant? In most jurisdictions, this forcible eviction needs to be preceded by a number of court-approved due process procedures before the landlord can take back his or her property.

B. Abusive Tactics

There are also classes of tort cases that involve the potential wrongful use of law enforcement to assist an individual in taking back their property. For example, in *State v. Dooley*, 26 S.W. 558 (Mo. 1894), a defendant's employee stole two horses from the employee's wife, using them to run a "bus" or stage-coach for the defendant. The wife offered a reward for the return of the horses. The local marshal and the local constable went to the defendant's employee with a warrant for his arrest for stealing the horses. The defendant's employee promptly offered to sell the horses to the defendant. The marshal and the constable took the horses from defendant's stagecoach and began to ride off with them. The defendant armed himself and rode after them, using threats to take back the horses. The court held that the defendant possessed the horses in good faith and the marshal and constable did not have a writ to say that they could take them. The court upheld the defendant's right to use force to take back the horses as long as it did not endanger life or cause great bodily harm, and concluded that the jury should have been so instructed.

Although such abusive conduct has sometimes been asserted in defense of certain types of property torts, it is far more likely to give rise to entirely separate intentional torts, known as abuse of process or misuse of process. These torts are discussed more thoroughly in Chapter 20, *infra*.

IV. Necessity

There are two branches of the necessity defense: private necessity and public necessity. A famous example of the private necessity defense is *Ploof v. Putnam*, 71 A. 188 (Vt. 1908), where the court justified a trespass where the trespasser attempted to dock his boat on another's property during a storm. When the landowner unmoored the boat, causing the boat to swamp and endangering the life of the boat owner and his family, the court announced that (private) *necessity* had justified his trespass and that the landowner's unmooring of the boat gave rise to liability.

It may follow that acts in defense of life might not only justify trespasses but also extend to other intentional torts. For example, does a private necessity ever justify the taking of one life to save another life? Moreover, does private necessity ever justify the taking of someone else's property merely to protect one's own property interests? These are just some of the questions that spin off from the principles announced in *Ploof v. Putnam. Vincent v. Lake Erie*, 124 N.W. 221 (Minn. 1910), is a famous example where the court found that an intentional taking of property out of private necessity was justified. Where a ship owner docked his ship, without negligence, and then a storm arose causing the continued mooring of the ship that damaged the dock during the storm, the court held that (private) *necessity justified* the ship's intentional continued mooring. Nevertheless, the court still ordered compensation for liability by the ship owner for the damage done to the plaintiff's dock. Its rationale was that public policy demanded compensation.

Of course, this is a curious result, as compensation is not ordered where others use force to defend self or property in other situations of valid defenses. *Vincent*, then creates a wild card in determining liability for intentional torts. It is a paradigm case for exploring the policies that undergird tort law: deterrence, compensation, and corrective justice. These policies also serve to move torts students to discussions about issues such as: insurance; who is the best cost avoider; what do we mean by the concepts of liability as opposed to blameworthiness; and what is the difference between attaching liabilities based on intent, negligence, or strict liability; as well as perhaps even certain issues involving causation.

The second branch of the necessity defense is public necessity. Here an actor may interfere with private property for the public good, and the public actor is not liable for *any* damage caused. For example, in *United States v. Caltex (Philippines), Inc.*, 344 U.S. 149 (1952), the U.S. Supreme Court, through Justice Vinson, found that no compensation was due to the plaintiff oil companies where the U.S. military had ordered the destruction of the plaintiff's oil facility to prevent it from falling into the hands of the Japanese after the bombing of Pearl Harbor. This case also raises a discussion of a *Vincent v. Lake Erie*-like analysis that is wrapped up in the Constitutional prohibition of government takings without just compensation. Where the actor is a city or state and the taking is to protect public health, public safety, or to promote economic development, the question is whether the municipal or state actor, even if otherwise privileged because of a public necessity, still needs to provide compensation. *Vincent v. Lake Erie* seems to hold as much. However, if there is truly a public necessity, like in time of war, flood, or local emergency, then the courts typically turn down compensation based solely on tort principles without more in the way of permission from the sovereign. *Cf. Wegner v. Milwaukee Mutual Ins. Co.*, 479 N.W.2d 38 (Minn. 1991). In these cases plaintiffs' lawyers might also choose to pursue other special remedies that have been provided by the legislature (like statutes creating "9-11" compensation) instead of litigation.

Checkpoints

- Consent can be a defense to an intentional tort if it is informed and un-coerced.

- Consent can be expressed or implied by conduct.

- When the tort is an intentional tort, assumption of the risk does not usually constitute a complete bar to recovery, especially where the jurisdiction is a comparative negligence jurisdiction.

- At common law, *assumption of risk* behavior is insufficient as defined in the context of negligence cases, and needs to fit into the definition of consent, in order for it to bar recovery for an intentional tort.

- Consent in medical malpractice saves a doctor from a cause of action for battery where the doctor's treatment would otherwise be an intentional harmful touching.

  - The doctor's treatment can still be negligence if the patient was not given information concerning all material risks (i.e., an informed consent).

  - Material risks are those that a reasonable person in the patient's position would likely attach significance to in deciding whether or not to forgo the proposed treatment.

  - Expert testimony is often required to establish the breach of this duty.

- Defense of self operates as a bar to recovery where the actor was reasonable in the belief that force was needed to defend his or her self from bodily harm and the use of such force was reasonable in the circumstances.

- Defense of others is similar to defense of self, though some jurisdictions do not allow its protection where the actor was, in fact, mistaken as to the need of the "other" for protection.

- Defense of property requires reasonable force, and so most often requires a request to stop before force calculated to cause bodily injury can be used.

- The tort of false imprisonment can occur from a business's attempts to protect itself from shoplifting, if the business does not have "probable cause" to believe that its property has been or is about to be taken.

- The "fresh pursuit" doctrine allows self-help in the defense of property only if the "taking" has just occurred or is still occurring.

- The "necessity" defense can provide justification for the use of force to protect one's self or one's family from unforeseen catastrophes.

    - In the case where life versus property is at stake, necessity can justify the destruction of property.

    - Where property versus property is at stake, while the resulting destruction may be said to be justified, or lawful, the court might still require the defendant to pay the plaintiff because of reasons of "public policy."

Chapter 4

Negligence

Roadmap

- Understand each of the elements of a negligence claim.
- Recognize when a person has a duty to act as a reasonably prudent person under the same or similar circumstances.
- Identify special situations when the duty standard varies from that of the reasonably prudent person.
- Learn how to determine whether an actor has breached a duty of care.
- Understand the role of custom evidence in determining breach of duty.
- Understand the significance of evidence that an actor has violated a criminal statute or a regulation.
- Recognize special circumstances where a court might infer breach of duty.

I. Introduction

Negligence is the second major category or basis of tort liability, and it forms the foundation of most all of modern tort law. To succeed in a negligence action, a plaintiff must prove the following elements:

(1) *Duty.* In most cases, an actor must behave as a reasonably prudent person would under the same or similar circumstances. This standard, however, varies under certain circumstances as described, *infra.*

(2) *Breach of Duty.* The plaintiff must prove that the defendant violated the relevant standard of care. Courts sometimes refer to this element alone as "negligence," although the cause of action also goes by this same name.

(3) *Causation.* The plaintiff must prove both "cause in fact" and "proximate cause." Cause in fact requires the plaintiff to connect the defendant's breach of duty to the resulting harm. In most cases, the plaintiff must show that (s)he would not have been injured "but for" the defendant's conduct. (*See* Chapter 5, *infra*, Cause in Fact). Proximate cause

requires the plaintiff to establish a sufficiently close connection between the breach and the harm. In most cases, the concept of foreseeability drives the determination of proximate cause. (*See* Chapter 6, *infra*, Proximate Cause).

(4) *Damages.* The plaintiff must prove that the defendant's breach caused some type of actual harm. (*See* Chapter 8, *infra*, Compensatory and Punitive Damages).

This chapter addresses the first two elements of a negligence claim—duty and breach. The remaining elements are addressed in subsequent chapters, as indicated *supra*.

II. Duty

Duty is a question of law (i.e., it is a matter for the judge to decide, rather than the jury). This means that while duty is technically an element of negligence, it is not something that a plaintiff must "prove." Instead, it is a judicially granted gateway to the remainder of his or her negligence claim. If a judge finds that no duty exists, the case is over. If the judge finds that a duty exists, the court (i.e., the judge) sets an appropriate standard of care by which the jury will then measure each party's conduct. Thus, duty is essentially a two-part process for the court to decide. First, the judge must determine that a duty is owed. Then, the judge also must determine the relevant standard of care with respect to that duty.

The first part of the process merits little attention in this chapter. It is only in unusual cases that a party owes no duty to another, and we will cover those situations in Chapter 9, *infra*, (Limited Duty). In most cases involving physical damage, an actor owes a duty to nearly everyone. The classic statement of this principle comes from the 19th century English case of *Heaven v. Pender*, 11 Q.B.D. 503, 509 (1883):

> [W]henever one person is by circumstances placed in such a position with regard to another that everyone of ordinary sense who did think would at once recognise that if he did not use ordinary care and skill in his own conduct with regard to the circumstances he would cause danger of injury to the person or property of the other, a duty arises to use ordinary care and skill to avoid such danger.

As the Wisconsin Supreme Court put it in more modern terms: "[E]veryone has a duty of care to the whole world." *Miller v. Wal-Mart Stores, Inc.*, 580 N.W.2d 233, 238 (Wis. 1998).

A. The Reasonably Prudent Person Standard

The second part of the process—the determination of the standard of care—requires more attention because the standard varies depending on the facts of each case. In most negligence cases, an actor owes the degree of care that would be exercised by a reasonably prudent person under the same or similar circumstances. This so-called "reasonably prudent person" standard is objective and, frankly, not always kind to the individual being evaluated. As A.P. Herbert famously once stated:

> [The reasonably prudent person] is an ideal, a standard, the embodiment of all those qualities, which we demand of the good citizen. . . . [The reasonably prudent person is] one who invariably looks where he is going, and is careful to examine the immediate foreground before he executes a leap or bound; who neither stargazes nor is lost in meditation when approaching trapdoors or the margin of a dock . . . and will inform himself of the history and habits of a dog before administering a caress . . . who definitely never drives his ball until those in front of him have definitely vacated the putting green which is his own objective; who . . . never swears, gambles, or loses his temper; who uses nothing except in moderation, and even while he flogs his child is meditating only on the golden mean.

A.P Herbert, Misleading Cases in the Common Law 12 (7th ed. 1932).

Perhaps the most famous early illustration of this principle comes from the English decision of *Vaughan v. Menlove*, 132 Eng. Rep. 490 (C.P. 1837). In *Vaughan*, the defendant built a hayrick on his property near the plaintiff's cottages. Others repeatedly warned the defendant about the perils (due to the risk of fire) created by his structure. The defendant responded by adding a chimney to the rick. In spite of this (or perhaps because of this), the rick burst into flames and burned down the cottages. When the plaintiff sued, the defendant argued that he should not be held liable because he personally did not know any better. The court refused to use such a subjective standard, noting the impracticalities of applying a rule that "would be as variable as the length of the foot of each individual." *Id.* at 493. Instead, the court ruled that an objective standard, based on the knowledge of an ordinary reasonable person, should be used to evaluate an actor's conduct.

Although the reasonable person is the general rule, subjectivity occasionally infiltrates the standard. For example, those with exceptional skills or knowledge are required to use them for the benefit of others. For example, a master electrician would be expected to use that knowledge when handling electrical equipment, and a champion sailor would need to exercise such talents in maneuvering a boat. In a sense, this principle can also be seen in the law's use of a separate standard for professional defendants, a topic discussed later in this chapter.

Subjective characteristics also count in situations where an actor has a physical disability. In these cases, the duty standard incorporates the disability so that an actor is compared to a reasonably prudent person with the same disability. For example, a deaf defendant would be compared to a reasonably prudent person who could not hear, or a blind person would be compared to a reasonably prudent person who could not see. As Justice Oliver Wendell Holmes explained:

> A blind man is not required to see at his peril; and although he is, no doubt, bound to consider his infirmity in regulating his actions, precautions requiring eyesight would not prevent his recovering for an injury to himself, and, it may be presumed, would not make him liable for injuring another.

Oliver Wendell Holmes, Jr., THE COMMON LAW 109 (1881).

However, this accommodation does not create a standard that one would describe as "higher" or "lower." In some cases, it might protect a person with a disability from liability where others would be negligent. Conversely, in different situations it might be unreasonable for a person with a disability to act where others could do so safely, and liability would result.

All that said, drawing the line between physical disability and mental disability is not easy, and courts have struggled in the gray areas. For example, should the standard applied to an elderly actor be somewhat subjective due to the effects of old age? What about a person with a diagnosed mental illness? In general, the law is unsympathetic to defendants in these types of situations. Absent specific physical conditions, old age alone is not relevant to determining the standard of care in a negligence case. Similarly, mental illness does not change the principle that a defendant is held to the conduct expected of a reasonably prudent person, although some courts do make exceptions when an actor's conduct is being considered for purposes of evaluating a *plaintiff's* conduct in a contributory or comparative negligence analysis.

B. The Duty Standard for Children

The law judges children by a special—and more subjective—standard of care. This standard acknowledges that children are less able to appreciate the risks and consequences of their choices. It also recognizes that they need an opportunity to live, learn, and develop as adults. Of course, children develop at different rates. To account for this, courts have long used a sliding scale that imposes more responsibility on children as they age.

Traditionally, courts followed the so-called "rule of sevens." Under this rule, children under the age of seven were presumed incapable of negligence (i.e., children of that age simply owed no duty of care to others). Children between seven and fourteen were also presumed to be incapable of negligence, but plaintiffs could rebut the presumption by showing that a particular child was capable of the negligent act in question. At fourteen and over, the presumption flipped. Children were presumed capable of behaving as reasonably prudent people, but the child could rebut the presumption and show that (s)he was not.

Today, most courts have moved away from the "rule of sevens" and apply a more flexible approach. Under this approach, children are deemed incapable of negligence until four or five years of age. After that, a child is simply compared to a reasonably prudent *child* of like age, intelligence, and experience. However, it is important to understand how this standard is different from the reasonably prudent person standard that is applied in cases involving adults. Here, "Little Johnny" is compared to a reasonably careful child, but one who is also just as young, just as immature, and just as inexperienced as "Little Johnny" himself. This actually makes the co-called child standard of care much more subjective than its adult counterpart.

There is one major exception to the duty rule regarding children. If the child engages in an adult activity, (s)he is held to the adult reasonably prudent person standard. The Restatement of Torts defines such an activity as "a dangerous activity that is characteristically undertaken by adults." RESTATEMENT (THIRD) OF TORTS: LIABILITY FOR PHYSICAL HARM §10. This definition includes activities such as operating automobiles, motorcycles, motorboats, or tractors. With other activities, however, the law is less clear. For example, recent authority suggests that using a firearm, even when hunting, is an adult activity, despite some older cases that disagree. On the opposite end of the spectrum, recent authority suggests that riding a bicycle is *not* an adult activity, as it is something commonly (perhaps even especially likely) done by children. Again, some courts and commentators disagree, asserting that children who injure others while cycling should not receive the benefit of the subjective child duty standard. Regardless, the key to making an argument in this area is to focus on both parts of the rule: the dangerousness of the activity and whether it is characteristically something that is done by adults.

C. The Duty Standard for Professionals

Those sued for negligence based on their professional conduct are also evaluated by a different duty standard. Professionals (i.e., doctors, lawyers, accountants, engineers, etc.) must behave as ordinary members of their profession under the same or similar circumstances. Once again, it is important to see how this standard is different from the reasonable person standard. In professional negligence cases, the profession itself, rather than the general community, sets the standard by which conduct is evaluated. The parties will need to introduce evidence (normally by expert testimony) to establish this duty standard, as a lay jury would not typically understand what is "ordinary" in a given profession.

In earlier cases, and particularly in medical malpractice cases, courts often included a locality component in the professional standard; that is, professionals were compared to members of their profession within the same community or those similar to it. The rationale behind this rule was to protect doctors in smaller communities who might not have access to cutting edge training or facilities. Today, the standard is essentially nationalized. As Professor Dan Dobbs wrote in his leading tort law treatise: "[T]oday's mainstream medical doctors are all trained in the same basic way throughout the country and all have access to continuing education and even to instant computer guidance. Medical and scientific facts are the same everywhere." DAN B. DOBBS, THE LAW OF TORTS 636 (West Group 2000). This is certainly true for medical specialists, who are often board-certified on a national level.

D. The Duty Standard for Land Owners and Occupiers

The duty standard in negligence cases brought against landowners and occupiers, for injuries both on and off the land, is a detailed and complex area of the law. In this realm, the rules often vary based on the relationship between the plaintiff and the land possessor. We will treat this issue separately in Chapter 10, *infra*, (Premises Liability).

III. Breach of Duty

A. Risk-Utility Balancing Test

Once the standard for evaluating conduct has been established, the next step is to decide if a person has breached (i.e., violated) those standards. When using the reasonably prudent person standard, most courts determine whether an actor created an unreasonable risk of harm by using some form of a risk-utility balancing test. The comments to the Restatement of Torts state that this balancing approach "rests on and expresses a simple idea. Conduct is negligent if its disadvantages outweigh its advantages, while the conduct is not negligent if its advantages outweigh its disadvantages." RESTATEMENT (THIRD) OF TORTS: LIABILITY FOR PHYSICAL HARM § 3, comment *d*.

The most famous articulation of the risk-utility balancing test comes from Judge Learned Hand's opinion in *United States v. Carroll Towing Co.,* 159 F.2d 169 (2d Cir. 1947). In *Carroll Towing,* a barge broke loose from a pier when its bargee was not present. The barge struck the propeller of a nearby tanker, causing the barge to leak, ultimately sink, and lose its cargo. The cargo owner and others sought to recover for damages from the barge's charterer based on the bargee's failure to be aboard the vessel at the time of the accident. Ultimately, the court found that the bargee's absence constituted negligence, but more important was Judge Hand's approach to the issue. Judge Hand stated that the determination of negligence was "a function of three variables: The *probability* that [the barge would] break away; (2) the *gravity* of the resulting injury, if she does; (3) the *burden* of adequate precautions." Hence, we have Judge Hand's famous formula for determining breach of duty—whether B (the burden) is less than P (the probability) multiplied by L (the gravity of the resulting injury or loss).

$$B < P \times L$$

Some prominent commentators, notably Judge Richard Posner of the Seventh Circuit U.S. Court of Appeals, assert that the Hand formula indicates that all tort law can be construed using economic cost-benefit analysis. "The Hand formula shows that it is possible to think about tort law in economic terms—that, in fact, a famous judge thought about it so. [T]he Hand formula—more broadly economic analysis—provides a unifying perspective in which to view all of tort law." RICHARD A. POSNER, TORT LAW, CASES AND ECONOMIC ANALYSIS 2 (1982). Others have challenged this perspective and argue that the risk-utility balancing approach does not dominate negligence determinations as much as many assume. *See* Richard W. Wright, *Hand, Posner, and the Myth of the 'Hand Formula,'* 4 THEORETICAL INQUIRIES IN LAW 145 (2003).

Scholarly debates aside, the Reporters for the current Restatement of Torts cite to a plethora of cases indicating that a large majority of U.S. jurisdictions do, in some form or fashion, use a balancing approach to determine breach of duty in negligence cases. RESTATEMENT (THIRD) OF TORTS: LIABILITY FOR PHYSICAL HARM § 3, cmt. *d*, Reporters' Note. Nonetheless, the fact that many courts use a balancing approach does not mean that judges or juries can (or should) attempt to apply the test with mathematical precision. Sometimes, evidence about the actual costs of precautions will be useful. However, even without exact figures it is appropriate to consider how an actor could have altered a particular negligent activity to make it safer. In rare instances, it is even possible to argue that it is unreasonable to engage in certain activities at any level. Balancing these considerations against the other side of the equation, the likelihood of harm, should be based on a consideration of what was foreseeable to the defendant when (s)he acted. Similarly, evaluating harm requires a consideration of foreseeable damage and not simply the plaintiff's actual injury.

B. Evidence of Custom

Some evidence carries special weight in determining breach of duty. One important example is evidence of custom. In cases that involve custom, parties essentially equate reasonableness with behavior that is typical. If it's typically done, the argument goes, it is reasonable to do it. If it is typically not done, it is reasonable not to do it.

As one might imagine, evidence of custom can be very powerful in a negligence case, but it is not dispositive. In other words, it is indicative of negligence (or the lack thereof) but such evidence is not conclusive on its own. Again, Judge Learned Hand wrote the classic opinion on this point in *The T.J. Hooper*, 60 F.2d 737 (2nd Cir. 1932). In *The T.J. Hooper*, several tugs, including the T.J. Hooper, left Virginia with barges of coal bound for New York. Shortly after passing the Delaware breakwater, they ran into bad weather and two of the barges sunk. The cargo owners filed a negligence action, arguing that the tugs were unseaworthy because they lacked a radio that could have received advance reports of the storm. The defendants argued that they did not breach the duty standard because such radio equipment was not customary among tug operators at the time. Judge Hand disagreed and stated that it is for courts to determine what is reasonable, regardless of custom:

> [I]n most cases reasonable prudence is in fact common prudence; but strictly it is never its measure; a whole calling may have unduly lagged in the adoption of new and available devices. It never may set its own tests, however persuasive be its usages. Courts must in the end say what is required; there are precautions so imperative that even their universal disregard will not excuse their omission. 60 F.2d at 740.

Bear in mind that it works the other way around, too. A defendant who departs from customary safety measures might avoid negligence liability if a judge or jury finds that the balancing test weighs against the custom.

C. Negligence *Per Se*

Another example of evidence that carries special weight in determining breach is when an actor has violated a criminal statute or a regulation. Legislative bodies sometimes enact laws that specifically designate specific civil consequences, but, here, we consider laws that impose criminal or administrative sanctions *without* reference to civil liability. The issue in such cases is whether violation of these statutes nonetheless constitutes negligence in a civil action. If so, courts often describe it as an example of "negligence *per se*."

In general, courts will find that violation of a statute constitutes negligence when the statute meets a two-part test. First, the statute must be designed to protect a class of persons within which the plaintiff falls. Second, the statute must be designed to protect against a type of risk that matches the harm that the plaintiff suffered in the case at hand.

The scope of the test's first part (i.e., the class of persons) varies widely. The class of persons might extend broadly to any individual who becomes injured as a consequence of the violation. On the other hand, a statute might be narrowly designed, say to protect workers in a given industry. In such a situation, a plaintiff from outside that industry would not be able to rely on a statutory violation to prove breach of duty for harm caused by the defendant's conduct.

The second part of the test (i.e., the type of risk) is not dissimilar to the proximate cause analysis that courts undertake in all tort cases. Here, a court must determine that the accident was within the scope of what the statute's drafters intended to prevent by enacting the law. A well-known example comes from the case of *Gorris v. Scott*, L.R. 9 Ex. 125 (1874). In *Gorris*, the plaintiff shipped a number of sheep on the defendant's ship. The defendant failed to put the animals in a pen, and they were washed overboard during a storm. A statute, the Contagious Disease Act of 1869, required ship owners to pen animals aboard their vessels. Adherence to this statute might have prevented the animals from going overboard, yet the court refused to find that its violation constituted negligence:

> [I]f we could see that it was the object, or among the objects of this Act, that the owners of sheep and cattle coming from a foreign port should be protected by the means described against the danger of their property being washed overboard, or lost by the perils of the sea, the present action would be within the principle.
>
> But, looking at the Act, it is perfectly clear that its provisions were all enacted with a totally different view; there was no purpose, direct or indirect to protect against such damage; but as is recited in the

preamble, the Act is directed against the possibility of sheep or cattle being exposed to disease on their way to this country. L.R. 9 Ex. at 129.

Even when the two-part test is satisfied, courts have carved out exceptions where a statutory violation is not always considered negligence. One such exception is where the actor's violation is otherwise reasonable, perhaps because (s)he has some recognized incapacity (minor status, physical disability, or physical incapacity) or simply because the actor used reasonable care in attempting to comply with the statute. As an example, a comment to the Restatement of Torts considers a statute requiring drivers to remain on the correct side of the road. The comment suggests that in some circumstances (e.g., an emergency on the road or adverse weather that blocked a lane) violating that law actually would be the reasonably prudent thing to do. *See* RESTATEMENT (THIRD) OF TORTS: LIABILITY FOR PHYSICAL HARM § 5, cmt. c.

In a sense, this exception overlaps with another well-settled exception to the negligence *per se* principle. In this second exception, compliance with the statute would be more dangerous than violating the statute. A classic example of this principle comes from *Tedla v. Ellman,* 19 N.E.2d 987 (N.Y. 1939). In *Tedla,* the plaintiff and her brother were walking along a highway shortly after dark, collecting junk for resale as part of their business. Instead of walking on the left-hand side of the highway and facing oncoming traffic, as required by statute, they walked on the right-hand side of the road, where traffic was much lighter, even though it approached them from behind. The defendant struck them with his car, hurting the plaintiff and killing her brother. The defendant's negligence was established at trial, but an issue was raised as to the plaintiffs' contributory negligence for violating the statute. The court refused to find that the violation constituted (contributory) negligence *per se,* as it would have been more dangerous for the plaintiffs to walk on the left side of the road, where traffic was heavier:

> If that be true, then the Legislature has decreed that pedestrians must observe the general rule of conduct, which it has prescribed for their safety even under circumstances where observance would subject them to unusual risk; that pedestrians are to be charged with negligence as a matter of law for acting as prudence dictates. It is unreasonable to ascribe to the Legislature an intention that the statute should have so extraordinary a result, and the courts may not give to a statute an effect not intended by the Legislature. 19 N.E.2d at 989.

Other examples of situations where courts will excuse a statutory violation in a negligence action include cases where an actor does not know, or should not know, about the facts that make the statute applicable, or even where the statute is sufficiently confusing in the way it presents its requirements to the public. As the comments to the Restatement explain, "ignorance of the law does not count as an excuse, [but] for negligence *per se* to operate fairly the legal system must avoid confusion in its communication of the law's obligations. Accordingly, if a statute is so vague or ambiguous that even the actor aware of the statute would need to guess as to its requirements, the actor who makes a reasonable guess is excused from negligence *per se*." RESTATEMENT (THIRD) OF TORTS: LIABILITY FOR PHYSICAL HARM § 15, cmt. *e*. Similarly, impossibility of compliance will ordinarily excuse a violation for purposes of maintaining a negligence *per se* action.

Before moving forward, it is worth clarifying several other points about negligence *per se*. First, a plaintiff who successfully proves that a statute fits the two-part test does not automatically win in a negligence case. Rather, it simply allows the plaintiff to prove breach of duty without using a balancing test. The plaintiff will still need to go forward and prove the remaining elements of the claim, notably causation and damages. Conversely, a plaintiff who fails to show that a statute satisfies the two-part test does not automatically lose in a negligence action. Such a plaintiff still can go forward and attempt to prove breach of duty using the normal balancing test. Finally, it is worth noting that actors sometime argue that they are not negligent because they have complied with a statute. In these types of situations, courts treat the actor's conduct as they do adherence to custom, i.e., it is evidence of reasonable behavior, but it does not insulate the actor from the possibility of negligence liability.

D. *Res Ipsa Loquitur*

In most cases, it is incumbent on the plaintiff to provide sufficient evidence (either direct or circumstantial) to demonstrate that the defendant has violated a standard of care. In some cases, however, providing such evidence is impossible. For example, in the famous case of *Byrne v. Boadle,* 159 Eng. Rep. 299 (Exch. 1863), the plaintiff was hit by a falling flour barrel as he walked on a sidewalk below the defendant's shop. The barrel undoubtedly came from the defendant's establishment, but the plaintiff was in no position to explain exactly how the defendant had been negligent. Did the defendant store the barrel in an unsafe fashion? Or did one of the defendant's employees handle the barrel in a careless fashion? Despite the plaintiff's inability to muster evidence, the court permitted him to proceed with his negligence action, explaining that: "There are certain cases of which it may be said *res ipsa loquitur*, and this seems one of them. . . . A barrel could not roll out of a warehouse without some negligence, and to say that a plaintiff who is injured by it must call witnesses from the warehouse to prove negligence seems to me preposterous." *Id.* at 300-301.

Res ipsa loquitur is a Latin phrase meaning, "the thing speaks for itself." In cases where the doctrine applies, courts allow a jury to infer negligence on the part of a defendant if the plaintiff is hurt in an accident that does not normally occur unless there is negligence by someone in a class of actors within which the defendant falls.

This basic test for *res ipsa loquitur* has evolved in recent years. It used to be common for courts to require a plaintiff to prove that the defendant had exclusive control of the instrumentality that caused the plaintiff's harm. Based on a long list of cases decided during the past thirty years, however, the current Restatement explicitly rejects "exclusive control" as an element of the test. The comments to the Restatement justify this on two grounds. One is that the test can be indeterminate in cases where several instrumentalities might have caused the plaintiff's harm. The second is the fact that exclusive control is sometimes a poor proxy for the ultimate question of which party was likely negligent. The comments provide an example of someone who buys a new car and has the brakes fail the next day, leading to an accident. Even though the driver had exclusive control of the car, it is unlikely that any negligence of the driver under these circumstances caused the accident. RESTATEMENT (THIRD) OF TORTS: LIABILITY FOR PHYSICAL HARM § 17, cmt. *b*.

A plaintiff who proves *res ipsa loquitur* does not automatically establish breach of duty. Instead, in most jurisdictions it simply spares the plaintiff from a directed verdict and creates an inference of breach as the case goes to the jury.

Checkpoints

- Duty is a question of law.
  - The judge decides whether the defendant owes a duty of care to the plaintiff in each individual case.
  - In most cases involving physical damage, the defendant owes a duty to the world at large.
- In most negligence cases, actors must behave as a reasonably prudent person would under the same or similar circumstances.

- This is an objective standard, and courts do not take account of an individual's mental deficiencies.

  - However, courts do consider some subjective characteristics. In particular, physical disabilities are considered when applying the reasonably prudent person duty standard.

  - Similarly, courts take account of an individual's exceptional knowledge and skills.

- Children are judged by a special duty standard.

  - In most jurisdictions today, courts compare children to a reasonably prudent child of like age, intelligence, and experience.

  - However, when children engage in a "dangerous activity that is characteristically undertaken by adults," they are judged by the objective reasonably prudent person standard.

- Professionals are judged by a special duty standard—a standard that is set by the profession itself.

  - In most cases, professionals must act as an ordinary member of their profession under the same or similar circumstances.

  - The professional standard normally must be established by expert testimony.

- In determining whether an actor has breached the reasonably prudent person standard, most courts use a balancing test, weighing the advantages and disadvantages of the actor's conduct. The most famous articulation of the balancing test is Learned Hand's formula from the *Carroll Towing* case (i.e., whether B<PL).

- Custom evidence is not dispositive on the issue of breach. It is admissible and may be used as evidence that a party has behaved reasonably (or not). But in the end, it is for a judge or jury to determine whether an actor has acted as a reasonably prudent person.

- Courts sometimes treat violations of a criminal statute or a regulation as negligence *per se* even if the statute or regulation is silent on the question of civil liability.

  - Courts do so only when the statute meets a two-part test. First, the statute must be designed to protect a class of persons within which the plaintiff falls.

  - Second, the statute must be designed to protect against a type of risk that matches the harm suffered by the plaintiff in the case at hand.

- There are several well-known exceptions to negligence *per se*.

  - One example is where the actor's violation of a statute is deemed reasonable, for example, where adhering to the statute would be more dangerous than violating its terms.

- • Another example is where an actor does not or should not know about facts that make the statute applicable.
- • When evidence of a defendant's breach of duty is unavailable, a plaintiff can sometimes proceed by using the evidentiary doctrine of *res ipsa loquitur*. In these cases, courts allow juries to infer negligence if the plaintiff is hurt in an accident that does not normally occur in the absence of negligence by someone in a class of actors within which the defendant falls.

Chapter 5

Cause in Fact

Roadmap

- Understand the essential link between causation and the negligent conduct of the defendant.
- Understand how to apply the "but for" test for determining cause in fact.
- Understand how to apply the "substantial factor" test for determining cause in fact.
- Learn how to allocate individual harms to specific causes.
- Recognize special problems in proving cause in fact, such as those involving the loss of a chance or the use of statistical proof.

I. Introduction: The Essential Link

Causation is fundamental to tort liability. In order to hold a defendant liable for an injury, the plaintiff must show that the defendant, by some tortious conduct, caused the injury. In tort law it is generally agreed that without this causal linkage, there is no just basis for making the defendant compensate the plaintiff. For this reason, causation is part of the plaintiff's *prima facie* case for almost every type of tort action, which the plaintiff must prove by a preponderance of the evidence. In tort law generally, but especially in negligence, this causal element is usually divided into two parts. The first part, the topic of this chapter, is called "actual cause" or "cause in fact." Cause in fact purports to determine as a matter of ordinary reasoning whether the defendant's tortious conduct brought about the harm to the plaintiff. (As we shall see, this inquiry is often not as pristine as the above statement might suggest.) The second part of the causation element is called "proximate" or "legal" cause, and that is the topic of the next chapter. In this second part of the analysis we determine whether the defendant's tortious conduct, shown to be a cause in fact, was also legally significant enough in bringing about the plaintiff's harm, so that it is otherwise appropriate to hold the defendant liable.

II. "But For" Test

The basic test of cause in fact is the "but for" test. The plaintiff must prove that "but for" the defendant's tortious conduct, (s)he would not have been injured. The way that courts apply this test can be illustrated by the following example.

Suppose that a car hits a pedestrian while (s)he is walking across an intersection controlled by a stop sign. The accident occurred because the driver was inattentive and did not see the stop sign, which we will assume was negligent conduct on the driver's part. The "but for" test asks: *but for* the driver's lack of attention, would the plaintiff have been injured? And the answer would be "no," the plaintiff would not have been injured, because an attentive driver would have seen the stop sign, stopped the car, and the pedestrian would have crossed safely.

Several aspects of this hypothetical deserve closer attention. First, the test focuses on the negligent aspect of the tortfeasor's conduct: in this case, on the driver's lack of attention. The test does not look more generally at the conduct, for example by focusing on the act of driving itself. In looking at the negligent act, the test then poses the counterfactual question of what would have happened if the negligent aspect of the conduct were removed from the picture. In the hypothetical, we therefore replace the driver's inattention with attention, which probably (i.e., "more likely than not") would have resulted in the driver's seeing the stop sign and avoiding the accident. It is apparent that the approach of the "but for" test is somewhat speculative, since no one can be certain what would have happened absent the negligent conduct. The burden on the plaintiff is to present sufficient proof of actual cause to satisfy the preponderance of the evidence standard.

In the hypothetical, *supra*, only a single negligent cause was involved. However, the "but for" test also works in many cases of multiple tortfeasors and multiple causes. A common example of this is the "intervening cause" problem that will be discussed in more detail in Chapter 6, *infra*, on Proximate Cause. In this type of case, one tortfeasor's negligence will create an unreasonably risky situation, while the second actor's negligence then triggers the harm to the victim. For example, in *Herman v. Markham Air Rifle Co.*, 258 F. 475 (E.D. Mich. 1918), the manufacturer of an air rifle negligently shipped it to a store already loaded with pellets. A customer in the store, examining the air rifle as a possible purchase, then negligently pulled the trigger while the rifle was pointed at the plaintiff, a salesclerk in the store. The rifle discharged a pellet, which struck the plaintiff and destroyed the sight in one eye.

The "but for" cause test works perfectly well in this type of multi-party tort. *But for* the negligence of the rifle manufacturer in shipping the rifle loaded with shot, the customer's negligent act of pulling the trigger while the rifle was pointed at the plaintiff would not have caused any harm. By the same token, however, *but for* the negligent conduct of the customer in pulling the trigger, the negligence of the rifle manufacturer would not have caused any harm either. Both acts of negligence were necessary in order to cause plaintiff's injury, and both are therefore "but for" causes of the harm. This illustration should make it clear to the student that the "but for" test should not be abandoned simply because more than one cause is operating to produce the plaintiff's injury.

III. Substantial Factor Test

Nevertheless, one type of multiple defendant or multiple cause situation does create problems for the "but for" cause test. This occurs when multiple causes not only exist (as in the previous case) but also cancel each other out. A familiar example of this problem is a multiple fire case such as the one in *Anderson v. Minneapolis, St. Paul & Sault Ste Marie Ry. Co.*, 179 N.W. 45 (Minn. 1920). The problem posed by this case involves two fires, one negligently started by the defendant railroad, and another fire of uncertain and possibly natural origin. Both fires threatened the plaintiff's property; either fire alone might be sufficient to destroy it. However, before either of the separate fires actually arrived at the plaintiff's land they merged, and the combined merged fire swept over and destroyed the plaintiff's property.

In this scenario, if neither fire was sufficient by itself to destroy the plaintiff's property, but the combined fire was, then both fires are "but for" causes and the test still works. If, on the other hand, each fire was sufficient by itself to cause the destruction, then it cannot be said that the defendant railroad's fire was a "but for" cause of the harm. By this hypothesis, the plaintiff's property still would have been destroyed by the other fire even if the defendant had not been negligent in starting the first fire. The issue can be made even starker by positing that the second fire was started, also negligently, by another railroad. We now have two negligent parties and two fires, but if the two fires joined, and each fire were sufficient by itself to have caused the destruction of the plaintiff's property, then neither fire was a but-for cause. Each defendant will point to the other and claim that its negligence was not a "but for" cause, since the other fire by itself still would have caused the harm. Courts have avoided this unpalatable result by aggregating the causes and holding both railroads jointly liable.

In *Anderson*, where the second fire may have been of natural origin and there was no second tortfeasor to join, the court solved the dilemma by telling the jury that it could hold the railroad liable if it found that the railroad's fire was a "material and substantial element" in causing the plaintiff's damage. The meaning of this so-called "substantial factor" test, unfortunately, is not entirely clear. However, the general idea seems to be that the jury should consider how significant the defendant's fire seemed to be in contributing to the harm. In other words, was it a big fire, with significant potential for harm? Or, on the other hand, was it a puny fire whose effects were overwhelmed by the other fire? In any event, the "substantial factor" test gives courts a way of finding causation in situations of redundant factors such as the fire cases. The test is an early example of relaxation of strict causation rules when the situation seems to demand it. Further examples will be discussed in the materials, *infra*, as well as in Chapter 7, *infra*, (Multiple Tortfeasors).

IV. Allocation of Harms to Causes

The "substantial factor" test has the effect of aggregating the causes of harm and imposing joint liability. In some situations, however, it is possible to allocate different harms to separate causes, and when this result is clear enough it is probably the proper thing to do. To continue with the multiple fires hypothetical, suppose that one fire burned down the plaintiff's apple orchard to the west, while the other fire burned the plaintiff's cornfield to the east, before the two fires joined and burned down the plaintiff's barn and farmhouse. If it is clear that different fires (or different tortfeasors) caused separable harms, then allocating the particular harm to the particular cause is a more accurate way of assessing responsibility. This approach, however, can still run into conflict with the "substantial factor" test.

An example of this conflict is found in *Dillon v. Twin State Gas & Electric Co.*, 163 A. 111 (N.H. 1932). A boy, while climbing on the steel girders of a bridge began to fall, and as he did so he reached out and touched an uninsulated power line maintained by the defendant utility. The boy was killed by electrocution. The court ruled that if the boy would likely have been killed or severely disabled by the fall itself, the negligence of the utility (in failing to insulate its power line) had only deprived the boy of seconds of life, or perhaps of a life of limited earning capacity due to a serious disability had the boy somehow managed to survive the fall. The recovery in the former case was so small as to be negligible, and in the latter had to be limited by the prospect of the boy's reduced future earning capacity. The key seems to be the presence of an existing source of harm, the fall.

If this approach were to be applied to the fire problem, however, it could be argued that the presence of a second fire of natural origin, capable of causing the destruction of plaintiff's property by itself, should limit any recovery. For example, if the railroad's fire burned the plaintiff's property before the other fire arrived, could one argue that the plaintiff could only recover the market value of the property in light of the looming disaster approaching from the other direction? The "substantial factor" test would say no, but the approach of allocating harms to causes might suggest such a limit. Here, the "substantial factor" test is the prevailing rule, even if the second fire is of natural origin. RESTATEMENT (SECOND) OF TORTS § 432, cmt. *d.*

V. Proof of Causation

The plaintiff generally bears the burden of proof that the defendant's negligence was a cause in fact of the harm. However, as we have already seen, this proof can be difficult when many causes and forces are operating. Plaintiffs can also run into problems when the exact mechanism of the injury is unclear, so that the contribution of the defendant's negligence is not demonstrated. For example, in *Paine v. Gamble Stores,* 279 N.W. 257 (Minn. 1938), the plaintiff's husband was found dead at the bottom of a stairwell that was guarded by a railing that was missing its top rail. The plaintiff alleged that the property owner negligently maintained the railing, but the problem was how to prove that the lack of the top rail was the cause of the fall. The plaintiff might have fallen on the stairs, or over a part of the railing that was in proper condition, but there was no direct proof as to what had caused the decedent's fall. Nevertheless, the plaintiff's counsel succeeded in proving a circumstantial case by an analysis of the position of the body, the condition of the stair treads, the lack of evidence of a struggle, and other items of physical evidence. By way of contrast, consider the situation in *Fleming v. Kings Ridge Recreation Park, Inc.,* 525 N.Y.S.2d 866 (N.Y. App. Div. 1988), which involved a child's fall from a diving board. There the plaintiff was able to prove that the railing on a diving board was too low, but was unable to provide any evidence of how the fall actually occurred. For this reason the suit was dismissed, because the plaintiff had not met her burden of showing that the negligent conduct (i.e., the low railing) caused her to fall. In cases such as this, although the defendant's negligent conduct may have increased the risk of such an accident occurring, the plaintiff still must marshal enough evidence to show that more likely than not the negligence was indeed the cause of the injury.

Many situations involving multiple tortfeasors present problems of proof of causation. Doctrines such as alternative liability, enterprise liability, and market share liability are responses to the inability of the plaintiff to prove cause in fact when multiple parties are at fault. These issues are discussed in Chapter 7, *infra*, (Multiple Tortfeasors).

VI. Loss of Chance, or "The Doctor Did It"

The burden of proof in civil cases is preponderance of the evidence (i.e., more likely than not). With advances in medical research, it is often possible to estimate a patient's chances of recovery from an illness. The problem of loss of chance occurs when the patient visits a doctor who negligently fails to diagnose the disease properly and therefore does not begin necessary treatment at the earliest possible time. If the patient subsequently dies of the disease, does the failure to diagnose early mean that the doctor is the cause in fact of the death? Under traditional rules, the doctor would not be liable if the patient had less than a fifty percent chance of recovery at the time of the misdiagnosis. In such a situation we cannot say that, more likely than not, the patient would not have died "but for" the doctor's negligent conduct. To the contrary, we can say that it is more likely than not that the patient would have died from disease no matter what the doctor did. On the other hand, the delay in treatment may well have measurably reduced the patient's chances of recovery below what they already were.

Herskovitz v. Group Health Coop. of Puget Sound, 664 P.2d 474 (Wash. 1983), responded to this scenario by allowing a suit for the wrongful death of the plaintiff's decedent based upon his lost chance of recovery. In that case the delay resulted in a reduction of the victim's chances from 39 percent to 25 percent. The court held that this reduction could be found by the jury to make the doctor's misdiagnosis a "substantial factor" in causing the death. The appearance of the "substantial factor" language here is not surprising, given that once again we have multiple causes for the injury: the disease itself (for which the doctor was not responsible) and the misdiagnosis. However, allowing this finding where the plaintiff initially had less than a fifty percent chance of recovery is a significant relaxation of the cause in fact standard.

Related to this issue is the question of how to award damages if loss of chance suits are recognized. Should the plaintiff recover the full amount possible under the wrongful death statute, or should that recovery be discounted in some way to reflect the plaintiff's diminished chances because of the pre-existing disease? Courts differ on the proper approach. Full damages is more in keeping with the "substantial factor" test, while a discounted recovery looks much like a form of allocation of harm to causes. One problem with the discount approach, however, is what to do in the case of a patient who goes to see the doctor with a fifty-five percent chance of recovery. Under traditional rules, such a victim would be entitled to full damages, since this patient did have a better than even chance of recovery if the doctor makes a correct diagnosis. Should this plaintiff also have damages discounted to reflect the forty-five percent chance of death even with a correct diagnosis? Consistency might seem to demand it, but the traditional rule would probably prevail in this situation.

VII. Statistical Proof

Toxic exposure cases often present challenging issues of causation, and statistical proof is often a vital element of the proof. In these cases the plaintiff must prove that the defendant caused the exposure and that the toxic substance is capable of causing the type of injury or disease complained of. In many cases, however, uncertainty still remains because the injury or disease also may occur even in the absence of toxic exposure. For example, suppose the plaintiff complains that the defendant's drug caused cardiac damage and a heart attack. The defendant will try to show that the plaintiff had heart problems already, and that the heart attack was caused by these pre-existing problems rather than by the drug. After all, many heart attacks do occur without exposure to any drugs. In order to try to establish causation, the plaintiff may turn to statistical analysis to show that persons taking the drug have a far higher incidence of heart problems than would be normal for a similar population. In this way the plaintiff will try to create the inference that the drug is responsible for the harm. Under the analysis of the Ninth Circuit in *Daubert v. Merrell Dow Pharmaceuticals, Inc.,* 43 F.3d 1311 (9th Cir. 1995), a plaintiff would have to prove that the drug doubled the risk of harm in order to show that it was more likely than not the cause of the harm.

Statistical evidence by itself, however, is often not sufficient to prove cause in fact. To improve the possibility of success, plaintiffs will often seek other sources of proof to bolster the inference. This may include proof that the particular disease is, in fact, linked to the toxic substance, proof of the amount of the exposure, proof of the timing of the exposure, as well as ruling out other possible causative factors for the harm.

Checkpoints

- First, try to apply the "but for" cause test. If it works, causation is established.

- Do not assume that multiple causes or multiple parties means that the "but for" cause test will not work.

- If the "but for" cause test does not work because causes cancel one another out, use the "substantial factor" test.

- If separate harms can be allocated to separate causes, do so.

- Consult the chapter on multiple tortfeasors for other solutions to problems of proving causation when more than one defendant is involved.

- In medical and toxic tort cases, statistical proofs are often important in demonstrating that the harm was caused by the defendant's conduct, but the inference must either be strong in itself or supported by other circumstantial evidence.

Chapter 6

Proximate Cause

Roadmap

- Learn how to apply the direct cause test.
- Understand how the concept of foreseeability imposes limits on the duty owed in a negligence case.
- Understand how the risk rule imposes limits on the concept of proximate cause.
- Understand the "thin-skulled plaintiff" rule and how it operates in regard to determining the extent of harm caused by a defendant's negligence.
- Distinguish between intervening and superseding causes.

I. Introduction: The Issue

Proximate cause deals with the issue of the proper extent of liability for a tortious act. It is a policy-based doctrine that limits liability even when the defendant is shown to have committed a tort that was a cause in fact of the plaintiff's injury. The need for such a limit exists because long and elaborate causal chains can be constructed, in which some remote act of a defendant is a cause in fact of harm suffered at some distance of time or space. However, liability for such remote consequences was thought to be inappropriate in many cases, as something that the defendant could not have anticipated and for which (s)he should not be made responsible. The great sticking point, of course, has always been how to draw this line in a principled way.

Although many fanciful scenarios can be concocted to illustrate the problem, let us begin with a simple example, our familiar hypothetical of a fire started by a negligently managed railroad engine. In Chapter 5, *supra*, on Cause in Fact, we addressed when such a fire might be considered a cause of the plaintiff's harm in the presence of other causal factors, such as a naturally occurring fire. However, suppose that fire spreads far beyond the point of origin. The railroad is clearly a cause in fact of all the resulting harm, but should it be held liable in tort no matter how far the fire may spread? New York has a special rule that strictly limits the scope of liability in these circumstances to the first or most immediate property damaged by the fire, but not to more remote victims. In *Ryan v. New York Central Railroad Co.*, 35 N.Y. 210 (1866), the court explained the reason for this limitation.

> That a building upon which sparks and cinders fall should be destroyed or seriously injured must be expected, but that the fire should spread and other buildings be consumed, is not a necessary or an usual result. That it is possible, and that it is not unfrequent, cannot be denied. The result, however, depends, not upon any necessity of a further communication of the fire, but upon a concurrence of accidental circumstances, such as the degree of the heat, the state of the atmosphere, the condition and materials of the adjoining structures and the direction of the wind. These are accidental and varying circumstances. The party has no control over them, and is not responsible for their effects. 35 N.Y. 210, at 212.

The court in *Ryan* was explicitly concerned that any other rule would impose too great a potential liability on defendants, who could insure their own property but not their neighbor's. The line was drawn, therefore, out of notions of public policy regarding the proper scope of liability. Other courts take a different view of policy and draw the scope of liability more broadly in this situation, but this determination still remains one of policy. In the case of the New York fire rule, that choice draws a hard and arbitrary line to limit the defendant's responsibility. As we will see, courts have searched for broader and more generally applicable approaches to decide this issue. Nevertheless, it is important to keep in mind that the application of these standards still requires a policy choice about the scope of liability.

II. Direct Cause Test

An early formulation of a rule for proximate cause was known as the direct cause (or "directness") test. This test focused on the sequence of events leading from the defendant's negligence to the plaintiff's injury, and denied liability if additional significant forces joined with the defendant's negligence to cause the harm. The language quoted from the *Ryan* case, *supra*, gives the flavor of this inquiry. The spread of the fire to the first structure can be seen as direct, since little in the way of additional force is required to spread the fire that far. Beyond that, other factors intervene to spread the fire, including the force and direction of the wind. The wind might be considered an intervening force that becomes the significant causal factor in the further spread of the fire.

The best known case illustrating the direct cause test in action is *In re Polemis and Furness, Withy & Co*, 3 K.B. 560 (C.A. 1921). There the defendants chartered a cargo ship, part of whose cargo included cans of petrol. While unloading in Casablanca, the stevedores, for whose conduct the defendants were responsible, dropped a wooden board into the ship's hold, sparking a rush of flame that destroyed the ship. The owners of the vessel claimed against the defendants, asserting that the stevedores were negligent in allowing the board to fall into the hold, where it must have caused a spark that ignited vapors from the petrol that had accumulated in the hold. The defendants argued that they could not anticipate that a wooden board would cause a spark or the resulting fire, and they claimed that the damages were therefore too remote.

The court in *Polemis* rejected the argument that foreseeability should be a limit on the defendants' liability. For the court, the lack of any intervening factors between the dropping of the plank and the igniting of the vapor proved decisive. Because the harm followed "directly" from the negligent act, the defendants were liable. This approach views foreseeability of the unreasonable risk of harm as relevant only to the issue of whether the defendant's act was negligent in the first instance. However, once an act is deemed negligent and therefore wrongful, the tortfeasor is liable for all the harm "directly" caused, even if the harm that occurred had no relationship to the types of foreseeable injury that made the conduct negligent in the first place. Under this approach the defendant is responsible, so long as no other significant cause has intervened to interrupt the direct causal connection between the defendant's wrong and the harm.

The direct cause test left the courts with the problem of distinguishing between intervening factors, identifying those that would cut off the defendant's responsibility from those that would not. Depending on how the courts drew this distinction, liability under this test could be expansive or narrow. Although the direct cause test does emphasize the importance of these intervening factors, it does not provide a principle, other than "directness," for making the decision. For this reason, courts have found the direct cause test unsatisfactory as a general approach to the problem of the scope of liability. Its major influence today lies in its identification of intervening forces as a crucial issue in determining proximate cause.

III. Foreseeability as a Limitation on Duty: The Unforeseeable Plaintiff

Searching for an appropriate principle to define the scope of liability, courts began to look to foreseeability as a better tool for proper line drawing. Already a part of the analysis regarding the existence of negligence, courts began to employ foreseeability as a limit on the scope of liability. This approach gave rise to the risk rule of proximate cause (*see* discussion in section IV., *infra*), as well as to a limitation on the scope of duties owed to unforeseeable victims.

Limiting the scope of the duty of due care that is owed by the defendant is another way of directly limiting the scope of that defendant's potential liability. The scope of duty can thus act as an alternative to proximate cause for a court looking to fashion a rule defining the extent of tort liability. As can be seen in the discussion in Chapter 9, *infra*, (Limited Duty), courts sometimes impose limits on duty as special rules for particular situations. One familiar example is the no duty to rescue rule. Another is the limited duty that a landowner owes to an unknown trespasser. However, in the famous case *Palsgraf v. Long Island R.R.,* 162 N.E. 99 (N.Y. 1928), the New York Court of Appeals used the concept of foreseeability in a much broader sense, to create a general limitation on the scope of duty, thus sparking an ongoing debate on the proper approach to limiting tort liability.

The plaintiff, Helen Palsgraf, stood with her daughters on the platform at a Long Island Railroad station, waiting for a train to Rockaway Beach. As a train bound for another destination pulled out of the station, two men ran to catch it. They managed to get on board, but in doing so a railroad employee caused one of the men to drop a small package, which, unknown to the railroad employee, contained fireworks. The package landed on the tracks and exploded. Either the concussion of the explosion itself or the subsequent stampede of frightened passengers knocked a railroad scale into the plaintiff, causing her injuries. Plaintiff succeeded in getting a jury award against the railroad on the basis of the employee's negligence in dislodging the package. Although the intermediate appellate court upheld the verdict, New York's highest court reversed by a 4–3 vote, on the ground that the railroad owed no duty to the plaintiff, at least in regard to the actions of the employee towards the man with the package. The reason offered for not recognizing any duty to the plaintiff Mrs. Palsgraf was that negligently handling the other passenger and his package created no foreseeable risk of harm to her. She stood "many feet away," and the package gave the employees no warning of its dangerous contents. The plaintiff, therefore, was found to be outside the zone of danger; she was an unforeseeable plaintiff.

The famous majority opinion by Chief Judge Cardozo laying out this "no duty" approach is matched by the equally famous dissent by Judge Andrews, who viewed the case as presenting an issue of proximate cause to be resolved, not by some mechanical formula, but as a matter of policy, fairness, and expediency. Judge Andrews rejected the idea, propounded by the majority, that duty required that harm to the plaintiff must be foreseeable. To Judge Andrews, a negligent act was a wrong to the public at large, so that the question was not who might foreseeably be harmed, but who was in fact harmed. Once the plaintiff established that the defendant's negligence was a cause in fact of the harm that occurred, the issue then became one of proximate cause rather than duty. Indeed, the issue of duty in *Palsgraf* might have rested on the relationship of Mrs. Palsgraf as a paying customer of the Long Island Railroad, since a common carrier at the time owed its customers the highest duty of care and watchfulness.

After identifying the issue as proximate cause, Judge Andrews stated that its resolution depended on a variety of factors. Foreseeability of harm is one such factor, but Judge Andrews applied it in a different manner than the majority. Rather than ask what was foreseeable from the standpoint of the negligent defendant before the accident occurred, he instead asked what the foreseeable results might be, given "prevision" of the presence of the fireworks in the package. This backwards-looking approach asks whether, given the presence of the explosives, a reasonable person would foresee the possibility of injury to Mrs. Palsgraf. Framing the inquiry in this way makes this approach a variant of the direct cause test, where the issue is simply the closeness of the connection between the defendant's wrong and the harm. The result would be unforeseeable in those situations in which other factors diverted the chain of causation out of the "natural and probable" sequence set in motion by the defendant's conduct.

Out of the vast amount of commentary about this case, only a few points can be emphasized here. First, the case makes clear the way in which both duty and proximate cause can be used to limit the scope of liability. However, because duty tends to be viewed as a question of law while proximate cause is often a question of fact, reliance on duty as a limitation will leave more of these decisions in the hands of judges rather than juries. For this reason, perhaps, courts today perform the duty analysis at a higher level of generality, such as the previously mentioned limited duty to rescue. However, this still leaves the need for a rule to guide juries if they are to determine the proper limits of proximate cause. Here it may be said that the *Palsgraf* case represents two approaches that courts today follow only to a limited extent. The "rule" derived from the majority opinion is often referred to as the "unforeseeable plaintiff" rule. It states that a defendant owes no duty to an injured victim unless harm to that particular victim was foreseeable. The suit by Mrs. Palsgraf fails under this test because she was situated outside the zone of any foreseeable danger created by other passengers and their packages. While the hindsight approach of the dissent has garnered some support over the years, courts have largely replaced it with a different test that looks to the foreseeable risks of the defendant's conduct to establish the proper scope of liability. This approach, often called the "risk rule," has become the dominant form of proximate cause analysis.

IV. The "Risk Rule"

The essence of the "risk rule" is that the defendant is liable for the generally foreseeable types of harm that made the conduct negligent in the first instance. As with all negligence cases, the analysis begins with the duty of care owed to the plaintiff. And as noted in the discussion, *supra*, the lack of any foreseeable danger to the plaintiff may cause the claim to fail at this first stage of analysis. However, if the court determines that a duty of care is owed, the defendant would breach that duty by conduct that created foreseeable and unreasonable risks of harm to the plaintiff. The "risk rule" asks at this point what those foreseeable risks of harm might be. These foreseeable risks are then compared to the harm actually caused by the defendant's conduct to determine whether that harm is "within the risk" that should have been anticipated. In performing this analysis, it is not necessary that the exact mechanism by which the harm came about was foreseeable, so long as the harm suffered is of the same general variety that was foreseeable as a result of the defendant's actions.

The "risk rule" came to the forefront in the cases involving a fire resulting from oil spilled by the steamship *Wagon Mound*. In the first of these cases, *Overseas Tankship (U.K.) Ltd. v. Morts Dock & Engineering Co., Ltd.*, [1961 A.C. 388], the claim was brought by the owner of a dock and repair facility located in the harbor of Sydney, Australia. The ship *Wagon Mound* had allowed a large quantity of fuel oil to spill into the harbor before its departure. The plaintiff suspended welding operations at its nearby dock pending an inquiry as to what substance was floating in the water and whether it was flammable. Upon receiving assurances that this type of oil could not burn when spread upon water, the plaintiff resumed its welding and repair work. Unfortunately, the assurance was mistaken. Molten metal falling onto the oil-covered water from the welding apparently ignited some floating debris, which in turn ignited the oil. The subsequent inferno destroyed the plaintiff's dock, as well as a ship that was under repair. The plaintiff charged the owners of the *Wagon Mound* with negligence in allowing the oil to leak into the waters of the harbor.

From the plaintiff's point of view, the case must have looked a good deal like *Polemis*. As in that earlier case, fire was not foreseeable as a result of the defendant's negligence (as the court so found). Nevertheless, the defendant's conduct was the cause in fact of the fire, even if somewhat less directly so. That conduct was also negligent, because it created unreasonable risks of harm from the fouling of the harbor facilities with the oil. Also, just as in *Polemis*, the defendant argued that it should not be liable for an unforeseeable type of harm. This time, however, the argument was successful. The court ruled that the owners of the vessel could not be liable for an unforeseeable fire risk even though it might be liable for other, foreseeable harms from pollution and fouling of the harbor. Fire was not within the foreseeable risks that made the defendant's conduct (i.e., spilling the fuel oil) negligent. The crucial and somewhat peculiar fact-finding regarding the unforeseeability of fuel oil burning, it should be noted, probably resulted from the plaintiff's concern that it would have been barred from recovery by contributory negligence if it disputed the defendant's contention that the fire was unforeseeable. If fire was a foreseeable risk, then the plaintiff should have suspended welding until the oil was gone.

The progression from *Polemis* (liable although fire was unforeseeable) to *Wagon Mound No. 1* (not liable because fire was unforeseeable) might suggest that the "risk rule" imposes greater limits on liability than the direct cause (or "directness") test that it replaced. As the second *Wagon Mound* case demonstrates, however, this is not necessarily true. In *Overseas Tankship (U.K.) Ltd. v. Miller Steamship Co.,* [1967] 1 A.C. 617, the owner of the ship that was under repair at Morts Dock also brought suit to recover for the fire damage. Not concerned with the problem of contributory negligence, the ship-owner secured a finding that the risk of fire was low, but not totally unforeseeable. Further, the potential damage from this low-probability event was severe. Finally, the conduct of spilling the oil and running this risk was negligent because it served no offsetting purpose, since the loss of the fuel oil was sheer waste for the owners of the *Wagon Mound*. The court found the defendant liable, since fire was now within the risk: one of a number of possible types of harm that a reasonably prudent person would have foreseen and taken steps to avoid. The concept of multiple foreseeable types of harm resulting from the single act of the defendant in fact makes the "risk rule" potentially more expansive in finding proximate cause.

The "risk rule" requires that all the elements of the plaintiff's *prima facie* case must integrate properly. It is not possible to say whether the defendant's negligence was the proximate cause of the harm without first considering exactly why the defendant's conduct was negligent (i.e., what unreasonable and foreseeable risks were created). The question of negligence itself also depends on the scope of the defendant's duty towards the plaintiff. The interrelation of these factors emphasizes the importance of very carefully defining the defendant's duty and describing the potential harms from the breach of that duty, in order that the plaintiff's injuries can be brought within the risk.

V. The Thin-Skulled Plaintiff: Extent of Harm

An important caveat in applying the "risk rule" is that it limits liability to the types of harm that were foreseeable, but it does not limit liability solely to the extent of harm that was foreseeable. The most important application of this principle is the "thin-skulled plaintiff" (or the "eggshell-skull plaintiff") doctrine. Under this rule, the defendant must take the plaintiff as (s)he finds him or her. The rule derives its name from a hypothetical plaintiff with a thin (even eggshell thin) skull, who suffers a fractured skull and resulting brain damage from a simple blow that would only have raised a lump on the head of a normal individual. The courts consistently hold that the "risk rule" does not allow the defendant to argue that the harm was unforeseeably severe. Instead, as long as the plaintiff's personal injury was within the risk of the defendant's negligent conduct, the defendant is responsible for the full extent of the injury that actually results.

Some courts have extended this rule to cover mental illness and psychological injury caused by the defendant's negligent conduct, even when that injury is unforeseeably severe. Sometimes also called the "thin-skinned plaintiff" rule, this principle is exemplified by *Steinhauser v. Hertz Corp.*, 421 F.2d 1169 (2d Cir. 1970), in which a minor automobile accident apparently caused the plaintiff to suffer such fright and upset that it triggered the development of paranoid schizophrenia. Recovery was allowed.

Any recovery under the "thin-skulled plaintiff" rule and its variants is still limited by the principle that damages must be adjusted for the likelihood that the plaintiff would have suffered the same harm even without the defendant's wrong. One example of this limitation is the use of estimated life expectancy evidence to calculate damages in a wrongful death case. Even if the defendant's negligence did cause in fact the victim's death, we know that the victim was not going to live forever. If the victim was suffering from a terminal illness with only a short time left to live, it is proper for the defendant to prove that the victim would not have enjoyed a normal life expectancy, but only a much-shortened one, in calculating such elements of damage as future lost wages. In the same way, the defendant also might be able to show that the victim was so vulnerable to injury that the same harm eventually would have occurred anyway, perhaps as the result of the progress of a degenerative disease or other weakness, and by so doing limit or reduce the amount of damages otherwise recoverable under the "thin-skulled plaintiff" rule.

VI. Intervening and Superseding Causes and the Risk Rule: The Basics

We have seen that the direct cause (or "directness") test focused on the causal chain between the defendant's tort and the plaintiff's injury, testing whether some force had intervened to the point of displacing the defendant's responsibility. The adoption of the "risk rule" did not make the problem of intervening forces go away, but it did suggest a different approach to resolving the issue. Rather than focus on the "natural and continuous sequences" of events, the logic of the "risk rule" asked whether the intervening force was foreseeable or not. An extraordinary and unforeseeable intervening force would cut off the liability of the defendant, because the harm would no longer be within the risk. Such a force is typically called a "superseding cause."

In a typical intervening cause situation, the defendant's negligence has set the stage for possible harm to the plaintiff, so to speak, by placing the plaintiff in a position of vulnerability, setting a trap, or placing some force in motion. However, it requires the action of some subsequent intervening force to change this potential harm into actual harm by triggering the plaintiff's injury. The well-known case of *Derdiarian v. Felix Contracting Corp.*, 414 N.E.2d 666 (N.Y. 1980), illustrates how this works. In that case, the plaintiff was the employee of a subcontractor working to install a gas pipe under a street, which required shutting down one lane of traffic near the excavation site. The defendant general contractor controlled the job site, and it negligently failed to place heavy equipment or a pile of dirt so as to prevent cars using the street from entering the area where the men were working. A motorist passing the job site suffered a sudden seizure and lost control of his car, crashing into the work area, striking the plaintiff, and dousing him with molten enamel that was being used to seal the gas pipe.

In this situation, the defendant's negligence in failing to place a sufficient barrier placed the plaintiff and the other workers in a vulnerable position. Of course, this by itself caused no harm. It required the intervening force of the driver who suffered a seizure to translate potential danger into actual catastrophic injury. The issue in the case was whether that intervening force superseded and cut off the defendant's responsibility for the plaintiff's injuries, so that the defendant's negligence was not considered to be the proximate cause of the harm. The defendant argued, in effect, that no one could foresee a driver having a seizure at that particular moment, making this event extraordinary and, thus, superseding. The court rejected this argument. Instead, the court explained that the foreseeable risk created by the defendant's negligence in failing to place a barrier capable of stopping a car that might negligently be driven into the work area and injure one of the workers was precisely the very risk that occurred. Indeed, this was the exact type of harm to be anticipated under the "risk rule." In other words, under this interpretation of the "risk rule," the defendant did not have to foresee the driver's seizure, but only the general risk of negligently driven cars in the work area. Had the defendant placed a proper barrier, it would have prevented the accident regardless of the reason for the intervening driver's conduct.

The "risk rule" approach asks whether the possibility of the intervening force was a foreseeable risk that the prudent person would have recognized and provided against. The intervening force might be a negligent third party, as in *Derdiarian, supra,* but it could also be a force of nature, or even the plaintiff's own non-negligent conduct. Nevertheless, as previously discussed, one important limitation on this approach still remains: the defendant must first have a duty to protect the victim against the risk. For example, the defendant's failure to rescue another from a threatening force might foreseeably result in injury to the victim, but it may still not result in liability under circumstances where the defendant had no duty to render aid to the victim in the first instance. Chapter 9, *infra,* (Limited Duty), addresses some of the more common situations where such a duty may be absent, as well as various arguments that have been utilized in expanding the scope of the defendant's duty so as to bring more injuries within certain categories of foreseeable risks.

VII. Within the Risk? Coping with Defendant's Negligence

One of the most common fact patterns that raise issues for the application of the "risk rule" often involves situations that deal with the subsequent effects resulting from the defendant's negligence. For example, someone fleeing a negligently started fire might trip and fall, sustaining injuries. While burn injuries are the most obvious type of harm that one might foresee as a risk created from a negligently started fire, it is also foreseeable that those threatened by the fire might run to get away from it, and in dong so that they well might suffer some other type of injury. Accordingly, injuries of this type are generally considered to be within the risk of the defendant's negligence.

Applying this same approach, the foreseeable risks of negligent driving, for example, do not end immediately after a collision occurs. If the damaged automobiles remain in the roadway, foreseeable risks remain, for example, in the form of a second collision. As one court put it when addressing a second collision scenario, "the consequences of such past negligence were in the bosom of time, as yet unrevealed." *Marshall v. Nugent*, 222 F.2d 604, 612 (1st Cir. 1955). That court did, however, recognize that the responsibility of the defendant for negligence should end once the "extra risks" created by the initial accident had entirely ended. Moreover, even here courts will draw the line if the second accident seems bizarrely unforeseeable, or where it involves a risk that is simply negligible.

An important example of the problem of follow-on risks occurs when a victim of the defendant's negligence is further harmed as the result of medical negligence (i.e., malpractice) in the course of treating the victim's original injuries. The initial tortfeasor will also be liable for these additional injuries (jointly with the negligent doctor), on the theory that this harm is an additional risk to which the defendant's original negligence exposed the victim. A further extension of this doctrine occurs when the ambulance transporting the victim of the defendant's original negligence to the hospital is involved in another accident, resulting in additional injuries to the victim. Here again the original tortfeasor will often be held liable. This was the result in *Anaya v. Superior Court*, 93 Cal. Rptr. 2d 228 (Cal. App. 2000), in which the victim died when the medical helicopter crashed while transporting her to the hospital following an automobile accident caused by the defendant's original negligence.

VIII. Within the Risk? Superseding Causes

If the intervening cause is sufficiently unforeseeable and extraordinary, it will cut off the defendant's responsibility for injury to the plaintiff. Such "superseding causes" are thought to be so independently important in causing the harm that the defendant's actions should no longer be considered causally significant enough to justify imposing liability. Superseding causes, in other words, are outside the risks created by the defendant's negligent conduct.

A commonly cited example of a superseding cause involves deliberate criminal misconduct by a third party. For example, in *Watson v. Kentucky & Indiana Bridge & R.R. Co.*, 126 S.W. 146 (Ky. 1910), the defendant railroad negligently caused a tank car of gasoline to derail, spilling a large quantity of gasoline. Of course, one foreseeable risk of such conduct is that the gasoline will ignite and injure people and property. Many natural and human sources of a spark can be imagined, and the resulting fire certainly would be within the risks that made the conduct negligent. In this case, the fire was started by a man who tossed a match aside after using it (supposedly) to light a cigar. If the man with the match were merely negligent, that would not be a superseding cause, but rather the sort of foreseeable event that could be anticipated as a foreseeable source of ignition for the gasoline. However, in *Watson, supra*, the railroad presented evidence that the man was actually a disgruntled former employee who threw the match deliberately, intending to start a fire. The court held that a criminal act like this was so unforeseeable that it would supersede the defendant railroad's original negligence, thereby relieving it from liability.

However, not all criminal acts supersede, because not all criminal acts are unforeseeable. In particular, criminal acts are foreseeable when the defendant has a duty to protect the plaintiff from them. For example, a landowner whose premises are open to the public for business owes a duty to the patrons as invitees. *See* Chapter 10, *infra*, (Premises Liability) addressing the duties of owners and occupiers of land for a further explanation of this duty. If the owner is on notice of the threat of criminal activity in the area, the owner may have a duty to provide a reasonable amount of security to protect against such attacks. If the owner breaches this duty and a patron is attacked, the owner may be liable and the attack will not be considered a superseding cause. In this situation, the harm is within the risk because the defendant's duty encompasses protection from otherwise foreseeable criminal attack. Evidence that the defendant had notice of prior criminal activity in the area may establish that a future attack is foreseeable and therefore within the risk created by not providing security. *Isaacs v. Huntington Memorial Hospital*, 695 P.2d 653 (Cal. 1985).

A duty to protect can also arise in other situations. For example, an exception to the no duty to render aid to a third party rule exists when the defendant's conduct has placed the plaintiff in a position of peril. *See* Chapter 9, *infra*, section I. (Limited Duty). If the defendant breaches this duty and then fails to take reasonable steps to protect the plaintiff from a foreseeable criminal attack, that attack will not be considered a superseding cause. *Brauer v. New York Central & H. R.R. Co.,* 103 A. 166 (1918).

The intervening negligent conduct of other persons may also be superseding, but such intervening negligence would have to be truly unforeseeable and independent of the conduct of the defendant. In the same way, unforeseeable and extraordinary natural forces can also constitute a superseding cause. However, if the defendant should have anticipated some sort of natural intervening force, the defendant is not excused simply because the force that occurred was unusually strong.

In the foregoing discussion of superseding cause, notice how the concept of duty keeps intruding into the discussion of proximate cause. This is not accidental. The legal concept of foreseeability helps define both duty and proximate cause, and the "risk rule" analysis requires frequent cross-referencing between these two elements. The way that the plaintiff's attorney describes the foreseeable risks that made the defendant's conduct negligent will later help to set the limits on the defendant's scope of liability when addressing the issue of proximate cause. But whether those risks in fact made the defendant's conduct negligent also depends on the duty of care that was owed by the defendant. Even foreseeable risks do not result in liability if the defendant had no duty to do anything about them. The task for the plaintiff's attorney, then, is to posture the case so that the defendant owes a duty to the particular plaintiff, to take precautions against a particular type of harm, which type of harm is in fact the injury that ultimately befell the plaintiff. In other words, all the elements of the negligence cause of action must fit together into a coherent whole in order for liability to be established.

Checkpoints

- Proximate cause deals with the issue of determining the proper scope of the defendant's liability.

- An older test for proximate cause, the direct cause (or "directness") test, based its analysis on the presence or absence of intervening causal factors. It is no longer much used, but the issue of intervening causes remains important.

- Foreseeability of the resulting harm is the more modern test. One application of this rule is that the plaintiff must be a foreseeable victim of the defendant's negligence.

- The general type of harm that the plaintiff suffered must also be foreseeable as a result of the negligence. We say that the harm must be "within the risk"; hence, this test is called the "risk rule."

- An important limitation on the "risk rule" is the "thin-skulled plaintiff" (or "egg-shell skull plaintiff") doctrine. Under this rule the defendant's liability for negligence is not limited simply because the extent of the victim's harm was greater than what was foreseeable.

- Intervening causes do not automatically cut off liability. If the intervening cause was foreseeable, the harm will likely still be within the risk.

- Efforts by the victim to cope with or to avoid the risk created by the defendant are considered foreseeable, at least if they are reasonable and foreseeable responses to the danger.

- Intervening causes that cut off liability are called "superseding" causes. Superseding causes are defined as extraordinary and unforeseeable intervening events.

- A cause will not be superseding if the defendant had a duty to protect the plaintiff from it.

Chapter 7

Multiple Tortfeasors

Roadmap

- Learn the meaning of joint and several liability.
- Understand the tension between traditional joint and several liability and comparative fault.
- Recognize how courts have addressed the problem of defendant indeterminacy (i.e., where a plaintiff cannot precisely identify who caused the harm but knows that the true cause is among a group of actors).
- Understand the concept of indemnity and identify examples of situations where it might apply.
- Analyze the traditional rule of pro rata contribution.
- Learn why many states today apply a rule of comparative contribution.

This chapter addresses cases where multiple actors are potentially responsible for a plaintiff's harm. The chapter is divided into three parts. First, it considers the traditional rule of joint and several liability. Second, it addresses cases where the cause of the plaintiff's harm is indeterminate. Finally, the chapter discusses how the law apportions loss among multiple tortfeasors after liability is established.

I. Joint and Several Liability

The starting point for any discussion about multiple tortfeasors is joint and several liability. Joint and several liability means that a defendant is responsible for the whole amount of the plaintiff's damages even if the conduct of another actor contributed to the loss. Joint and several liability is consistent with tort law's historical "all-or-nothing" nature whereby traditionally, a plaintiff either recovered full damages from a defendant or the plaintiff recovered nothing whatsoever.

The all-or-nothing principle is perhaps best illustrated by contributory negligence, an affirmative defense that once totally precluded a plaintiff from
recovering damages in a negligence action if the harm was due in any part to
the plaintiff's own fault. (*See* Chapter 12, *infra*, Defenses to Negligence). The
principle also manifested itself in cases where more than one actor injured
fault-free plaintiffs. A classic illustration is *Carolina C. & O. Ry. v. Hill*, 89 S.E.
902 (Va. 1916). In *Hill*, the defendant railway company damaged the plaintiff's property. At the same time, a lumber company engaged in activity that
could have caused the same harm. The railway company argued that it should
not be responsible for the full amount of the loss, but the court disagreed,
explaining that:

> The doctrine is thoroughly established that where there are several
> concurrent negligent causes, the effects of which are not separable,
> though due to independent authors, either of which is sufficient to
> produce the entire loss, all are jointly or severally liable for the entire
> loss. 89 S.E. at 903.

As the quote, *supra*, indicates, joint and several liability applies only where
multiple actors cause the plaintiff to suffer an *indivisible*, or non-separable,
harm. If portions of a plaintiff's harm are logically divisible, then the defendant is liable only for those losses associated with the component that (s)he
actually caused.

Even in cases of indivisible harm, however, tort law's "all-or-nothing" nature
has changed in recent years. During the latter half of the 20th century, nearly
every jurisdiction has adopted some form of comparative fault in an effort to
better align liability with culpability. (*See* Chapter 12, *infra*, Defenses to Negligence). As this movement has progressed, however, courts have struggled to
harmonize comparative fault with the traditional rule of joint and several liability. In other words, if a state allows the allocation of fault between a plaintiff and a defendant under principles of comparative negligence, why not also
do so among multiple defendants?

States have dealt with this issue in different ways. In fact, the approaches
are so splintered that the Restatement of Torts refuses to endorse a single position. Instead, the Restatement sets out five separate "tracks" to describe the
competing approaches. *See* Restatement (Third) of Torts: Apportionment of Liability §§ 27A–E. The first track reflects jurisdictions that retain
joint and several liability even after adopting comparative fault. The second
track describes an opposite approach, limiting liability to a portion of the
plaintiff's damages based on the percentage of fault that a fact finder assigns
to each defendant. In these states, liability is said to be "several" only. The

remaining tracks reflect jurisdictions that come down somewhere in the middle. One permits the imposition of joint and several liability, subject to a reallocation of "unenforceable" shares among all parties in proportion to their level of fault. An example of an unenforceable share might be one assigned to an insolvent entity. Another track describes states that impose joint and several liability for a plaintiff's economic damages, but only several liability for non-economic harm, such as pain and suffering. A final track describes jurisdictions that impose joint and several liability against defendants only if they are assigned a percentage of fault exceeding a designated legal threshold. Among states that follow this approach, that threshold ranges from 10 to 60 percent.

In sum, the traditional concept of joint and several liability means that a defendant is responsible for the whole amount of the plaintiff's non-separable harm, even if another actor has contributed to that same loss. However, the advent of comparative fault has muddied the waters in terms of how, or even whether, modern courts will apply the rule.

II. Indeterminate Causation

Cases involving multiple tortfeasors often raise causation issues. These issues are particularly acute when a plaintiff knows that the actor who caused the harm is among a defined group, but cannot identify the particular culpable party. In these cases, it is often impossible for the plaintiff to prove cause in fact since it is impossible to demonstrate that his or her damages would not have occurred "but for" the conduct of a particular actor. Normally, this would preclude the plaintiff from recovery in a negligence action. In some situations, however, courts have determined that the plaintiff should not bear the consequences of this uncertainty.

One example involves situations where multiple defendants share joint control of a risk. This is a concept that courts and commentators sometimes call "enterprise liability." A well-known example comes from the case of *Hall v. E. I. DuPont de Nemours & Co.*, 345 F. Supp. 353 (E.D.N.Y. 1972). In *Hall,* thirteen children were injured in separate "blasting cap" incidents. Those children filed claims against six blasting cap manufacturers that, together, comprised nearly the entire blasting cap industry. The plaintiffs, however, could not show which company produced the individual caps that caused their injuries. To remedy this unfairness, the *Hall* court shifted the burden of proof onto each defendant to demonstrate that it did not manufacture the relevant caps at issue. The court justified this decision by pointing to evidence that each defendant, through a common trade association, had cooperated in the development of inadequate industry safety standards. Therefore, each member of the industry was culpable for contributing to the overall risk of harm.

Perhaps the most well-known theory for adjusting causation rules in multiple tortfeasor cases is "alternative liability." This theory originated in *Summers v. Tice*, 199 P.2d 1 (Cal. 1948), a decision of the California Supreme Court. In *Summers*, three quail hunters arranged themselves in a triangular formation. At nearly the same moment, two of the hunters negligently fired their shotguns while standing at points equidistant behind the third hunter. Pellets from at least one (although possibly both) of the shotguns hit the third hunter's eye and lip. However, the injured hunter could not identify which of his companions fired the shot(s) that caused the injury. This uncertainty prevented the plaintiff from establishing "but for" causation in a negligence action against either of the two defendants. To avoid an unfair outcome, the California Supreme Court shifted the burden to both of the other shooters to prove that they did not cause their companion's harm. If the negligent hunters could not exculpate themselves, either could be jointly and severally liable for the damages.

"Alternative liability" represents a significant exception to the normal cause in fact rule insofar as it permits a finding of liability against a defendant even though the plaintiff cannot prove "but for" causation by a preponderance of the evidence. Constrained to the unique facts of *Summers*, this exception would apply only in very limited circumstances. However, one notable extension comes from a line of cases articulating a related theory called "market share liability."

The market share liability cases involved a prescription drug called diethylstilbestrol ("DES"), which was widely used during the 1950s and 1960s to prevent pregnant women from suffering miscarriages. However, in the 1970s, scientists discovered that DES caused a rare form of cancer in the adolescent daughters of women who took the drug. Given the passage of time, and the multitude of companies that manufactured DES, these daughters were in no position (causally) to connect their disease to any particular manufacturer's product. Analogizing this situation from the one in *Summers v. Tice, supra*, a handful of courts, including the high courts of New York and California, obviated this unfairness, once again, by shifting the burden of proof on causation to the manufacturers.

Jurisdictions that have adopted "market share liability" vary in their approach to its details. However, one consistent component is to largely divorce "market share liability" from joint and several liability. In other words, defendants in "market share liability" cases are not automatically liable for the full amount of a plaintiff's harm. Instead, liability is limited to only a percentage of the plaintiff's harm based on the share of DES that each defendant sold in the relevant market at the relevant time. Some jurisdictions view the relevant market narrowly. Others view it as encompassing the entire country. All, however, reflect tort law's broader movement toward liability that is proportional to the fault of each actor.

III. Indemnity and Contribution

When one defendant's liability exceeds that defendant's individual *pro rata* or proportional share among multiple tortfeasors, (s)he sometimes can seek reimbursement from other actors that contributed to the plaintiff's harm. Two different approaches are available for doing so: indemnity and contribution.

A. Indemnity

The concept of indemnity provides for a complete reimbursement, and it applies only under limited circumstances. The most common circumstance is where one party contractually agrees to indemnify another party for liabilities. A typical example is found in construction contracts, where a subcontractor agrees to indemnify a general contractor who might face tort liability for the subcontractor's work. Another example is where a party contracts with an insurance company to provide insurance protection against the insured's potential liability to a third party for negligence.

Indemnity can also apply in some cases even where the actors are not in a contractual relationship. An example is where one party pays a judgment or settlement based on vicarious liability. For example, suppose that the owner of a shipping company hires a driver to transport goods across town. While en route, the driver negligently runs a stop sign and hits a pedestrian. The pedestrian might be able to recover damages from the owner using a theory of vicarious liability. (*See* Chapter 13, *infra*, Vicarious Liability). The owner then has the right to file a separate indemnity action seeking full reimbursement from the negligent driver.

Another example comes from the area of products liability. A retailer might be liable to a consumer if it sells a defective product that subsequently injures the consumer. If the retailer pays a judgment or reasonable settlement, it then can seek reimbursement from the product's manufacturer, even absent a contractual agreement to do so. Indemnity applies in such situations, however, only if the retailer is not independently liable for the consumer's harm. In most cases, this means that the retailer could not have discovered the product's defect through reasonable inspection before selling the product to the consumer. (*See generally* Chapter 15, *infra*, Products Liability).

B. Contribution

Contribution permits only partial instead of complete reimbursement among multiple tortfeasors. As this conflicts with the traditional all-or-nothing nature of tort law, it is not surprising that contribution developed through legislation rather than through common law.

Before the advent of comparative responsibility, contribution statutes contemplated *pro rata* reimbursement. For example, suppose that three negligent actors—A, B, and C—contributed to a plaintiff's harm. Suppose further that the plaintiff sued only A, and received a $300,000 judgment reflecting full compensation for the harm. Under traditional contribution, A could still seek to recover $100,000 in *pro rata* reimbursement from both B and C, assuming that A could establish that each of them was also negligent in causing the plaintiff's harm. The ultimate effect of *pro rata* contribution is to make each multiple tortfeasor responsible for paying only his or her *pro rata* share of the plaintiff's loss. Of course, if B or C (or both) is insolvent or otherwise incapable of paying their share of the contribution to A, then A (in this example) will not be reimbursed for their share(s) of the loss.

Today, most jurisdictions have amended their contribution statutes to reflect tort law's movement to comparative fault. In these "comparative contribution" jurisdictions, reimbursement is proportional to the share of fault that a fact finder has assigned to each individual tortfeasor, rather than to merely the total number of tortfeasors involved (as in *pro rata* contribution). Using the previous example, *supra*, suppose that A's jurisdiction is one that retains traditional joint and several liability, making A liable for the full $300,000 judgment. Suppose further that, in a subsequent contribution action, a jury found A to be 50% at fault for the plaintiff's harm, while assigning 25% fault to B and C, respectively. Here, A could recover $75,000 from B (i.e., B's 25% of the $300,000 judgment) and $75,000 from C (i.e., C's 25% of the $300,000 judgment), leaving A responsible for the other half of the plaintiff's damages (i.e., $150,000) in accordance with the percentage of fault that the jury assigned to each of the three tortfeasors.

In states that have abolished joint and several liability, contribution is rarely an issue, as it will be unusual for a defendant to pay damages beyond the percentage consistent with the degree of fault assigned to each individual defendant. However, without joint and several liability the plaintiff must bear the risk of actually collecting the assigned amount against each respective defendant. Nevertheless, regardless of a state's rule on joint and several liability, a defendant that enters into a reasonable settlement with a plaintiff is insulated from a contribution claim brought by a tortfeasor that later pays a judgment or enters into an additional settlement.

Checkpoints

- Joint and several liability means that a defendant is responsible for the whole amount of a plaintiff's harm, even if the conduct of another actor contributed to the loss.

  - The rule traditionally applied in cases where a plaintiff suffered an indivisible loss at the hands of more than one actor.

  - No consensus has emerged about how the advent of comparative fault affects joint and several liability.

- Cases involving multiple tortfeasors often raise causation issues because the plaintiff cannot identify which individual defendant caused the harm.

  - In limited circumstances, courts have created special doctrines to avoid unfair outcomes.

  - These doctrines include "enterprise liability," "alternative liability," and "market share liability."

- Indemnity means complete reimbursement.

  - It often applies in situations where one party contractually agrees to indemnify another for liabilities.

  - Indemnity also applies in limited circumstances where parties are not in a contractual relationship.

- Contribution is only a partial reimbursement.

  - Traditionally, it permitted a defendant who had paid a judgment to recover *pro rata* shares from other culpable tortfeasors.

  - With the advent of comparative fault, however, most states have moved to a system of comparative contribution.

Chapter 8

Compensatory and Punitive Damages

Roadmap

- Understand the nature of pecuniary losses caused by physical injury, including past and future medical expenses and past and future lost income.
- Understand why future pecuniary losses must be discounted to their present value.
- Understand the nature of non-economic losses and how they are measured.
- Understand the distinctions between non-economic damages for pain and suffering, loss of consortium, and loss of enjoyment of life.
- Understand why some jurisdictions have imposed legislative caps on certain types of damages.
- Understand the purpose for and the function of the collateral source rule.
- Learn the purposes and the requirements for punitive damages.
- Recognize the Constitutional challenges to the recovery of punitive damages.

The term "damages" refers to the monetary award for a legally recognized harm. In tort cases, the normal remedy is compensatory damages awarded in a lump sum. The fundamental goal of damage awards is to restore the plaintiff as closely as possible to his or her condition before the accident. In a few tort cases, courts have ordered restitution (requiring defendants to return any gains made in a transaction), or have issued an injunction (forbidding threatened actions or requiring the defendant to take some action to repair the consequences of harmful conduct), but these are rare. In addition to compensatory damages, plaintiffs may also be awarded punitive damages in special cases. Punitive (or exemplary) damages are usually available only when the tortfeasor has committed serious misconduct with a bad intent or a bad state of mind such as malice.

The term "moral" damage is not used in the U.S, as it is in other countries. Instead, all damages that are not punitive damages are regarded as compensatory damages. This large category of compensatory damages is then further divided into "pecuniary" damages and "non-pecuniary" damages. The former category is said to consist of damages that are capable of precise calculation and set on market-based measures. The latter are supposed to be intangible damages that are not capable of precise measurement and for which there is often no market value. In the vocabulary of U.S. tort law, however, non-pecuniary damages are nevertheless actual damages and their award serves to compensate plaintiffs for real losses, even if hard to quantify. Damages for pain and suffering are examples of non-pecuniary damages.

I. Pecuniary Damages

Before looking more closely at non-pecuniary damages and punitive damages, we should briefly review the main components that make up the pecuniary portion of the compensatory damage award. First and foremost, plaintiffs can recover for any medical expenses proximately resulting from the tortious injury, including costs of doctors, drugs, medical devices, artificial limbs, etc. Future medical expenses are also recoverable, including the costs of medical monitoring after exposure to a toxic substance.

The next big-ticket item of pecuniary damage is wage loss. Plaintiffs can recover for the loss of wages or lost earning capacity when injuries prevent work. This includes lost future earnings, including wage increases or fringe benefits that would have been collected in the future. Most courts do not limit plaintiffs to the recovery of actual lost earnings, but allow recovery for lost earning *capacity*. Lost earning capacity reflects the value of work the plaintiff could have done, but for the injury. If the plaintiff did not work in the labor market but works without pay in the family business or in the household, for example, (s)he should be allowed to recover for the lost capacity to work, measured in terms of opportunity cost.

Under U.S. tax law, a plaintiff pays no income taxes on those compensatory damages representing past pecuniary losses for physical injury, thus actually netting more than (s)he would have received from taxable earnings had the injury not occurred. However, the award of damages representing *future* pecuniary losses is typically adjusted to account for the effects of future inflation as well as discounted to their "present value," reflecting that fact that money received today as compensation for future damages may be invested over the period of the actual future loss. This is an economic concept that will usually require the use of expert witnesses during trial.

The basic notion of "present value" is fairly easy to understand. If the tort victim was earning $50,000 a year and had a normal work life of 20 more years, that would generate potential future earnings of about $1,000,000.00. However, it should be obvious that receiving $1,000,000.00 in one lump sum at the end of the trial is a much different experience than receiving $50,000 a year over the next 20 years (as that income would actually have been received had the victim earned it normally throughout the remainder of his or her lifetime). If the entire lump sum of $1,000,000.00 received as a result of the trial verdict was invested over the subsequent 20-year future period at even a modest rate of interest, it would produce significantly more than the $50,000 of annual earnings that the damage award was intended to compensate for the victim's loss during that same future period. This might be seen as "over-compensating" the victim who, by the end of the future period in question, could have accumulated a sum that far exceeded the original amount intended as compensation for the victim's lost future earnings. To avoid any potential unfairness, the concept of reducing the plaintiff's future pecuniary damage recovery to its "present value" basically involves computing a sum of money that, if invested in one lump sum at today's investment rates, would generate roughly $50,000 a year over the next 20 years (in order to replace the victim's actual future loss over that same future period of time). That number, of course, would be substantially less than the full $1,000,000.00 verdict amount. Some jurisdictions require no reduction to "present value," assuming that whatever amount that the plaintiff would have earned over the future period would simply be offset by the ravages of future inflation. However, most jurisdictions require the parties to calculate the expected difference between investment interest rates and future inflation rates, and modify the award accordingly to reflect its inflation-adjusted "present value."

II. Non-Pecuniary Damages

Pain and Suffering. Plaintiffs are entitled to recover for all forms of suffering caused by the tortious injury, including future suffering. The recovery for "pain and suffering" includes virtually all forms of conscious suffering, both emotional and physical. Suffering can encompass, for example, terror at an impending injury (e.g., pre-impact fright) or worry over whether exposure to a substance will lead to disease (e.g., fear of AIDS or fear of cancer). Expert testimony can be offered to address pain, but frequently the jury will be able to simply to infer that the plaintiff has suffered pain from the nature of the injury and the kind of medical attention that it required. In cases of physical harm, if pain is established, some courts have even insisted that the jury include an amount for pain and suffering beyond medical expenses.

Awards for pain are not easy to evaluate because there is no objective criterion for assessing pain, making it difficult to set rational limits on such awards. It is thought that juries may sometimes use a baseline or anchor for determining the amount of damages for pain and suffering, often perhaps some multiple of the pecuniary damage amount. Despite great variability in awards, however, the severity of the injury is usually a good predictor of the size of the pain and suffering award.

Although awards for pain and suffering in cases of physical injury are well established, they have become the subject of increasing academic criticism and statutory tort reform. Defendant-oriented scholars stress the imprecision of such non-pecuniary awards and argue that they do not really serve the purpose of restoring plaintiffs to the position they were in before the accident. Past pain is harm, an injury, but to their way of thinking neither past pain nor its compensation has any consistent economic significance. The past experience is not a loss except insofar as it may have produced a present deterioration in the plaintiff's earning capacity. They also argue that variation in tort awards proves that the system is inequitable because all similar harms are not treated alike. A common argument put forward by economics-minded scholars is the "optimal insurance" view. Proponents of this view argue that the value of pain and suffering should be measured by whether a person would have bargained and paid for insurance against such a loss. They then reason that such a bargain would not be rational because supposedly money is worth less to a person in an injured state than it is to a healthy person. Other critics of pain and suffering awards do not necessarily want to abolish these awards, but they wish to limit the jury's discretion in determining the amount of the award. One proposal, for example, would inform jurors about the spectrum of prior awards and would instruct the jurors that if they wish to make an award in the top (or bottom) quartile of past results, they must justify their decision by pointing to specific facts in the case that tilt it to the high (or low) range.

Scholars who defend awards of pain and suffering emphasize the expressive function of law. They stress that tort judgments are not only about money, even though the award of damages is the principal tort remedy. Instead, a judgment also functions as a way of demonstrating the importance placed on human relationships and legal rights. These interests deserve legal recognition, even though they may lack precise market valuation. We also know that freedom from pain is something people value highly, based on empirical studies asking healthy persons how much money they would want to sell their good health in exchange for certain injuries or how much they would pay to avoid such injuries. These valuations are often higher than the awards actually given in tort cases for pain and suffering. With respect to the problem of variability of awards, defenders of pain and suffering awards argue that pain and suffering is highly individualistic and that we should not blame or penalize a plaintiff for not experiencing the "modal" amount of pain, just as certain plaintiffs are not penalized under the "eggshell skull plaintiff" rule if they happen to receive physical injuries that are more extensive than those normally experienced by other similarly injured persons.

Loss of enjoyment of life. One distinctive form of suffering is the plaintiff's sense of loss at being unable to engage in the activities (s)he enjoyed prior to the accident. For example, even if the plaintiff's injury makes it impossible to see a sunset, hear music, or engage in sexual activity, (s)he may have no physical sensation, but (s)he is still conscious of suffering a loss. It is a loss of a positive experience rather than the infliction of a negative experience. Most courts hold that such loss of enjoyment of life, or *hedonic* damages, is as compensable as any other emotional state. However, the controversy today is whether the plaintiff can recover for suffering in the form of lost enjoyment as a separate item of damages independent of pain and suffering.

For example, court decisions are split as to whether a plaintiff who is in an irreversible coma may recover damages for the lost enjoyment of life, even though (s)he is not aware of the loss. In such a case, ordinary language permits us to say that the plaintiff has lost enjoyment of life. However, if loss of enjoyment is merely an aspect of conscious suffering, then there should be no recovery. Most jurisdictions prohibit expert testimony on the subject of the value of damages for loss of enjoyment of life, although many courts do allow the plaintiff to personally testify as to such losses. Another issue that often arises is whether the jury should be instructed to make an award for pain and suffering and a separate award for the loss of enjoyment of life. Defendants commonly object to such an instruction because they believe that it will result in a duplicative recovery for the same injury. Plaintiffs, on the other hand, prefer a number of separate pegs by which the jury can consider and assess nonpecuniary losses that otherwise are often hard to describe and express.

Loss of consortium, companionship, and society. One special type of claim for intangible injuries is given to certain designated family members who suffer as a result of a physical injury to their spouse or child or parent. Claims for the "loss of consortium" and for "loss of companionship" are relational harms; the essence of these claims is to compensate for the change in the relationship brought about by the injury. Technically, there is a significant difference between the emotional grief and sorrow that a person may experience due to any injury to a loved one (typically referred to as "loss of companionship"), and the "loss of consortium" (defined as the mutual right between *spouses* in a marriage relationship to each other's love, support, cooperation, aid, companionship, services, and sexual relations). Although historically some courts have not always clearly articulated the distinction between these two separate relational interests, today most jurisdictions do allow recovery for both types of relationships in appropriate situations. Evidence showing the difference in the overall quality of the particular relationship before and after the victim's injury is usually sufficient to prove damages for these types of emotional injuries. In the U.S., claims for "loss of consortium" are strictly limited. Typically, only a spouse in a legally recognized marriage relationship is allowed to sue for "loss of consortium" damages (i.e., known as the "deprived" spouse) as a result of injuries to the other spouse (often referred to as the "impaired" spouse). In addition to the deprived spouse's claim for "loss of consortium" damages resulting from an injury to an impaired spouse, in some states parents may also sue for "loss of companionship" damages when their minor child is injured. Similarly, in a few states minor children may even have a separate "loss of companionship" claim for the loss of a parent's society and guidance. When a parent, child, or spouse dies as a result of tortious action, certain designated surviving family members may also have a claim for wrongful death. Wrongful death recoveries in the U.S. are governed by statute. As a result, only some states provide for recovery of non-pecuniary losses, such as loss of companionship and society, and grief. (*See* Chapter 11, *infra*, Wrongful Death and Survival).

III. The Movement to Cap Damage Awards

In the last two decades, many business groups have lobbied state and federal legislatures to restrict tort recoveries. As a result, well over half the states have enacted some kind of cap on recoverable damages. Some statutes only apply to certain types of claims, such as medical malpractice claims or suits against public entities. Some impose an absolute cap on all damages, while others only restrict non-pecuniary damages. The caps vary from state to state. For example, California's cap for "pain and suffering" damages is $250,000. Many plaintiffs have challenged caps as being unconstitutional, on a variety of grounds including equal protection and separation of powers. The results of these constitutional challenges are mixed, with approximately half of these challenges being successful in invalidating the caps.

Critics of caps argue that even if there is a need to reduce recoveries, caps are the wrong way to do it. By their nature, caps allow full recovery to the least injured but only partial recovery to those who are the most seriously injured. They also argue that the most controversial awards are often those that are least affected by caps (i.e., those involving sizeable "pain and suffering" awards when the economic losses are low).

IV. The Collateral Source Rule

One important doctrine in the law of damages that has also been the subject of "tort reform" statutes is the collateral source rule. In many cases, the injured plaintiff receives some compensation for injuries from sources that have nothing to do with the defendant (e.g., the plaintiff's own insurance, job benefits, or donations from friends). The traditional rule is that compensation from "collateral sources" is none of the defendant's business and does not go to reduce the defendant's obligation to pay damages. Some jurisdictions have distinguished between *gratuitous* collateral sources (i.e., support provided by family members that are not counted against what the defendant owes) and *nongratuitous* collateral sources (i.e., those paid for through premiums or taxes, for which the defendant will need to compensate the plaintiff).

It might seem that the injured plaintiff would be better off after the injury than before because (s)he may be able to collect both the insurance benefits from a collateral source and also a full tort award against the defendant, thus obtaining, in effect, a "double recovery." However, in many cases, to the extent that an insurer pays the plaintiff under the terms of an insurance policy, the insurer will acquire the plaintiff's right to sue the tortfeasor in order to be reimbursed for the amount that it has previously paid to the plaintiff insured (through a process known as subrogation). The collateral source rule is thus sometimes justified on the ground that it protects the insurer's subrogation right, without which insurance premiums might rise. Nevertheless, about half the states have abolished or limited the collateral source rule for certain claims, most often medical malpractice claims. In such states, plaintiffs are sometimes still able to recover their insurance premiums from the defendant.

V. Punitive Damages

In the vast majority of states, the jury is permitted but not required to assess punitive damages in special cases. Punitive damages represent a sum in excess of any compensatory damages, and they are usually available only when the tortfeasor has committed quite serious misconduct with a bad intent or bad state of mind. It is usually stated that punitive damages are awarded to punish or to deter such egregious misconduct. Damages serve as punishment or retribution because it is considered appropriate for the defendant to suffer for these types of misconduct, expressing the community's view of the anti-social nature of such actions. Damages serve as deterrence because a sufficient sum should be extracted from the defendant to make repetition of the misconduct unlikely. In some cases, deterrence is also necessary because the defendant's activity is profitable or the defendant retains gains even after compensation has been paid.

In addition to punishment and deterrence, punitive damages sometimes also serve other goals. They provide a source of funds to the plaintiff to aid in financing costly litigation. In the U.S., each party pays his or her own attorneys' fees, regardless of whether they are ultimately successful. Thus, a winning plaintiff may still be out of pocket considerable sums if the damage award is less than the costs of the litigation.

In some cases, punitive damages also serve a compensatory function, particularly in cases of dignitary harm, civil rights violations, etc., where the invasion of the plaintiff's rights is serious but there has been little economic loss or physical injury. One commentator has called punitive damages "extra compensatory damages," perhaps to suggest that punishment of the tortfeasor is not the only objective.

The courts have approved punitive damages in a wide variety of cases, ranging from traditional intentional tort cases (e.g., battery, fraud, sexual assault), to drunk driving, environmental harm, and products liability cases. The standard used to determine the appropriateness of punitive damages generally requires an extreme departure from acceptable conduct, as well as a bad state of mind, although reckless indifference to a great risk may at times also suffice. The defendant's abuse of power or a special relationship is another marker for punitive awards (e.g., an insurer who refuses to pay off on a policy or an employer who maliciously and wrongfully discharges an employee).

Because punitive damage awards have often been in the millions and even billions of dollars, the issue of the appropriate amount of such awards is the burning question in the courts and among many commentators. Despite huge amounts in celebrated individual cases, empirical studies conducted in the mid 1990s report that punitive damages are awarded in less than 10% of jury trials, with a median award of only $50,000 and a mean (because of high end awards) of $534,000. Very often, trial judges or appellate courts reduce the excessively huge awards. Nevertheless, because the amounts are so unpredictable and potentially huge, there is perhaps no issue in tort law more controversial than punitive damages.

Although there is no objective measure for determining the amount of punitive damages, courts have tried to provide a framework for assessing punitive damages by considering several factors including: (1) the reprehensibility of the defendant's misconduct, (2) the defendant's net wealth, (3) the profitability of the misconduct, (4) litigation costs, and (5) the aggregate of all civil and criminal sanctions against the defendant. Some courts also maintain that the punitive damage award should bear some reasonable relationship to either the potential harm caused by defendant's conduct or the actual damages suffered by the plaintiff.

Punitive damages are unusual in that the defendant's financial status is a factor in determining the right amount of punitive damages. The theory is that the trier of fact must know something about the defendant's financial condition in order to inflict a liability that will have an appropriate sting, for a small punitive damage award against a wealthy person may have little of its intended effect. However, in order to protect against the threat that juries will be more ready to impose liability when they are also informed as to the wealth of the defendant, some courts have permitted bifurcated trials, so that evidence of the defendant's wealth is not introduced for purposes of determining punitive damages until after liability has been established against the defendant.

One problem for corporate defendants is the risk that they will be punished several times over, as successive plaintiffs sue for injuries caused by defective products. Punitive damages are not subject to the prohibition against double jeopardy. Therefore in order to limit the threat of aggregate punishment, judges may review the punitive damages awarded against the defendant in prior cases and consider the potential for such awards in the future.

Since 1996, the U.S. Supreme Court has placed nationwide limits on awards involving punitive damages. It held that grossly excessive awards violate due process and, thus, it required trial judges and appellate courts to review punitive damage awards and cut down on the amount of excessive awards. The case that established these new requirements was *BMW v. Gore*, 517 U.S. 559 (1996). Gore had purchased a new car, which had been damaged while still in BMW's possession, probably from acid rain. BMW repainted the car and sold it as a new car without disclosing the repair. In terms of actual economic harm sustained by the plaintiff customer, the fact that the car had been repainted before it was sold as a "new" car might have reduced its resale value by $4,000. Nevertheless, the jury awarded $4 million in punitive damages, which the Alabama court reduced to $2 million.

Nevertheless, the Court ruled that the adjusted award was still grossly excessive and instructed courts in the future to follow the following guideposts in their review of punitive damages. They should consider the reprehensibility of the defendant's conduct; the disparity between the harm (or potential harm) suffered by the plaintiff and the size of the punitive damage award (i.e., the ratio of punitive to actual damages); and the difference between this remedy and civil penalties authorized or imposed in similar cases. This last guideline was new and seemed clearly to favor defendants. In *BMW*, the Court compared the punitive damage award with statutory fines for consumer fraud, concluding that the punitive damage award was far higher.

BMW v. Gore was not the Supreme Court's last word on punitive damages. In *Cooper Industries, Inc. v. Leatherman Tool Group, Inc.*, the Court determined that punitive damages would no longer be a question of fact left to the jury. 532 U.S. 424 (2001). In *Cooper*, the jury had found by clear and convincing evidence that the defendant, Cooper, had acted with malice, recklessness, and outrageous indifference to a highly unreasonable risk of harm in passing off Leatherman Tool's product as its own, and awarded the plaintiff $50,000 in compensatory damages and $4.5 million in punitive damages. *Id.* at 429. On appeal, the Supreme Court remanded the punitive damages decision. Despite two centuries of common law to the contrary, the Court declared that punitive damage determinations were questions of law, not of fact, and needed to be reviewed, *de novo*, rather than under an "abuse of discretion" standard. *Id.* at 437. The Court, in *Cooper*, upheld a mixed rationale of reprehensibility and deterrence for punitive damages. The Court explained that juries act capriciously because they are not bound by the "optimal deterrence rationale." Justice Stevens, for the Court, said:

> However attractive such an approach (optimally efficient deterrence) to punitive damages might be as an abstract policy matter, it is clear that juries do not normally engage in such a finely tuned exercise of deterrence calibration when awarding punitive damages. After all, deterrence is not the only purpose served by punitive damages. And there is no dispute that in this case, deterrence was but one of four concerns the jury was instructed to consider when setting the amount of punitive damages. Moreover, it is not at all obvious that even the deterrent function of punitive damages can be served only by economically "optimal deterrence." "[C]itizens and legislators may rightly insist that they are willing to tolerate some loss of economic efficiency in order to deter what they consider morally offensive con-

duct, albeit cost—beneficial morally offensive conduct; efficiency is just one consideration among many." *Id.* at 438–39.

While Justice Stevens saw a need for flexibility in determining the underlying purpose of punitive damages, he then went on to hold that juries were less able to apply this mix of rationales. Juries were found to be particularly inept at considering the third *Gore* criteria (comparing fines in criminal cases with punitive damage).

It wasn't long after *Cooper* that the Supreme Court got a chance to exercise its own *de novo* review of a punitive damages award. In April 2003, the Supreme Court decided *State Farm Mutual Automobile Insurance Co. v. Campbell.* 538 U.S. 408 (2003). In an underlying suit, the Campbells had been sued in tort for injuries arising from an automobile accident and had been defended by their insurance company, State Farm. Their insurance policy required State Farm to defend the Campbells and act in good faith in the resolution of the claims on their behalf. State Farm, however, refused to settle the claims for $50,000 (the policy limit) and insisted on a trial. State Farm assured the Campbells that their liability would be limited to the policy limit. *Id.* at 440. The Utah jury, however, awarded damages in an amount over three times the policy limit. (The award was $187,000.) After the verdict, State Farm refused to take an appeal and suggested that the Campbells put their house up for sale. The Campbells sued State Farm for bad faith in refusing to accept the plaintiff's settlement offer (which had been within the policy amount). State Farm initially defended, but then, before trial and after their appeal was denied, agreed to pay the Campbells' judgment. At trial, the Campbells exposed the true reason why State Farm had previously refused settlement in the underlying lawsuit (i.e., the settlement would not have allowed State Farm to meet certain nationwide targeted profitability goals set by the company). Campbell proved that State Farm routinely denied justified claims and lied to the policyholders about their personal liability at trial in order to meet its profitability targets.

In her dissent, Justice Ginsberg explained that State Farm's Performance Planning & Review (PP&R) scheme (1) functioned, and continues to function, as an unlawful scheme to deny benefits owed to consumers by paying out less than fair value in order to meet preset, arbitrary payout targets, (2) adversely affected Utah residents when State Farm falsified and withheld evidence in claim files, (3) subjected claimants to unjustified attacks on their character, reputation, and credibility, which further prejudiced claimants against the jury if their case went to trial, (4) exposed its claims agents to intolerable and recurrent pressure to reduce payouts below fair value, (5) instructed its agents to pad files with "self-serving" documents and omit critical information, (6) destroyed documents in the Campbells' file, and (7) deliberately crafted their business plan to prey on consumers who were unlikely to defend themselves (i.e., the elderly, the poor, and other consumers who were infirm).

The jury awarded the Campbells $2.6 million in compensatory damages and $145 million in punitive damages. The trial court subsequently reduced the damages to $1 million and $25 million, respectively. When the Utah Supreme Court reinstated the jury verdict, State Farm appealed to the U.S. Supreme Court, which reversed and remanded (Justices Scalia, Thomas, and Ginsberg dissented). The Court used *Gore*'s three-part analysis to justify its decision. In applying the reprehensibility factor, the Court held that a state does not have a legitimate concern in imposing punitive damages to punish a defendant for *unlawful* acts committed outside the state's jurisdiction, unless those unlawful acts have a specific nexus with their acts against the plaintiffs. This is significantly different from *Gore*, where the Court held that Alabama had no jurisdiction to punish for acts *lawful* in other jurisdictions, when determining the degree of reprehensibility.

The Court found that State Farm's denial of other claims outside of Utah, pursuant to its PP&R policy, were dissimilar acts, independent from the acts upon which liability was premised, and, therefore, could not serve as the basis for punitive damages. The Court instead analyzed the acts of the individual agent who (1) instructed the Campbells to reject the settlement, (2) counseled them not to get a separate attorney, (3) told them State Farm would not appeal, and (4) informed them that they had no rights to redress against State Farm. The Court found no similarity with what State Farm did to its other insureds with respect to homeowners' claims, fire claims, or other insurance claims, even though there was proof that other agents had engaged in similar devious behavior.

Justice Kennedy explained that retribution remains a major factor in the award of punitive damages. In addition, however, he stated that punitive damages should usually not exceed a single-digit multiplier to the compensatory damages suffered by the plaintiffs unless the retribution factor warranted it. In combination with that limitation, state courts only consider acts occurring in that state. This outside multiplier usually will serve as a significant cap for jury verdicts. Such an analysis shows that the Supreme Court is following an economic efficiency, or deterrence-based, rationale for punitive damages that takes individual compensation as its prime reference point. Thus, a deterrence-based rationale for punitive damages, especially one that has an augmented damages component, seems to be one important rationale supporting punitive damages. The *Campbell* decision severely cramps the ability of a court to provide augmented damages. In addition, it may also severely limit the ability of the jury to exact retribution. On the other hand, when a particular defendant's behavior warrants it, states like California continue to allow awards of punitive damages well in excess of the single digit cap. *See, Simon v. San Paolo U.S. Holding Co., Inc.,* 35 Cal. 4th 1159 (2005).

VI. Statutory Reform

A number of states have also recently placed limits on punitive damages in the form of caps and other measures that make it even more difficult to award punitive damages. Some of the caps place flat dollar limits on the amount of the award, while others limit punitive damages to some multiple (e.g., two or three times) of compensatory damages. As with other types of damage caps, caps on punitive damages do not address excessive awards at lower levels and there is some evidence that juries may actually tend to balloon the award to the cap level.

The most intriguing reform enacted in some states is to allocate a portion of the punitive award to be paid directly to a state agency, rather than award it to the plaintiff. The theory is that if the purpose of punitive damages is to punish or deter the defendant, the award will accomplish its objective even if it does not end up in the hands of the plaintiff. There is no good reason why plaintiffs should get a windfall recovery. This argument, however, ignores the other purposes for punitive damage awards, namely financing the litigation and compensating plaintiffs for hard-to-measure, but nevertheless actual, harms.

Checkpoints

- A tort award for physical injury can include pecuniary losses, such as recovery for past and future medical expenses.

- A tort award for personal injury can include an award for past and future lost income.

- In some jurisdictions, awards of damages for future losses (e.g., future medical expenses or lost income) must be discounted to present value.

- A tort award for physical injury may also include damages for so-called "pain and suffering."

- A tort award for physical injury can include an award for "loss of consortium" to the injured person's spouse. It can sometimes also include an award for the "loss of companionship" to minor children or even parents of an injured family member.

- In appropriate situations, courts may award damages for "wrongful death."

- Some states place legislative caps on certain types of damages, particularly "pain and suffering."

- Damage awards may be limited by the collateral source rule.

- In an appropriate case, punitive damages may be awarded in a torts case, but the U.S. Supreme Court has placed constitutional limits on the size of punitive damage awards.

Chapter 9

Limited Duty

Roadmap

- Understand the distinctions between the legal concepts of "nonfeasance" versus "misfeasance," and how they limit the duty owed in a negligence case.

- Understand the limitations imposed upon the concept of "duty" with respect to the tort of negligence under the "rescue rule."

- Understand the limitations imposed upon the concept of "duty" by virtue of "voluntarily assumed duties."

- Understand the limitations imposed upon the concept of "duty" based upon the existence of certain "special relationships" between the defendant and the plaintiff.

- Recognize the different types of "special relationships" that can be utilized to impose an affirmative duty to act on the defendant.

- Understand the limitations imposed upon the concept of "duty" by virtue of the "public duty rule."

- Recognize the duties imposed by express contractual agreements.

- Recognize the distinctions between the rules pertaining to the recovery of damages based upon the negligent infliction of *purely* emotional injuries and the recovery of "parasitic" emotional distress damages in an ordinary negligence action.

- Understand the special problems created when bystanders seek to recover damages for their *purely* emotional distress injuries sustained as a result of injuries negligently inflicted by the defendant on a third person.

This chapter expands upon the general concept of "duty" with respect to the tort of negligence discussed in Chapter 4, *supra*. Specifically, it addresses some special limitations that have been imposed upon the scope of the legal duty of care that is owed in negligence cases. Although negligence is most commonly asserted in relation to some type of affirmative misconduct by the defendant that violates a legally-recognized standard of care owed to the plaintiff, this chapter will examine a variety of situations where the defendant has simply not engaged in any sort of *mis*conduct whatsoever, but where the law, nevertheless, still imposes upon the defendant *an affirmative duty to act* in a certain manner.

I. No Duty to Act (Non-Feasance Versus Mis-Feasance)

Traditionally, the law of negligence declined to impose any legal duty whatsoever upon a defendant who merely failed to take action to protect the plaintiff or who failed to prevent an injury to the plaintiff in a situation where one could otherwise have been avoided, as long as no legal duty otherwise was owed by the defendant to the plaintiff in the first place. As morally reprehensible as it might seem for the defendant to stand idly by and decline (or even refuse) to offer assistance to a plaintiff in distress, the courts have consistently upheld the defendant's legal right to do so, citing as their primary justification the distinction between legal as opposed to moral or ecumenical duties.

A typical early case to articulate this concept was *Yania v. Bigan*, 155 A. 2d 343 (Pa. 1959). There, the defendant landowner had asked the plaintiff's decedent to assist him in starting a pump to remove water from his strip-mining trench, but then just stood by and watched as the decedent, while attempting to assist the defendant, drowned when he jumped into a steep-sided water-filled trench. The court, in upholding the dismissal of the plaintiff's complaint, explained that:

> The mere fact that [the defendant] saw [the decedent] in a position of peril in the water imposed upon him no legal, although a moral, obligation or duty to go to his rescue unless [the defendant] was legally responsible, in whole or in part, for placing [the decedent] in the perilous position: RESTATEMENT, TORTS § 314. *Id.* at 345-346.

Cases such as *Yania, supra*, eventually came to stand for a principle in negligence law known simply as "non-feasance." Under this principle, absent any legally recognized duty of care owed to the victim by the defendant, the law of negligence requires no affirmative duty to act whatsoever. *See* W. PROSSER, HANDBOOK ON THE LAW OF TORTS § 56, p. 340 (West Publ. Co. 4ᵗʰ ed. 1971). Thus, negligence law does not impose any affirmative duty on the part of anyone to render aid or assistance to another person who is in peril, so long as the defendant has done nothing to cause that peril (i.e., non-feasance).

As harsh and repugnant as the non-feasance rule may appear to the moral sensibilities of many people, to others a contrary rule may be equally reprehensible to society's notions of individual autonomy and the freedom to act (or not to act) in a certain way, regardless of the personal reason or motivation of the actor for doing so. The law of negligence must seek to maintain a proper balance between both of these competing societal interests. In an effort to provide just such a balance, the common law has developed a competing doctrine that is sometimes referred to as "misfeasance."

Under the doctrine of "misfeasance," even though a defendant may owe no duty to act affirmatively in traditional non-feasance situations (i.e., in those situations where the defendant initially has not caused or created the victim's peril), where the defendant nevertheless has acted in any manner that otherwise causes or creates a position of peril with respect to the victim (i.e., misfeasance), a duty will be imposed upon the defendant to act in a non-negligent manner. If the defendant breaches this duty, liability can be imposed, just as in any other situation involving negligent conduct. Thus, where the defendant affirmatively acts in some manner to actually create a danger that places the plaintiff in peril (i.e., misfeasance), the defendant will not be able to refrain from taking further action merely by relying upon the doctrine of "non-feasance." Instead, a misfeasant defendant will be required to make reasonable efforts to aid or assist anyone who otherwise has been imperiled by the defendant's previous misconduct.

While these two doctrines (i.e., non-feasance and misfeasance) reflect clearly distinct legal concepts, the differences between them are not always easy for courts to recognize, or even to articulate. For example, in a situation such as that involved in the *Yania* case, discussed *supra*, did the defendant initially (as the *Yania* court concluded) really do "nothing" at all to place the decedent in danger of drowning (i.e., non-feasance)? Or, as another court might just as easily conclude, did the defendant act initially in a negligent manner by asking the decedent to assist him to start a pump that he knew to be submerged in the deep water-filled trench, without also warning the decedent about the dangerous depth of water in that trench (i.e., misfeasance)? Obviously, this difference is much more than merely a semantic one, since a determination of non-feasance means that the defendant owes no duty of care whatsoever to the victim and, thus, as in *Yania*, cannot be negligent at all. Conversely, a finding of misfeasance could lead to the imposition of liability for the tort of negligence against a different defendant in a different case based upon these identical facts. Therefore, since the outcome in any given negligence scenario may depend upon whether the court analyses the facts from the perspective of "non-feasance" or "misfeasance," it is important to understand how these two concepts can be distinguished.

Over the years, courts have struggled with this question, offering a variety of possible responses. Among these, perhaps one of the most articulate attempts was provided by Judge Cardozo, in *H.R. Moch Co., Inc. v. Rensselaer Water Co.*, 159 N.E. 896 (N.Y. 1928), wherein he suggested the following test:

> The query [in distinguishing between non-feasance and misfeasance] always is whether the putative wrongdoer has advanced to such a point as to have launched a force or instrument of harm, or has stopped [short of such a point] where inaction is at most a refusal to become an instrument for good. *Id.* at 898.

Of course, in applying this or any other test to distinguish between "non-feasance" and "misfeasance," most jurisdictions do agree that since this determination pertains to the issue of duty, it is ultimately a question that must be made solely by the court, as a matter of law. But, if the court does determine that the defendant's duty is one addressed merely by the doctrine of "non-feasance," does this necessarily end the matter? That is the subject of the next section, *infra*.

II. Exceptions to the "No-Duty" (Non-Feasance) Rule

Even under the so-called "no duty" rule established by the doctrine of "non-feasance," courts have created numerous "exceptions" whereby a legal duty has nevertheless been imposed in negligence cases. Several of the more common of these exceptions are addressed here.

A. Where Defendant's Initial Negligence Imperils a Rescuer

Where the defendant has acted initially in some negligent manner that creates a victim who is otherwise in need of being rescued from some position of peril, many courts recognize this as an exception to the general "non-feasance" rule, and impose upon the defendant a legal duty of care with respect to any person(s) who foreseeably may attempt to rescue the originally imperiled victim. Often referred to simply as the "rescue doctrine," this rule states that where the defendant's negligence places any person in a position of peril, the defendant owes an affirmative duty to anyone else who may be injured while attempting to rescue that victim (even though originally no duty may have been owed to the rescuer). Once again, the rationale for this rule was eloquently stated by Judge Cardozo in *Wagner v. International Railway Co.*, 133 N.E. 437 (1921):

> *Danger invites rescue.* The cry of distress is the summons to relief. The law does not ignore these reactions of the mind in tracing conduct to its consequences. It recognizes them as normal. It places their effects within the range of the natural and probable. The wrong that imperils life is a wrong to the imperiled victim; it is a wrong also to his rescuer. *Id.*

However, the scope of the duty to act that is affirmatively owed to the rescuer under this rule is not always the same as that which may have been owed by the defendant directly to the victim of the initial negligence. As with any duty in negligence, it is measured in relation to the defendant's exercise of reasonable care under the circumstances. Thus, in these situations the defendant is not actually required to succeed in rescuing an imperiled rescuer, so long as (s)he at least reasonably attempts to do so. In most cases, the reasonableness of any rescue attempt ultimately remains a question of fact to be resolved just as in any other negligence situation. Therefore, a defendant whose negligence toward the original victim places a foreseeable rescuer in some life-threatening peril is still not required to risk his or her own life in order to attempt to save the rescuer. Nevertheless, this duty does require that the defendant take at least some affirmative steps to attempt an effective rescue, such as providing otherwise available lifesaving equipment, or at least summoning emergency assistance. Additionally, in no event will a defendant who is found to owe such an affirmative duty be permitted to impede reasonable rescue attempts offered by third persons.

B. Where Defendant Voluntarily Assumes a Duty

Even where the defendant owes no duty whatsoever to another person, whenever (s)he voluntarily undertakes to act with respect to anyone, a duty automatically arises to perform such actions in a non-negligent manner. Thus, a mere passerby who happens upon the scene of a personal injury accident may owe no legal duty (i.e., "non-feasance") whatsoever with respect to any of the accident victims encountered at that scene. However, if (s)he begins to offer any type of assistance (such as attempting an actual rescue, or providing emergency medical aid, or even summoning for help), a duty then arises to perform that assistance in a non-negligent manner (i.e., "misfeasance.") By affirmatively taking any action whatsoever with respect to the accident victims, the defendant has voluntarily assumed a legal duty to non-negligently complete that action.

One rationale sometimes offered for this exception to the "no duty to act" rule is merely that by voluntarily assuming a duty with respect to anyone, the defendant causes (or at least encourages) that person's reliance upon the defendant's actions. As a result of such reliance, the victim is induced to relinquish possible alternative options for rescue that otherwise may have been available, all to the victim's eventual detriment if the defendant then negligently performs. In this sense, the argument is very similar to one based upon the equitable concept of estoppel: by voluntarily acting in respect to the plaintiff, the defendant cannot later discontinue that action in a negligent manner, and leave the plaintiff in a position in which (s)he is worse off than before the defendant ever offered to act.

Under this exception to the traditional "non-feasance" rule, once a defendant does voluntarily assume a duty by acting in some manner with respect to the plaintiff, just how long does that duty last? Does the defendant now become duty-bound to continue that voluntary performance to its ultimate conclusion? The answer, of course, depends upon the exact nature of the duty that was assumed, as well as the particular circumstances involved. Generally, courts are guided by ordinary negligence principles in determining just how long the defendant's voluntary performance must continue once it has begun, but most would probably agree that it cannot be terminated so long as the plaintiff remains at a disadvantage by virtue of having initially relied upon defendant's voluntarily assumed performance. Referring again to the case of *H.R. Moch Co., Inc. v. Rensselaer Water Co.*, 159 N.E. 896 (N.Y. 1928), Judge Cardozo offered the following observation in regard to this doctrine, stating that:

> The hand once set to a task [i.e., a voluntarily assumed duty] may not always be withdrawn with impunity though liability would fail if it had never been applied at all. *Id.* at 898.

In general, most courts require that the initial occasion that gave rise to the defendant's voluntarily assumed duty must have come to an end, so that it is no longer reasonable to expect the plaintiff's continued reliance upon the defendant's continued performance.

C. Where Some Type of "Special Relationship" Exists Between the Plaintiff and the Defendant

By far the most frequently asserted exception to the traditional "no duty to act" (i.e., non-feasance") rule arises when the plaintiff alleges the existence of some "special relationship" between the parties, for which the law of negligence otherwise recognizes an affirmative duty owed by the defendant to act in some prescribed manner with respect to the plaintiff. The history of the common law of negligence is replete with examples, almost too numerous to list, of legal duties that have been based upon the existence of such "special relationships." For example, courts have imposed affirmative duties on behalf of defendants to act in "special relationship" situations involving "common carrier-passenger," "employer-employee," "parent-minor child," "doctor-patient," "teacher-student," "jailer-inmate," "landlord-tenant," "business invitor-invitee," as well as a myriad of other types of special legal relationships. Although this "special relationship" exception is most frequently asserted as an exception to overcome claims by the defendant that "no duty to rescue" was owed to the plaintiff victim, it can also arise as an exception to various other "no duty" applications as well. Moreover, this same "special relationship" exception has also been asserted as a source of imposing affirmative duties even with respect to controlling the actions of third persons for whom the defendant is claimed to have responsibility by virtue of some "special relationship" with that person. *See* RESTATEMENT (SECOND) OF TORTS § 315 (1965).

Once recognized as an exception for imposing a duty of care in "nonfeasance" cases, there is, at least potentially, no end to the theoretical applicability of this "special relationship" rule, as the case of *Farwell v. Keaton*, 240 N.W. 2d 219 (Mich. 1976), clearly illustrates. In *Farwell*, the young defendant and his friend were engaged in a purely social outing one evening, when they attempted to engage a group of young girls in a drive-in restaurant. The girls complained to some other boys at the restaurant who subsequently chased the defendant and his companion, eventually catching the companion and beating him severely. Afterwards, the defendant returned to his companion, applied ice to his head, and then drove him around for a couple of hours before returning the companion to his home, where the defendant then simply left him asleep in the backseat of his car that he parked outside in the friend's driveway. The following morning the companion was discovered unconscious in the backseat of the car, and subsequent attempts to revive him were unsuccessful, due to the severe head injuries that he had sustained the night before. Relying upon the "special relationship" which it found to exist "between companions on a social venture" who were "engaged in a common undertaking," the court rejected the defendant's assertion that he owed "no duty to rescue" his companion (i.e., the "non-feasance" rule) and re-instated a jury verdict for negligence against the defendant.

Of course, the outcome in *Farwell, supra,* could just as easily have been sustained on the basis of either of the other exceptions to the "no duty rule" of "non-feasance" discussed, *supra*. For example, when the defendant and his companion originally decided to engage the young girls in the restaurant, despite the girls' objections, the defendant's actions in running away from the danger as the group of boys chased them, instead of simply driving away in their car, might easily have been determined to be negligent, and as a result of that negligence, the defendant placed both himself and his friend in danger of attack from the boys, thereby creating *an affirmative duty to rescue* his friend from the danger that this conduct created. Moreover, when the defendant (who did run away to escape this danger) later returned to aid his friend, he this time may have *voluntarily assumed a duty* to rescue his friend by providing some limited medical assistance that he performed in a negligent manner. By removing his friend from the lot near the restaurant where he was beaten, and not driving him immediately to a hospital (or at least calling for emergency assistance), and by placing him in the backseat of his car and then leaving the scene unannounced with the car parked in the driveway outside the decedent's home, the defendant significantly decreased his friend's chances of being successfully treated for his injuries in a timely manner, as well as the possibility that anyone else might have found the decedent in time to seek proper medical attention.

As the foregoing discussion indicates, the traditional "no duty" rule of "non-feasance" with respect to the defendant's duty to act affirmatively in the context of the tort of negligence, has, to a fairly significant extent, now been almost completely replaced by any number of "exceptions" that can be utilized to justify the imposition of a duty of ordinary care in most negligence situations today. Thus, armed with the proper "exception," any court can almost always articulate some legitimate legal basis upon which to define a duty in most situations, regardless of whether an initial duty to act is otherwise apparent or not.

III. Public Versus Private Duties

Thus far in this chapter, the primary focus of the discussion of affirmative duties to act has involved the imposition of such duties upon *private* individuals in "non-feasance" situations where the traditional rules of negligence simply did not recognize any duty to act in the first place. In this section, the focus of that discussion now shifts to the duty of various *public entities* to act affirmatively in similar situations where otherwise no such duty is owed to the individual plaintiff.

A. The "Public Duty" Rule

Historically, the law of negligence has addressed this issue somewhat differently, depending upon whether the defendant was a private individual or a public entity. The reasons for doing so are primarily based upon public policy, relating to the potentially adverse economic implications of imposing affirmative duties to act upon various public entities with respect to specific situations in which a public entity is legally required to act for the benefit or protection of individual citizens. For the most part, the legal rules pertaining to the affirmative duties owed by public entities are not really all that different from those involving ordinary private defendants, discussed *supra*. However, they are typically applied a little differently in public duty situations, where courts usually require a somewhat closer degree of relationship between the public entity and the individual plaintiff. Thus, where a public entity, although under no duty to take any action whatsoever with respect to a given individual citizen, nevertheless voluntarily undertakes to do so anyway, the public entity will be required to act in a non-negligent manner with respect to that particular individual, just as in any negligence situation. However, where the legal justification for imposing an affirmative duty to act on a public entity is based solely upon the existence of some "special relationship" between the victim and the public entity, most courts will require a stronger showing as to the nature of that relationship before requiring the public entity to take specific action where otherwise no duty was owed. This special limitation upon the ordinary duty owed by public entities is often referred to as the "public duty" rule.

Under the "public duty" rule, an affirmative duty to act will not be imposed upon a public entity for the benefit or protection of any individual citizen merely by virtue of the relationship that exists between public entities and their citizens. The economic burden of sustaining such a duty would simply be too great for most public entities to bear. Instead, before any such affirmative duty will be imposed upon a public entity, some uniquely-identified "special relationship" must be found to exist between the public entity and the specific victim involved that otherwise justifies requiring the entity to act in some specific manner with respect to that particular victim rather than merely the public at large. For example, under this rule, the mere threat posed to the community at large from general criminal activity will not provide a sufficient legal basis for imposing a duty on the police department to protect all citizens against injuries inflicted by such criminal activity by requiring the police to hire more officers or to increase patrols in the community. Even though it is quite foreseeable that injury to some citizens in the community (at least statistically) could be reduced by either of these actions, the economic burden imposed upon the police department (and ultimately the taxpayers) by requiring such a duty does not justify this additional expense. However, where the police department has been made aware that a specific criminal threat was directed against a specifically identified citizen or group of citizens in the community, an affirmative legal duty to take reasonable steps to avert such a threat may be imposed against the public entity. Of course, the actual extent of those additional steps still might not require the police department to hire additional officers where the money to do so is simply not available from the public entity. However, it might still be reasonable to require the police to increase their patrols in response to such a specific identified threat. The policies and concerns pertaining to many of these issues are explored by the California Supreme Court in its majority and dissenting opinions in *Thompson v. County of Alameda*, 614 P. 2d 728 (1980).

B. Voluntarily Assumed Public Duties

Just as in the case of duties that have been voluntarily assumed by private defendants (*see* section II.B., *supra*), a public entity can also be liable for negligently performing a duty that it has voluntarily undertaken, even though initially it may not have had any affirmative legal obligation to do anything in the first place. A classic illustration of this type of duty is provided by the case of *Florence v. Goldberg*, 375 N.E. 2d 763 (N.Y. 1978). In *Florence*, the plaintiff's young child was struck and injured by a taxicab in a school crosswalk at which the defendant municipality had previously provided a crossing guard during normal school hours. However, on the day of the accident, the regular guard did not report to work and the defendant municipality failed to provide a substitute or otherwise to warn parents that a guard was not available. Declining to apply the traditional "public duty" rule as asserted by the defendant municipality, the court explained that by providing the crossing guard at this particular intersection (even though initially there was no duty to provide any guard), the defendant municipality had voluntarily assumed such a duty, which it was now obligated to perform in a non-negligent manner.

Having once voluntarily assumed a duty under this limited exception to the "public duty" rule, does this mean that the public entity is then obligated to continue to perform that duty forever? The court in *Florence, supra,* explained that even voluntarily assumed duties can be discontinued, provided that all of the affected citizens are given proper notification and sufficient time in which to make other arrangements. Thus, even though a duty has been voluntarily assumed by a public entity which otherwise would not have owed any duty under the "public duty" rule, that voluntarily assumed duty still can be discontinued, provided that this too is done in a non-negligent manner.

IV. Contractual Limitations on Duty

The common law rules pertaining to the "limited" duties that are imposed upon both private individuals as well as public entities by the law of negligence (discussed *supra*) are generally well established and fairly consistent among most American jurisdictions. However, there is one additional limitation that deserves at least some mention. As with most other situations involving autonomous individuals and/or public entities, sometimes the parties expressly agree to alter their normal legal duties with respect to each other by contractually agreeing to assume certain additional duties that might not otherwise have been imposed by the common law. In most instances, at least absent some specific public policy reason that would prevent the enforcement of the parties' contract altogether, courts will not interfere with the contractual re-allocation of negligence duties in some way that may differ from the traditional common law, provided that such agreements clearly articulate the parties' respective duties. Thus, even where the common law might not recognize any duty on the part of the defendant to act in a given set of circumstances, a court might still impose such a duty where the defendant has contracted with the plaintiff, expressly agreeing to assume such a duty.

V. Negligent Infliction of Purely Emotional Distress Injuries

A. Purely Emotional Distress Injuries Inflicted upon Direct Victims of Tortious Misconduct

In Chapter 2, *supra*, we addressed the tort of "intentional infliction of emotional distress" (IIED) within the context of our discussion of intentional torts. There, we saw that the law of torts provides protection for *purely* emotional injuries to persons that have been *intentionally* inflicted by the defendant. In this section, we will discuss whether the law allows similar protection for such injuries when they have merely been *negligently* inflicted. The short answer to this question is "yes," and the specific tort theory of liability that addresses these types of injuries is referred to as "*negligent infliction of emotional distress*" (or NIED). However, tort liability for *purely* emotional distress injures that have been negligently inflicted is not without some serious limitations, and for this reason the specific tort of "negligent infliction of emotional distress" is often regarded as a special adaptation of some of the "limited duty" rules that are discussed throughout this chapter.

At the very outset of this portion of our discussion, it should be noted that some courts actually treat this issue as a matter of "proximate cause," rather than duty. These issues are addressed more fully in Chapter 6, *supra*. However, in this discussion, the defendant's liability for negligent infliction of emotional distress will be analyzed from the perspective of determining the duty of care that is owed by the defendant in these factually limited situations.

Historically, courts made a very clear distinction between purely emotional injuries that had been *intentionally* inflicted on the plaintiff (and for which recovery was allowed by the common law tort of "intentional infliction of emotional distress") and those that were due to the defendant's mere acts of negligence. As to the latter types of injuries, the majority of courts simply declined to recognize any liability at all. *See Spade v. Lynn & Boston R.R.,* 168 Mass. 285 (1897). Given the then commonly held notion among most courts that purely emotional injuries were just too easy for plaintiffs to "fake," they simply declined to recognize any action based upon negligence where the plaintiff claimed solely emotional injuries. However, a few courts were somewhat more inclined to permit recovery for these same types of purely emotional injuries in situations where the defendant had acted intentionally to inflict such injuries, so gradually the tort of "intentional infliction of emotional distress" came to be recognized in most jurisdictions, but with the express qualification that such harm must have been specifically intended by the defendant. (*See* Chapter 2, section I.D., *supra*). The defendant's culpable misconduct in specifically intending to inflict extreme emotional distress upon the plaintiff was thought to provide sufficient evidence that the plaintiff's resulting emotional distress injuries were legitimate and not feigned. By contrast, with respect to purely emotional distress injuries allegedly resulting from merely negligent misconduct by the defendant, most courts considered it simply unreasonable to require defendants to anticipate and then to take appropriate precautions against causing such consequences due to their merely negligent actions. As a result, at least absent some additional evidence to corroborate them, damages were not allowed by most courts whenever purely emotional distress injuries were negligently inflicted.

The one exception to this approach was where the emotional distress injuries were also accompanied by other types of harms sustained at the same time by the plaintiff as a result of the defendant's negligence. Thus, where the defendant's negligence caused some other type of physical harm, for example a broken leg or some other physical injury, courts have always allowed the plaintiff to recover for any accompanying emotional distress damages that (s)he may have sustained, such as worry about the life-altering impact of a serious physical injury, or the emotional distress resulting from the loss of enjoyment of some activity in which the plaintiff can no longer participate because of an accompanying permanent physical injury. Often referred to as "parasitic" harms, these types of emotional injuries are thought to be much more reliable (and, thus, less likely to be "faked") than purely emotional distress claims, because they are accompanied by a more easily provable physical injury as well. As such, "parasitic" emotional distress damages are always recoverable, if proven, when they are accompanied by other physical injuries resulting from the defendant's negligence. (See Chapter 8, *supra.*). Thus, in this chapter, the reference to *purely* emotional distress injuries refers only to those emotional harms in which there has been no accompanying tortiously inflicted physical injury.

In negligent infliction of emotional distress cases, initial fears that it was too easy to "fake" purely emotional distress harm in the absence of an accompanying physical injury gradually gave way to what became known as the "impact rule." Under this rule, plaintiffs were permitted to recover damages for purely emotional distress injuries, even in the absence of any accompanying physical injuries, if they were able to prove that the emotional injuries resulted from at least some type of physical impact that was also caused by the defendant's alleged negligent act. The "impact rule" was often subject to very technical interpretations for determining initially whether the defendant owed any duty at all. Thus, a plaintiff under the "impact rule" would still be denied any recovery for purely emotional injuries allegedly resulting from a "near miss" accident caused by the defendant's negligence, whereas that same plaintiff could recover fully for a purely emotional harm if there was at least some actual physical impact with the plaintiff's person, however slight and regardless whether that impact resulted in any physical injury to the plaintiff.

B. Purely Emotional Distress Injuries Inflicted upon Bystanders

It is one thing for the plaintiff in a negligent infliction of emotional distress case to personally seek damages for purely emotional harm that has been inflicted upon the plaintiff as a direct result of the defendant's negligence with respect to the injured plaintiff (*see* section A., *supra*), but it is quite another thing if the person claiming the distress damages is not even the primary victim of the defendant's negligence. For example, what if the plaintiff is a bystander who merely watches as a third person sustains some type of injury as a result of the defendant's negligence? Just how far should the defendant's duty of care be allowed to extend in negligent infliction of emotional distress cases brought by such bystanders? Should the law of negligence extend the defendant's duty of care with respect to these types of purely emotional harm injuries even to include bystanders situated well beyond the initial victim who may nevertheless claim some type of emotional distress merely by watching or otherwise observing an injury that was negligently inflicted by the defendant onto the original victim? These are the kinds of questions that courts must address when responding to this issue.

In a sense, the "impact rule" provided its own form of authentification for all injuries sustained by the plaintiff, since these damages arose directly and personally from a physical impact caused by the defendant's negligence toward the original victim. Aside from the purely fortuitous circumstance where the bystander plaintiff was not also *physically* injured by the impact, even though *emotionally* harmed, the defendant in this situation can hardly assert that no duty was even owed to the bystander in the first place, since at least some physical impact to the victim did occur. However, how should the defendant's duty be analyzed when the plaintiff bystander is physically situated so far away from the impact with the original victim that there is no longer even a possibility that the plaintiff also could have been "physically impacted" by the defendant's negligence? This issue has resulted in several different approaches being taken by the courts.

Expanding upon the original "impact rule," some courts have concluded that as long as the plaintiff bystander was physically situated within such close proximity to the original victim of the defendant's negligence that an actual physical impact with the bystander at least *might* have occurred, this will suffice for imposing a duty on the defendant to avoid negligently inflicting emotional distress injuries to such a bystander. Known as the "zone of impact" or "zone of danger" rule, this doctrine denies recovery for purely emotional distress injuries that have been negligently inflicted by the defendant unless the defendant's original negligence also created at least a risk of actual bodily harm to the plaintiff bystander as the result of a physical impact. *See* RESTATEMENT (SECOND) OF TORTS § 313(2) (1965). Thus, under such a rule, the plaintiff bystander must have been situated in close physical proximity to the actual injured victim before any recovery for the plaintiff's purely emotional distress damages will be allowed. In that regard, the so-called "zone of impact" rule is actually quite similar to the basic formulation of duty that was expressed by Judge Cardozo in *Palsgraf v. Long Island R. Co.*, 162 N.E. 99 (N.Y. 1928). (*See* Chapter 6, *supra*).

But what happens in situations where the plaintiff bystander is physically situated well outside of the so-called "zone of impact," but nevertheless still sustains purely emotional distress injuries from witnessing or otherwise observing an injury negligently inflicted by the defendant on an accident victim. While some courts, fearing the possibility of "faked" emotional distress claims, have simply refused to allow any recovery at all in such circumstances, other courts have attempted to formulate a rule that further defines the scope of the defendant's duty, even in these types of situations.

In *Dillon v. Legg*, 441 P.2d 912 (Cal. 1963), the California Supreme Court became the first court to formally extend the scope of the defendant's duty in such cases to bystanders situated beyond the actual "zone of impact," by adopting a test for determining the defendant's duty of care based upon the degree of foreseeability with respect to each individual plaintiff bystander's emotional distress harm. Known today as the *"Dillon* rule," this approach actually incorporates three different considerations into the court's determination as to whether to extend the defendant's duty of care to bystanders situated outside the physical "zone of impact." Specifically, these factors are:

(1) whether the plaintiff bystander was situated in close proximity to the actual site of the original victim's injury;

(2) whether the plaintiff bystander's emotional shock resulted from a direct, contemporary, sensory observation of the original victim's injury, or from merely learning about it from some other source after the fact; and

(3) whether the plaintiff bystander and the original victim were closely related, and if so, to what degree, as contrasted with a mere stranger.

While a number of other courts have subsequently applied the *"Dillon* rule" in these types of bystander negligent infliction of emotional distress cases, there is still a general lack of agreement as to the formal legal effect to be afforded each of the individual factors (*supra*) that were addressed by the California Court. *See, e.g., Dzionski v. Babineau*, 380 N.E. 2d 1295 (Mass. 1978). For example, some courts merely consider the general impact of these three factors as they pertain to the overall reliability of sustaining a claim for the plaintiff's claimed emotional distress injuries. However, other courts are more inflexible, regarding each of the so-called *"Dillon"* factors as an essential threshold requirement that must be satisfied before any duty of care will be imposed upon the defendant with respect to purely emotional distress injuries negligently inflicted upon a bystander. As a result of these different interpretations of the defendant's duty of care with respect to negligently inflicted emotional distress in these bystander-injury cases, the *"Dillon* rule," as originally formulated by the California Supreme Court, has now become even more restricted, requiring that the plaintiff *must*:

(1) be closely related to the originally impacted victim;
(2) be physically present at the scene of the original accident, actually witnessing the injury to the original victim; and
(3) suffer severe emotional distress as a result of witnessing the accident. *See Thing v. La Chusa*, 771 P. 2d 814 (Cal. 1989).

Checkpoints

- "Non-feasance" refers to situations in which the law of negligence does not impose any affirmative duty upon the defendant to act whatsoever.
- The doctrine of "misfeasance" refers to situations where the defendant *has* acted, but in some manner that the law regards as negligent.
- Where the defendant initially has not caused or created the victim's peril but subsequently acts to cause or create a position of peril with respect to the victim, a duty will be imposed upon the defendant to act in a non-negligent manner.
- Under the "rescue rule," if the defendant negligently places any person in a position of peril, the defendant will also owe an affirmative duty to anyone else who may be injured while attempting to rescue that victim.
- Under the "voluntarily assumed duty rule" a defendant who voluntarily takes any action with respect to the plaintiff, even though under no duty to do so, voluntarily assumes a legal duty to non-negligently complete that action.
- Where a "special relationship" is found to exist between the defendant and the plaintiff, courts often impose an affirmative duty to act.
- Courts have recognized a wide variety of different types of "special relationships," including those of:
  - common carrier-passenger;
  - employer-employee;
  - parent-minor child;
  - doctor-patient;
  - teacher-student;
  - jailer-inmate;
  - landlord-tenant; and
  - business invitor-invitee.

- Under the "public duty" rule, an affirmative duty to act will not be imposed upon a public entity for the benefit or protection of any individual citizen merely by virtue of the existence of the "public entity-citizen" relationship.

- Before any affirmative duty to act will be imposed upon a public entity there must be some uniquely-identified special relationship existing between the public entity and the specific victim.

- Even in the absence of a common law duty on the part of the defendant to act in a given set of circumstances, the courts will generally enforce contractually imposed duties, as long as they are not otherwise against public policy.

- Emotional distress damages in negligence actions may be fully recovered by the victim where they are "parasitic" in relation to other recoverable damages.

- Defendants owe only a limited duty to victims with respect to damages resulting from the negligent infliction of *purely* emotional injuries.

- Courts have recognized a variety of different approaches restricting the scope of a defendant's duty owed to bystanders with respect to damages for their *purely* emotional distress injuries sustained as a result of injuries negligently inflicted by the defendant on a third person, including:

  - the "impact rule";

  - the "zone of impact rule"; and

  - the "*Dillon* rule."

Chapter 10

Premises Liability: Duties of Owners and Occupiers of Land

Roadmap

- Understand the traditional basis for determining the duty of care owed by owners and occupiers of land with respect to persons who are injured on the premises.

- Appreciate the historical background in which the special rules for determining the duty of care owed by landowners and occupants of premises were derived.

- Distinguish between the landowner's duties owed with respect to injuries caused by *dangerous conditions* and those caused by various *activities* conducted on the premises.

- Learn the duty of care traditionally owed by landowners and occupants to *trespassers*.

- Learn the duty of care traditionally owed by landowners and occupants to *licensees*.

- Learn the duty of care traditionally owed by landowners and occupants to *invitees*.

- Recognize the common exceptions that are traditionally applied to alter the landowner's duties owed to special categories of entrants such as "child trespassers," "discovered trespassers," "fire-fighters," "social guests," and "recreational entrants."

- Understand the rationale for abolishing or modifying the traditional rules for determining the duties owed by landowners and occupants of premises based upon the "status" of the entrant, as well as how the new rule based solely upon the exercise of reasonable care under the circumstances has fared after its adoption in some jurisdictions.

- Understand the landlord's traditional "no duty" rule with respect to injuries sustained by tenants and their guests upon leased property, as well as the modification of that no-duty rule by the application of various special common law exceptions.

Premises liability represents probably one of the most unique areas in all of the law of torts today. Basically, the concept of "premises liability" simply refers to the tort liability of various owners and occupiers of real property with respect to persons who are injured on the premises. However, unlike most other areas of the law where the defendant's liability for the tort of negligence is generally based upon traditional common law rules that define the defendant's duty in relation to the exercise of reasonable care under the circumstances, in premises liability cases the defendant's duty of care traditionally is determined solely according to the legal classification of the injured plaintiff. This chapter will explore precisely how and why these special premises liability rules came into existence, as well as many of the current applications of these rules. It will also examine some of the more important legal doctrines that have developed in relation to this fascinating area of the law, and address precisely how they fit within the overall structure of the law of torts.

I. Historical Background

In order to fully appreciate the many different rules and doctrines that pertain to the modern law of premises liability, it is necessary first to understand where they came from and how they were derived. As with most other areas of modern American law, the various premises liability rules and doctrines developed almost exclusively from the early English common law. At that time England was primarily a rural, agrarian society in which the ownership of land still reflected many of the social and economic influences of early English feudal society. Land itself represented a symbol of wealth and power, and as the common law rules pertaining to the tort liability of landowners and occupants gradually began to develop, courts often favored the creation of rules that gave greater protection to the landowners in claims brought by various persons who were injured after entering upon the land. Thus, the traditional concept of duty with respect to the tort of negligence in ordinary situations (*see* Chapter 4, *supra*), took on entirely different characteristics when it was applied within the context of premises liability. Instead of focusing upon the overall reasonableness of the defendant's conduct, as it applied in most other types of different duty situations, premises liability cases created entirely separate and distinct legal duties of care that were owed to different types of injured entrants upon the land. Thus, the duty of care owed by the defendant landowner or occupant to any given plaintiff in a premises liability case was determined solely by the classification of the injured entrant either as a *trespasser*, a *licensee*, or an *invitee*. As the injured entrant's classification changed from one category to another, so did the defendant's duty that was owed to the plaintiff.

Since colonial American society, like its English ancestor, was still largely rural and agrarian, early American courts quite readily applied and enforced these common law categories as the sole means of determining the defendant landowner's legal duty of care in premises liability cases, often with somewhat harsh results that usually favored the landowner. Over time, as American society evolved, becoming more urban and industrialized, courts began to create additional classifications of entrants, as well as new "exceptions" to existing classifications, in an effort to lessen the harshness of the results that often occurred when the limited duty rules pertaining to the traditional status classifications were applied in unique circumstances. For the most part, these rules and exceptions continued to be developed and applied by most American courts throughout much of the last century, resulting in the creation of an entirely separate body of "premises liability law" that still persists today in most American jurisdictions. As a result, courts in a majority of jurisdictions continue to resolve premises liability cases by applying the numerous special "duty" rules, exceptions, and limitations that have been fashioned around the traditional common law classifications based solely upon the legal status of the injured entrant. While sometimes criticized [*see Kermac v. Compagnie Generale Translantique*, 358 U.S. 625 (1959) where the U. S. Supreme Court partially rejected some of these classifications in an admiralty case, referring to the then existing body of rules and exceptions as a "semantic morass"], with only a relatively few significant departures [*see Rowland v. Christian*, 443 P. 2d 561 (1968), discussed *infra*], the majority of American jurisdictions continue to apply most, if not all, of these traditional common law doctrines in premises liability cases. Among the main reasons for doing so, most courts cite their continued commitment to the doctrine of *stare decisis* and the overall importance in American common law of adhering to case precedent. They are also quick to point out that as complicated (and at times even confusing) as these different premises liability "duty" rules and exceptions may appear, in the majority of situations whenever these traditional rules are applied courts generally have been able to reach consistently fair results. Thus, criticisms over the basic fairness of the original common law rules as a means of determining the landowner's duty of care owed to injured entrants that once prompted a movement away from the traditional tri-partite classification scheme have now generally been replaced by a recognition among most courts that the existing premises liability rules and exceptions are more than adequate to provide just and consistent outcomes without the necessity and added confusion created by over-ruling vast numbers of prior cases in an attempt to produce essentially similar results.

As a result of these historical developments, most jurisdictions today continue to recognize an entirely separate scheme for determining the duty of care owed by landowners and occupants in any case in which an entrant onto the premises has been injured. *See generally* N. Landau & E. Martin, Premises Liability: Law and Practice, §§ 1.05[2]-[4] (Matthew Bender Co. 2016). Although the vast majority of these cases involve the traditional common law tort of negligence (*see* Chapter 4, *supra*), the concept of "duty" in premises liability cases is generally determined in accordance with a completely different set of legal principles. These principles are discussed in the sections that follow.

II. "Conditions" Versus "Activities" on the Land

Before addressing landowners' different duties of care as determined on the basis of the particular legal classification of each individually injured entrant, it is important to understand that the traditional common law rules applicable in most premises liability cases generally pertain only to those injuries that are caused by *dangerous conditions* existing on the property rather than by dangerous activities that also might be conducted on such property. When an entrant has been injured by some *activity* while on the land (as opposed to a dangerous condition), courts generally apply the standard duty based upon the defendant's exercise of "ordinary, reasonable care under the circumstances" that is applicable to all traditional negligence cases. (*See* Chapter 4, *supra*, Negligence). Thus, the special "duty" rules based upon the classification of the injured entrant as a trespasser, a licensee, or an invitee are generally applicable only where some type of dangerous condition on the premises has caused the injury.

Basically, a dangerous condition for purposes of applying these special duty rules is simply a static hazard that exists on the land. Since it does not move on its own, a dangerous *condition* is a static, or passive, defect that cannot exist apart from its relationship to the specific premises upon which it is found. Thus, a slippery rug on the floor, or a loose handrail or tread on a set of stairs, or a puddle of water on the floor are all typical examples of dangerous conditions. By contrast, an *activity* may generally be defined as anything that involves movement with respect to the actual source of the entrant's injury, as opposed to some type of static hazardous condition. Thus, operating a tractor, or mowing the lawn, or chopping down a tree are typically classified as activities. Moreover, an activity can occur anywhere and is not dependent upon any particular type of premises or location. In premises liability cases, although the entrant's activities may certainly involve some type of movement while on the premises, the actual cause of the plaintiff's harm is due to the existence of a hazardous (static) condition on the property.

The distinction between a truly static *dangerous condition* (for which the special duty rules of premises liability are applicable) and a mere *activity* (for which the traditional common law duty of reasonable care under the circumstances applies) is not always an easy matter to resolve. For example, in *Baldwin v. Gartman*, 604 So. 2d 347 (Ala. 1992), the plaintiff neighbor entered the defendant's property to assist in the construction of a walkway and was injured when a large slab that had been precariously balanced on a transport dolly suddenly fell onto him. Arguing that since he had been injured by a dangerous activity conducted on the defendant's premises (i.e., moving the large slab with a dolly), the plaintiff claimed that the defendant's duty of care should be based upon the traditional common law duty of "reasonable care under the circumstances." However, the Alabama Supreme Court disagreed, and concluded that the plaintiff's injury was caused by a dangerous condition that existed on the property (i.e., a large slab that had been precariously balanced on a moveable dolly). As such, the Court declined to apply the traditional duty based upon the defendant's exercise of reasonable care and applied, instead, a lower standard of care based upon the plaintiff's classification as a mere "licensee" on the premises.

III. Common Law Categories of Entrants

As discussed, *supra*, in most premises liability cases, the duty of care owed by the defendant landowner or occupant to any person who is injured on the premises will be determined, at least in the majority of jurisdictions, entirely on the basis of the injured entrant's legal classification as either a *trespasser*, a *licensee*, or an *invitee*. As the injured entrant's legal classification changes from that of a trespasser to a licensee to an invitee, so does the defendant's corresponding duty of care, increasing from virtually no duty being owed to a trespasser, to only a limited duty that is owed to a licensee, and reserving the traditional common law negligence's basic duty to exercise "ordinary, reasonable care under the circumstances" solely to invitees who have been injured on the defendant's premises. To better understand just how these different duties are applied, we need to look more closely at each of these major categories of entrants, as well as some of the more important exceptions and limitations that have been developed by the courts when applying these different categories.

A. Trespassers

For purposes of applying the special rules pertaining to premises liability, a "trespasser" has been defined as someone who enters or remains on the land of another without any permission or an invitation to do so. Generally, with respect to trespassers, the only duty that is imposed upon the owner or occupant of the premises is simply to refrain from wilfully or wantonly inflicting an injury upon them. In most jurisdictions, this rule can be stated as follows:

> *A landowner or occupant owes no duty to a trespasser, except to avoid inflicting a wilful or wanton injury.*

Although this duty is often characterized as a "no duty" rule, it still offers at least some slight protection, even with respect to outright trespassers, since the landowner is never permitted to wilfully or wantonly inflict any injury upon them. Thus, where a landowner digs a camouflaged pit across a path that is known to be used by trespassers, or hides an electrified fence along the boundary of the property in an effort to discourage entry by trespassers, most courts would have little hesitancy in allowing a jury to determine whether such actions by the landowner constituted "wilful or wanton" misconduct for which liability for negligence could still be imposed against the defendant.

B. Licensees

A "licensee" is a person who enters or remains on the land with the permission or consent of the landowner (either express or implied), but not under such circumstances as would justify treating the entrant as a true "invitee" for purposes of the landowner's duty of care. Since they enter the land with at least some knowledge of the landowner or occupant (and in some cases even with the owner's permission), licensees are entitled to a little more protection than mere trespassers (*see* section III.A., *supra*), but still not as much as would be owed to an "invitee." Thus, under the traditional common law scheme for classifying entrants, the status of a "licensee" represents something of a "catch-all" category for those entrants who cannot be fit within either the "trespasser" or the "invitee" categories. Whenever there is any doubt as to an entrant's formal classification status, this is the category into which most are placed. And, not surprisingly, this is also the category that has given courts the greatest difficulty when attempting to define an appropriate duty of care that is otherwise owed by the landowner or occupant.

In general, the landowner has no duty to prepare the land for entry by a licensee. Instead, licensees generally are required to accept the premises as they find them. The legal duty of care owed to licensees is merely to warn them of hidden or concealed dangerous conditions that exist on the premises. *See* RESTATEMENT (SECOND) OF TORTS § 342 (1965). However, this duty to warn only exists to the extent that such conditions are actually known to the landowner or occupant. In other words, at least in most jurisdictions, this rule may be stated as follows:

> A landowner or occupant only owes a duty to warn licensees of known, hidden dangerous conditions that exist on the premises.

Such a duty means, of course, that if the landowner or occupant is otherwise unaware of the existence of some dangerous condition on the premises, there is still essentially no duty owed to any licensee that may be injured by that condition. As distinguished from the significantly greater duty owed to "invitees" (*see* section III.C., *infra*), this also means that landowners and occupants have no duty even to inspect the premises in advance of an entry by a licensee in order to discover the presence of any potential hidden dangerous condition. Moreover, even where the landowner knows about a particular dangerous condition on the premises, if that condition is not otherwise hidden (i.e., latent), the landowner or occupant still has no affirmative duty to provide any warning of such a danger to a mere licensee.

C. Invitees

The most favored (and legally protected) category of entrants under the common law's traditional tri-partite system of classification is that of "invitees." Basically, an invitee is any person who enters or remains on the premises (either at the express or implied invitation of the landowner or occupant), for some purpose that is associated with the owner's business (either directly or indirectly), or for some other purpose for which the premises are held open for entry by members of the general public. *See* RESTATEMENT (SECOND) OF TORTS § 332 (1965). With respect to invitees, landowners and occupants are required to exercise "reasonable care under the circumstances" in maintaining their property and keeping it safe from dangerous conditions that might cause injury to such persons. In this respect, the landowner's duty of care owed to invitees is essentially the same as the traditional common law duty owed in any other situation involving a claim based upon the tort of negligence. (*See* Chapter 4, *supra*, Negligence). In most jurisdictions, this rule may be stated as follows:

> *A landowner or occupant owes a duty to exercise reasonable care in maintaining the premises in a condition that is reasonably safe for entry by invitees. In most instances, such a duty requires the landowner or occupant to (1) make a reasonable inspection of the premises, and then to (2) either warn or (if appropriate) repair or remove the hazard.*

Instead of merely warning of those dangers that are otherwise known to exist on the premises (as in the case of the landowner's duty owed to licensees, *supra*), the landowner or occupant is actually required to inspect the premises in order to discover the presence of any dangers that do exist. Then, once discovered, the landowner's duty of reasonable care further requires the landowner to make the premises safe for entry by invitees. While in some cases it may suffice for the landowner or occupant merely to provide a warning of the danger (as in the case of the duty owed to licensees, once a hidden danger has been discovered, *supra*), in the majority of cases involving injuries to invitees the duty of reasonable care to make the premises safe for entry by invitees actually requires the landowner or occupant either to repair or to remove the dangerous condition altogether.

IV. Exceptions to the Common Law Category Classifications

Historically, the rationale for imposing different duties of care upon landowners and occupants based upon the legal classification of each individual entrant onto the property made sense to the early common law courts. It was simply too burdensome to require all landowners and occupants to inspect their entire property and then to make it safe for entry by everyone who might happen to come upon the land, regardless of the entrant's purpose in doing so. Thus, rather than applying a single duty of care with respect to all entrants, the courts applied these different legal duties to entrants, depending upon how each individual entrant was classified in relation specifically to the landowner or occupant. As a result, courts in premises cases soon became absorbed in determining *how* individual entrants should be classified in each individual case.

Aside from obvious inconsistencies resulting from different classifications being applied to individual entrants in factually similar situations, it quickly became apparent that courts could also pre-determine the outcome in any given premises liability case, merely by placing the entrant into a higher (or lower) duty category. Additionally, in order to avoid the occasionally harsh results obtained by relying upon just three primary "status" classification categories (i.e., trespassers, licensees, and invitees), courts gradually expanded their options even further by creating entirely new sub-categories of entrant classifications. Special groupings of entrants such as "bare licensees," "discovered trespassers," "child trespassers," "social guests," "fire-fighters," and many others began to appear in which the legal duties owed by landowners and occupants to entrants to these special classes could more easily be shifted from one traditional "status" category to another. While this did provide the courts with much greater flexibility in resolving premises liability cases, enabling them to attain fairer outcomes in some cases, it also created an even greater potential for inconsistent results in many cases involving factually similar situations. These issues are explained further as we examine a few of the more significant exceptions to the original common law "status" categories that have been recognized by most American jurisdictions.

A. Child Trespassers

One of the first situations in which courts found the need to expand the traditional tri-partite classification scheme utilized in defining the landowner's duty in premises liability cases involved trespassing minor children. Often, because of their young age and lack of maturity, minor children are injured after trespassing onto the land of another and encountering some type of dangerous condition on the property. Under the traditional common law scheme for classifying entrants, these children would normally be classified as "trespassers," to whom the landowner's only duty was to refrain from wilfully inflicting injury. *See* section III.A., *supra*. However, in order to avoid the unfairness that often resulted from classifying these young children as "trespassers," common law courts created a new category of entrants for these types of situations, along with an entirely new duty that was owed by the landowners and occupants that actually required them to anticipate the presence of trespassing young children on the premises in certain situations. Known initially as the "turntable doctrine" (because it was derived originally from railroad turntable injury cases), or the "playground theory," or the "dangerous instrumentality doctrine," the present version of this rule is generally referred to as the "attractive nuisance doctrine." *See* RESTATEMENT (SECOND) OF TORTS § 339 (1965).

Specifically, under this doctrine a young child's status as a "trespasser" no longer conclusively determines the duty that is owed by the landowner. Instead, a duty of *reasonable care* may still be imposed upon any landowner or occupant who has reason to anticipate the presence of trespassing young children on the premises where a dangerous condition exists which, by virtue of the child's young age and inexperience, the child is unable to appreciate. Although there are currently many different variations of this doctrine, when applied in appropriate child trespasser situations they all have the same legal effect of elevating the child's classification status from that of a "trespasser" to essentially that of an ordinary "invitee," at least with respect to the actual injury-causing condition.

The RESTATEMENT (SECOND) OF TORTS version of the "attractive nuisance" doctrine, as set forth in section 339, does not apply to all types of conditions on the landowner's property. Instead, this version of the doctrine is currently applicable only to those conditions that are: (1) artificial and (2) highly dangerous to trespassing young children. Individual variations of this rule sometimes impose additional restrictions on the applicability of the "attractive nuisance" doctrine. A minority of jurisdictions still requires the injured child's initial trespass onto the property to have been enticed or caused by the actual condition that subsequently produced the injury. Thus, under this application of the doctrine a child who trespassed initially onto the defendant's property for some other reason (e.g., to retrieve a ball) and then was subsequently injured by some dangerous artificial condition encountered only after that entry would not be entitled to rely upon the higher duty imposed by this doctrine. *See, e.g., Hughes v. Union Pac. R.R.*, 757 P. 2d 1185 (Idaho 1988).

B. "Discovered" Trespassers

The "attractive nuisance" doctrine, discussed *supra*, is one way in which courts have attempted to ameliorate some of the harshness of the traditional "no duty" rule imposed with respect to trespassing young children. However, the common law "no duty" rule still barred recovery by all adult trespassers, even in situations that sometimes produced harsh or unfair results. To remedy those situations, courts in certain situations simply re-classified the adult trespasser into a higher duty category. They reasoned that in situations where the landowner has discovered the presence of a trespasser on the premises (either actually or, at least, indirectly such as through the discovery of a well-worn footpath across the property), the trespassing entrant's status changed from that of a mere "trespasser" to that of a "discovered trespasser" to whom the landowner or occupant owed a higher duty, such as that normally reserved for "licensees" or in some cases, even "invitees." Thus, a landowner who becomes aware (or who has reason to know) that unknown persons are trespassing onto the property may be required to exercise a greater degree of care with respect to such persons. *See, e.g., Gladdon v. Greater Cleveland Regional Transit Auth.*, 662 N.E. 2d 287 (1996).

C. Fire-fighters

The great flexibility of the common law tri-partite system of classifying entrants upon the land of another also means that courts have a ready tool by which they can easily adjust the duty of care owed to entire groups of entrants all at once. Moreover, these adjustments in the duty of care can not only be made in favor of expanding the landowner's liability (as in the situations discussed, *supra*, regarding trespassing minor children and "discovered" adult trespassers), but also in situations where, for reasons of policy or otherwise, the courts wish to restrict or limit the landowner's duty of care.

One of the most controversial of these types of situations involves injuries sustained by fire-fighters, police officers, and other public safety individuals who enter onto the premises in the performance of their official responsibilities. Applying the traditional classification categories, these persons would almost certainly fall within the "invitee" category, to whom the landowner or occupant would owe a duty of "reasonable care under the circumstances" to prepare the premises for their safe entry. However, for various policy reasons most courts have agreed that it would simply be unreasonable to impose this higher duty upon landowners to protect these types of entrants, since they often enter the premises at unusual times and under often difficult or extraordinary circumstances as a part of their public safety responsibilities. As a result, courts in almost every American jurisdiction treat these special types of entrants as mere "licensees" to whom the landowners and occupants only have a duty to warn of known hidden dangerous conditions that exist on the premises. (*See* section III.B., *supra*).

Aside from the basic unfairness of imposing a duty to inspect and make their premises safe for entry by fire-fighters, police officers and other public safety employees, courts have also asserted a number of other justifications for treating these types of entrants as "licensees" rather than "invitees." For example, in *Chapman v. Craig*, 431 N.W. 2d 770 (Iowa 1988), the Iowa Supreme Court upheld the continued application of its so-called "fireman's rule" to a police officer who was injured by an intoxicated patron after being summoned to a bar to make an arrest, despite the injured officer's assertion that it violated equal protection laws. The court explained that for reasons of public policy, the lesser duty owed by landowners to fire-fighters, police officers and other public safety employees under this special classification was justified, given the special training and compensation that is otherwise provided for such individuals.

D. Social Guests

Another category of entrants entitled to somewhat lesser protection under the traditional rules applicable in many premises liability cases is that of social guests. Although these persons, like fire-fighters, police officers, and other public safety officials discussed *supra*, have been expressly invited onto the premises by the landowner or occupant, most courts have nevertheless declined to classify them as "invitees." They reason that since social guests are present on the premises purely for social purposes and not for any business or other purpose for which the premises are otherwise held open to the general public, landowners should not be responsible for making their premises as safe for social guests as might otherwise be appropriate for traditional invitees. *See* RESTATEMENT (SECOND) OF TORTS, section 330, comment h. As a result, social guests who sustain injury while visiting on the landowner's premises are ordinarily treated as mere "licensees," to whom the landowner or occupant must only warn of known hidden dangerous conditions that exist on the property.

The justification most frequently offered in support of classifying social guests into this lesser duty category of entrants is, once again, based upon the perceived unfairness of requiring landowners and occupants to first inspect and then to make their property safe from dangerous conditions in advance of any entry by invited guests. Instead, with respect to mere social guests, most courts have simply concluded that they should not be entitled to receive any greater protection from unknown dangerous conditions that exist on their host's premises than would be afforded to members of the host's own family.

Attempts to classify individual entrants as "social guests" have met with numerous fact-specific issues as they seek to determine exactly who constitute "social guests." For example, what if the guest also provides some incidental services such as cooking, cleaning, or babysitting to the host? Would this alone be a sufficient basis for concluding that the landowner or occupant has received an "economic benefit" for which the guest should be treated as an "invitee"? (*See* section III.C., *supra*). The courts have disagreed on these issues, as well as articulating any specific parameters for defining the scope of the "social guest" category. *See, e.g., Hambright v. First Baptist Church-Eastwood*, 638 So. 2d 865 (Ala. 1994) (concluding that an entrant who fell while attending a social dinner at her church was a mere "social guest" and not an "invitee" of the church.) As a result, some jurisdictions have simply re-classified all expressly *invited* social guests within the broader "invitee" category for purposes of determining the landowner's applicable duty of care in such situations. *See, e.g., Beresford v. Starsky* 571 N.E. 2d 1257 (Ind. 1991). Other courts have addressed this problem by simply abolishing the "licensee" category of entrants altogether, retaining only the more easily defined "trespasser" and "invitee" categories. *See* the discussion in section V., *supra*.

E. Recreational Premises

Another unique area in which entrants normally classified as "licensees" are given uncharacteristically different treatment in premises liability cases involves situations where persons are injured after being gratuitously permitted to enter onto rural land for the purpose of engaging in various types of "recreational" activities. While these entrants would normally be classified as either "invitees" (*see* section III.C., *supra*), or at least "licensees" (*see* section III.B., *supra*), doing so in these situations would be particularly burdensome upon the landowners or occupants of rural premises, who scarcely could inspect and discover, or even warn about, every potential dangerous condition that might exist on the property. As a result, the legislatures in virtually every state have sought to address this problem by statute, enacting what are commonly referred to as "recreational use" statutes. *See generally* N. LANDAU & E. MARTIN, PREMISES LIABILITY: LAW AND PRACTICE, ch. 5, "Recreational Premises" (Matthew Bender Co. 2016).

Essentially, these statutes treat persons who gratuitously enter onto rural lands with the permission of the landowners and sustain injury while engaged in some recreational pursuit on those premises as mere "trespassers" for purposes of defining the scope of the landowner's duty of care. This means that the only duty owed by landowners and occupants with respect to injuries sustained by recreational entrants on their property is to refrain from wilfully or wantonly inflicting any injury. (*See* section III.A., *supra*).

Although the specific requirements for imposing this lesser statutory duty of care with respect to landowners and occupants of recreational property varies somewhat from one jurisdiction to another, most "recreational use" statutes share at least a couple of common features. For example, they all pertain to only certain types of specified recreational activities that are usually listed or otherwise described by each statute, and they are all inapplicable whenever the landowner or occupant charges a fee for the entry or otherwise receives some valuable consideration from the entrant. Of course, where a "recreational use" statute is otherwise found to be inapplicable, the landowner's duty of care owed to an injured entrant will be determined according to the entrant's traditionally recognized status as either a "licensee" or an "invitee."

V. Modifications to Common Law
Category Classifications

As we have seen in the preceding discussion, *supra*, throughout the past couple of hundred years the American law of premises liability has continued to develop and expand in response to the changes in society's needs with respect to the duties of care that are imposed upon the owners and occupiers of land for injuries to persons who enter onto their property. For the most part, these duties are determined according to the traditional classification of each individual entrant into one of three basic categories as either a "trespasser," a "licensee," or an "invitee." However, as we have also seen, these classifications can, at times, be somewhat complicated and confusing to apply, and determining the landowner's duty solely on the basis of the injured entrant's legal "status" can occasionally produce results that may seem unfair or at least inconsistent from case to case. As a result of increasing criticisms of this traditional tri-partite common law system of classifying entrants for the purpose of determining the duty owed in premises liability cases, some courts have made significant modifications in the traditional classification scheme, and a few have even abolished it altogether.

The very first case to do so was *Rowland v. Christian*, 443 P. 2d 561 (Cal. 1968). There, the plaintiff was an invited social guest who was visiting in the defendant's apartment when he severely cut his hand on the handle of a defective faucet that he was attempting to use in the defendant's bathroom when the handle suddenly broke. Although prior to the defendant's injury the defendant had been personally aware that the handle was cracked, she had not warned him of that danger. Despite the fact that the plaintiff would nevertheless have been entitled to recover for the defendant's failure to warn him (a licensee) of the dangerous hidden condition of the faucet handle under the defendant's traditional duty owed to all licensees, the California Supreme Court nevertheless concluded that defining duty in any negligence case (even one involving premises liability) based solely upon the plaintiff's rigid classification into one of these traditional common law "status" categories was simply too anachronistic and would no longer be followed. Instead, the court adopted a duty based solely upon the exercise of reasonable care under the circumstances with respect to the landowner's management of the premises, regardless of the entrant's former status as a trespasser, licensee, or invitee. In doing so, the court explained that: "although the plaintiff's status as a trespasser, licensee, or invitee may in light of the facts giving rise to such status have some bearing on the question of liability, the status is not determinative." *Id.* at 568.

The immediate effect of the *Rowland* decision meant that the outcome of every premises liability case would no longer be determined exclusively by the entrant's "status" classification (usually done by the court) alone. Instead, juries in most instances would now have to assess whether each individual landowner or occupant had exercised the appropriate degree of care (i.e., reasonable care) as applied to the specific circumstances of each and every premises liability case. For example, if the entrant was a trespasser, then the jury would still need to determine whether reasonable care under such circumstances required somewhat less preparation or warning from the landowner than if that same entrant had been a license or even an invitee. While the legal duty owed was the same in all cases (i.e., reasonable care under the circumstances), the actual conduct required in the exercise of that duty might still vary from case to case, depending in large part upon the classification of the entrant. The *Rowland* decision abolished the traditional common law system whereby the court defined the applicable duty of care owed to entrants in premises liability cases merely by relying upon the entrant's "status" classification pursuant to the traditional tri-partite categories. However, this decision did not abolish the necessity for determining the entrant's classification according to these same categories. Instead, it simply shifted the responsibility for making that determination away from the court (as it had been done under the traditional common law system of classification) and onto the jury, to be applied on a case-by-case basis (and, at least presumptively, without the added benefit of *stare decisis* and case precedent to aid in making such determinations).

Initially, the *Rowland* decision was fairly well received by courts in several other jurisdictions which quickly followed suit by abolishing their rigid adherence to the former common law status classifications as the sole means by which courts determined the duty owed to entrants by landowners and occupants. However, after only a few years, this so-called trend stopped, and even reversed itself somewhat as more and more courts began to re-evaluate the role of the court (as compared with that of the jury) in determining the landowner's duty of care in premises liability situations. As a result, today the majority of American jurisdictions still continue to adhere to the traditional common law categories (*see* section III., *supra*) for classifying the duty of care owed by landowners and occupants in premises liability cases.

Nevertheless, a significant number of jurisdictions today have at least partially altered the traditional common law classification scheme in premises liability cases. In these jurisdictions, the categories of "licensee" and "invitee" simply have been combined into just one category, that of the "invitee," for which landowners and occupants owe a duty of "reasonable care under the circumstances" to prepare the premises and to make them reasonably safe for entry by both of these former groups of entrants. *See, e.g., Jones v. Hansen*, 867 P. 2d 303 (Kan. 1994); *Poulin v. Colby College*, 402 A. 2d 846 (Me. 1979); *Mounsey v. Ellard*, 297 N.E. 2d 43 (Mass. 1979). Among these jurisdictions, as well as the still majority of jurisdictions that continue to recognize all three categories of entrants in determining the duty of care applicable in premises liability cases, the classification of each injured entrant into the appropriate category continues to be largely a determination that is made by the court (as opposed to juries).

VI. Lessors

As we have seen, in almost all types of premises liability litigation, the duty of care owed by the landowner or occupant is normally determined on the basis of the injured entrant's legal status in relation to the actual premises in question. However, there is one important category of premises cases for which the duty is determined solely upon the basis of a special legal relationship that exists between the injured entrant and the landowners and occupants, rather than the nature of the entrant's relationship to the property itself. That category of cases is based upon the special relationship that exists in the eyes of the law between landlords and their tenants/lessees. Even though a tenant (or lessee) might very properly have been classified as an "invitee" under the traditional tri-partite system of entrant categories, at common law most courts simply refused to impose any duty whatsoever upon landlords with respect to their tenants, or even to an injured guest of the tenant, where the injury occurred on the leased premises. This rule was known simply as the doctrine of "*caveat lessee*" (i.e., let the lessee beware) by analogy to the similar common law sales doctrine of "*caveat emptor*" (i.e., let the buyer beware).

However, just as with the ever-expanding set of rules and exceptions that gradually developed whereby courts began to expand and enlarge the traditional tri-partite status category duties owed by landowners to the various different categories of entrants (*see* section IV., *supra*), courts also gradually began to create special "exceptions" to the no-duty rule regarding the liability of landlords and lessors of residential property. The legal effect of most of these so-called "exceptions" was to recognize a duty of "reasonable care under the circumstances" owed by landlords and lessors of real property in a variety of special situations. Among the most common of these special "exceptions" are the following scenarios in which landlords today are generally required to exercise reasonable care with respect to injuries sustained by their tenants (and often even invited guests of those tenants):

(1) where the injury occurs in a "common area" of the leased premises over which the landlord has retained exclusive control;

(2) where the landlord voluntarily undertakes to make some repair(s) to the leased premises, and performs those repairs in a negligent manner;

(3) where the leased premises contains a latent (i.e., hidden) defect that existed at the time of the leasing; and,

(4) where the premises were leased for use by the public.

In addition to these specific situations, *supra*, over the years many courts have also continued to develop numerous other exceptions as well. Nevertheless, although many jurisdictions now determine duty in landlord-tenant cases based upon the application of one of these many "exceptions" to the traditional "no duty" rule, a few courts have abandoned the traditional "no duty" rule (and its attendant "exceptions") altogether, replacing it with a single duty, as in other negligence cases, based entirely upon the landlord's exercise of "reasonable care under the circumstances." *See, e.g., Pagelsdorf v. Safeco Ins. Co. of America*, 284 N.W. 2d 55 (Wis. 1979).

VII. Conclusion

The specific rules pertaining to the liability of owners and occupiers of land with respect to injuries to various persons who enter onto the premises have a long tradition in the common law that still continues to this day in most American jurisdictions, even though many of these rules have been significantly modified by numerous exceptions, limitations, and doctrinal qualifications. Despite the seeming complexity of this myriad of premises liability rules, as well as their potential for producing, at least at times, somewhat inconsistent results, they are still amazingly accurate (at least when properly applied) in guiding courts who seek to determine the appropriate duty of care that is owed by the landowner or occupant in most situations. Perhaps it is for this reason that the majority of courts continue to apply these rules in defining the landowners' duties to persons injured as a result of various types of premises-related conditions and defects.

Nevertheless, once the duty of care owed by the landowner or possessor of the property has been determined in a premises liability case, the remaining elements of liability are essentially the same as in any other negligence action. The plaintiff must still establish breach, causation [including both cause in fact (*See* Chapter 5, *supra*,) as well as proximate cause (*See* Chapter 6, *supra*)], and damages (*See* Chapter 8, *supra*). Moreover, since all premises liability cases represent just one very specialized instance of negligence, the applicable defenses are the same as in any other negligence case (i.e., contributory negligence, comparative negligence, and assumption of the risk). (*See* Chapter 12, *infra*.)

Checkpoints

- In premises liability cases the duty of care owed by owners and occupiers of real property is determined according to the legal classification of the persons who are injured on or in relation to that property.

- The special duties owed by landowners and occupants to entrants who are injured in premises liability cases are only applicable with respect to *dangerous conditions* on the premises.

- Where entrants are injured by various *activities* conducted on the premises, the landowners and occupants of such premises are generally required to exercise reasonable care under the circumstances.

- A "trespasser" is someone who enters or remains on the land of another without any permission or an invitation to do so.

- Generally, a landowner or occupant owes no duty to a trespasser, except to avoid inflicting a wilful or wanton injury.

- A "licensee" is a person who enters or remains on the land with the permission or consent of the landowner (either express or implied), but not under such circumstances as would justify treating the entrant as a true "invitee" for purposes of the landowner's duty of care.

- Generally, a landowner or occupant only owes a duty to warn licensees of known, hidden dangerous conditions that exist on the premises.

- An invitee is any person who enters or remains on the premises (either at the express or implied invitation of the landowner or occupant), for some purpose that is associated with the owner's business (either directly or indirectly), or for some other purpose for which the premises are held open for entry by members of the general public.

- Generally, a landowner or occupant owes a duty to exercise reasonable care in maintaining the premises in a condition that is reasonably safe for entry by invitees. In most instances, such a duty requires the landowner or occupant to (1) make a reasonable inspection of the premises, and then to (2) either warn or (if appropriate) repair or remove the hazard.

- Under the "attractive nuisance" doctrine a landowner or occupant who has reason to anticipate the presence of trespassing young children on the premises that may, by virtue of their young age and inexperience, be unable to appreciate its highly dangerous condition, owes a duty of reasonable care to the child, even though that child may have the status of a "trespasser."

- A "discovered trespasser" is an adult trespasser whose physical presence on the premises has been discovered by the landowner or occupant (either actually, or at least, indirectly) and by virtue of which the landowner or occupant owes a higher duty, such as that normally reserved for "licensees" or in some cases even "invitees."

- Fire-fighters, police officers and other public safety individuals who enter onto the premises in the performance of their official responsibilities, for reasons of public policy, are treated as mere "licensees" upon the premises to whom the landowners and occupants only have a duty to warn of known hidden dangerous conditions existing on the premises.

- "Social guests" are persons who have been expressly invited onto the premises by the landowner or occupant purely for social purposes and not for any business or other purpose for which the premises are otherwise held open to the general public.

- Most courts have declined to classify "social guests" as "invitees." Instead, "social guests" are ordinarily treated as mere "licensees," to whom the landowner or occupant must only warn of known hidden dangerous conditions that exist on the property.

- Most jurisdictions have enacted legislation typically known as "recreational use" statutes by which persons who gratuitously enter onto rural lands with the permission of the landowners and sustain injury while engaged in some recreational pursuit on those premises are treated as mere "trespassers" for purposes of defining the scope of the landowner's duty of care.

- The only duty owed by landowners and occupants with respect to injuries sustained by recreational entrants on their property is to refrain from wilfully or wantonly inflicting any injury, provided the entrant was engaged in an approved recreational activity, and that the landowner or occupant has not charged a fee for the entry or otherwise received some valuable consideration from the entrant.

- A minority of courts have modified the traditional common law tri-partite "status" classification scheme by either abolishing one or more of the traditional entrant categories altogether, or by combining the two categories of "licensee" and "invitee" into just one category (i.e., that of the "invitee" category).

- Only a few jurisdictions have abolished the traditional tri-partite "status" based system of determining duty altogether, replacing the duty owed to all of the entrant categories to just a single duty based upon the exercise of "reasonable care under the circumstances."

- Under the traditional doctrine of *"caveat lessee,"* landlords owed no duty with respect to their tenants, or even an injured guest of the tenant, with respect to any injuries occurring on the leased premises.

- Several special "exceptions" to the common law no-duty rule of *"caveat lessee"* have been recognized whereby landlords and lessors of real property owe a duty of "reasonable care under the circumstances." Those exceptions include:

  - where the injury occurs in a "common area" of the leased premises over which the landlord has retained exclusive control;

  - where the landlord voluntarily undertakes to make some repairs to the leased premises, and performs those repairs in a negligent manner;

  - where the leased premises contains a latent (i.e., hidden) defect that existed at the time of the leasing; and

  - where the tenant leases the premises for some public use.

- A few courts have abandoned the traditional "no duty" rule (and its attendant "exceptions") altogether, replacing it with a single duty, as in other negligence cases, based entirely upon the landlord's exercise of "reasonable care under the circumstances.

Chapter 11

Wrongful Death and Survival

Roadmap

- Identify the sources of law for wrongful death and survival claims.
- Understand the basic differences between wrongful death and survival claims.
- Recognize who the proper plaintiffs are for both types of actions.
- Recognize the damages recoverable in both types of actions.
- Distinguish between the proper beneficiaries of recoveries in both wrongful death and survival claims.

I. History of Wrongful Death and Survival

"Wrongful death" and "survival" claims are something of an oddity in tort law. Most tort law causes of action developed out of the common law. Thus, they were created by the common law court system with the courts developing all aspects of the claims. By contrast, at common law, there were no actions for either "wrongful death" or "survival."

The common law prohibition (against recovery for wrongful death) assumed that there could be no claim for injuries when the injured person died. There were two generally stated and recognized reasons for this position. First, it was assumed that personal injury actions were personal to the individual who suffered them, and therefore only the person who suffered the injury had the right to bring the action; and when that injured person died, the claim for those injuries died along with him or her. Second, any potential tort action was considered to merge with the corresponding crime. This is because when a person was killed in a wrongful manner, a criminal action would be brought for that death. The law assumed that the criminal action would take precedence over any possible civil claim. Thus, under the so-called "felony merger" doctrine, only the criminal action could be brought. This secondary reason also had a practical point. At common law, a conviction for the crime of murder often resulted in the execution of the defendant, and the government would confiscate all of the property of the defendant as a further punishment to the defendant and the defendant's family. Since the defendant was dead and no property remained, there was no possibility of recovering damages from that person.

The absence of claims after the death of a tort victim, while allowing such claims if the victim was only injured, gave rise to an odd circumstance. If the defendant injured a plaintiff, that defendant might be forced to pay a substantial civil judgment. If, however, the defendant outright killed the other person, there could be no tort claim and, therefore, no judgment to pay. Having a situation where liability was avoided by increasing the level of harm to the victim did not seem to be a rational plan for compensation.

Since there was no common law right to a "wrongful death" or a "survival" action, most American jurisdictions have legislatively created both types of claims. In other words, they have enacted two different types of statutes, one that allows certain designated family members of a deceased tort victim to seek recovery for their own individual damages when a wrongful act has brought about the death of their decedent (i.e., known as a "wrongful death" statute), and one that allows the legal representative of the estate of the deceased victim to seek recovery for whatever damages that the decedent personally could have recovered as the result of a wrongful act had the decedent lived and not died (i.e., known as a "survival" statute). Since this is purely a matter of state statutory law, there are quite a few differences among the states on the exact details of these claims. More recently, some states have actually combined their separate "wrongful death" and "survival" statutes into just a single "death" statute that allows specific individual items of damages to be recovered by various specific beneficiaries. In reviewing the law in this area for any particular state, it is necessary to study closely the exact language of the relevant statutes to make sure that the details are fully understood. However, there are sufficient similarities among these different statutes to allow this text to point out some of the general details.

One of the most important distinctions to be noted is that statutory "wrongful death" claims and statutory "survival" claims represent two entirely separate and distinct claims that may be brought for the recovery of separate and distinct items of damages resulting from the death of the victim by a wrongful act. Moreover, the specific items of damages permitted under each of these individual statutory claims are only recoverable by certain specific designated persons under each statute. Although many states, where appropriate, now do allow for both types of these claims to be joined in one action and also for both of them to be brought at one time, it is still important to understand the differences between these two types of claims, since the damages recoverable under each type of statute are quite different.

The "survival" claim typically allows any claims that the deceased victim could have brought, had that person lived, to survive the decedent's death. (This explains the name of the claim insofar as the statute allows the tort claim that otherwise would have died with the deceased at common law to *survive* the victim's death.) *See* section III., *infra*. Such a claim allows the court to award those damages that the deceased *personally* could have recovered from the period between the date of the injury and the date of the decedent's normal life expectancy had (s)he lived and not been prematurely killed by the tortfeasor's wrongful act. Typically, this would include such damages as the decedent's medical bills, pain and suffering, and lost wages. However, it also includes any proven *net* lost future earnings that the decedent would have received throughout the remainder of his or her normal anticipated life expectancy had the decedent survived and not been killed. Recovery of only the *net* future earnings as part of the estate's "survival" damages reflects any deductions from the gross amount of the decedent's lost future earnings to account for the costs of the decedent's normal living expenses, as well as any gifts to various beneficiaries, and other payments, etc. that otherwise would have been paid out during the decedent's lifetime and, thus, would not have been a part of the decedent's estate upon his or her death. Using only the *net* amount for this component of the estate's "survival" recovery also eliminates any possibility for a "double recovery" of this same damage component (i.e., lost future earnings) by a beneficiary under a "wrongful death" statute. *See* section II.D., *infra*.

By contrast, the "wrongful death" claim allows recovery by certain designated beneficiaries of the decedent for each of *their* own unique damages resulting from the decedent's death. Typically, these damages include more intangible losses due to each individual beneficiary's own personal emotional distress and grief caused by the decedent's death, although it could also include, if proven, any lost future economic support that each beneficiary might have received from the decedent had (s)he lived and not died prematurely.

These principles set out some of the basic differences between "wrongful death" and "survival" claims. However, there are several additional issues that need to be addressed in regard to both of these different statutory causes of action.

II. Wrongful Death

A. Statutory

As noted, claims for "wrongful death" were not part of the early common law, since all personal injury actions died with the person that could have brought them. To remedy this situation, most all states have passed legislation actually *creating* an entirely new cause of action for "wrongful death." These statutes expressly create a cause of action (where none had existed at common law), identify which designated beneficiaries are entitled to bring the action, and usually specify what items of damages may be recovered by those designated beneficiaries. However, because the precise language used in these statutes may differ slightly in each jurisdiction, it is imperative to read each individual statute closely and carefully. For a computer lesson on the topic, *see* Damages for Injuries that Cause Death (CALI).

B. Bases of Claims

The mere fact that a victim has been killed is not a separate basis for bringing a "wrongful death" claim. Rather, the victim's death must be caused by some specific tortious act for which liability otherwise may be asserted under one of the three traditional bases of liability in tort: intent, negligence and strict liability. Thus, to incur liability for a victim's wrongful death, it is still necessary for the plaintiff to establish a proper legal cause of action by asserting any one or more of these traditional bases for recovering damages in tort. "Wrongful death" statutes merely recognize the right of certain designated individuals to maintain those tort claims on their own behalf in order to recover for *their* own personal and unique damages caused by the decedent's death when liability for that death can otherwise be established (just as in any other case).

For example, an intent claim for "wrongful death" could arise as the result of an intentional murder. The defendant may be charged with the crime by the state and have to go through a criminal case. However, the family members of the deceased may also bring an action for "wrongful death" and seek whatever damages they individually and personally sustained as a result of their relative's death. Since the claim would be based on the defendant's intentional conduct, the family might also be able to obtain punitive damages. With the large number of murders occurring within the United States each year, there could also be a large number of intentional, "wrongful death" claims brought. However, it is important to remember that the purpose of a tort claim, including a "wrongful death" claim, is to recover damages. If the defendant does not have any money or property, then there is no reason to bring the tort claim. Even if the plaintiff recovers a large judgment, the defendant (who would possibly also be in jail for the crime) would not have the money to pay it. However, in the rare case where a defendant has sufficient money to pay damages, the family is likely to bring the action.

Negligent "wrongful death" claims are more common. When an automobile accident occurs, claims for damages typically are based on negligence. Individual victims who are personally injured due to the negligence of the party(ies) responsible for causing the accident often recover compensatory damages for their injuries. (*See* Chapter 8, *supra*, Compensatory and Punitive Damages). However, if an accident victim dies from the accident, that person's family members might also bring their own separate action(s) for "wrongful death." The proof of negligence in order to establish their "wrongful death" claim would be the same as in any other negligence action. The only difference would be that the recovery of *their* damages under the "wrongful death" statute is limited to those items necessary to compensate them individually for their own unique personal losses due to the decedent's death. It is important to note that these damages are significantly different from those items of compensatory damages that would be recoverable by the decedent's personal estate in a typical "survival statute." *See* section III., *infra*.

Strict liability "wrongful death" claims may also be brought. Here, the most common example would be a death caused by a defective product. In modern products liability cases, people injured by a defective product often bring a "strict liability in tort" claim to recover for their injuries. (*See* Chapter 16, *infra*, Products Liability). However, if the defective product actually kills the decedent, members of the decedent's family may bring their own "wrongful death" claims, asserting the same basis of recovery (i.e., "strict liability in tort"). Of course, there are also other types of strict liability claims. For example, a person who was killed by attacking animals or some abnormally dangerous activity on the defendant's land might also give rise to sufficient facts to allow the decedent's family members to bring a "wrongful death" claim(s) based upon traditional common law strict liability in tort.

C. Proper Party Plaintiff

One of the difficulties in any "wrongful death" case is to determine the proper plaintiff. This is where it is important to read carefully the specific language of the "wrongful death" statute at issue, since each statute expressly designates those specific categories of persons who may bring the action. Apart from these specific named individuals, no other persons can bring a "wrong-ful death" action. Generally, most courts strictly construe "wrongful death" statutes, since they are considered to be in derogation of the common law (which did not recognize any cause of action for "wrongful death"). Never-theless, most "wrongful death" statutes do permit an action to be brought by the decedent's surviving spouse, children, and parents to recover "wrongful death" damages for their own personal losses caused by the death of the dece-dent. In most instances, these damages include primarily intangible losses for each designated beneficiary's own personal emotional distress, grief, and loss of companionship and society resulting from the decedent's death. *See* the next section *infra*, for a more detailed discussion of the individual components of "wrongful death" damages.

D. Recovery of Damages

The purpose of bringing a "wrongful death" claim is to permit the dece-dent's statutorily designated *beneficiaries* to recover damages for *their* own per-sonal losses sustained as the result of the decedent's death. For this reason, the method of determining damages under a "wrongful death" statute is sometimes referred to as a "loss to survivors" or a "loss to beneficiaries" rule, since each individual beneficiary must establish damages based upon the uniqueness of his or her own personal loss resulting from the death of the decedent.

In most "wrongful death" cases, the major portion of each beneficiary's award is for the loss of emotional support, grief, and the general society and companionship of the decedent. Of course, the very nature of these rather intangible losses means that they will vary significantly from one statutory beneficiary to another, depending upon the nature and quality of each bene-ficiary's personal relationship with the decedent. While most statutory ben-eficiaries will likely suffer at least some degree of grief and emotional distress resulting from the decedent's death, those with a closer emotional dependency upon the decedent will likely experience a greater personal loss from his or her death than those who may have had a more distant relationship. For this reason, surviving spouses typically incur the greatest emotional losses from the death of a spouse. However, under most "wrongful death" statutes, a sur-viving spouse is not allowed to recover additional separate damages that extend beyond the period of the joint lives of both spouses. Often referred to as dam-ages for "post-mortem" loss of emotional support, grief, and the general soci-ety and companionship of the decedent, these damages are said to terminate in any marriage relationship upon the death of whichever spouse had the shorter life expectancy. Likewise, even among minor siblings of a deceased parent, one child may have a different emotional experience from the death of the decedent than another. This also explains why most "wrongful death" statutes limit the number of potential beneficiaries primarily to immediate family members, as opposed to the wide variety of other potential claimants who might otherwise seek to recover "wrongful death" damages resulting from the loss of any number of other types of "close relationships" with the decedent.

In addition to damages for emotional distress, grief, and loss of companionship with the decedent that are generally recoverable by most beneficiaries of "wrongful death" statutes, some statutory beneficiaries may also be able to obtain actual pecuniary damages based upon their loss of future economic support from the decedent. For example, a wife who must now seek future employment to replace the economic support that her deceased husband had been providing, may be able to obtain damages based upon the amount of the additional future financial support that her husband would have provided during his remaining life expectancy had he not been prematurely killed. Likewise, minor children often can recover for their loss of financial support that they otherwise would have received from a deceased parent had (s)he not died, or for the loss of a college education that will no longer be provided to them because of the decedent's death. It is important to note when calculating the amount of lost future economic support that each beneficiary can receive in a "wrongful death" claim, that each individual beneficiary must prove the specific future amount(s) of money that the deceased likely would have contributed individually to him or her, taking into account all of the decedent's other financial obligations to creditors as well as to other family members, including even other "wrongful death" beneficiaries.

When proving these types of issues, regardless whether they involve the loss of emotional or future financial support, each plaintiff beneficiary in a "wrongful death" action must establish the uniqueness of his or her own personal relationship with the decedent in order to support each claimed loss. The proof will need to show the decedent's age at the time of death, as well as the decedent's overall condition of health, normal life expectancy, and other relevant circumstances, especially including the overall nature and quality of the plaintiff's personal relationship with the decedent. Keep in mind that the parties may also argue that the time period for calculating future losses should be longer or shorter than the decedent's normal life expectancy, depending upon how these various factors may relate to their individual circumstances. Thus, defendants also may seek to prove that the deceased had latent health problems that would have shortened his or her life, even while plaintiffs seek to prove that the deceased was very healthy.

"Wrongful death" beneficiaries will need to establish actual figures to support any claims for their loss of future economic support from the decedent. Figures such as the decedent's wages, as well as the decedent's own personal expenses and debts as of the time of death, are a good starting point for making these determinations. However, the parties often will have to offer substantial other evidence as well. For example, plaintiffs may claim that the deceased was well educated and would have received substantial income increases in the future, whereas defendants may claim that the job market would not have produced such increased income.

As discussed, *supra*, because of the lack of uniformity among the various different state "wrongful death" statutes, each of these claims must be closely researched. Some jurisdictions may also allow the recovery of other additional items of damages, whereas others do not.

E. Distribution of Awards

Once a plaintiff's verdict has been returned, it is necessary to determine who shall receive the award. Ordinarily, the "wrongful death" statute specifies who will receive the damages. This money does not usually pass under any will that the deceased may have left since the "wrongful death" recovery is not considered part of the deceased's estate. These funds, instead, are proceeds of the separate "wrongful death" action, and the statute specifying the distribution must be followed. Because of this, "wrongful death" recoveries by the statutory beneficiaries are typically not subject to the payment of any debts that may have been owed by the decedent's estate.

One of the current technical problems being discussed in tort law is whether the statutory designation of the term "spouse" also includes long-term partners. Such partners may be opposite sex partners or even same sex partners that had been living with the deceased. Since most "wrongful death" statutes frequently use the term "spouse," courts have struggled with the proper legal definition of that term. In the absence of some legislative history to the contrary, a "spouse" traditionally was assumed to mean a party to a *legal* marriage. Thus, in some states persons living in "common law marriages" have been denied the right to bring "wrongful death" claims because the law requires a legal marriage. However, in light of a recent U.S. Supreme Court decision re-defining the traditional definition of "marriage" to include same sex partners, it is likely that "wrongful death" benefits will now also be extended to include even same-sex couples who can provide proof of a legal marriage relationship. *See Obergefell v. Hodges,* 576 U.S. ____, 135 S.Ct. 2584, 192 L.Ed.2d 609 (2015).

III. Survival

A. Statutory

As with "wrongful death" claims (*see* section II., *supra*), "survival" claims were not allowed at common law. When an injured person died, whatever claim for any injuries that person may have had also died. To address this problem, most jurisdictions have passed "survival statutes" that allow claims for damages to survive the death of the litigant. Those statutes usually allow recovery for any damages that the deceased personally could have sought had (s)he not died. In situations involving the death of the claimant, the time period for measuring those losses is the period between the date of the injury and the date of the decedent's normal life expectancy had (s)he lived and not been prematurely killed by the tortfeasor's wrongful act. In order to avoid confusion, it is a good idea to again review the basic difference between "wrongful death" and "survival" claims. *See* section I., *supra*.

As a matter of civil procedure, depending upon the jurisdiction, "survival" claims are sometimes brought in the same action as the "wrongful death" claim. In fact, many jurisdictions actually mandate that if there is to be both a "wrongful death" and a separate "survival" claim, those claims must be joined together in the same action. Other jurisdictions allow these statutory claims to be filed either separately or jointly.

B. Bases of Claims

As noted in the discussion of "wrongful death" claims (*see* section II., *supra*), the "survival" claim is not a separate basis of liability. Instead, the "survival" statute merely grants the right to *continue* (after the decedent's death) any existing claim(s) that the injured party may have had during his or her lifetime. The only difference is that the "survival" claim must be filed by the personal representative of the decedent's estate to recover whatever losses the decedent personally could have recovered had (s)he not died. Thus, just as in the discussion of "wrongful death" claims, *supra*, the injured party may have had a cause of action against the tortfeasor based on intent, negligence or strict liability. However, once the injured party dies, that action then "survives" to the personal representative of the decedent's personal estate who must now prosecute the decedent's original tort claim for damages, and any subsequent recovery goes directly to the decedent's estate. The discussion of the various different bases of claims in the section on "wrongful death," *supra*, provides examples that would be equally applicable to "survival" claims. *See* section II.B., *supra*.

C. Proper Party Plaintiffs

Given the very nature of any "survival" action, the injured party obviously cannot personally bring the action because (s)he is dead. Therefore, since the law needs a live person to act as plaintiff, the "survival" statute usually specifies who may bring the action. In most "survival" statutes, the legal representative of the estate of the deceased victim is designated as the person who may bring the "survival" claim. Depending on the circumstances and the state law, this person may have one of several different titles. For example, the person may be called the executor or executrix if there is a will, or the administrator or administratrix who is typically appointed by the court to handle the probate of the estate of a deceased individual who dies intestate without a will. The decedent's legal representative is also responsible for ensuring that the assets of the estate are collected, debts of the estate are paid, and that any remaining property is distributed according to the decedent's will or the state law of intestate succession. Thus, this individual makes the ideal person to act as the plaintiff of behalf of the decedent in any "survival" claim that may be brought.

D. Recovery of Damages

The damages to be recovered in the "survival" action are those damages that the deceased party could have recovered had that person lived and not died. In many respects, therefore, this claim is very much like the typical personal injury claim. (*See* Chapter 8, *supra*, Compensatory and Punitive Damages).

The measure of the decedent's recoverable pecuniary losses in a typical "survival" statute will be past medical bills and lost past wages and earnings for the period of the loss. Just as in a personal injury claim had the decedent not died, non-pecuniary damages for the decedent's conscious "pain and suffering" would also be recoverable in a "survival" action. However, these "pain and suffering" damages are limited only to the period from the date of the initial injury until the time of the decedent's death. There is also one fairly significant difference between the decedent's future damages that are recoverable in a "survival" claim and those that are recoverable in an ordinary personal injury claim. Since the injured party is now dead, in a "survival" claim the decedent will not be incurring any additional *future* medical bills or *future* "pain and suffering," so these items, although typically present in an ordinary personal injury damage recovery, are generally not available in a "survival" claim.

In a typical "survival" action the decedent's estate can also recover the *net* amount of money that the deceased would have earned during his or her normal lifetime. However, when calculating these damages it is important to understand that this *net* amount is not the same total amount as what the decedent has lost in future earnings. Instead, it represents only the *net* amount of money that would have remained in the decedent's estate at the end of his or her normal life expectancy as a result of all future earnings (i.e., all of the decedent's *gross* future earnings, including employment, as well as all other investments, possible inheritances, etc.). These proven gross future earnings must then be reduced to reflect all anticipated future costs and expenses associated with the decedent's own personal living expenses, debts, future payments and expenditures, etc. that likely would have been paid out over the decedent's lifetime. Thus, even where the estate might be able to prove that the decedent would have had a substantial loss of *gross* future earnings over the remainder of his or her life expectancy, the actual future *net* amount of money that still remained in the decedent's estate at the normal end of that time may be significantly smaller where the defendant can establish that the decedent also had large debts, or probable future medical expenses or other sizeable future expenditures. Emphasizing primarily the economic or pecuniary aspect of the estate's loss, "survival" actions have sometimes been referred to as claims for "loss to estate" damages, although the estate's actual losses, as explained *supra*, typically include both non-pecuniary as well as pecuniary damages.

One issue that sometimes can arise with "survival" damages is where the decedent suffers instantaneous death. Imagine, for example, that the accident victim is injured and dies instantly in a plane or automobile crash. Since the period between the time of the decedent's injury and the time of death is virtually instantaneous, there would appear to be very little basis for awarding any significant amount of damages for the decedent's "pain and suffering" in a "survival" action due to the very brief period during which the decedent could have suffered. Nevertheless, courts have developed a rule that permits the decedent's estate to recover "pain and suffering" damages even for these relatively brief periods, provided that it can prove that the decedent was at least conscious (and thus presumably able to experience the feeling of "pain and suffering") during even a brief period. Otherwise, absent such proof, the decedent's "pain and suffering" damages are generally not recoverable in a "survival" action where death occurs instantaneously.

A somewhat related issue arises in "survival" claims where the decedent dies as the result of an accident caused by a slower developing injury, such as an airplane crash. Even though the decedent's death was instantaneous upon impact of the airplane in a crash, in many instances the plaintiff's attorney may be able to prove that the deceased was aware that his or her death was imminent as a result of the impending crash. Often referred to as "pre-impact" suffering, some courts have permitted recovery of the decedent's emotional distress in these situations as part of the decedent's "pain and suffering" recoverable in the "survival" claim, even though the deceased died instantly when the plane hit the ground.

E. Distribution of Awards

The damages recovered in a "survival" claim are typically included directly into the decedent's estate. As such, the decedent's "survival" damage recovery becomes just another asset of the decedent's estate that will be distributed either according to the terms and directives of the decedent's will or by the rules of intestate succession where the decedent dies without a will. Of course, this also means that any "survival" damage recovery by the decedent's estate will also be subject to reduction in order to satisfy the decedent's funeral and burial expenses, as well as any debts and other claims of the decedent's creditors, including also any taxes that may be owed by the decedent's estate.

One constant source of confusion in regard to a proper understanding of the distinction between "wrongful death" and "survival" claims arises from the fact that in many (if not most) situations, the same individuals who are designated as beneficiaries to recover damages in the "wrongful death" action (i.e., spouses, children, and parents) are usually also among the very same class of individuals who most typically are named as beneficiaries of the decedent's will. Thus, upon a mere cursory glimpse at these two different statutory schemes, initially it might appear that the same individuals are impermissibly receiving a "double recovery" of damages by pursuing both types of claims. However, since each of these statutes, as explained throughout the discussion *supra*, is designed to award damages for completely separate and distinct losses, the fact that the same person(s) might receive a recovery for their own individual losses under a "wrongful death" statute and then later also receive a distribution as the beneficiary of the decedent's estate for a portion of the decedent's own personal losses recoverable under the "survival" statute is of no consequence. Nevertheless, because of this confusion, some jurisdictions have concluded that the same individual cannot maintain both a "wrongful death" action and also a "survival" action. Most jurisdictions, however, do permit both actions to be maintained by the same individual, at least where no overlapping damages are recovered. A growing number of jurisdictions has sought to remedy this confusion altogether by replacing their individual "wrongful death" and "survival" statutes with more comprehensive "death" statutes that specify precisely what individual damage components may be recovered by which individuals.

Checkpoints

- "Wrongful death" and "survival" claims are usually matters of state statutory law.

- "Survival" claims allow recovery by the decedent's estate for damages suffered by the decedent as a result of the death of that person.

- "Wrongful death" claims allow recovery of damages for personal losses suffered by designated statutory beneficiaries due to the death of the decedent. They are usually calculated from the date of the decedent's death until the end of the decedent's normal life expectancy.

- The usual proper party plaintiffs in "survival" actions are the legal representatives of the estate of the deceased. The usual proper party plaintiffs in a "wrongful death" action are designated in the statute, and typically include the decedent's spouse, children, and parents.

- "Wrongful death" damages typically include damages for each beneficiary's loss of emotional support, grief, and the general society and companionship of the decedent, as well as the loss of any proven future economic support that each beneficiary would likely have received from the decedent.

- "Survival" damages include all of those damages that the deceased personally could have recovered had the deceased lived. They typically include the ordinary medical bills, "pain and suffering," and lost wages of the decedent from the time of injury to the time of death, as well as the decedent's *net* lost future earnings for the period up to the decedent's normal life expectancy.

- "Survival" damages are recoverable directly as assets of the decedent's estate. As such, they are subject to reduction for the claims of the decedent's creditors, as well as such things as funeral expenses and administration of the estate. Afterwards, the decedent's "survival" damages are distributed to the decedent's beneficiaries as part of the decedent's estate in accordance with the terms of the decedent's will or in accordance with the rules of intestate succession if there is no will.

Chapter 12

Defenses to Negligence

Roadmap

- Follow the development of the traditional common law defense of contributory negligence.
- Understand the "last clear chance" doctrine and the special problems associated with distinguishing between "helpless" versus "inattentive" plaintiffs.
- Understand the traditional common law defense of assumption of the risk.
- Appreciate the distinctions between express and implied assumption of the risk, and between primary and secondary assumption of the risk.
- Understand the special problems involving assumption of the risk in sports injury cases and in implied consent cases.
- Follow the development of the modern defense of comparative negligence.
- Understand the distinctions between comparative negligence, and common law contributory negligence and common law assumption of the risk.
- Understand the distinctions between statutes of limitation and statutes of repose.
- Distinguish between defenses and immunities.
- Learn to recognize different types of immunities, including family, charitable, and governmental.
- Distinguish between "discretionary" and "proprietary" functions as they pertain to governmental immunity.

I. Defenses Based on Plaintiff's Conduct

A. Common Law Contributory Negligence

The common law doctrine of contributory negligence is said to have its origins in the progenitor case of *Butterfield v. Forester*, 103 Eng. Rep. 926 (K.B. 1809). In that case, the plaintiff was riding his horse as fast as it would go through the streets of Derby at about eight o'clock at night. The defendant, in the process of repairing his house, had placed a pole across the road. The plaintiff did not see the pole because he was riding his horse so fast, even though a person riding with reasonable and ordinary care would have seen it. The court held the plaintiff could not recover because of the plaintiff's own conduct.

The opinions in the case were not completely clear as to whether its holding was based on a finding that the defendant's negligence did not cause the plaintiff's injury because, as Bayley, J., said, "the accident appeared to happen entirely from [the plaintiff's] own fault." *Id.* at 927. Lord Ellenborough, C.J., was a little clearer, explaining that since there was an absence of ordinary care on the part of the plaintiff, he could not recover, even though the obstruction in the road was the fault of the defendant. Although in *Butterfield*, there may have been some confusion over whether the holding was based on *causation* (i.e., that the plaintiff caused his own injury), or whether it was based on the defendant's showing that the plaintiff was at fault, as the common law of contributory negligence developed it came to require the defendant to carry the burden of proving that the plaintiff was contributorily negligent. This meant that the defendant must prove by a preponderance of evidence not only that the plaintiff was negligent, but also that the plaintiff's negligence proximately caused the plaintiff's own injuries. As a result, the defendant, in proving contributory negligence, takes on cause in fact burdens, proximate or legal cause burdens, as well as a burden to show that the plaintiff's conduct fell below a reasonably prudent person's standard of care.

The basic negligence analysis (i.e., determining duty-breach) is said to be essentially the same as the analysis used for determining the defendant's behavior. However, because a finding of contributory negligence completely bars the plaintiff's ability to recover at common law, the courts strained to develop doctrines that would still provide the plaintiff recovery. The doctrine of "last clear chance" (*see Davies v. Mann* 152 Eng. Rep. 588 (1842) for the progenitor case), as well as other legal concepts such as "gross negligence" and "slight negligence," reflects just some of the resourceful techniques that courts developed to protect plaintiffs from the otherwise harsh results produced by contributory negligence. In addition, since the courts permitted the jury to determine negligence, causation, and damages for both plaintiffs as well as defendants, jurors often compromised their verdicts by merely reducing damages in exchange for their undisclosed determinations of fault on the part of the plaintiff (that otherwise would have totally barred a contributorily negligent plaintiff's recovery).

1. The "Last Clear Chance" Doctrine

"Last clear chance" is a doctrine that works only in favor of the plaintiff as a means of avoiding the plaintiff's contributory negligence in situations where the defendant is said to have had the last clear chance to avoid injury to an otherwise contributorily negligent plaintiff. The doctrine is limited to situations where a plaintiff has given the court proof of the defendant's negligence, the defendant has presented *prima facie* evidence of the plaintiff's negligence, and then the judge decides that the circumstances of the proof warrant a further jury instruction on the question of whether the defendant, despite the plaintiff's contributory negligence, still had the "last clear chance" to prevent the harm. Thus, this doctrine would never under any circumstances be asserted on behalf of a defendant.

Originally, the inquiry was a time sequenced based inquiry: did the defendant have knowledge of the plaintiff's situation or condition such that the defendant's further exercise of less than ordinary care ultimately still caused the plaintiff's harm? In situations where the defendant's failure to exercise reasonable care contributed to the defendant's own failure to discover the plaintiff's situation or condition, the courts came to instruct juries further that the defendant's subsequent conduct was the "last clear chance" because the defendant "should have known" of the situation and then been able to prevent it. In these situations it could not be said that the defendant's original negligence followed after the contributory negligence of the plaintiff; instead, the defendant's failure to exercise the "last clear chance" came to be seen as an overriding "different" or more substantial negligent act. This raised the possibility at common law that a defendant must have also anticipated and protected against the foreseeable contributory negligence of a plaintiff.

In order to further address the foreseeability by the defendant of the plaintiff's contributory negligence, the Restatement distinguishes between plaintiffs who are "helpless" and those who are merely "inattentive." For example, where a contributorily negligent plaintiff is "helpless" (e.g., drunk, or unconscious, or in a car without brakes, or with a stuck accelerator), the defendant's failure to anticipate such helplessness may become an entirely new, overriding negligent act under the "last clear chance" doctrine if the plaintiff proves that had the defendant been exercising reasonable care, (s)he would have known or otherwise discovered the plaintiff's perilous situation in time to avoid the injury. By contrast, where a contributorily negligent plaintiff's peril has arisen because the plaintiff was merely "inattentive" (e.g., not watching where (s)he is going, or reading a roadmap while stopped at an intersection, or driving too fast and failing to notice how slippery the road has become), the plaintiff must show that the defendant actually knew of the plaintiff's perilous situation and disregarded it, before the "last clear chance" doctrine can be invoked. In some jurisdictions this particular application of the "last clear chance" doctrine is also referred to as the "discovered peril" doctrine, since it requires the defendant to actually *discover* the contributorily negligent plain-tiff's perilous situation *before* the defendant's "last clear chance" to avoid the injury will even arise.

Sections 479 and 480 of the Restatement (Second) Torts provide a good exercise in careful and close reading of a text. Look at the difference between how each of these sections is articulated.

§ 479. Last Clear Chance: Helpless Plaintiff

A plaintiff who has negligently subjected himself to a risk of harm from the defendant's subsequent negligence may recover for harm caused thereby if, immediately preceding the harm,

    (a) the plaintiff is unable to avoid it by the exercise of reasonable vigilance and care, and

    (b) the defendant is negligent in failing to utilize with reasonable care and competence his then existing opportunity to avoid the harm, when he (i) knows of the plaintiff's situation and realizes or has reason to realize the peril involved in it or (ii) would discover the situation and thus have reason to realize the peril, if he were to exercise the vigilance which it is then his duty to the plaintiff to exercise.

§ 480. Last Clear Chance: Inattentive Plaintiff

A plaintiff who, by the exercise of reasonable vigilance, could discover the danger created by the defendant's negligence in time to avoid the harm to him, can recover if, but only if, the defendant

    (a) knows of the plaintiff's situation, and

    (b) realizes or has reason to realize that the plaintiff is inattentive and therefore unlikely to discover his peril in time to avoid the harm, and

    (c) thereafter is negligent in failing to utilize with reasonable care and competence his then existing opportunity to avoid the harm.

In the "helpless plaintiff" scenario addressed by Section 479, *supra*, notice that the "last clear chance" doctrine is triggered whenever the defendant either *knows* (i.e., has actual knowledge) or *should have known* (i.e., has construc-tive knowledge) of the contributorily negligent plaintiff's perilous situation. But, in the absence of having actual knowledge of the peril, how does a defen-dant acquire knowledge that (s)he *should have known*? By maintaining a proper lookout, in anticipation of encountering any potentially perilous situations involving "helpless plaintiffs." By contrast, under Section 480 a defendant has no affirmative duty even to anticipate the presence of merely "inattentive" contributorily negligent plaintiffs, and the "last clear chance" doctrine does not come into play at all unless the defendant actually discovers the "inattentive" plaintiff's peril.

2. Assumption of the Risk as a Bar to an Employer's Negligence

In addition to the common law defense of contributory negligence, early common law courts sometimes also denied an injured employee's recovery in negligence for injuries allegedly caused by the plaintiff's own assumption of risk. In early employment cases prior to the enactment of workers' compensation laws, a plaintiff could not sue his or her employer or even a fellow worker for work-related injuries, because employees were said to have "assumed the risk" of injury merely by virtue of accepting the employment.

In these early cases, even where an injured employee may not have been acting at all negligent at the time of the plaintiff's injury, the employee was considered to have voluntarily assumed the risk of injury by virtue of his or her conduct showing that the plaintiff knew of the risk and nevertheless continued to work in the face of such a risk of injury. In other words, the plaintiff may have been innocent of any contributory negligence, and indeed may have even acted reasonably by continuing to work in the face of certain known risks, but nevertheless, many common law courts held that the employee was barred from any recovery for negligence against the employer, having "waived" any right to sue the employer, or "impliedly consented," or "voluntarily proceeded in the face of a known risk of injury." In effect, the defendant employer simply owed no duty to an employee, and as such, employers essentially were immune from suit at early common law.

Again, the common law responded to the harshness of these rules, and started to narrowly apply the plaintiff's assumption of risk only to those risks that actually were known to the plaintiff at the time of his or her injury. Proving the plaintiff's knowledge of the risk required the defendant to show not only that the plaintiff was in fact aware of the risk, but also that (s)he appreciated and understood the specific danger presented by that risk. In some jurisdictions assumption of the risk also came to require that the defendant prove that the plaintiff's injury factually occurred just as it indeed had happened. (e.g., California.)

In addition, where a particular risk was deemed "unreasonably dangerous," some courts held that the defendant simply owed a "non-delegable" duty to protect the plaintiff from such risks. Over the years, courts have struggled to distinguish which cases involved unreasonably dangerous risks, such as those where an employee was asked to wash windows on skyscrapers, or to handle toxic chemicals without being provided with proper protective gear. Gradually, the assumption of the risk doctrine expanded beyond employment situations, and eventually it developed into the affirmative defense known as "assumption of the risk" that operated as a total bar to the defendant's negligence in cases involving all types of plaintiffs in all types of different factual scenarios. (*See* Section I.C., *infra*.) As we will also see, many of these same early common law doctrines that eventually developed into the somewhat harsh "all-or-nothing" "contributory negligence" and "assumption of the risk" defenses often continue to re-emerge today as entirely new issues that must be addressed by cases in "comparative negligence" jurisdictions. (*See* Section I.B. *infra*.)

B. Comparative Negligence

Criticism of the common law "all-or-nothing" aspect of contributory negligence gave rise to the comparative negligence doctrine. Instead of totally barring a contributorily negligent plaintiff from any recovery at all, the concept of comparative negligence seeks to reduce the plaintiff's award in the amount that the plaintiff was at fault, basically mimicking what was believed to be going on in the jury at the time. Juries, under the harsh contributory negligence defense, often would find in favor of the plaintiff on the issue of contributory negligence, but then turn around and reduce the damages awarded to that plaintiff, presumably to reflect the presence of at least some degree of contributory negligence by the plaintiff.

Bradley v. Appalachian Power Company, 256 S.E.2d 879 (W. Va. 1979), provides a thorough review of various jurisdictions' treatment of contributory and comparative negligence. Almost all tort scholars are dissatisfied with the doctrine of contributory negligence, which bars recovery in any case where the plaintiff is even slightly at fault. Some jurisdictions, however, continue to resist comparative negligence. (Alabama, Virginia, Maryland, North Carolina and District of Columbia are five such jurisdictions.)

As an alternative to so-called *pure* comparative negligence (which allows the negligence and/or contributory negligence of both parties to be compared across the full spectrum of potential liability, ranging from 0 percent to 100 percent, and reduces the plaintiff's damage recovery proportionately), several legislatures and courts have adopted rules creating what is known as *modified* comparative negligence that allow a negligent plaintiff to recover at least some damages, but only as long as that negligence does not exceed a certain threshold percent, usually around 50 percent. In modified comparative negligence jurisdictions, once the plaintiff's negligence exceeds the designated threshold percentage, the plaintiff is then totally barred from recovering any damages, just as in common law contributory negligence. (*See* section I.A., *supra*). Students should read these statutes and decisions carefully, giving particular attention to the precise wording that is used. For example, in some modified comparative negligence jurisdictions the plaintiff can recover as long as his or her (contributory) negligence *does not exceed* the defendant's negligence, thereby allowing recovery at a 50/50 split which is a fairly common outcome in close jury cases (e.g. Connecticut, Delaware, Hawaii, Illinois, Indiana, Iowa, Massachusetts, Michigan, Minnesota, Montana, Nevada, New Hampshire, New Jersey, Ohio, Oklahoma, Oregon, Pennsylvania, South Carolina, Texas, Vermont, Wisconsin, and Wyoming). Other modified comparative negligence jurisdictions allow recovery only if the plaintiff's (contributory) negligence is found to be *less than* the negligence of the defendant(s), thus allowing recovery for the plaintiff's contributory negligence only up to 49 percent (e.g. Arkansas, Colorado, Georgia, Idaho, Kansas, Maine, Nebraska, North Dakota, Tennessee, Utah, and West Virginia).

In addition, there may be other ambiguities as to how these statutes work in situations involving multiple defendants. For example, if the plaintiff is 40 percent (contributorily) negligent, and Defendant A and Defendant B are both only 30 percent negligent, can the plaintiff recover as to either one of these defendants? What if one defendant is not joined in the case, or has settled out, or is bankrupt? These fairly common scenarios often raise interesting questions of joint and several liability, subrogation, and setoff. (*See* Chapter 7, *supra*, Multiple Tortfeasors). Some comparative negligence statutes address these questions specifically, while others leave it for the courts to work out solutions if and when these issues arise. However, where a court, as opposed to a legislature, has adopted comparative negligence, the court typically will address these issues as they are presented to it. The West Virginia Supreme Court's opinion in *Bradley v. Appalachian Power Company*, 256 S.E.2d 879 (W. Va. 1979), provides an example of just some of the issues that must be addressed when a court decides to judicially adopt the defense of comparative negligence in place of the former common law contributory negligence defense.

Four states have judicially abolished contributory negligence in favor of a *pure* comparative negligence system that allows a (contributorily) negligent plaintiff to recover, but requires the jury to reduce the award according to the percentage of the plaintiff's negligence, without imposing any limitations on the extent of the plaintiff's own (contributory) negligence. Advocates of the *pure* comparative negligence approach view the *modified* (i.e., the 50 percent) approach discussed, *supra*, as establishing an arbitrary line for recovery.

The *pure* comparative approach is often criticized, however, because it allows a plaintiff who is almost totally at fault still to recover at least some damages. Some critics of comparative negligence see this type of scenario as contributing to a crisis in municipal liability from the practice by plaintiffs of joining the city or locality in every traffic accident where allegations are made about negligence in regard to the failure to reasonably design or fix roadways (e.g., New York City and Philadelphia both teeter on bankruptcy as a result of these kinds of practices).

However, perhaps a more serious criticism of *pure* comparative negligence is that it favors whichever party has the most damages. Depending upon the nature and extent of both parties' injuries, in some situations *pure* comparative negligence can actually result in greater damages being awarded to a negligent defendant who is seriously injured by a contributorily negligent plaintiff than what that same plaintiff could have recovered against the defendant. The prime example is where a $300,000 Rolls Royce driver who is 90 percent at fault becomes involved in an accident with a $3,000 VW whose driver is only 10 percent at fault. Assuming that both cars are completely totaled and that neither driver was harmed, the VW driver (despite being only 10 percent negligent) would still end up having to pay $30,000 to the Rolls Royce driver, while only receiving $2,700 from the driver of the Rolls Royce.

This previous example, *supra*, also raises interesting questions about insurance and set off. For example, should the parties in this example "off set" the amounts they would otherwise end up paying to each other? This means that the VW driver would receive absolutely nothing and the 90 percent negligent driver of the Rolls Royce would end up with $27,300.00 (i.e., $30,000 minus $2,700). If the parties have insurance, the answer seems to depend on the subrogation rights of each of their respective insurance companies in regard to the outcome of the lawsuits. If neither has subrogation rights, then each driver would prefer no set off, since they are not personally paying the money to the other side. Where neither has insurance (note that insurance is mandatory in most jurisdictions so this is highly unlikely) then set off seems to make more sense. Where one driver, perhaps the Rolls Royce driver, has insurance it seems that set off would not be favored unless the VW driver is judgment proof. In that situation, the Rolls Royce driver would get nothing either way, so it is likely neutral on the question of what amount the VW driver gets from his or her insurance company. If the insurance company has subrogation rights in its policy with the Rolls Royce driver, the insurance company may prefer to pay nothing to the VW driver, as it will get nothing in return for its payment to the Rolls Royce driver.

Moreover, this situation can get even more complicated when there are multiple parties involved. Since the sum of all damages in a negligence action must equal 100 percent, and it is the jury's job to apportion the individual degree of negligence among all the parties, this problem becomes even more exacerbated in *modified* comparative negligence jurisdictions where any party can recover damages, but only as long as that party's negligence is not equal to or greater than the combined negligence of the other parties. Where insurance is paying, the ultimate determination as to which party gets what often turns on the terms of each individual party's policy. For example, in a first party payout situation (e.g., the driver buys extra insurance from the rental car company when (s)he rents their car, requiring that insurance company to pay directly for any damage done to the rented car as well as damage done to others, as opposed to the driver's own car insurance that covers the driver and that may or may not pay the entire amount of liability, depending on the terms of its policy and deductible with the driver) the driver's protection is provided directly for the damage done to the car and by the car.

As the preceding example, *supra*, illustrates, insurance law is extremely important to the lawyer's ability to predict final outcomes to his or her client. Therefore, it is vital for the parties to discover both the existence of all possible policies that might provide coverage to the parties (personal liability policies, business policies, homeowners insurance, and third party policies of individuals or entities) as well as the limits and terms of those policies. Insurance law sets up reservation of rights provisions, good faith obligations, and affirmative duties by insurance companies to pay under the terms of the policies. These principles apply not only in automobile cases, but also to complex litigation concerning environmental issues, products liability (e.g. defective consumer products, asbestos, etc.), and they often raise additional questions of successor corporate liability and who among various insurers might have the responsibility to provide coverage for the liability of the corporate actors.

There is normally no change to the proximate cause analysis under comparative negligence rules, and proximate cause must be proven in order for any of the parties to recover. (*See* Chapter 6, *supra*, Proximate Cause). Also, under comparative negligence there is generally no change to a plaintiff's ability to sue joint tortfeasors, unless the rules in a particular jurisdiction specifically require otherwise. Similarly, the laws of contribution and *pro rata* credit are also unchanged if the jurisdiction has adopted its comparative fault through the common law. (*See* Chapter 7, *supra*, Multiple Tortfeasors). As a result, the lawyer must examine both the cases and statutes following the adoption of comparative negligence in every jurisdiction to determine its current position regarding which party will finally pay what to whom.

In comparative negligence jurisdictions, courts typically use general verdicts to determine the total amount of damages to be awarded to each party, and then they often use special interrogatories to assign the percentage of fault that is attributed to each individual party. In some jurisdictions, the "last clear chance" doctrine has been preserved under comparative negligence, whereas in others, that doctrine is folded into the juries' consideration of all the other comparative fault considerations. *See* the discussion in section I.A.1., *supra*.

An interesting example of the interplay between contributory negligence defenses that existed before the adoption of comparative negligence and the law after its adoption is found in *Law v. Superior Court*, 755 P.2d 1135 (Ariz. 1988). In that case, Cindy Law was driving her parents' car when she pulled out in front of James Harder. Harder swerved to avoid the collision, and overturned his car. Harder and his wife, who were not wearing seatbelts, were thrown through the sunroof of their car and injured.

Harder sued Law and her parents for negligence. During discovery, the defendants sought information about the Harders' seatbelt use. The trial court, relying upon its earlier developed law under a contributory negligence regime, issued a protective order regarding the seatbelt issue, concluding that there was no duty to wear seatbelts. The court of appeals vacated on grounds that the doctrines of avoidable consequences and damage mitigation allowed the inquiry. The problem had been (prior to the adoption of comparative negligence) that the plaintiffs' failure to wear seat belts under a contributory negligence regime would have barred their recovery altogether if such conduct was found to be contributorily negligent. However, since the plaintiffs' contributory negligence occurred prior to the accident, it was said to not "contribute" to the accident. Instead, it only contributed to their harm. As such, the court concluded that the plaintiffs' failure to wear a seatbelt could be taken into account by the jury either to mitigate their damages, or to avoid the consequences of such damages, but it could no longer be considered as contributory negligence under the comparative negligence regime.

As illustrated by the *Law* decision, *supra*, the change to comparative negligence, along with the fact that seatbelts became required in all vehicles and their use mandatory, has definitely put pressure on some courts to incorporate the seatbelt defense into the juries' consideration of comparative negligence. And, as accidents are clearly foreseeable, the duty to wear the seatbelt becomes an increasingly important consideration. Since courts hold auto manufacturers liable for providing reasonable protection for the occupants of their vehicles, it is certainly reasonable for courts also to require occupants to use such protective devices when available. Moreover, since statistically seatbelts are more likely to reduce harm than to cause harm, the court concluded that their use may well be "part of the obligation to conduct oneself reasonably in order to minimize damages and avoid foreseeable harm to oneself." *Id*. at 1141.

Addressing the doctrine of "avoidable consequences" within the context of the seatbelt issue, the court reasoned that this doctrine includes both pre- and post-accident conduct because of the impact of the comparative negligence statute. Explaining that comparative negligence allows the jury to reduce the plaintiff's award by the degree to which the plaintiff's conduct is a proximate cause of the injury or death, the court modified the traditional post-accident concept of the "avoidable consequences" rule by folding it into the determination of comparative fault. In opposition, the dissent in *Law, supra*, pointed out that this issue might be better left for the legislature to resolve in jurisdictions where the legislature had been responsible for instituting comparative fault, noting, in effect, that the court's holding changes comparative fault into comparative causation.

As the foregoing discussion illustrates, jurisdictions vary considerably as to how issues such as the seatbelt defense should be resolved under a comparative negligence regime. Some jurisdictions require seatbelt use, but make evidence of their non-use inadmissible in civil actions. Others allow the defense, but limit the percentage of damage reduction under comparative negligence. Still other courts allow full reduction of damages. Finally, some courts completely disallow the defense altogether.

C. Common Law Assumption of the Risk

In order to understand how the traditional common law defense of assumption of risk is currently handled under a comparative fault regime, we must go back and understand the different types of assumption of risk that the courts developed under the common law "contributory" negligence regime. Traditionally, the result under the common law application of assumption of the risk was always the same. Regardless of the particular type of assumption of risk, the plaintiff's recovery was totally barred. Because of this, courts throughout much of our common law history were less than precise in their use of the term "assumption of risk," and this has led to considerable difficulty and confusion for the courts today in their efforts to conform these earlier cases into the comparative negligence regime. (*See* section I.D., *infra*.)

As discussed previously (*see* section 1.A., *supra*), the original doctrine of assumption of the risk came from the common law concept that one who consents is not legally injured. Based upon this notion of consent, common law courts began to recognize two different kinds of consensual assumption of the risk. One kind was "expressed," or based on the freedom of an individual to contract around risk, and the other kind was "implied." However, the recognition of implied contracts by the courts also raised the possibility for courts to create a second type of assumption of risk known as "implied" assumption of the risk. Both types of common law assumption of the risk are discussed *infra*.

1. Express Assumption of the Risk

"Express" assumption of the risk in negligence cases raises many of the same problems as those presented by classic contract cases in regard to both the proof of the actual words used (i.e., oral or written), as well as the meaning of those words when used to express the risk(s) being assumed. In addition, factual questions were often presented as to whether the risk at issue was fully understood and freely bargained for by the parties to be bound. Thus, just as in any contract dispute, the party seeking to enforce an express assumption of the risk agreement had to overcome any assertions that the contract was one of adhesion, or that it had been improperly obtained by coercion or fraud.

Although parties are generally free to contract around a risk to which they mutually agree, courts in "express" assumption of the risk cases are generally wary when the contract involves health and safety. Therefore, in negligence cases where the plaintiff typically has sustained some type of personal injury, courts have an even greater incentive to interpret the language against the drafter, and in favor of the person who is said to have assumed the risk.

Of course, all "express" assumption of the risk agreements in torts do not necessarily involve personal injuries. For example, in *Wolf v. Ford*, 644 A.2d 522 (Md. 1994), the plaintiff received $145,700 in a settlement from an auto accident. In 1986, the plaintiff and her mother visited the defendant to discuss investing the money in order to pay for a college education and to preserve most of the money. The day after the visit, the defendant sent the plaintiff a letter with three enclosures for the plaintiff to sign. Among the enclosures was an agreement authorizing the defendant to buy, sell, and trade securities for the plaintiff. In that agreement the plaintiff also expressly agreed to relieve the defendant of liability for any losses. Although the plaintiff did reserve the power to direct or terminate the sale or purchase of securities, the agreement itself could not be terminated. The plaintiff signed and returned the agreement, depositing $135,000 with the defendant, which the defendant then used to buy stocks.

Later, the plaintiff decided to begin making large ($5,000) withdrawals from the account. The defendant's company sent plaintiff a letter asking if she wanted to terminate the discretionary agreement, and the plaintiff returned a letter indicating that she did not. The plaintiff kept withdrawing money from the account, eventually withdrawing a total of $64,650. Each withdrawal necessitated a sale of stock. Finally the plaintiff terminated the defendant's discretionary authority, transferred the remaining balance, and closed the account. The plaintiff then filed suit, but the trial judge granted the defendant's motion to dismiss on grounds that the defendant was only liable for losses occurring from gross negligence or intentional misconduct. The plaintiff appealed, arguing that the agreement was void as against public policy.

The court began by examining the case law applicable to exculpatory clauses in contracts. Citing *Winterstein v. Wilcom,* 293 A.2d 821 (Md. Ct. Spec. App. 1972), the court explained that exculpatory clauses are generally valid, since they serve the public policy of freedom of contract. Nevertheless, the court did recognize several exceptions whereby certain intentional harms and extreme forms of negligence are not excused. Thus, if a party is at such an obvious disadvantage as to put him or her at the mercy of the other's negligence, then such conduct is not excused. Likewise, where the transaction affects a significant public interest, then the conduct is not excused. Explaining that transactions affecting these types of public interests are hard to define, the *Wolf* court reviewed a legal "test" from *Tunkl v. Regents of the University of California,* 383 P.2d 441 (Cal. 1963) that considered several factors:

(1) Was the business of a type suitable for public regulation?
(2) Was the party seeking exculpation performing a great service to the public?
(3) Was the defendant willing to perform its service for any member of the public?
(4) Did the party invoking exculpation have an advantage of bargaining strength?
(5) Was the property of the purchaser placed under another's control and subject to his carelessness?

However, after examining the *Tunkl* test, the court in *Wolf* discarded it, saying that *Tunkl* was supposed to be just a rough guide, but it had, instead, become a rigid measurement. *Wolf* concluded that there was no reason for the exculpatory clause not to be enforced because it did not fall within any of the three exceptions for doing so: 1) there had been no allegation of fraud or willful misconduct, because the plaintiff had testified to the contrary, 2) there was no disparate bargaining advantage, because the plaintiff was eighteen, had sought out the defendant, etc., and 3) stockbroker/client relationships are not ones that affect public interest so significantly as to overturn the contract. Some courts have adopted this same analysis in favor of mandatory arbitration clauses and other damages limitations to restrict plaintiffs' abilities to recover in tort.

Other courts, however, continue to use the *Tunkl* factors and rule against a private agreement that restricts mandatory arbitration and other damage limitations to plaintiffs' abilities to recover in tort. This issue has taken on new importance in the light of the rise of the use of mandatory arbitration clauses as a condition of using certain internet websites for buying goods and services.

2. Implied Assumption of the Risk

As discussed, *supra*, "implied" assumption of the risk does not occur from what the plaintiff says or has expressly agreed to, but from the plaintiff's *conduct* in voluntarily encountering a known risk of injury. In the absence of an actual agreement expressing the plaintiff's consent to assume the risk, courts simply implied the necessary consent by examining the plaintiff's conduct in relation to encountering that risk. Under the traditional common law defense of implied assumption of the risk, courts typically require the defendant to prove three things:

(1) that the plaintiff had actual knowledge of the danger;
(2) that the plaintiff (subjectively) understood and appreciated the risk(s) associated with that danger; and
(3) that the plaintiff voluntarily exposed himself or herself to the risk(s).
See Borders v. Board of Trustees, VFW Clubs 2875, Inc., 500 S.E. 2d 362, 365 (Ga. App. 1998).

Unlike "express" assumption of the risk situations where the plaintiff's personal (i.e., subjective) understanding of the risk and willingness to encounter it can be fairly easily proven just from the agreement itself, in implied assumption of the risk situations it is not always a simple matter to prove what the plaintiff subjectively knew and understood and whether the plaintiff specifically agreed to encounter the particular risk in question. When such evidence was available, courts traditionally have had no trouble in barring the plaintiff's recovery under the "all-or-nothing" defense of implied assumption of the risk, just as they did with respect to express assumption of the risk agreements. *See Wirtz v. Gillogly*, 216 P.3d 416 (Wash. App. 2009). However, as explained *supra*, implying a plaintiff's subjective "agreement" to assume a certain risk is not always easy to do from mere proof of the plaintiff's conduct alone.

An illustrative early case is *Murphy v. Steeplechase Amusement Co., Inc.*, 166 N.E. 173 (N.Y. 1929). In *Murphy*, the defendant operated an amusement park with an attraction called "The Flopper." The Flopper had a moving belt, running on an inclined plane, with padding on the floor and both sides. People would sit or stand on the belt and then, usually, be thrown off. The plaintiff, along with his wife and some friends, got on The Flopper. All were thrown, but the plaintiff landed and fractured his kneecap.

The plaintiff contended that the belt was dangerous and improperly equipped to prevent injuries to unknowing users. The defendant argued that there was nothing wrong with the belt. The belt was moving when the plaintiff put his foot on it, and it kept moving. The plaintiff knowingly accepted the dangers when he stepped on the belt. The dangers were obvious and the result was what normally happens whenever a person steps onto a moving belt. There was also nothing wrong with the padding. Judge Cardozo, writing for the court, concluded that the plaintiff had assumed the risk and gave judgment for the defendant. However, the rationale of the decision also included language suggesting that the defendant did not even owe the plaintiff a duty. Under such a "no duty" rationale, the plaintiff would also be barred from recovery in a comparative negligence jurisdiction, since the plaintiff's implied assumption of the risk would be regarded as "primary," and, as such, the defendant could not be said to have been negligent at all. Therefore, the plaintiff's *prima facie* case would simply fail. (*See* section I.D.2., *infra*, for a further discussion of "Primary" Implied Assumption of the Risk).

D. Implied Assumption of the Risk under a Comparative Fault System

1. *"Reasonable" Versus "Unreasonable" Implied Assumption of the Risk.*

The implications of this "no duty" rationale suggested in the *Murphy* case, *supra*, are that assumption of risk under a comparative fault system would still bar recovery, because the defendant is not shown to have breached a duty to the plaintiff. On the other hand, since the common law recognized implied assumption of the risk as an affirmative defense, the burden of proof is usually imposed on the defendant; it is not an affirmative obligation as part of the plaintiff's *prima facie* case to prove the lack of assumption of the risk. The court in *Knight v. Jewitt*, 834 P. 2d 696 (Cal. 1992), tried to sort out some of these complexities. In *Knight* the plaintiff was injured during a game of touch football. Early in the game, the defendant ran into the plaintiff during a play. The plaintiff told the defendant not to play so rough or she would stop playing. Defendant, on the other hand, simply remembered this encounter as a warning for him to "be careful." On the next play, according to the defendant, the defendant leapt into the air to intercept a pass and collided with the plaintiff, knocking her over. When he landed, he stepped on her hand, injuring it.

The plaintiff, along with another participant, contended that the other participant had already caught the ball when the defendant ran into the plaintiff from behind, knocked her down, and then stepped on her hand. He also then tackled the other participant. The injury to the plaintiff's little finger resulted in three operations and, finally, amputation.

After the plaintiff initiated suit, the defendant filed an answer and moved for summary judgment on grounds that implied assumption of the risk was a complete defense, as the plaintiff had impliedly agreed to reduce the duty of care owed by her joining the game. Plaintiff opposed summary judgment on grounds that implied assumption of the risk had been eliminated by the adoption of comparative negligence, and that by participating she only assumed the risk of a "mellow" game that could, at worst, have resulted in bumps and bruises. Plaintiff admitted having assumed a risk; just not a risk that she believed would result in having her finger amputated. After addressing the potential impact of the traditional common law defense of implied assumption of the risk on the outcome of the plaintiff's case (*see* section I.C.2., *supra*), the court explained that the outcome under a comparative negligence regime required a more careful analysis as to precisely what kind of "assumption of risk" this case presented. To do that, the court referred to *Li v. Yellow Cab Co.*, 532 P. 2d 1226 (Cal. 1975), where the California Supreme Court had previously adopted *pure* comparative negligence and discussed its effect on traditional common law tort doctrine. The court in *Li* explained that implied assumption of the risk already had been partially merged into comparative negligence in situations where a plaintiff *unreasonably* encounters a known risk. However, the court then distinguished those situations from others where the plaintiff was totally barred from any recovery at all (under the traditional common law defense of implied assumption of the risk) when (s)he had *reasonably* encountered that same risk. Pointing out the irony of such a distinction, the *Li* court explained that under comparative negligence principles this meant that a plaintiff who "reasonably assumed" a risk would be *completely* barred from any recovery whereas a plaintiff who unreasonably encountered that same risk would merely suffer a reduction in his or her damages. As a result of this perceived unfairness, the court in *Li* completely abolished the traditional defenses of contributory negligence and implied assumption of the risk (including both the "reasonable" as well as the "unreasonable" varieties), and replaced them both with *pure* comparative negligence.

2. *"Primary" Versus "Secondary" Implied Assumption of the Risk.*

Relying upon the *Li* decision, the plaintiff in *Knight* asserted that her implied assumption of the risk no longer constituted a total bar to her recovery; instead, she claimed that it would merely result in a reduction of her damages under *pure* comparative negligence. However, the *Knight* court disagreed, explaining that *Li* had been misinterpreted by subsequent California cases. Instead, according to *Knight*, the distinction involving *reasonably* assumed risks did not pertain to those situations where there was "no duty" owed by the defendant in the first instance to protect the plaintiff from a particular risk. This is a legal concept known as "primary" implied assumption of the risk. By contrast, "secondary" implied assumption of the risk covers situations where a duty is owed to the plaintiff, but the plaintiff knowingly encounters the risk of injury caused by a breach. According to the court in *Knight*, a plaintiff's "secondary" implied assumption of the risk, regardless whether it is of the reasonable or unreasonable variety, is merely compared under pure comparative negligence, but "primary" implied assumption of the risk is still a complete bar to recovery.

In "primary" cases, where no duty is owed, the reasonableness (or unreasonableness) of the plaintiff's conduct simply does not matter. The determination of which cases involve "primary" (i.e., no duty) implied assumption of the risk, and which cases do not, usually remains a question of law for the court, just as in any duty case. For the most part, these cases typically involve various types of sporting events in which participants (or in some cases even spectators) have been injured while participating in (or watching) the activity in question. As in California, "secondary" implied assumption of the risk has been merged with comparative negligence in many other comparative negligence jurisdictions as well. Thus, in "secondary" cases, where a duty has been breached, the defendant may not be entirely relieved of liability by the plaintiff's implied assumption of the risk, depending upon the jurisdiction and the type of comparative negligence involved. Moreover, the legal question in these cases also depends upon the sport in question and the defendant's relationship to the plaintiff.

There are several reasons why the traditional implied consent rationale does not withstand analysis when applied to these types of situations. The argument that a plaintiff who knowingly encounters a risk has impliedly consented to that risk would apply equally to both reasonable as well as unreasonable risks. However, it seems wrong to suggest that a plaintiff, when engaging in a sporting contest, actually "consents" to a breach of duty by the defendant that makes the sport more dangerous. In the *Knight* case, the dissent's reliance upon pre-*Li* cases makes the application of the traditional defense of implied assumption of the risk dependent upon proof of the plaintiff's knowledge of the particular injury-causing risk involved, and such proof is often hard to ascertain. The real question in these types of cases, given the nature of such sporting injuries, is whether the defendant has breached a duty that was owed to the plaintiff in the first instance.

In most negligence situations, people normally have a duty to avoid injuries to others. However, in sporting injury cases this duty often changes, due to the nature of the particular sport in question. Although defendants generally do have a duty to avoid increasing the risks associated with any given activity in which they may be involved, that duty does not extend to certain risks that are inherent in the very nature of the activity itself. Thus, in sporting injury cases, courts must first determine what risks are inherent in the particular activity in question, and the duty approach as adopted by the *Knight* majority allows them to do this. In this case, both participants were engaged in a touch football game. Most cases of this sort have not found liability for ordinary careless conduct by the defendant, but only for conduct that is intentional or reckless, given the nature of the sporting contest itself.

Here, the defendant was at most careless or negligent in his conduct, and because of this, at least according to the majority of the court, no legal duty of care owing to the plaintiff was ever breached, and, hence, there could be no negligence. As such, the *Knight* case clearly falls into the "primary" implied assumption of the risk category, whereby the defendant is relieved of liability entirely.

The dissent in the *Knight* case saw the case differently, arguing that the majority's approach transformed tort law entirely, by moving the plaintiff's implied assumption of the risk from being a question for the jury and making it a legal duty inquiry for the court. This effectively abolishes the traditional defense and makes the lack of assumption of the risk part of the plaintiff's burden of proof. Arguably, it also eliminates the legal "reasonable person" as the applicable standard of care between participants in sporting contest cases.

Part of the confusion as exemplified by the *Knight* case lies in the overlap between the court's role in granting summary judgment concerning issues of fact, and its separate role in determining whether a given plaintiff's actions constitute "primary" implied assumption of the risk or "secondary" implied assumption of the risk. In the comparative negligence context, the court is free to decide questions of fact so long as reasonable jurors could not conclude otherwise on those same facts. Therefore, a court in concluding that the plaintiff had impliedly assumed a given risk in the "primary" sense as to whether the defendant even owed a duty to the plaintiff, might actually not be any different than allowing a court to determine as a matter of law that no jury could conclude that the defendant had actually breached any duty that might have been owed, or that any such negligence by the defendant was simply not the proximate (i.e., legal) cause of the plaintiff's harm. The outcome in any of these situations would be exactly the same.

Thus, in comparative negligence cases a determination by the court that the plaintiff's recovery is barred because the plaintiff's conduct impliedly "assumed the risk" might actually mean any one of several different things. It could mean that: 1) the defendant simply owed no duty in the first instance (i.e., "primary" implied assumption of the risk); or, 2) in a modified comparative negligence jurisdiction the plaintiff's own negligence simply contributed to more than 50% of the responsible cause of the plaintiff's harm; or 3) even in a pure comparative fault jurisdiction the plaintiff's conduct was so egregious (e.g., trying to cross six-lanes of speeding highway traffic to change a tire) that no reasonable jury could conclude that the defendant's original negligent conduct in exposing the plaintiff to danger was the proximate (i.e., legal) cause of the plaintiff's injury.

II. Non-Conduct Defenses, Limitations, and Immunities: Statutes of Limitation and Repose

Both statutes of limitation and statutes of repose bar untimely claims brought too long after the time when the claim originally accrued, because such claims are simply too old to be given legal recognition. This is done for two reasons: 1) memories can fade and evidence can disappear, resulting in unfairness to one side or the other in proving claims, and 2) there is value to both sides in having finality, certainty and settled expectations as to unfiled potential tort claims that might otherwise linger indefinitely.

A. Accrual

For statutes of limitation, time is measured from the moment the cause of action is complete (i.e., from the moment when all of the required elements for the *prima facie* cause of action are legally present). In personal injury cases, this begins the moment of the injury, or when knowledge of the injury otherwise would have been discovered by the reasonable person. For a child the cause of action may toll (i.e., be temporarily paused or suspended) until the child reaches the age of majority. In toxic exposure cases, the injury may not even show up until long after the plaintiff has been exposed to the injury-causing toxin, thus delaying the accrual of the plaintiff's action. Likewise, in medical malpractice cases, the combination of issues regarding the point in time when the injury was reasonably discoverable, as well as often lengthy periods of unconsciousness, and injuries to child patients, can sometime combine to extend, or toll, the statute until long after the treatment takes place.

For statutes of repose, accrual begins at the completion of a certain act, no matter when the plaintiff's subsequent injury may arise. Legislatures have developed statutes of repose to get around some of the potential tolling problems that occur with statutes of limitation. However, unlike statutes of limitation which are usually fairly short in length (typically varying between one and four years depending upon the type of claim involved and the jurisdiction), statutes of repose tend to be for much longer periods, extending as much as ten or twenty years after accrual.

Failure to file claims within the period allowed by the applicable statutes of limitation or repose is the subject of many plaintiffs' malpractice lawsuits against their attorneys, because these statutes can be hard to calculate. In addition, statutes of limitations can also raise questions of insurance coverage concerning whose policy was in effect when the tort action accrued. Moreover, different limits are placed not only on different tort causes of action, but also whether the cause of action is in tort or in contract. Finally, when the statute operates to actually bar a plaintiff from seeking a remedy before it was even possible to bring a case, plaintiffs have sometimes succeeded in raising challenges to the statutes based upon various constitutional grounds.

An example of a tort versus contract statute of limitations conflict is found in *Garcia v. Texas Instruments, Inc.*, 610 S.W.2d 456 (Tex. 1980). There, Texas Instruments sold sulfuric acid to Mostek Corporation. Garcia, a Mostek employee, was injured when he dropped a carton made of fiberboard that contained four 1-liter bottles of acid. Three years and eight months after his injury, Garcia sued for damages alleging breach of implied warranty of merchantability under the UCC. No tort theory was alleged, and the statute of limitations under the UCC was four years. Texas Instruments filed a motion for summary judgment, which was granted by the trial court and affirmed on appeal, on the basis that since Garcia's suit was for personal injuries, the claim was barred by the two-year tort statute of limitations. Garcia argued that the UCC expressly authorized the suit, and that the four-year statute should govern the suit. Garcia also argued that the Texas Supreme Court did not abandon the statute by adopting strict liability. Texas Instruments countered that since all personal injury actions, even though based on breach of implied warranty of merchantability, were in reality common law tort actions, they should be governed by the two-year tort statute of limitations.

The court framed the issue as whether a cause of action existed under the UCC for personal injury resulting from the breach of an implied warranty of merchantability. The court explained that before enactment of the UCC all determinations as to whether an action was for personal injury or contract were based solely upon the type of damages sought. Here, since the plaintiff chose to bring the action under the UCC, the plaintiff was limited to UCC damages. However, the court concluded that since the UCC also provides for damages for personal injury, the UCC's four-year statute of limitations applied under its own terms. Thus, the UCC allowed the plaintiff to recover statutory damages rather than tort damages. However, those statutory damages in this case also included the plaintiff's personal injuries. Privity of contract was also not a requirement in this suit, so the case was reversed and remanded for trial.

The *Garcia* case also raises the specter of other types of non-conduct defenses that may potentially limit plaintiffs' ability to recover damages. One is the limitation in some jurisdictions of not being able to recover certain types of damages under wrongful death statutes (e.g., damages for "pain and suffering"). (*See* Chapter 11, *supra*, Wrongful Death and Survival). Closely related to wrongful death limitations are judicial decisions that simply prohibit plaintiffs from recovering certain types of damages altogether, for example those supposedly arising from "wrongful life." Finally, most jurisdictions also restrict plaintiffs from seeking specific categories of damages in certain types of cases. For example, commercial buyers who sustain purely economic losses are generally not permitted to assert claims based upon "strict liability in tort" for allegedly defective products. (*See* Chapter 16, *infra*, Products Liability).

An interesting statute of limitation case involving multiple issues such as tolling and even a constitutional "open court" challenge is *Nelson v. Krusen*, 678 S.W.2d 918 (Tex. 1984). There, the Nelsons brought suit on their own behalf for "wrongful birth" and on their infant son's behalf for "wrongful life." The Nelsons had one child with Duchenne's Muscular Dystrophy when they learned that Mrs. Nelson was pregnant with another child. They consulted Dr. Krusen who advised them that Mrs. Nelson was not a carrier of the disease based upon a test reported by Baylor University Medical Center. The Nelsons claimed that Dr. Krusen had negligently advised them, or, in the alternative, that Baylor University Medical Center had negligently conducted or reported the tests. Relying upon the doctor's advice, the Nelsons chose not to terminate the pregnancy, and three years later, after it became medically evident that their child had Duchenne's Muscular Dystrophy, the Nelsons sued.

Dr. Krusen and Baylor moved for summary judgment, which was granted and affirmed on appeal, on the basis that the plaintiff's suit was barred by a two-year statute of limitations. Dr. Krusen and Baylor both argued that the two-year limitations period had run before the plaintiffs' claim was filed, whether it began accruing at the time of the Nelsons' last visit to the doctor or the birth of the child three years earlier. The Nelsons challenged the constitutionality of the statute of limitations on several grounds, but the court took note of the "open court" challenge. Under an "open courts" constitutional provision, the court explained that legislatures, unlike the courts, are not permitted to create statutory remedies that are contingent upon the occurrence of an impossible condition. Here, the court explained, the Nelsons would have had to initiate their lawsuit even before the time when they knew of the injury. As such, the court held that the statute was unconstitutional, and the plaintiffs' cause of action was not barred by the statute of limitations.

B. Immunities

Immunities protect the defendant from suit based solely upon the legal status of the defendant. Traditionally, the common law recognized three types of immunities: family immunity, charitable immunity, and governmental immunity. Family and charitable immunities have been severely limited or eliminated by judicial decisions. However, governmental immunities still play a major role in protecting governments from suits by their citizens.

1. Family Immunities

At common law, one spouse could not sue the other because they were legally considered to be just one person. This rule has been abrogated over time so that generally no immunity exists today based solely on the marital relationship. However, a second family immunity was also recognized, and that immunity still raises its head today: the immunity of parents from tort actions brought by their minor children.

This immunity served two functions: it preserved family harmony and it was said to help eliminate collusive lawsuits. This later function was necessitated as a means of discouraging the natural parental impulse to admit negligence if it would get the parent access to insurance proceeds that would help compensate for their child's injuries.

Courts first began to allow suits where the injured child was working for his or her parents and for intentional torts where insurance was involved. Some have also allowed negligent supervision claims based upon a "reasonable parent" standard, although other courts have disallowed this. A few jurisdictions have even abolished the immunity altogether. So, in *Bonte v. Bonte*, 616 A.2d 464 (N.H. 1992), the defendant mother was hit by a car while crossing a street. At the time, she was seven months pregnant with the plaintiff, who was delivered by C-section on the following day. The plaintiff was born with cerebral palsy, and was severely and permanently disabled, requiring care for the rest of her life. The plaintiff's father brought suit individually, and on the child's behalf, alleging negligence based upon the defendant mother's failure to use reasonable care in crossing the street and her failure to use a designated crosswalk. The insurance company representing the mother raised family immunity as a defense. The first issue addressed by the court was whether a child, born alive, may even bring suit for injuries suffered while in the womb. The court held, based upon an earlier case [*Bennett v. Hymers*, 147 A. 2d 108 (N.H. 1958)], that a child, born alive, may bring suit to recover for prenatal injuries. The second issue was whether a child may sue the mother. The court in *Bonte* abolished the parental immunity doctrine in New Hampshire, and concluded that a mother's duty to her fetus should be recognized. The court explained that by doing so the mother is not deprived of her rights; instead, she merely has the same duty of care that she otherwise would have owed when the child is born.

However, compare *Bonte, supra*, with the result in *Shoemake v. Fogel, Ltd., A.T.*, 826 S.W.2d 933 (Tex. 1992), where the Texas court dismissed a cause of action on the grounds of parental immunity. Miranda Gilley nearly drowned in the swimming pool at her apartment complex, owned by defendant Fogel. She was rescued, but later died of her injuries. Miranda Gilley's mother (Shoemake) brought suit on her own behalf against the apartment complex owners for "wrongful death" damages and also as representative of her deceased child's estate for "survival" damages. At trial, the jury awarded Shoemake $285,492.28 for her "wrongful death" damages, and $50,969.00 for the estate's "survival" damages. The "wrongful death" award was reduced by 45%, as the jury found that Shoemake was 45% comparatively negligent in failing to properly supervise the decedent which contributed to the child's death. Fogel argued that the estate's separate "survival" action should also be reduced by that same 45%, to reflect the amount of contribution that was owed by Shoemake to Fogel, but the trial court rejected this. The court of appeals reversed.

At issue here was whether the estate's "survival" damages from Fogel should also be reduced to reflect the mother's (Shoemake's) same 45% comparative negligence that had reduced Shoemake's own "wrongful death" claim against Fogel. Shoemake asserted that since any claim on behalf of her deceased child against her personally would have been barred by parental immunity, she had no liability at all. The court agreed, explaining that Fogel's right to receive contribution from Shoemake, a joint defendant, was dependent upon the decedent's estate's right to recover in the "survival" action against her mother. However, since Shoemake (the mother) was immune from any liability to her daughter (or her deceased daughter's estate) by virtue of parental immunity, this also meant that Fogel had no claim for contribution from her. The court explained that in Texas the only recognized exceptions to parental immunity included lawsuits arising from the parents' business activities, and automobile tort actions. However, since neither of these exceptions involved ordinary negligence claims such as this one alleging that Shoemake had been negligent in the management, supervision, and control of her daughter, the court held that the parental authority granted Shoemake also operated to bar Fogel's derivative claim for contribution with respect to her deceased daughter's "survival" action.

The Court in *Shoemake, supra*, explained that the parental immunity doctrine was designed to avoid judicial interference with parental discretion, and that this immunity even survives the death of the child. Thus, since the child (Gilley) had no claim against her mother (Shoemake), likewise Fogel had no derivative claim against Shoemake. As a result, the estate's "survival" damages were not reduced.

Another way to view the *Shoemake* case is as an example of the "both ways" test. Also sometimes described as imputed contributory negligence, under the "both ways" test the negligence (or contributory negligence) of a parent (or a child) may be imputed "both ways" (i.e., one to the other). Under this doctrine, some courts have held that the contributory negligence of a parent in driving a car that was involved in an accident may be imputed to the parent's non-negligent child who was also injured while riding as a passenger in the car to bar the child's claim against a third party whose negligence otherwise may have caused the accident. Similarly, a court might invoke the "both ways" test by reasoning that if the child can't sue the parent (as in this case, because of the parent Shoemake's immunity), then the defendant (Fogel) should also not be able to get contribution from that parent for any damages the party seeking contribution (Fogel) otherwise had to pay to the child.

The "both ways" test creates some interesting anomalies in its application. Moreover, the outcome is often complicated by the court's usual practice of imputing any negligence of the child to the parent in determining the total amount of damages the parent will be allowed to recover. However, in those jurisdictions that have adopted comparative negligence (i.e., where the child's contributory negligence will not bar the parents' recovery altogether), the court may simply disregard the "both ways" test, and either impute liability of the child to the parent or the parent to the child, in order to reduce recovery as appropriate in regard to whichever one happens to be the plaintiff in the particular tort action before the court.

2. Charitable Immunity

Courts originally allowed immunity to all charities on grounds that it would protect and encourage those who tried to provide charitable benefits. As the nature of charities changed, (e.g. charitable hospitals), and charities adopted more standard business practices, including the purchase of insurance, the courts' attitudes toward this immunity also changed. Today, the immunity has been abrogated more or less completely, as recognized by the Restatement (Second) of Torts, Section 895E, which totally precludes it.

3. Governmental (Federal, State, and Municipal) Immunity

The liability of governmental entities for torts committed by their agents is large enough for a stand-alone course in many law schools. This entire area of governmental tort liability encompasses many complex issues such as constitutional separation of power problems that arise when the judicial branch attempts to assess the liability of the executive branch. This "second-guessing" of executive power can lead to policy-based arguments that providing any tort remedy against a governmental entity simply usurps executive and legislative authority altogether. *See* section II.B.4., *infra*. Obviously, however, such issues are well beyond the scope of this basic text.

To begin with, it is important to note that the whole concept of governmental immunity originated from the earliest days of the English common law where any lawsuits against the King (i.e., the sovereign) were simply barred altogether. In doing so, courts typically cited the Latin maxim, "*rex non potest peccare*," which translated as: "the King can do no wrong" (at least in the legal sense). After the American Revolution, this doctrine was brought into the jurisprudence of most American jurisdictions by their adoption of English common law as it stood prior to the Revolution. In one form or another it largely continued as a bar to any suits brought against the federal as well as the various state governments (i.e., sovereigns in their own right), until the adoption of the Federal Tort Claims Act [28 U.S.C. § 1346(b), § 1402(b), § 2401(b), and §§ 2671-2680] in 1946, at which time Congress granted a limited waiver of immunity, thereby allowing lawsuits for negligence to be maintained against the federal government in certain situations. Soon afterwards, most states adopted their own state versions of the Tort Claims Act, each of which provided similar limited waivers of state sovereign immunity. *See* the dissenting opinion of Henry, J. in *Cooper v. Rutherford County*, 531 S.W.2d 783, 786-787 (Tenn. 1975) for a thorough review of the early history of sovereign immunity in the United States. As a result, today the Federal Tort Claims Act (FTCA) waives sovereign immunity for certain types of claims against the federal government, and individual State Tort Claims Acts provide similar waivers of state sovereign immunity on a limited basis for certain types of claims in most jurisdictions.

Nevertheless, not all governmental entities are sovereign. Municipal, as well as various other local governmental entities, as creatures of state law, were never sovereign, so at common law they did not have any sovereign immunity. However, since municipal governmental entities often perform certain governmental functions for which the federal or a state government would have been immune at common law, courts have sometimes extended something called "governmental" immunity to them. And, since the FTCA and the various state Tort Claims Acts did not remove the common law sovereign immunity against municipalities and other local governmental entities, courts have extended immunity for those types of activities said to constitute "governmental" functions. These "governmental" functions are said to involve the exercise of an entity's governmental "discretion," which must be distinguished from other activities sometimes also engaged in by municipalities when they act more like businesses, or in a "proprietary" manner.

Case law has developed in most jurisdictions seeking to establish what specific types of activities are considered to represent immune "governmental" functions and which activities represent non-immune "proprietary" functions. Unfortunately, there is no bright-line rule that defines the difference between governmental and proprietary activities. *Cuffy v. City of New York*, 505 N.E.2d 937 (N.Y. 1987) represents a good example of the difficulties that can arise when courts attempt to draw a distinction between them. In *Cuffy*, Joseph and Eleanor Cuffy lived in the upper apartment of their two-family house. The Cuffys leased the lower ground apartment to Joel and Barbara Aitkins. The Cuffys and the Aitkinses had a history of repeated confrontation and police intervention. The night before the incident in this case, Joel Aitkins physically attacked Eleanor Cuffy. The officer that responded to the attack had been to the house a few times before, and determined that no arrest was needed, as this was a landlord-tenant dispute. Joseph Cuffy, with a neighbor, went to the police and asked for protection, saying that he intended to move out of the apartment if no arrest was made. The officer at the station responded to Cuffy's complaint by saying that an arrest would be made in the morning.

Mr. Cuffy then returned home and ordered his wife to unpack their things. However, the police took no action the next day, and at 7:00 that evening Aitkins attacked the Cuffys' son, Ralston, when he came for a visit. Both families then joined the fray, and all three Cuffys were severely injured. The Cuffys brought suit against the City of New York, claiming that the police were under a special duty to protect them. At trial, the Cuffys won a large judgment that was affirmed on appeal. In the *Cuffy* decision, even though providing a police force and allocating how and when individual police officers are to be deployed might certainly appear to represent a quintessential "governmental" function, the court explained that there is a narrow exception whereby a citizen might still be able to recover from a municipality for its negligent failure to provide police protection when a promise of protection was made to a particular citizen, creating a special duty owed just to that citizen, and where the promise of protection was relied upon by the citizen who subsequently suffered a causally related injury.

In order to determine if this special duty or relationship had arisen, the court considered four requirements:

(1) the assumption of a duty by the municipality, by word or action, to act on behalf of the injured party;

(2) knowledge by the municipalities' agents that inaction could lead to harm;

(3) direct contact between the municipalities' agents and the injured party; and,

(4) the injured party's justifiable reliance on this duty.

Reliance is probably the most critical element, because most courts recognize the potential unfairness that otherwise would arise if the injured party is lulled into a false sense of security. However, when the reliance element is not present or causally related, then this concern is not applicable. The direct contact element is also needed to establish the special relationship and limit the number of citizens to which this duty can be applied. Here, the court found that the Cuffys' son had no direct contact with the municipalities' agents, since there was no evidence that he even knew of the promise of protection made to his parents. Therefore, the court denied the son's claim. Likewise, even as to the Cuffys' claims the court concluded that since the police did not come to their tenants' apartment on the next morning to arrest the tenant as they had promised, the Cuffys could not justifiably have relied to their detriment on such a promise.

The tricky nature of trying to impose liability against a municipality for negligence is further illustrated by another example, this one examining a municipality's role in designing its roads and traffic lights. In *Aguehounde v. District of Columbia*, 666 A.2d 443 (D.C. 1995), Aguehounde was hit by a car driven by Davis. Aguehounde was standing on the corner. He looked left and did not see any vehicles approaching. He looked right and traffic was stopped. He cannot remember what the "walk" sign said. However, he stepped out into the crosswalk just as Davis was driving toward it. She saw the light facing her turn to green when she was a block away. She was traveling 20 mph when she saw Aguehounde step out in front of her, never looking in her direction. She put on the brakes, but she still hit him. Aguehounde brought suit against the municipality for negligence, alleging that the District of Columbia did not follow the proper engineering standards when setting the "clearance interval" of the traffic signal at the intersection. This failure created a clearance interval that was too short to allow cars safely to clear the intersection before the light changed. Because of this, Davis's car was already within the intersection when Aguehounde stepped into the crosswalk on a green light.

At trial, the city moved for judgment as a matter of law, claiming immunity on the basis that setting the intervals was a discretionary act. The motion was denied. The jury found the municipality's failure to set a proper clearance interval to be a proximate cause of the accident, and awarded Aguehounde $7 million and his wife $600,000. The city then renewed its motion for judgment as a matter of law, and it was granted.

On appeal, the court explained that the clearance interval is the time the yellow light is illuminated between the green light for one street and the green light for the crossing street. Some intersections also have an "all-red" setting which adds another second or two for clearance. The purpose of the interval was to allow drivers time to stop or clear the intersection and to keep traffic and pedestrians from entering the intersection until it was clear. In this case, the clearance interval had been 4.5 seconds, but the defendant city changed the interval to 4.0 seconds.

The court explained that municipalities are immune for actions that are "discretionary," which it defined as those involving the *formulation of policy*. However, municipalities are not immune for actions that are merely "ministerial." Ministerial acts relate to the *execution of policy*. Barring suits for "discretionary" acts prevents judicial second-guessing of the executive branch. To determine if an act is "discretionary," the court must decide if it involves a policy *judgment*. If so, then it is said to be "discretionary," and the municipality is immune, unless there is some specific directive removing discretion and thereby making the action "ministerial."

The trial court in *Aguehounde, supra,* had found that the decision to set the clearance interval involved the weighing of factors such as safety, commerce, and convenience, as well as ascertaining facts. As such, the court found that the city's decision was "discretionary," and its decision regarding the clearance interval for the traffic light should not be the subject of judicial second-guessing. The appellate court agreed. It should be noted, however, that had the plaintiff in *Aguehounde* been able to prove factually that the timing interval of the traffic light at the intersection in question was actually only 3.5 seconds (or even less), then he could have argued that the city had negligently failed to *execute* its policy-based decision of setting the traffic light clearance intervals at 4.0 seconds. If proven, such a fact could possibly have formed the basis for claiming that the city had negligently performed its "ministerial" responsibility by improperly setting the traffic light timing interval at an interval other than the one that had been specifically designated by the city's "discretionary" policy.

4. Federal Immunity

Federal immunity cases (also involving subject matter jurisdiction issues) often deal with questions of statutory interpretation. The common law establishes the background against which the federal government can be sued and, as discussed in section II.B.3., *supra*, this assumes that no suit will be allowed against the federal government unless the sovereign permits it. As a result, most sovereign immunity cases today typically deal with interpretations of the Federal Tort Claims Act (FTCA) or with the meaning of the language found in some other federal statute that provides a limited waiver of the federal government's immunity, such as the Federal Employers Liability Act (FELA.)

Sometimes in actions against the federal government the court deals with the legitimate exercise by the government through its agencies of its political discretion to carry out its mandate to govern. These cases raise separation of powers concerns. However, when an agency fails to act in a manner that is consistent with its own mandates, and thereby causes harm, can that agency be said to have "exercised its political discretion" or is it even "governing" at all?

In *Berkovitz v. United States*, 486 U.S. 531 (1988), Berkovitz, at 2 months old, took Orimune, an oral polio vaccine made by Lederle Laboratories. In less than a month, Berkovitz contracted polio and was almost completely paralyzed as a result. Berkovitz and his parents brought suit under 28 U.S.C. §§ 1346(b), 2674, alleging that the Division of Biologic Standards (DBS), a part of the National Institute of Health at the time, acted negligently in *licensing* Lederle to produce Orimune, and also that the Bureau of Biologics of the Food and Drug Administration (FDA) acted negligently in *approving* the particular lot of the vaccine that contained Berkovitz's dose.

At trial, the government moved to dismiss for lack of subject matter jurisdiction because it contended that its actions were immune "discretionary"
functions. The District Court denied the motion, and, at the government's
request, the decision was immediately certified to the 3rd Circuit, who reversed.
The Supreme Court then granted certiorari. After determining that it did have
jurisdiction, the court asked, "whether the discretionary function exception
of the Federal Tort Claims Act, 28 U.S.C. § 2680(a), bars a suit based on the
Government's licensing of an oral polio vaccine and on its subsequent approval
of the release of a specific lot of that vaccine to the public"? *Id.* at 433.

In discussing the "discretionary" exemption, the Court held that the nature
of the conduct determines if an action is discretionary. Discretionary conduct
involves a choice of judgment. If a federal statute, regulation, or policy tells
the federal employee exactly what to do, then there is no choice and, thus, no
discretion. However, if there is an element of choice, then the court must decide
if the choice is one that the exception was meant to shield. The court explained
that actions and decisions based on public policy are the only ones that Congress meant to shield because the purpose of the exception was to prevent judicial second-guessing. Moreover, regulatory functions are not excepted, as the
language of the statute only excepts "discretionary" functions. This is also supported by legislative history and previous opinions.

In *Berkovitz, supra,* it was alleged that DBS had violated the federal statute
and regulations by granting Lederle a license to make Orimune, and that the
FDA had also violated the federal statute and regulations by approving the
release of the particular lot of vaccine containing the Orimune that Berkovitz
took. The court discussed the procedure by which under federal law for marketing live oral polio vaccine, the manufacturer must obtain a product license.
The court explained that to obtain a product license, the manufacturer must
make a sample of the vaccine, conducting tests during the manufacturing process. After manufacturing and testing, an application for license must be sent
to the DBS, along with test data and a product sample. Before licensing, DBS
was required by statutory and regulatory provisions to 1) receive all required
data, 2) examine the product, and 3) determine that the product complies with
safety standards.

The Court concluded that the plaintiffs' first assertion was not barred by
the "discretionary" function exception, since the exception only applies to
conduct that involves a policy judgment. The court explained that the issuance of the license did not involve a policy judgment because statutory and
regulatory provisions required DBS to have certain things before issuing the
license. The court held that because the license did not involve a policy judgment, the "discretionary" function exception did not apply. The court also

addressed the plaintiffs' second assertion, explaining that although it was unclear from the complaint and briefs, the plaintiffs' may have meant one of three things: 1) DBS licensed the vaccine without determining that it met regulatory safety standards, 2) DBS found that the vaccine did not comply with regulatory safety standards, but issued a license anyway, or 3) DBS made a determination of compliance, but that determination was incorrect.

The court explained that if the assertion was based upon either #1 or #2, *supra*, then the discretionary function exception did not bar the claim. Since the "discretionary" exception only applies to conduct that involves a policy judgment, the court concluded that the license did not involve a policy judgment because statutory and regulatory provisions required DBS to have certain things before issuing the license. Thus, the court held that the "discretionary" function exception did not apply to bar the plaintiffs' assertions #1 or #2.

Considering the plaintiffs' assertion #3, *supra*, the court explained that the question becomes whether this was a policy choice or not. The petitioners contended that since the standards were objectively scientific, the "discretionary" function was not a bar to their claim. The Court concluded that the regulations, however, were obtuse, and should be left for District Court determination given the scanty record. The Court explained that when issuing lots by the FDA's Bureau of Biologics, the Bureau can examine any lot and prevent distribution of non-complying ones, but the Bureau is not required to do so. Because the Bureau is not required to do so, the "discretionary" function exception bars any claims that challenge the Bureau's formulation of policy as to the regulation or release of the lots. In addition, if officials from the Bureau are permitted to make independent policy decisions, then the exception bars claims against those decisions as well.

The petitioners also claimed that the Bureau had a policy of testing all lots of the vaccine, to prevent non-complying lots from being released, and that it had knowingly released a non-compliant lot. The Court concluded that if this claim were correct, then the "discretionary" exception also would not bar the plaintiffs from recovery. Therefore, it would appear that where a federal agency fails to act and where that failure is in the face of statutory mandates or internal regulations that require it to act, there is no "discretionary" immunity from suit.

Checkpoints

- At common law, contributory negligence on the part of the plaintiff barred the plaintiff's recovery.

- Only Alabama, Maryland, North Carolina, Virginia and Washington, D.C., still bar recovery completely if the plaintiff is contributorily negligent.

- Even in a state where contributory negligence is no longer a complete bar, the plaintiff's own negligence still forms the basis for comparing the plaintiff's behavior with that of the defendant for purposes of determining if (and/or how much) the plaintiff may recover from the defendant.

- If the plaintiff violated no duty, acted reasonably under the circumstances, or was not the cause in fact nor the proximate cause of his or her own injuries, then the jury will have nothing to compare when comparing negligence among the different parties.

- In common law jurisdictions, to avoid the harsh consequences of the contributory negligence bar, the courts developed the doctrine of "last clear chance" (LCC).

- As the LCC doctrine has evolved, the jury is asked to distinguish between a merely "inattentive" plaintiff and a truly "helpless" plaintiff.

- An "inattentive" plaintiff is given less protection from the defendant's negligence than a "helpless" plaintiff.

- At common law, the defense of assumption of the risk (AR) by a plaintiff also operated as a complete bar to the plaintiff's recovery.

- Assumption of the risk (AR) can be either express or implied; if implied, assumption of the risk can be either "primary" or "secondary."

- While most comparative negligence jurisdictions have done away with implied assumption of the risk as a complete defense, the plaintiff's express assumption of the risk will still bar the plaintiff's recovery, even under comparative negligence, as long as the agreement is not against public policy.

- Under the concept of "primary" implied assumption of the risk the defendant simply owes no duty whatsoever to the plaintiff.

- In sports injury cases, if the plaintiff impliedly consents to the risk of injuries that ordinarily can occur in that particular sport, the plaintiff's recovery will be barred under the doctrine of "primary" implied assumption of the risk (in which no duty is owed) in many jurisdictions.

- *Pure* comparative negligence allows the negligence and/or contributory negligence of both parties to be compared across the full spectrum of potential liability, ranging from 0 percent to 100 percent, and reduces the plaintiff's damage recovery proportionately.

- *Modified* comparative negligence allows a negligent plaintiff to recover at least a portion of his or her damages, as long as that negligence does not exceed a certain threshold percent, usually around 50 percent. If the plaintiff's negligence exceeds the threshold amount, then the plaintiff's recovery is totally barred just as in common law contributory negligence.

- Statutes of limitation run from the time of accrual of the plaintiff's cause of action, including a reasonable period during which the plaintiff should have discovered the injury.

- Statutes of repose run from some other fixed point, like the date of signing of a contract or the date of completion of construction of a building.

- While some types of immunity (such as charitable immunity) have receded with the prevalence of liability insurance, family immunity can sometimes still be asserted when minor children seek to sue their parents for negligence.

- In cases where both a child and the child's parents sue a third party, and the child's parents are also negligent, the court may allow the parents' negligence to be imputed to the child, especially in situations where the parents are otherwise immune from suit directly by the child.

- Governmental immunity turns upon the particular nature of the governmental entity's actions by determining whether the allegedly negligent act involves the exercise of an immune governmental "discretion" or a merely non-immune "proprietary" or "ministerial" function.

Chapter 13

Vicarious Liability

Roadmap

- Learn about the concept of "vicarious liability."
- Understand the distinction between "indirect" and "direct" liability, and the different legal implications involved in asserting them.
- Discover the origins of the doctrine of *respondeat superior*.
- Recognize the various situations in which the doctrine of *respondeat superior* can be asserted to impute vicarious liability against an employer for injuries tortiously inflicted by an employee.
- Learn the different factors utilized in determining "scope of employment" for purposes of imputing vicarious liability against an employer for injuries tortiously inflicted by an employee.
- Understand the application of the "going and coming rule" exception to the "scope of employment" for purposes of imputing vicarious liability against an employer for injuries tortiously inflicted by an employee.
- Learn the most commonly asserted exceptions to the "going and coming rule," and understand how each is applied to impute vicarious liability against an employer for injuries tortiously inflicted by an employee while going to or coming from the place of employment.
- Understand the difference between a "frolic" and a "detour" for purposes of imputing vicarious liability against an employer for injuries tortiously inflicted by an employee.
- Understand the "dual purpose" test and its application to vicarious liability in situations involving intentional torts committed by an employee.
- Recognize the circumstances and policy arguments that justify the imputation of vicarious liability against an employer for the aggravated tortious misconduct of an employee.
- Recognize the distinctions between an "independent contractor" and an "employee" with respect to imputing vicarious liability against an employer for injuries tortiously inflicted by an independent contractor.
- Understand the different situations when vicarious liability can be imputed against the employer of an independent contractor.

- Recognize the legal distinctions between a "joint enterprise" and a "joint venture," as well as the different situations in which vicarious liability can be asserted against each.

"Vicarious liability" refers to any number of different situations in which the tort liability incurred by one party (i.e., the "active" tortfeasor) is *imputed* (at least in the eyes of the law) to another party (i.e., the "responsible" party) for reasons that are primarily based upon policy rather than the traditional legal concept of "fault" that we have been addressing in most of the chapters of the text to this point. Of course, whenever any defendant is found liable for damages in a tort action, that person is typically responsible for the payment of damages to the aggrieved victim, regardless of whether (s)he is classified as an "active" tortfeasor or merely a "responsible" party. However, in vicarious liability situations tort liability is not assessed on the basis of any act or omission by the responsible party defendant. Instead, the primary justification for imposing vicarious liability is typically the existence of some type of "special relationship" between the "active" tortfeasor and the "responsible" party. Thus, "vicarious liability" may be seen as a kind of transition between cases asserting truly fault-based intentional tort (*see* Chapter 2, *supra*, Intentional Interference with Person or Property) and negligence (*see* Chapter 4, *supra*, Negligence) causes of action and those in which the no-fault concept of "strict liability" is imposed (*see* Chapter 14, *infra*, Common Law Strict Liability).

However, before examining any of these "special relationships" that give rise to the imposition of "vicarious liability," as well as the specific policy arguments that support them, it is absolutely crucial to recognize one very important distinction between the legal concept of "vicarious liability" and most other forms of tort liability that we have studied thus far. Vicarious liability is *indirect* tort liability, meaning that the "responsible" party really has not *done* (or failed to do) anything for which the law of torts imposes any legal culpability. Therefore, even if some policy of the law otherwise favors the imputation of tort liability (vicariously or indirectly) without a showing of any fault on the part of the so-called "responsible" party, in any "vicarious liability" situation there still must be a legal basis for establishing some underlying tort liability. In other words, somebody must have committed an actual tort against the victim who is now seeking to recover damages (vicariously) against the defendant whom the law recognizes as being responsible for that underlying tortfeasor's actions. That person is referred to as the "active" tortfeasor, and before any form of "vicarious liability" can be asserted against the defendant (i.e., the "responsible" party), the plaintiff victim must first establish the existence of an actual tort that has been committed by the "active" tortfeasor. In this sense, "vicarious liability" is not a tort theory or cause of action at all (i.e., a plaintiff does not sue the defendant for the *tort* of "vicarious liability" because there is no such tort). Instead, the plaintiff in every "vicarious liability" situation must *first* allege and prove a traditional tortious act that has been committed by the "active" tortfeasor (i.e., direct liability), and *then also* allege and prove the existence of a "special relationship" or some other legal basis for imputing that original tort liability vicariously to the party otherwise legally "responsible" for paying the damages caused by the underlying tort (i.e., indirect liability). This is why "vicarious liability" is referred to as *indirect* liability. It can only be imposed indirectly in relation to the existence of some underlying tort committed directly by the "active" tortfeasor.

I. *Respondeat Superior*

As explained, *supra*, the most common legal basis for imputing liability vicariously upon a tortfeasor (i.e., the "responsible" party) for the tortious conduct of another (i.e., the "active" tortfeasor) is based upon the existence of some type of "special relationship" between these two parties. In Chapter 9, *supra*, (Limited Duty) we examined a number of "special relationship" situations in which the law of torts recognizes a legal basis for imposing a duty of care *directly* owed by one person to another with respect to the tort of negligence. Many of those very same types of "special relationships" can also be utilized as a basis for *indirectly* imputing tort liability (i.e., vicariously) from one individual to another. In vicarious liability situations, by far the most commonly asserted of these "special relationships" pertains to the employer-employee relationship. As a result, many of the special rules and doctrines that are currently utilized in *respondeat superior* situations, although potentially applicable to many different types of "special relationships," were derived originally within the unique context of employer-employee relationships.

Historically, English common law courts first imposed vicarious liability against employers (referred to as "masters") for the tortious acts committed by their employees (referred to as "servants") while in pursuit of the master's business. Known originally by the Latin phrase *"respondeat superior,"* (meaning literally, "let the master respond"), this term is still used today in most jurisdictions in relation to the imposition of vicarious liability in situations where an employee has inflicted a tortious injury to the plaintiff while that employee was engaged in the course of employment for the defendant employer.

Both the history of the doctrine of *respondeat superior*, as well as the primary philosophical rationales for imputing liability vicariously to the active tortfeasor's employer, are thoroughly addressed in the classic case of *Fruit v. Schreiner*, 502 P. 2d 133 (Alaska 1972). There, the court explained that the doctrine of *respondeat superior*, while originally asserted as a means of justifying the transfer of tort liability onto an employer who at least implicitly had ordered the employee to act in some manner that caused injury to the plaintiff (i.e., the so-called "control" rationale), was gradually expanded to include all types of situations where the plaintiff's injury resulted from any acts whatsoever committed by the employee, provided that those acts were performed within the scope of employment for the employer (i.e., the so-called "enterprise" rationale). Today, most courts tend to prefer the "enterprise" rationale as a means of justifying the imposition of "vicarious liability" against employers for the tortious acts of their employees while engaged in the course of their employment, since the employee's actions have benefited, at least in general, the employer's business enterprise. Nevertheless, some courts still utilize a "control" rationale to justify imputing "vicarious liability" against employers, particularly in situations where the economic benefit of the employee's actions to the employer may not be quite as apparent, or where the employee has acted in some manner that is even contrary to the employer's stated business policy.

A. Scope of Employment

Regardless of which rationale is asserted in support of imputing "vicarious liability" against an employer for the tortious acts of an employee (*see* discussion, *supra*), the legal "test" applied by most courts is whether the conduct of the "active" tortfeasor employee was within the "scope of employment" at the time of the injury. *See generally* RESTATEMENT (SECOND) OF AGENCY § 228 (1958). "Scope of employment" is largely a factual issue that in most cases is left for the jury to determine after consideration of all the surrounding circumstances. When making this determination, most jurisdictions typically rely upon some combination of the following specific factors:

(1) the general character of the employment;
(2) the nature of the employee's tortious act;
(3) the purpose of the employee's act; and
(4) the time and place of the injury.

See also Griffith v. George Transfer & Rigging, Inc., 201 S.E. 2d 281, 287 (W. Va. 1973).

Regardless of what specific criteria are utilized in applying this "scope of employment" test in "vicarious liability" cases, it is important to remember, as stated *supra*, that in most "vicarious liability" situations today the majority of jurisdictions permit these determinations to be made by the jury (usually on a case-by-case basis). However, this is completely different from current "no-fault" worker's compensation laws wherein the court applies essentially this same "test" as a matter of law, since jury trials are seldom allowed in worker's compensation proceedings. What this means is that a fairly sizeable and separate body of case law has been developed in cases addressing "scope of employment" issues in which the courts (applying "no-fault" worker's compensation laws) have already previously defined certain types of activities as being within (or outside of) the "scope of employment." Construing and applying these so-called "no fault" worker's compensation "scope of employment" cases within the context of separate fault-based tort clams asserting "vicarious liability" can often result in confusion for students, as well as the courts. Although any study of worker's compensation law, with its attendant doctrines, rules and exceptions, is well beyond the scope of this text, students should understand that courts in "vicarious liability" situations arising within our traditional fault-based tort system often still attempt to rely upon many of these same "no-fault" doctrines and legal concepts that were developed exclusively for application within the worker's compensation system when attempting to address "vicarious liability" issues involving factually similar types of situations. *See generally* 1 LARSON's WORKMEN's COMPENSATION LAW § 16.10 (1972).

1. The "Going and Coming" Rule

While the "scope of employment" aspect of most employment situations is usually quite apparent in the typical employment setting, there are still a number of special circumstances in which the courts (again applying traditional "no-fault" worker's compensation principles) have recognized certain "exceptions" to the traditional notion of "scope of employment." For example, what about situations where a tortious injury is inflicted while the employee is still en route to (or from) the place of employment? To resolve this question, courts developed the so-called "going and coming" rule.

Under this rule, an injured worker is ordinarily denied worker's compensation coverage for any injury that occurs while (s)he is traveling en route to (or from) the employer's place of employment. Injuries sustained by an employee within such times, even though necessitated by some work purpose of the employer, are generally regarded, at least for traditional worker's compensation purposes, as being outside the "scope of employment." Relying upon a similar rationale, many courts have declined to impute "vicarious liability" in situations involving injuries tortuously inflicted upon third parties by employees who are still en route to (or from) their regular places of employment, reasoning that such injuries did not occur within the employee's formal "scope of employment." Other courts, recognizing the potential unfairness of such a rule when applied either to the employee (for purposes of denying worker's compensation benefits) or in a traditional lawsuit to a third party plaintiff who has been injured by such an employee, have recognized a number of different exceptions. Among the most common of these, are situations:

(1) where the employee, while traveling to or from the place of employment, is (either expressly or impliedly) rendering a "*special service*" to which the employer has consented; or

(2) where the employee, while traveling to or from the place of employment, is rendering some "*incidental benefit*" to the employer that is not otherwise common to ordinary commuting; or

(3) where the employee, while traveling to or from the place of employment, is actually subjected to some "*special hazard*" not common to ordinary commutes.

Thus, where the employer has expressly instructed a particular employee to pick up supplies or to perform some other type of service for the employer before arriving at work (or after leaving the work premises), courts have been more willing to extend that employee's "scope of employment" to include such activities, or at least to permit a jury to consider them as such. *See Skinner v. Braum's Ice Cream Store*, 890 P. 2d 922 (Okla. 1995). Likewise, while merely traveling to an employer's remote job site might not otherwise satisfy the "scope of employment" test, where the employee is also required to drive the employer's own special-purpose vehicle (i.e., providing an "incidental benefit" to the employer), or to transport explosives to that remote jobsite (subjecting the employee to a "special hazard" of the employment), it is much more likely that such types of activities would qualify under one of these exceptions to the "going and coming" rule for purposes of imputing "vicarious liability" to the employer for tortious injuries inflicted onto the plaintiff victim by an employee while en route to (or away from) the jobsite. *See, e.g., Faul v. Jelco, Inc.*, 595 P. 2d 1035 (Ariz. App. 1979).

2. "Frolics" versus "Detours"

Even when an employee is engaged in the general "scope of employment," there may be certain times when the employee at least temporarily leaves that employment to engage in some errand of a purely personal nature. When an injury is tortiously inflicted upon the victim by the employee who is engaged in one of these "personal errands," a question arises as to whether the employee is still acting within the "scope of employment" for purposes of imputing "vicarious liability" to the employer, and, if not, when does the employer's potential "vicarious liability" resume once the employee has finished the personal errand and returned to his or her regular employment activities? These and related questions are often resolved by the courts in "vicarious liability" situations by characterizing the employee's action as to the nature and extent of its departure from the regular duties associated with the employee's general "scope of employment."

Once again, derived from the application of "no-fault" worker's compensation laws (*see* section I.A.1., *supra*), courts typically characterize these types of temporary departures from an employee's "scope of employment" as either "frolics" or "detours." Since certain types of temporary departures from regular employment duties are all too common in many types of employment situations, these classifications are based upon their overall scope and extent, as well as the employee's own particular motives in engaging in them. A "detour" refers to only a minor deviation from the employee's regular employment duties that still sufficiently relates to the employer's business to justify imputing "vicarious liability" to the employer for injuries inflicted upon the plaintiff victim by the employee. *See Laird v. Baxter HealthCare Corp.*, 650 N.E. 2d 215 (Ill. App. 1994). Most "detours" tend to be foreseeable departures that only slightly deviate from the employee's "scope of employment." By contrast, a "frolic" is generally classified as a substantial departure from the employee's "scope of employment" that is completely unrelated to the employment and is of such a purely personal nature that the employer will not be vicariously liable.

In most cases, the determination as to whether a particular departure from the employee's regular employment duties is so significant as to represent an actual "frolic," or whether it is considered a mere "detour" will be questions for the jury. In addition to the actual scope and duration of the departure itself, other factors relating to the nature of the employer's business, as well as its physical location, may also be used. Thus, a greater degree of "departure" may be allowed for an employee who has been hired as a traveling salesperson and whose job responsibilities necessarily requires driving a personal vehicle from one physical location to another when calling upon business customers, than to an employee who has been hired to work on an assembly line situated exclusively within the employer's factory and whose job responsibilities do not involve the use of any vehicle whatsoever outside of the employer's workplace.

Once an employee enters upon an actual "frolic," any injury that is tortiously inflicted upon the plaintiff by that employee will be considered outside the "scope of employment," and "vicarious liability" will normally not be imputed against the employer until such time as the employee has once again resumed his or her designated employment activities. In most situations this means that the employee must physically return to a location that is at least reasonably near to the actual place of employment, with the intention of resuming service to the employer. *See* Restatement (Second) of Agency § 237 (1958).

3. Intentional Torts and the "Dual Purpose" Test

So far, this discussion has focused upon the employer's "vicarious liability" for tortious injuries inflicted upon the plaintiff as a result of the negligent conduct of the employee. Based upon the various policy-based reasons discussed in section I.A., *supra*, it is certainly one thing to impute civil liability onto an employer (i.e., the "responsible" party) for injuries that have been *negligently* inflicted by an employee (the "active" tortfeasor) who is acting within the "scope of employment." However, it is a very different matter to impute such liability when the tortfeasing employee has *intentionally* inflicted those same injuries upon the victim. How do these same policy considerations relate to the imputation of liability against the employer when an employee has committed intentional torts while acting within the "scope of employment"?

Obviously the easiest response to this issue would be simply to deny the imputation of "vicarious liability" against any employer whose employee has intentionally inflicted a tortious injury upon the plaintiff victim, reasoning that such intentional misconduct by an employee is so unforeseeable as to presumptively fall outside the "scope of employment." But, is this always true? What about those special categories of employees who are hired to work in environments or under circumstances in which even intentionally tortious behavior is at least sometimes foreseeable by the employer due to the very nature of the employment? For example, consider a tavern owner who hires a "bouncer" to maintain order on the tavern premises and to remove those patrons who exhibit dangerous or unruly behavior toward the other patrons, or a bill collector who is sent to repossess an automobile against an angry debtor, or a police officer who must subdue a suspect who is resisting a lawful arrest. In these and other similar types of situations it is very foreseeable that the employee, while engaged in the exercise of employment duties that (s)he was specifically hired to perform, at least occasionally may act in such a manner as to inflict even an intentional injury upon the plaintiff. How should the doctrine of "vicarious liability" respond in these types of situations?

Where the actual duties of an employee's job make it otherwise foreseeable to the employer that the employee might commit an intentional tort even while acting within the "scope of the employment," many courts utilize what is known as the "dual purpose" doctrine to justify imputing "vicarious liability" to the employer. Under this doctrine, liability even for an employee's intentionally tortious acts can still be imputed vicariously to the employer if at least some part of the employee's actions were intended to further the employer's business. *See* RESTATEMENT (SECOND) OF AGENCY § 235 (1958). Thus, even where the employee's actions may have exceeded the scope of express instructions from the employer or where the employee may have been motivated, at least in part, by some purely personal motive, as long as some part of the employee's actions are still performed in furtherance of the employer's business, the "dual purpose" doctrine allows for the employer to be "vicariously liable" even where the plaintiff victim's injuries may have been intentionally inflicted.

Under the "dual purpose" test, the cases are still a bit unclear as to exactly how much (or how little) of the employee's conduct actually must be motivated by the employee's own personal reasons (as opposed to the employer's business purpose). While most departures from the "scope of employment" in "dual purpose" cases are generally matters for the jury to determine just as in other "scope of employment" situations, potentially inconsistent outcomes are likely, depending upon whether the application of this doctrine focuses on the employee's own personal *motive* in committing the tortious activity, or the particular *activity* that gave rise to the plaintiff's injury. Evidence that an employee has acted for purely personal motives or that (s)he has used clearly excessive force remains highly probative in determining whether liability for such injuries will be vicariously imputed to the employer. *See* RESTATEMENT (SECOND) OF TORTS § 245 (1958). Likewise, evidence that the employee's tortious misconduct was inextricably intertwined with some aspect of the employee's job-related activity often favors the imputation of "vicarious liability" against the employer.

However, there is one particularly troublesome category of intentionally tortious behavior by employees that does deserve special attention. Even if somewhat foreseeable in certain employment situations, courts have not always agreed as to an employer's "vicarious liability" for sexual assaults committed upon tort victims by employees. Given the "dual purpose" doctrine's focus upon the individual employee's own personal motives, some courts have questioned whether such a test is even appropriate at all in sexual assault cases? Consider the case of *Plummer v. Center Psychiatrists, Ltd.*, 476 S.E. 2d 172 (Va. 1996). There, the defendant had employed a licensed clinical psychologist in its clinic who, in the course of providing counseling and therapy to a female patient, also sexually assaulted the patient as part of her "treatment." Even though the employee's sexual misconduct was clearly unethical and certainly well beyond the scope of the employee's job description, the court nevertheless concluded that it was for the jury to determine whether the employee had acted beyond the "scope of employment" for purposes of imputing "vicarious liability" to the defendant employer. However, in determining whether the employee had been personally motivated at least in part by some purpose of serving the employer's business, the court declined to apply a subjective test (as typically utilized in "dual purpose" cases) to determine the offending employee's own personal motives for engaging in the sexual activity. Instead, the court explained that an objective test was more appropriate under these circumstances to determine whether the employee's sexual activities with a patient were within the "scope of employment" for psychotherapists in general.

B. Punitive Damages

Even in situations where it otherwise may be appropriate to impute "vicarious liability" against an employer for injuries inflicted upon the plaintiff as the result of certain types of intentionally tortious behavior by an employee, a question still remains as to whether the employer can also be held legally responsible for the payment of any *punitive* damages (apart from ordinary compensatory damages) that may be additionally imposed as a result of such intentional misconduct. As discussed in Chapter 8, *supra*, (Compensatory and Punitive Damages) punitive damages are only imposed against individual tortfeasors who engage in certain types of aggravated misbehavior that is either intentional or otherwise in wanton disregard for the plaintiff's safety. Unlike compensatory damages, which are intended to compensate the plaintiff for his or her actual loss caused by the defendant's tortious action, punitive damages are designed for entirely different purposes. They are either intended to provide a deterrent against future acts of misconduct, or as punishment against specific wrongdoers, or both. However, in "vicarious liability" situations, the actual wrongdoer (i.e., the "active" tortfeasor) is usually not solvent or, for various other reasons, is typically unable to pay any judgment (and certainly one involving punitive damages). That is primarily why the whole concept of *respondeat superior* was created in the first place: to provide a *financially* "responsible" party against whom the plaintiff's damages could be appropriately assessed (and ultimately recovered).

While "vicarious liability" has generally been permitted in regard to the recovery of ordinary *compensatory* damages by a plaintiff who sustains an injury due to the misconduct of the defendant's employee while acting within the "scope of employment," the rationale for doing so hardly seems appropriate where the plaintiff also seeks to recover *punitive* damages against the defendant employer who is only *indirectly* responsible for the employee's misconduct. As a result of such concerns, many courts have simply declined to apply the doctrine of *respondeat superior* to justify vicariously imposing liability for separate punitive damages against the *active* tortfeasor's employer. Others have questioned whether doing so is at all consistent with any of the traditionally asserted policies in support of punitive damages. However, some jurisdictions do apply the doctrine, even with respect to the vicarious imputation of liability (indirectly) for punitive damages against a non-tortfeasing employer. *See generally* J. GHIARDI & J. KIRCHNER, PUNITIVE DAMAGES LAW AND PRACTICE Ch. 24, 36–39 (1987).

One somewhat unique situation in which courts have upheld "vicarious liability" for punitive damages against an employer for the aggravated tortious misconduct of an employee arises where the employer has become *directly* involved in authorizing or subsequently ratifying certain types of aggravated misconduct by employees. Often referred to as the "complicity theory," this rule is intended to protect both the interests of the public in preventing irresponsible or even directly tortious misconduct by employers, as well as the interests of those employers who do attempt to protect members of the public by implementing reasonable precautions against certain foreseeable aggravated misconduct by their employees. *See* RESTATEMENT (SECOND) OF TORTS § 909 (1977); RESTATEMENT (SECOND) OF AGENCY § 217C (1958). The "complicity theory" actually represents a form of *direct* liability rather than indirect liability, as we will see in the next section, *infra*.

C. Direct versus Indirect Liability

Thus far in this chapter we have only been addressing the defendant's "vicarious," or *indirect*, liability for the tortious misconduct of another person. In each of these "vicarious liability" situations, the defendant against whom liability is being asserted has not actually done (or failed to do) anything for which tort liability could be *directly* imposed. Instead, for reasons of policy that we have already discussed, *supra*, the plaintiff is seeking to hold the defendant legally responsible for the tortious misconduct of another person (i.e., the "active" tortfeasor). However, in many of these same situations, tort liability could also be imposed directly against the responsible defendant based upon some type of actual tortious misconduct that has been committed directly by that defendant. In these situations, rather than merely seeking to vicariously (i.e., indirectly) impute liability onto the defendant for the tortious misconduct of another person, the plaintiff may also wish to assert tort liability directly (as opposed to vicariously) against the defendant as an "active" tortfeasor.

Consider the following scenario that is often encountered in these types of cases. The defendant employer hires an unqualified and inexperienced employee to perform a certain task and then, without providing any training or supervision, puts that employee to work on the assigned task, whereupon the employee negligently injures the plaintiff, an innocent third person. Quite obviously, as we have already discussed, the defendant employer can be sued by the injured plaintiff based upon the doctrine of *respondeat superior* (*see* section I.A., *supra*), and if the plaintiff can establish that the tortfeasing employee was engaged within the "scope of employment" at the time of the injury, the defendant employer can *indirectly* be held vicariously liable for the plaintiff's injuries. However, in this situation, the plaintiff may also wish to assert liability *directly* against the defendant employer by alleging that:

(1) the defendant employer *negligently hired* an inexperienced and untrained employee to perform a task for which more training and experience was required; or that

(2) the defendant employer *negligently failed to provide proper training and supervision* of the employee with respect to the assigned employment task.

If the plaintiff is able to prove either of these allegations against the defendant employer, then *direct* liability for negligence can also be imposed against the defendant. This means that instead of indirectly imputing "vicarious liability" for the employee's negligence onto the defendant employer (as a legally "responsible" party), the defendant employer now becomes *directly* liable for its own negligence as an "active" tortfeasor.

But, what difference does all of this really matter, since the defendant employer is ultimately responsible for paying for the damages sustained by the injured plaintiff in either case? There are several important reasons for distinguishing between direct and indirect liability. Perhaps the most obvious reason relates to the defendant employer's legal responsibility for the payment of punitive damages. Many jurisdictions (as discussed in section I.B., *supra*), simply do not permit liability for punitive damages to be vicariously imputed at all. Another reason relates to the additional requirement in all "vicarious liability" cases for the plaintiff to prove the existence of some type of "special relationship" between the "responsible" defendant and the "active" tortfeasor. In addition to the ordinary requirements for establishing that a tort was committed by the "active" tortfeasor, the plaintiff in "vicarious liability" cases has the additional burden of proving the existence of some "special relationship" between these two parties that otherwise would justify holding the "responsible" party legally accountable for the payment of the plaintiff victim's damages. While this may be a relatively easy matter to prove in some cases, we have also seen that there are many other situations, especially in *respondeat superior* cases, in which proving that an employee was actually acting within the "scope of employment" at the time of the injury-causing conduct may be quite difficult. (*See* discussion in sections I.A.1-3., *supra*).

Finally, perhaps the single most important reason for asserting liability *directly* against the "responsible" defendant rather than just vicariously (i.e., indirectly) pertains to the very nature of all "fault-based" tortious misconduct. Remember that since "vicarious liability" merely imputes tort liability *indirectly* rather than directly, "vicarious liability" is often said to be "without fault." (*See* section I.A, *supra*). By contrast, *direct* liability (at least insofar as it asserts claims based upon either negligence or an intentional tort) is normally considered to be "fault-based." Since "no-fault" (i.e., "vicarious") liability is often considered by juries to be somewhat less culpable than other "fault-based" forms of tort liability, most plaintiff attorneys prefer to assert claims that seek to impose "fault-based" liability. This is because juries are far more likely to return a higher damage award in response to a defendant's *direct* negligence than in response merely to a defendant's indirect negligence. Therefore, when choosing between claims that assert potential tort liability either "directly" or "indirectly," it is usually preferable in most situations for the plaintiff to at least try to establish direct liability first. Of course, in many "vicarious liability" situations, the plaintiff will assert claims based upon both "direct" and "indirect" liability.

II. Independent Contractors

Traditionally, the common law recognized that any person who hired an "independent contractor" could not be held vicariously liable for injuries that were tortiously inflicted onto the plaintiff by the independent contractor. Although subject to many exceptions which have developed over the years, for the most part this basic rule continues to be applied in most jurisdictions today. See RESTATEMENT (SECOND) OF TORTS § 409 (1965).

An independent contractor may be defined generally as someone who performs work for hire for the defendant, but who is not considered to be an employee. Courts have developed many tests for distinguishing between "independent contractors" and "employees." Basically, they all focus upon the defendant's legal right to control the actual means and methods by which the work is performed, rather than merely the final result of that work. Where the employer seeks to control the actual details of the work (e.g., by furnishing tools, setting work schedules and activities, and directly supervising the work) a court is more likely to classify the worker as an "employee," for which "vicarious liability" can be imputed to the employer. (*See* section I.A., *supra*). However, in situations where the employer retains little, if any, control over the manner in which the work is actually performed (e.g., where the worker provides his or her own tools, equipment, and insurance, establishes his or her own work schedule, as well as the means of accomplishing the work) the worker is more likely to be classified as an "independent contractor." *See* RESTATEMENT (SECOND) OF AGENCY § 220 (1958). Often referred to as the "independent contractor" rule, this doctrine provides that tort liability is normally not vicariously imputed to the employer for the tortious misconduct of an "independent contractor." Of course, merely stating within the terms of a contractual agreement that the worker is an "independent contractor" for purposes of the work performed usually does not, in the absence of a consideration of these other factors addressed, *supra*, determine the worker's true legal status for purposes of applying this rule.

There are, however, a number of commonly recognized exceptions to the general rule denying the imputation of liability against the employer for the tortious conduct of an independent contractor. Among the most common of these exceptions involve situations where:

(1) the work to be performed is "intrinsically dangerous;" or
(2) the work subjects the worker to a "peculiar risk" that is different from the ordinary risks associated with the activity in question; or
(3) the employer has a legally non-delegable duty to perform the work in question.

Intrinsically (also sometimes referred to as inherently) dangerous activities are those that, by their very nature, present a special danger that simply cannot be eliminated, even by the exercise of the greatest degree of care. *See* RESTATEMENT (SECOND) OF TORTS § 427 (1965). An intrinsic danger stems from the nature of the activity itself, rather than the particular manner in which it is performed. Thus, under this exception courts have refused to apply the "independent contractor" rule to injuries inflicted upon plaintiffs during the performance of certain types of intrinsically dangerous work activities, such as blasting with explosives or spraying poisons. *See*, e.g., *Alamo Nat'l Bank v. Kraus*, 616 S.W.2d 908 (Tex. 1981).

As distinguished from "intrinsically dangerous" activities, a "peculiar risk" is merely one that involves some degree of special danger that is uniquely different from the ordinary foreseeable risks associated with the particular work activity in question. For example, the risk of injury to a construction worker as the result of a cave-in at an excavation site would probably not be classified as a "peculiar risk" under this exception with respect to performing excavation work, since such risks, although quite dangerous, are nevertheless very foreseeable, and even commonplace with respect to excavation work. Instead, "peculiar risks" related to a particular work activity involve those which are not routine and which ordinarily are unforeseeable. Thus, the risk of a cave-in at an ordinary construction site caused by the sudden and unanticipated subsidence due to the presence of an underground "sinkhole" might very well be classified as a "peculiar risk" with respect to the excavation work activities, whereas the ordinary collapse of a wall at that same excavation site would not. Under the so-called "peculiar risk" exception to the "independent contractor" rule, an employer may be vicariously liable for injuries to plaintiffs that arise from work that involves a "peculiar risk" of such harm. *See* RESTATEMENT (SECOND) OF TORTS § 416 (1965). As a practical matter, whether the work is "intrinsically dangerous" in and of itself, or whether some aspect of it merely involves an unforeseeable "peculiar risk," the result is pretty much the same: "vicarious liability" for injuries to a third party tort victim *can* be imputed (indirectly) to the employer, even in situations where the tortious injury was actually inflicted by an independent contractor.

The law also recognizes any number of other legal responsibilities of employers with respect to particular activities in which they may be involved. Sometimes, these legal responsibilities are formally imposed by statute, such as a statute requiring employers to erect and maintain safe scaffoldings at all construction sites, *See* RESTATEMENT (SECOND) OF TORTS § 424 (1965). Other legal duties may simply be imposed by the common law as a matter of public policy intended for the protection of certain members of the public, such as a rule that prohibits employers from hiring independent contractors who are financially insolvent or otherwise legally incompetent to bear the responsibility for their tortious actions, or rules that prohibit the creation of public nuisances. *See* RESTATEMENT (SECOND) OF TORTS § 411 (1965). In these situations, courts often simply refer to the existence of a non-delegable duty that is owed by the employer to the community at large as a basis for imputing vicarious liability, even where the actual injury to the plaintiff was caused by the actions of an independent contractor.

The rationale for declining to permit an employer to avoid liability for injuries in these types of "non-delegable duty" situations merely by hiring an independent contractor is primarily based upon public policy. As one court has explained, these responsibilities owed by the employer "are deemed so important to the community that the employer should not be permitted to transfer these duties to another." *See Bagley v. Insight Communications Co., L.P.*, 658 N.E. 2d 584, 587–588 (Ind. 1995).

III. Joint Enterprises and Joint Ventures

Apart from imposing "vicarious liability" in settings that involve employer-employee relationships (*see* section I.A., *supra*) and certain limited exceptions arising within the context of injuries inflicted by independent contractors (*see* section II., *supra*), there are also a variety of other situations in which liability for the tortious actions of one person will be vicariously imputed to another. As we have already discussed, most all of these situations involve the existence of some type of legally recognized "special relationship" between the "active" tortfeasor and the "responsible" party. (*See* section I.A., *supra*). However, in addition to all of these situations, there is one other unique setting in which vicarious liability is also commonly asserted. This situation arises when the defendant has agreed, in advance of any tortious activity, to participate with other persons in a specific activity, which then subsequently produces an injury to the plaintiff victim. Depending upon how each of these individual agreements is structured, as well as the specific jurisdiction involved, they are typically referred to as either "joint ventures" or "joint enterprises."

Essentially, a "joint venture" involves a special relationship among two or more persons with respect to a single business activity (that is usually undertaken for profit), whereas a "joint enterprise" involves a similar relationship among two or more persons more typically with respect to a non-business related activity. *See Cullip v. Domann*, 972 P. 2d 776 (Kan. 1999). While each individual participant in both a "joint venture" as well as a "joint enterprise" can be vicariously liable for injuries tortiously inflicted onto third persons by any other members, in a "joint venture" each member *also* owes a duty of care *directly* to each other member of the "joint venture" (whereas no similar duty is owed to one another among individual members of a "joint enterprise"). *See St. Joseph Hospital v. Wolff*, 94 S.W. 3d 513 (Tex. 2002). Although the individual elements of these two very similar types of special relationships do vary somewhat from one jurisdiction to another, they each basically share at least the following minimum requirements:

(1) some type of agreement (either express or implied) among all of the participants in the activity in question;

(2) a common purpose; and

(3) an equal "right of control" over the activity involved.

The "agreement" necessary to create either a "joint venture" or a "joint enterprise" need not be in writing (although typically a written agreement is more commonly associated with "joint ventures" because of their profit-related purposes). Moreover, such agreements can be either express or implied from the participants' conduct in relation to such activity. For example, a simple decision by three friends to go hunting together or to attend a concert would likely qualify as an "agreement" for purposes of this requirement, despite the lack of any formal writing or even an express statement of agreement among them. The mere fact that they all loaded their gear and got into the car together with the intention of traveling to a common destination would probably be sufficient evidence from which such an agreement could at least be implied.

The "common purpose" necessary for either a "joint venture" or a "joint enterprise" merely refers to the uniting purpose that gives rise to the occasion for the group's association. Thus, going hunting together, attending a concert together, taking a vacation together, or jointly entering a contest is each sufficient to satisfy this "common purpose" requirement in a majority of jurisdictions. In most instances, the subjective "motive" of each individual participant in the group activity is irrelevant, so long as each person's participation at least objectively appears to be for the same common purpose or goal. *But see Salmeron v. Nava*, 694 A. 2d 709 (R.I. 1997).

The "equal right of control" requirement for creating either a "joint venture" or a "joint enterprise" must not be confused with the concept of actual physical control. It is each participant's equal *right* to control or to direct the activities of the group that is important here and not the actual physical exercise of that control. For example, if three persons agree to take a vacation trip to the beach, sharing all of their expenses on the trip and taking turns in driving, at any given point in time obviously only one person will have actual physical control over the car in which all three participants of the group are riding. Nevertheless, all three participants are said to have an "equal right of control" over their "joint enterprise," since each individual participant can direct that whoever is driving the car must stop for food or gas. Even if the other two members of the group disagree and ultimately overrule such a request, each member at least has had an equal say in the outcome of the decision. Contrast this situation with one involving a traditional employer-employee relationship. If the employer instructs the employee to drive along a certain route or in a particular manner and the employee disagrees, the employee may certainly choose to voice his or her opposition, but this does not reflect an equal right of control, since by doing so the employee risks getting fired. The employer always retained the sole *right* of control, and even if the employer accedes to the employee's request, the employer still has not relinquished the sole legal right to make decisions that determine the ultimate direction or manner in which the car travels.

In recognizing the business or profit-related purpose that distinguishes a "joint venture" from a "joint enterprise" in most jurisdictions, courts often add an additional requirement referred to as a "community of interest" with respect to "joint ventures." Generally, this refers to some actual economic or profit-related goal for which the venture was established, rather than merely a common economic interest in the relationship. Thus, in the illustration, *supra*, the three friends may also have a common economic interest in sharing their expenses as they travel to the beach together, however such an interest probably would not qualify as sufficiently profit-related to classify their relationship as one involving a "joint venture." Instead, they would more likely be engaged in a "join enterprise."

Sometimes a "joint venture" can even be confused with a "partnership." However, in most instances, a "partnership" generally involves an *ongoing, long-term* business relationship between two or more persons, whereas a "joint venture" is typically based only upon a single, one-time business transaction. In the case of potential liability incurred by individual members of a "partnership" for injuries that have been tortiously inflicted onto the plaintiff victim by any one of the partners, any subsequent tort claims are usually not directed at the "partnership" itself, since most "partnerships" are not recognized as separate legal entities that can be sued directly. Instead, any recovery would normally come directly from the assets of the individual partners themselves.

Checkpoints

- "Vicarious liability" refers to situations in which the tort liability of one person (i.e., the "active" tortfeasor) is imputed to another person (i.e., the "responsible" party) even though the "responsible" party is otherwise not at fault in actually causing the plaintiff's injury.

- "Vicarious liability" is *indirect* as opposed to direct liability in which the liability of the tortfeasor is imputed (or transferred) to the defendant for reasons of public policy based solely upon the nature of the relationship that exists between the two parties rather than on the basis of any legal "fault" of the defendant.

- It is usually preferable whenever possible to assert claims based upon *direct* liability, since such claims are generally more "culpable" and typically result in greater damage awards.

- The doctrine of *respondeat superior* refers to a special category of cases in which "vicarious liability" is imputed against an employer for injuries to the plaintiff that have been tortiously inflicted by an employee who was acting within the "scope of employment."

- Under the "going and coming rule," some courts have declined to impute "vicarious liability" against the employer in situations involving injuries inflicted upon third parties by employees who are merely en route to (or from) their regular places of employment.

- Courts have recognized a number of special exceptions to the "coming and going" rule where the employee, while traveling to (or from) the place of employment, is (either expressly or impliedly):

  - rendering a "*special service*" to which the employer has consented; or

  - rendering some "*incidental benefit*" to the employer that is not otherwise common to ordinary commuting; or

  - actually subjected to some "*special hazard*" not common to ordinary commutes.

- A "detour" refers to a minor deviation from the employee's regular employment duties that still sufficiently relates to the employer's business to justify imputing "vicarious liability" to the employer for injuries inflicted upon the plaintiff by the employee.

- A "frolic" is generally classified as a substantial departure from the employee's "scope of employment" for which the employer will not be vicariously liable when that departure is:

  - completely unrelated to the employment; and

  - of a purely personal nature.

- When an employee commits intentionally tortious acts that cause injury to the plaintiff, such actions are usually considered to be outside the "scope of employment."

- Under the "dual purpose" doctrine, "vicarious liability" may be imputed to the employer even for an employee's intentionally tortious acts if at least part of the employee's actions were intended to further the employer's business.

- "Vicarious liability" is generally permitted in regard to the recovery of ordinary *compensatory* damages by a plaintiff who sustains an injury due to the misconduct of the defendant's employee while acting within the "scope of employment."

- Courts have generally declined to apply the doctrine of *respondeat superior* to justify imposing vicarious liability for separate punitive damages against the employer.
- Under the "complicity theory," punitive damages may still be vicariously imputed against an employer for the aggravated tortious misconduct of an employee where the employer has become *directly* involved in authorizing or subsequently ratifying certain types of aggravated misconduct by employees.
- An independent contractor is someone who performs work for hire for the defendant, but who is not considered to be an employee.
- Traditionally, any person who hires an "independent contractor" cannot be held vicariously liable for injuries that are tortiously inflicted onto the plaintiff by an independent contractor.
- Exceptions to the "independent contractor" rule are recognized whereby "vicarious liability" can be imputed against the employer of an independent contractor for injuries sustained by the plaintiff where:
  - the work to be performed is "intrinsically dangerous;" or
  - the work subjects the worker to a "peculiar risk" that is different from the ordinary risks associated with the activity in question; or
  - the employer has a legally non-delegable duty to perform the work in question.
- A "joint venture" involves a special relationship among two or more persons with respect to a single business activity (that is usually undertaken for profit).
- A "joint enterprise" involves a special relationship among two or more persons with respect to a non-business related activity.
- Each individual participant in both a "joint venture" as well as a "joint enterprise" can be vicariously liable for injuries tortiously inflicted onto third persons by any other members.
- In a "joint venture" each member *also* owes a duty of care *directly* to each other member of the "joint venture."
- In a "joint enterprise" each member does not owe a duty of care *directly* to each other member of the "joint enterprise."
- Both a "joint venture" and a "joint enterprise" requires:
  - some type of agreement (either express or implied) among all of the participants in the activity in question;
  - a common purpose; and
  - an equal "right of control" over the activity involved.
- A "partnership" generally involves an ongoing, long-term business relationship between two or more persons.

- A "joint venture" is typically based upon only a single, one-time business transaction, rather than any on-going, long-term business relationship.

- Since most partnerships are not recognized as separate legal entities that can be sued directly, recovery of any damages resulting from liability incurred by individual members of a "partnership" for injuries that have been tortiously inflicted onto the plaintiff third party victim by any one of the partners normally comes directly from the assets of the individual partners themselves rather than the "partnership" assets.

Chapter 14

Common Law Strict Liability

Roadmap

- Understand the common law rules that impose strict liability for injuries caused by wild and domestic animals known to be dangerous.
- Analyze the early English case of *Rylands v. Fletcher*, and understand both the broad as well as the narrow versions of its holding.
- Understand the Restatement (First) of Torts approach to strict liability for "ultra-hazardous" activities.
- Understand the Restatement (Second) of Torts approach to strict liability in sections 519 and 520 with respect to "abnormally dangerous" activities.
- Understand Judge Posner's approach to strict liability in tort as addressed by Restatement (Second) of Torts, section 520, factor (f).
- Distinguish between the evidentiary doctrine of *res ipsa loquitur* and the tort of strict liability.

I. Common Law Strict Liability

A. Wild Animals and Domestic Animals Known to Be Dangerous

In addition to strict liability principles that show up in the English common law cases of trespass to land, trespass to chattels and conversion (i.e., mistake is no defense), the first types of cases where strict liability language is explicitly found in the law of torts is where wild or dangerous animals escape and cause harm to others.

In wild animal cases there are basically two elements of contention. The first is the classification of whether the animal is a wild animal or a domestic animal. This is crucial to whether a negligence analysis will be used or whether the court will find liability simply as a risk associated with the keeping of the animal. Where liability is based solely upon the keeping of a wild animal, it follows that if the animal causes harm its keeper is responsible, regardless of how carefully the keeper has kept the animal. Wild animals may be defined as animals that are not "by custom devoted to the service of mankind at the time and in the place in which they are kept." RESTATEMENT (SECOND) TORTS, Section 506(1) (1977). The second element involves whether the wild animal has acted in a manner that is characteristic of that type of animal.

Domesticated animals, on the other hand, are those that are "by custom devoted to the service of mankind at the time and in the place in which they are kept." RESTATEMENT (SECOND) TORTS, Section 506(2) (1977). Strict liability only attaches in domesticated animal cases where the owner *knows or has reason to know that the animal is abnormally dangerous.* Most of these cases involve dogs that are rabid, or that have bitten others previously.

In domestic animal cases, the proof problems usually revolve around whether the animal was known to be dangerous. To some extent, these cases involve an analysis that is similar to that used in certain intentional tort cases. Did the owner or keeper of the animal know with substantial certainty of the offending animal's dangerous propensity to cause substantial injury to others or was the owner merely reckless in that regard? For example in *Sinclair v. Okata,* 874 F. Supp. 1051 (D. Alaska 1994), the defendants avoided summary judgment in a dog bite case, despite the fact that the plaintiff put on testimony to the effect that the dog in question had bitten at least four and maybe five other people before biting the two-year-old plaintiff. The defendant's expert claimed that those other incidents did not amount to conclusive evidence that the dog presented an abnormal danger to others. So the court left it to the jury to determine whether the defendant knew or should have known that the dog was dangerous.

The Third Restatement of Torts reflects from the case law some evidence of a change in the definition of "wild" animal to include animals that belong "to a category which has not been generally domesticated, and which is likely, unless restrained to cause physical injury." RESTATEMENT (THIRD) TORTS: LIABILITY FOR PHYSICAL HARM, Section 22(b) (2001). Thus, in a jurisdiction that has adopted the Third Restatement, the class of animals that could be classified as "wild" animals appears to have expanded. Perhaps the drafters of this latest version of the Restatement may have had Dobermans and Pit Bulls in mind when they formulated this new definition.

To say that a case is governed by strict liability principles still does not mean that the defendant is automatically liable. It seems there is often an inverse relationship between strict liability principles that lessen the burden of proving some type of fault and the triggering definitions of whether the case is of the general type for which strict liability is appropriate.

In strict liability cases, more emphasis is typically placed on the element of proximate cause. Since the Restatement dictates in animal injury cases that strict liability will only attach to the type of injury that makes the animal dangerous, some courts have been reluctant to impose liability for certain types of damages. For example, the mother of a child who experiences emotional distress after she witnesses her child being bitten by a dog may have a harder time recovering for damages in strict liability, than if she had brought her claim for negligent infliction of emotional distress. (*See* Chapter 9, section V., *supra*, Limited Duty).

In modern urban environments, many states have significantly broadened the responsibility of dog owners to prevent harm to others from their dogs. Many states have enacted leash laws as well as various other types of statutes that even further expand the scope of animal owners' responsibility. Violations of these statutes, typically characterized as negligence *per se*, often have almost the same legal effect as imposing strict liability.

The traditional common law distinction between strict liability and negligence is lessened somewhat in jurisdictions that allow comparative fault defenses in strict liability cases. As a practical matter, if the jurisdiction allows the defendant to argue a reduced recovery due to the plaintiff's own simple (i.e., comparative) negligence, then such plaintiffs will be motivated to provide proof of the defendant's negligence in both the knowledge of the animal's dangerous propensities, as well as in the way the defendant handled the animal at the time of the attack.

B. Livestock

At early common law, strict liability was generally applied to the owners of livestock that trespassed upon another person's real property. This rule likely originated from the fact that landed gentry had superior rights over their subjects in regard to the exclusive use of their land. (*See* Chapter 10, section I., *supra*, Premises Liability). In the U.S., there is a very interesting history involving the battle between farmers and ranchers for superior rights of land use and the risk of injury from wandering cattle. In states situated generally East of the Mississippi River, statutes were enacted that required the owners of livestock to enclose their animals within proper fences in order to prevent them from trespassing onto neighboring property. Under these so-called "fencing in" statutes, livestock owners were strictly liable for any damage done by their escaping livestock who were not confined within proper fenced enclosures. By contrast, in the West where land was far more plentiful, many states typically enacted "fencing out" statutes whereby individual landowners were required to fence their land before strict liability could be asserted against a rancher whose cattle had wandered onto the land and caused damage.

Strict liability is generally limited in these cases to situations where the animal actually trespasses onto another's real property. In other situations involving injuries caused by livestock, where, for example, a motorcyclist hits a cow that has wandered onto a public highway, the cow owner's liability may be limited to negligence. As we will see, one way to describe this principle is to say that strict liability attaches whenever the defendant's behavior causes risks of harm to the public that are "non-reciprocal."

C. Abnormally Dangerous Activities— *Rylands v. Fletcher*

Most tort teachers and state bar examiners require that lawyers know the rule found in the famous English case of *Rylands v. Fletcher, House of Lords, 1868, 37 L.J. Ex. 161, S.C.L.R. 3 H.L. 300, 19 L.T.N. S. 220.* This rule can be understood either broadly or narrowly. In a broad sense, it announces principles of strict liability whenever a person conducts an "abnormally dangerous activity" that causing injury to another person. Narrowly understood, it is limited to the facts of the original case, and no more. Therefore, to understand both its majority (i.e., broad) and narrow interpretations we must first examine its facts.

The plaintiff was a coal mine operator. The defendants ran a mill. To supply water to their mill, the defendants decided to build a reservoir. Despite hiring engineers and contractors to complete the project, the reservoir was ultimately built above some old filled-in mine shafts belonging to the plaintiff. After the defendants completed building the reservoir and then began filling it with water, the mine shafts underneath the reservoir gave way and the entire mine was flooded. Because of the flood, the plaintiff had to stop mining.

To understand the narrow holding of *Rylands*, it is important to know that the trial court found as a fact that the defendant was not at fault for the plaintiff's property being flooded with water, because the defect in the mine was said to be latent (i.e., hidden). The coal mine had been dug out years earlier, but the defendant had no knowledge of this. Further, the lower court found that the engineers and contractors were otherwise competent, and in the course of the digging workers discovered the filled-in mines, but they had no idea that the old shafts were connected to anything. The only issue in the case that the high court could consider was the liability of a person who lawfully brings onto his land something that is harmless while it is on the land (i.e., impounded water), but naturally does great harm when it escapes.

The rule that the lower court used in resolving this narrow issue is also the basis for a broader understanding of the case: the court decided that anyone who brings onto their land something that is likely to do mischief if it escapes, is *prima facie* answerable (i.e., strictly liable) for any damage that it causes if it does escape. The defendant may defend on grounds that the escape was solely the plaintiff's fault or was due to an act of God. The trigger seems to be the nature of the activity and whether it is capable of causing great harm, while the place of the injury, the land, seems to be immaterial.

The early seeds of an interventionist and extensive environmental law movement may also be seen in the lower court's language. As a result, today it is fairly well recognized that if a by-product, manufacturing process, or even waste caused by a business pollutes or is toxic to others situated outside the land, and this by-product escapes and causes harm to others, then the business responsible for producing the injury-causing substance is strictly liable for the harm that is caused to the land, and if to another's land, then certainly to the person of another as well.

The High Court in *Rylands*, however, slightly modified the original rule in this case by adding some key language (i.e., language pertaining to whether the use of the land was *natural* or *non-natural*). By doing so, the *Rylands* court arguably put greater emphasis on the fact that the injury to the landowner was done by a neighboring landowner. The defendants could have used their land for anything for which such land might have been used in the ordinary course of enjoyment. If water had merely collected on the land naturally and happened to cause this same damage, then so be it. However, the defendants here decided to use the land for what the court termed a "non-natural" use when they constructed the reservoir. "Non-natural" uses are those uses that are for the purpose of introducing something that was not naturally on the land (in this case, water that had been impounded in the reservoir). Because this use was "non-natural," the defendants acted at their own peril and, thus, were strictly liable for any damage that ensued.

U.S. courts still follow the rule of *Rylands v. Fletcher* today. However, later courts have interpreted the "natural/non-natural" distinction of this rule to apply only to extraordinary or abnormal activities. This application makes sense because, relating it back to the previous discussion of wild or domesticated animals (*see* section I.A., *supra*), a person is generally only strictly liable for keeping a wild animal (i.e., an abnormal activity) or a domesticated animal when that animal is known to have an abnormally dangerous propensity to cause harm. The same principle can be said to apply here.

II. The Restatement and Strict Liability

A. Historical Background

Over the years, the A.L.I. Restatement has evolved beyond *Rylands* in its understanding of what triggers a strict liability analysis. Sections 519 and 520 of the First Restatement used the word "ultrahazardous" to describe the trigger, and it did not limit the harm solely to harm done by a neighbor to a neighbor's land. In the Second Restatement, William Prosser argued that the phrase "abnormally dangerous" should be substituted in place of the phrase "ultrahazardous," and the A.L.I. subsequently adopted his suggestion in its description of the general principles that defined when strict liability would apply.

The Second Restatement section 520 went on to describe a "factors-analysis" to help courts in determining whether an activity was "abnormally dangerous." Specifically, those factors include the:

a. existence of a high degree of risk of some harm to the person, land or chattels of others;
b. likelihood that the harm that results from it will be great;
c. inability to eliminate the risk by the exercise of reasonable care;
d. extent to which the activity is not a matter of common usage;
e. inappropriateness of the activity to the place where it is carried on; and
f. extent to which its value to the community is outweighed by it dangerous attributes.

So, for example, blasting, operating a hazardous waste site, transporting nitro glycerin, and firing rocket motors have all been held to be "abnormally dangerous activities." On the other hand, the manufacture and sale of firearms, and the use of uninsulated power lines is not. Courts are divided in their analysis as to whether large underground storage tanks for storing oil are considered to be "abnormally dangerous activities." For example, courts in Colorado say they are abnormally dangerous, while Maryland and Virginia courts say they are not.

Even situations strikingly similar to *Rylands* involving the storage of large amounts of groundwater may not always be considered "abnormally dangerous activities" for which strict liability would be appropriate. For example, in Texas and Oklahoma, a properly conducted oil or gas well that used underground water might be considered natural, or so valuable to the community that it might not be regarded as an "abnormally dangerous activity," at least when conducted in a rural area. However, a different conclusion has been reached in Kansas and Indiana. *See* Second Restatement section 520(f), comment k.

One famous commentator, Professor George P. Fletcher, has suggested the paradigm of *reciprocity* to describe those situations when a strict liability analysis should be used. *See Fairness and Utility in Tort Theory*, 85 Harv. L. Rev. 537 (1972). Alternatively, Richard Epstein argues that the language of causation adequately captures when liability ought to be imposed, and that burdening tort law with claims based upon negligence and strict liability is unnecessary if the concept of causation is correctly understood. *See* Richard A. Epstein, *A Theory of Strict Liability*, 2 J. Legal Stud. 151 (1973).

Regardless of the exact language used to trigger a strict liability analysis, the famous case of *Siegler v. Kuhlman*, 502 P.2d 1181 (Wash. 1972), is a prime example of its modern use. The facts are important to the holding. In *Siegler*, the defendant was driving a truck and trailer, fully loaded with gasoline. Before leaving the gasoline plant, the defendant inspected the trailer and found nothing wrong. A few hours later, as he was driving downgrade on a freeway offramp, he felt a jerk and realized that the fully loaded trailer was no longer attached to the truck. The defendant stopped the truck without skidding the tires, got out of the truck, and saw that the trailer had crashed through a fence and came to rest upside down on the road below. The defendant then heard a sound and the trailer began burning. Carol House died in the flames of the explosion when her car hit the un-illuminated trailer tank. The reason the trailer disengaged is unknown.

The plaintiff tried to prove negligence on the part of the driver and the owner of the truck, attempting to use the evidentiary doctrine of *res ipsa loquitur*. Defendants, on the other hand, tried to prove due care. At trial, the jury found for the defendants. The principal objection at trial was the failure to give a *res ipsa loquitur* instruction. However, according to the Washington Supreme Court, the instruction did not matter, because strict liability as a matter of law should have been applied. Hauling gasoline is no more unusual than hauling water, but it is far more dangerous. And, according to the court, when gasoline is carried as cargo, it becomes even more hazardous, much like large quantities of water when they are impounded (as occurred in *Rylands v. Fletcher, supra*). Dangers multiply from the quantity, bulk, and weight. Additionally, the court explained that the very nature of gasoline also results in the destruction of evidence to prove or disprove negligence if the gasoline is ignited. The court gave as reasons for applying strict liability in the case the fact that the gasoline was:

a. a highly flammable, volatile, and explosive substance;
b. carried at a high rate of speed;
c. on the public highway; and
d. subject to ignition and explosion if it escapes.

The court applied Restatement (Second) § 519, noting that three factors supported the application of strict liability: 1) transport of gasoline involves a high degree of risk; 2) the risk is potentially one of great harm and injury; and 3) the dangers cannot be eliminated by the exercise ordinary care. The court remanded the case solely for a determination of damages.

Nevertheless, could a different cause of action have been used? This example provides a good opportunity in which to review some earlier tort concepts that we have discussed in order to develop a better understanding of the differences between negligence and strict liability. For example, the evidentiary doctrine of *res ipsa loquitor* could have been applied, as the plaintiffs had contended. Still, *res ipsa loquitor* raises at most, only a rebuttable presumption of negligence. However, by relying upon strict liability the court does not allow for the defendant even to rebut this presumption of negligence with proof, because the effect of strict liability is to make the defendant's liability absolute, at least in the absence of any defense.

B. Posner and Factor (f)

In *Indiana Harbor Belt Railroad Co. v. American Cyanamid Co.*, 916 F. 2d 1174 (7th Cir. 1990), Judge Posner, of law and economics fame, argued that factor (f) is the prime factor for determining whether to apply strict liability. In *Indiana Harbor*, American Cyanamid loaded a railroad car leased from North American Car Corporation with acrylonitrile at its manufacturing plant in Louisiana. A train from the Missouri Pacific Railroad picked up the car from the plant for delivery in New Jersey. Conrail, which serviced New Jersey and, as a consequence, the Missouri Pacific Railroad, took the car to a yard just south of Chicago that was owned by the Indiana Harbor Belt Railroad. The Indiana Harbor Belt Railroad had a contract with Conrail to switch cars onto Conrail's system.

When the car arrived in the plaintiff's yard, a yard employee noticed that the car was gushing fluid from an outlet on the car that had a broken lid. The leak was finally stopped, but due to the flammable, toxic, and possibly even carcinogenic nature of the chemical (acrylonitrile), all surrounding homes were evacuated and the car in question was moved to a remote part of the yard. Only a quarter of the chemical actually leaked. Nevertheless, the Illinois Department of Environmental Protection ordered Indiana Harbor Belt Railroad to pay nearly 1 million dollars for decontamination. Indiana Harbor Belt Railroad then sued American Cyanamid to recover for those costs.

The first count of the complaint charged Cyanamid with negligently maintaining the railcar (in which the acrylonitrile had been transported), while the second count charged Cyanamid with strict liability for the "abnormally dangerous activity" of transporting acrylonitrile in bulk. The issue in the case was whether the shipper of a hazardous chemical should be held strictly liable for accidents caused by the shipment while en route to its destination, and Judge Posner found Restatement (Second) of Torts, section 520 to be controlling under Illinois law.

The court relied upon a nineteenth century case, *Guillen v. Smith*, 19 Johns. 381 (N.Y. 1822), in which a man who was hot-air ballooning in New York City landed unintentionally in the plaintiff's vegetable garden, to show the roots of the principles articulated by section 520. Judge Posner argued that strict liability is necessary when the accidents associated with the activity cannot be prevented by the exercise of due care, at least in respect to the overall value of the activity to the community. He defined "due care" as "average care." Against this backdrop, Posner then began his analysis, finding that acrylonitrile was flammable and toxic, even though it did not burn or explode in this case. The substance was listed on a table of 125 hazardous materials that are shipped in the highest volume on railroads, in which it was ranked at 53. Based upon such evidence alone if the court held the defendant strictly liable in this case, then all similar shippers would also be strictly liable, and that would be too broad a rule to impose.

The court saw no reason that negligence could not remedy and deter this same behavior. In this case, the leak had not been caused by the inherent dangerous properties of acrylonitrile, but by ordinary carelessness (i.e., either that of Cyanamid or of North American Car Corporation or of Missouri Pacific Railroad or of Indiana Harbor Belt Railroad). Accidents that can be remedied simply by taking "due care" can be avoided on a traditional negligence theory. While this accident had occurred in a densely populated area, the acrylonitrile had to be shipped through such areas due to the nature of the nation's railroad system. Nevertheless, under these circumstances, the mere shipping of acrylonitrile was not so hazardous as to impose a duty to re-route such shipments through lesser-populated areas.

Judge Posner held that the primary emphasis of section 520 is upon choosing a liability regime to control accidents most efficiently, and not to redistribute wealth by finding the deepest pocket. In short, the court held that strict liability was not applicable here because the plaintiff had failed to show that an ordinary negligence regime would not have provided the necessary and adequate deterrence against the defendants.

Under this rationale, Judge Posner has, in effect, imposed a new burden upon the plaintiff: to demonstrate that negligence law would otherwise not be adequate to deter the accident. Of course, the accident did occur, and someone could always have exercised greater care, or something could always have been done more safely. On an incremental level, each activity, whether to check that a valve had been closed, or a fuse lit properly, or nitroglycerine was adequately packed, is always a matter of exercising "due" (or average) care under the circumstances. Additionally, where *res ipsa loquitur* is widely available as an evidentiary aid in proving negligence, then the plaintiff is actually hurt by any arguments that (s)he might otherwise wish to make in support of *res ipsa*. For example, the mere claim that at least someone was likely negligent, for example, in letting the dog loose, or in using dynamite to blast in a densely populated area, or whatever, can be harmful to the plaintiff's assertion of strict liability against the defendant, since the more likely that an accident is caused as the result of someone's negligence (even if not negligence by the defendant), then the less likely that strict liability would be appropriate as a proper theory to be asserted at all. If negligence against someone is a likely cause of the accident, then under Judge Posner's approach to strict liability, the law of negligence can adequately deter the injury-causing behavior. And there is no need to impose strict liability.

Likewise, even if the evidentiary doctrine of *res ipsa loquitur* is not available, as we have seen in many cases that now require the plaintiff to show an inability to prove negligence with respect to each individual defendant, whenever the plaintiff uses a probability analysis to show that negligence likely existed even though it cannot be specifically proven as to any particular defendant, such proof will still probably suffice in defeating the claim for strict liability, since it clearly establishes that a negligence regime would have provided adequate accident deterrence. Similarly, there is another trap when the plaintiff actually sues multiple defendants, since any evidence of negligence on the part of any defendant, even if otherwise insufficient to prove negligence against that particular defendant, will likely be sufficient to defeat the imposition of strict liability under Restatement (Second) of Torts, section 520, comment (f). *See* William K. Jones, *Strict Liability for Hazardous Enterprises*, 92 Colum. L. Rev. 1705, 1752-53 (1992).

One additional consideration that also used to be relevant whenever the court was trying to determine whether or not to apply strict liability was that the defendant could not assert the defense of contributory negligence in claims alleging strict liability. However, this is no longer the case in most comparative negligence jurisdictions. (*See* Chapter 12, section I.B., *supra*). Further, strict liability is usually limited to recovery for only those damages that actually made the activity "abnormally dangerous," so emotional distress experienced by bystanders to an injury do not usually fall within the umbrella of damages that can be recovered.

Interestingly, the English courts have come full circle from the early *Rylands* decision, and most courts in England today have determined that strict liability will not apply *unless* the harm from the defendant's dangerous activity was specifically foreseeable. So, in *Cambridge Water Co. v. Eastern Counties Leather PLC.*, 1 All E.R. 53 (H.L. 1994), the defendant was a leather manufacturer that used perchloroethene (P.C.E.) in its leather tanning facilities. The P.C.E. apparently seeped through the groundwater and into the plaintiff's borehole. The plaintiff sued on three theories: negligence, nuisance, and strict liability. The court narrowed the issue to nuisance and strict liability because the defendant, like the defendant in *Rylands v. Fletcher, supra*, had collected something on its land that was likely to do mischief if it escaped. However, the court observed that while nuisance liability is generally strict if the defendant is responsible for the creation of the nuisance, this rule is limited by the notion of a reasonable use, and if the use is reasonable, the defendant is relieved of liability for nuisance. Explaining that the concept of strict liability was more appropriate for Parliament to adopt than for the courts, the court then interpreted *Rylands v. Fletcher* to include the additional requirement of foreseeability before liability will attach in a strict liability case.

Checkpoints

- Strict liability at common law had its origins in the law regarding the keeping of wild animals.

- Strict liability attaches to the owners and keepers of both wild animals and also domestic animals with known dangerous propensities.

- *Rylands v. Fletcher* applied strict liability principles to damage caused by the non-negligent escape of water kept artificially on the defendant landowner's land that caused harm to a neighbor's land.

- Principles announced in *Rylands v. Fletcher* provided the impetus for *Restatement (Second) of Torts*, Sections 519 and 520, regarding strict liability for "abnormally dangerous" activities.

- Judge Posner used comment (f) of *Restatement (Second) of Torts*, section 520 to place new emphasis upon the examination of whether the exercise of due care would have avoided the accident. Where the exercise of due care would have prevented the accident, strict liability principles are unnecessary and wasteful because they over-deter the actors.

- *Res ipsa loquitur* is not the same as strict liability, as it only provides an evidentiary mechanism for getting past the defendant's motion to dismiss the plaintiff's case of negligence, and, depending on the jurisdiction, it may shift the burden of production (of evidence) onto the defendant, but it does not change the standard from one of due care.

- England has retreated from its former use of strict liability by, in effect, limiting the case of *Rylands v. Fletcher* to its facts.

Chapter 15

Nuisance

Roadmap

- Understand the distinctions between the two types of nuisance: public and private.
- Understand the proper legal bases for imposing liability for the nuisance torts.
- Understand the requirement of "substantial harm" as it relates to the nuisance torts.
- Identify the appropriate remedies for nuisance.
- Identify the appropriate defenses for the torts of nuisance.

Nuisance is an area of tort law that can be quite complex. It is a combination of claims that, on their face, often appear unrelated. There are basically two types of nuisance: public nuisance and private nuisance. Each of these requires separate analysis, but a brief statement of some general concepts is useful at the outset of our discussion.

A public nuisance is a substantial interference with the public's right to health, safety, comfort or convenience. A public representative ordinarily brings this action. However, a public nuisance claim can be brought by a private individual where that individual has suffered an injury that is different in kind and not merely in degree from the general public.

A private nuisance is brought to protect a landowner's (or possessor's) right to the peaceful enjoyment and use of land. Students may find, for example, that private nuisance is frequently covered in both the basic Torts class as well as the basic Property class. A plaintiff may seek compensatory damages for the harm done by the nuisance, but typically of even greater importance the plaintiff in a nuisance action will also seek an injunction to stop the nuisance.

It has been suggested that generally, a nuisance is just a thing in the wrong place. A traditional comment is that a nuisance is like a "pig in a parlor." It just does not belong where it is found.

I. Public Nuisance

A. Types of Claims

As stated, *supra*, a public nuisance action is designed to protect the public's right to health, safety, comfort and convenience. A public representative usually brings the action. Many public nuisance claims involve attempts to enforce minor criminal laws. For example, defendants who have been engaged in inappropriate or illegal conduct may be sued in public nuisance in an attempt to seek public damages, as well as to obtain an injunction to prevent similar misbehavior in the future.

Most cities have comprehensive zoning laws and regulations that assure that land use is done in a planned, organized manner, and also that there are similar uses in similar areas. Under these laws, for example, residential homeowners can be assured that they will not find themselves living next door to a heavy industry or a commercial area. Prior to modern zoning, nuisance actions had to be used, and then the courts had to decide which use was appropriate to the area. Such actions would litigate the proper location of industries, taverns, funeral homes and other sensitive uses. A public nuisance action might also have been brought against businesses that were inappropriate to a particular location. In addition, public officials could seek injunctive relief to close houses of prostitution or illegal shows and acts.

Even with modern zoning laws, however, nuisance actions to litigate land use are still available. Thus, a business may be in an area that is properly zoned for that business, but the method of conducting the business may be inappropriate. A bar or tavern, for example, may locate in a properly zoned area for bars or taverns. However, if the bar owner allows excessive trash, noise, lighting, or other problems, an action for public nuisance may be brought to remedy those issues.

It would seem that modern public nuisance actions could be brought to resolve pollution problems, and indeed some pollution issues have been addressed by such actions. When the polluter and the source of the pollution are clearly identified, a public nuisance action may be useful. However, many pollution issues are sufficiently complex to cause confusion in nuisance litigation. Citywide pollution due to the size of the city, the use of automobiles and the presence of heavy industry, often leaves public officials without a clear plaintiff or clear source of the problem. For this reason, legislation and regulatory agencies have been more successful methods for controlling these types of pollution. Nevertheless, actions for public nuisance are, at times, still used to supplement those primary pollution control methods.

Public nuisance has been and continues to be a method to protect the public's right to the use of public roads and waterways that are available for the public's safety, comfort and convenience. Members of the public use those thoroughfares to get to places of employment, travel for recreation, and to make sure that fire trucks and ambulances may reach appropriate destinations. When someone blocks such a public way, (s)he is subject to an action for public nuisance.

One common problem with public thoroughfares involves interference by adjoining landowners. For example, a landowner may allow trees or bushes to block the road or place impediments to travel in the road. Alternatively, tree growth may not completely block the roadway, but it may impede clear sightlines necessary for safe travel. Such conduct is a classic example of a public nuisance. The blocking of the public road is an interference with the public's rights.

Conduct that the public finds offensive has, at times, been the subject of nuisance actions. In the late 1800s, the federal government sought to eliminate polygamy and to confiscate property owned by those engaged in that practice. Although initially these actions were of several types, they ultimately took the form of public nuisance. For example, the federal government alleged that the practice of polygamy was contrary to the public health, safety and morals, and had to be stopped. More recently, the State of Tennessee sought to bring an end to the practice of snake handling in certain religious ceremonies. Again, the government claimed that the practice was a threat to the public safety. Although governments have obtained some success with such litigation tactics, the practices at issue often continue in less overt forms.

B. Bases of Claims

Nuisance is not a new and separate basis of liability. Instead, it is an area of the law that combines all three traditional categories of tort liability: intent, negligence, and strict liability. A public nuisance may, therefore, be grounded in any of those three bases of liability.

A defendant who is engaged in blasting may disrupt the public's right to safety, health, or convenience. The blasting may be showering a public road with debris or causing substantial damage to numerous other property owners. Even if the defendant is using the highest degree of care, blasting is conduct that has traditionally been subject to strict liability. (*See* Chapter 14, *supra*, Common Law Strict Liability). A person engaged in blasting may be liable regardless of the degree of fault. Under such circumstances, an action for public nuisance could be brought and the basis of the claim would be strict liability.

Another defendant could be an operator of a factory. Due to the failure to use reasonable care, the defendant's factory might allow the release of pollutants or materials that disrupt the public's rights. Again, the interference with the public's rights of health, safety, comfort, and convenience give rise to liability for a public nuisance. When the defendant's conduct is a failure to use reasonable care, the basis of the public nuisance claim is negligence. (*See* Chapter 4, *supra*, Negligence).

Finally, it is also possible that the defendant's conduct could be intentional. For example, a defendant factory owner may know that certain pollutants are being released and purposefully decide to do nothing to stop it. That level of knowledge would likely meet the definition of intent, in which case the basis of the public nuisance action would be intent. (*See* Chapter 2, *supra*, Intentional Interference with Person or Property).

Interestingly enough, there are even times when a single defendant may be subject to liability on more than one theory of liability. Imagine, for example, that the defendant is negligently releasing water that covers a public road. The defendant may not know of the interference with the public way. If the action is brought immediately, the basis of the claim would be negligence. Assume, however, that a public official notifies the defendant that the water is covering the public way. At that point, the defendant now knows of the interference. If the defendant still does nothing to remedy the problem, the conduct on the part of the defendant may become intentional, since the defendant now knows that the interference with the public way is at least substantially certain to occur.

Since a nuisance action may be based either on intent, negligence, or strict liability, a question may arise as to why the parties would be concerned about the basis of liability. The reason for such concern is that damages and available defenses may be affected by the basis of the claim. Punitive damages, for example, may be available if the nuisance is intentional. However, such damages are not available for strict liability and negligent nuisances. In regard to defenses, the basis of the claim will also indicate the nature of defenses that may be asserted. Consent, for example, is an appropriate defense for intentional nuisances, whereas in most jurisdictions comparative fault is the appropriate defense for negligence and strict liability.

C. Proper Party Plaintiff

Ordinarily, a public representative will bring the action for public nuisance. Since a public right is being threatened and, frequently, the conduct is a minor crime, the public official is the most appropriate plaintiff. The public official may bring a criminal action to prosecute the crime and then seek civil damages and injunctive relief for public nuisance. Any damages recovered in the action would be used to compensate for the harm caused, and the injunctive relief could insure that the conduct would not continue.

There are several possible public officials that may seek to bring the public nuisance action. If a public nuisance threatens the public on merely a local level, the county attorney or district attorney would be the appropriate plaintiff. If the nuisance were on a statewide level, the appropriate public official would be a state attorney general. Likewise, if the nuisance were federal or national in scope, the appropriate party would be the U.S. Attorney.

D. Private Action for Public Nuisance

Although the action for public nuisance is designed to protect the public at large, there are times when such conduct may have a special impact on an individual member of the public. In certain special circumstances, a private individual may also bring a private action for a public nuisance. There are two conditions that typically give rise to the right of a private individual to bring the action for a public nuisance. Those conditions are: (1) the private individual has suffered special harm that is *different in kind* from the harm to the general public and not just different in degree; (2) the private individual has suffered a private nuisance in conjunction with the public nuisance.

The first type of claim, where the private individual has suffered an injury different in kind from that of the general public, may be the most difficult for the private individual to bring. Imagine, for example, that one of the defendant's trees has fallen and has blocked a public way. The injury to the public is a general inconvenience in using the roadway. The plaintiff may claim that (s)he must travel this road twice a day on the way to work. The blockage causes substantial loss of time by having to detour around the tree. The courts would probably hold that the damages suffered by the plaintiff were merely different in degree and not in kind. The plaintiff is suffering greater inconvenience, but not a different kind of injury, since all members of the public who travel this same road would also be inconvenienced by this same blockage. Imagine, however, that the tree struck the plaintiff as it fell on the road blocking the roadway, or that the plaintiff tripped and fell over the tree while attempting to pass around it. That plaintiff has now suffered a special personal injury and not just inconvenience. That would be an injury different in kind and not merely in degree.

Pollution problems may also give rise to a private action for a public nuisance. When a defendant pollutes water or air, obviously the public at large is harmed by the worsening air quality or water quality. Most individuals will not have an independent claim for public nuisance since they all suffer from that same type of injury. This is true even for individuals who claim special personal injury due to the pollution (e.g., individuals with lung problems who claim that they suffer more seriously due to the air pollution). The defendants will argue that the problems suffered by those plaintiffs, while of a greater magnitude than those experienced by the general public, are still of the same type. In order for an individual to bring a private action for pollution, that individual would have to show an injury that is different in kind. If it is possible to show that the individual's work was disrupted, or some special type of personal injury arose, then that affected individual could bring the action directly.

In the previous example, *supra*, if the individual plaintiff could show that the public (pollution) nuisance also created an interference with the individual's use or enjoyment of his or her own land, then an action for public nuisance could be brought by the plaintiff individually. Such an injury is different in kind than the type of harm that it causes to the general public. Of course, this type of harm also constitutes a private nuisance and, independently, would allow the individual to bring this also as a separate cause of action. Claims for the tort of private nuisance are more fully discussed, *infra*.

II. Private Nuisance

A. Types of Claims

The claim for private nuisance is substantially different from the claim for public nuisance. Where the claim for public nuisance is designed to remedy an interference with the *public's right* to health, safety, comfort or convenience, the action for private nuisance is to protect a *private interest*. That private interest is a narrow and limited one: the plaintiff's use and/or enjoyment of his or her own private land. For a computer lesson on this topic, *see* Damages for Harms to Interests in Use and Enjoyment (of land) (CALI).

Private nuisance is, therefore, a tort claim used to protect an interest in real property. As noted earlier, private nuisance is a topic that is frequently taught in Property as well as Torts courses in law school. As a claim to protect an interest in land, it should be compared and contrasted with the tort of trespass to land. That tort is, of course, also designed to protect an interest in land. So, what is the difference between these two different causes of action?

Trespass to land is a claim that protects the possessor of land's exclusive right of *possession*. If a defendant interferes with that exclusive right of possession, then the trespass action is the appropriate remedy. Interference with the right of possession occurs merely when someone enters upon the land of another. In addition, the trespasser may commit that trespass by placing something on the land of another. (*See* Chapter 2, section III.A., *supra*, Trespass to Land).

Private nuisance is a claim that protects the possessor's right to *the use and/ or enjoyment* of the land. For this tort to occur, it is not necessary for the defendant actually to enter upon the land or even to place anything on the land. Interference with use and enjoyment may occur in numerous ways. It is that *interference* with use and enjoyment that creates the private nuisance claim.

One distinction between trespass to land and nuisance is apparent. Typically, the tort of trespass requires a physical invasion in order to be actionable. If there is such a physical invasion, then trespass and not private nuisance is the correct claim. Nuisance, however, may occur even when some type of transitory or outside circumstance gives rise to the interference. If there is no physical invasion, then trespass to land is simply not available as a claim. In such cases, the only possible claim is private nuisance. Examples of different types of interference may help illustrate the differences.

Where someone enters or walks upon the land of another, the appropriate claim is trespass to land. Obviously, the defendant has interfered with the plaintiff's exclusive right of possession. Where, however, the defendant remains entirely outside the residential property of the plaintiff but plays loud music all night long, the plaintiff could bring a claim for private nuisance. Although there has been no physical invasion to create a trespass to land, the plaintiff's use and enjoyment of his or her residence has been disrupted.

Noise is obviously one of the most common issues raised in private nuisance cases. Unusual or sustained noise in the wrong place can be treated as an interference with the use and enjoyment of land. Lights may also be treated as a private nuisance. For example, if a plaintiff's use and enjoyment of land becomes impaired because a neighbor shines excessive lights onto his or her land, the plaintiff's action would involve a private nuisance claim. Conversely, sometimes even the absence of light could also give rise to a private nuisance claim. Thus, the plaintiff might also allege that a neighboring landowner who erects tall buildings or fences to such an extent that they shut out light and air from reaching the plaintiff's land has created a private nuisance.

Odors or smells could also be raised as a possible private nuisance claim. A plaintiff who is concerned that the defendant has produced such strong odors or smells on the neighboring property as to make it difficult for the plaintiff to remain on his or her own land may have a claim for private nuisance.

Sometimes it is not always clear whether the proper claim is one for private nuisance or trespass to land. For example, consider situations where smoke drifts onto the plaintiff's land because of some activity conducted on the defendant's neighboring property. Scientists and engineers recognize that smoke is usually the combined presence of super-heated gases and tiny particles. As this combination of gases and particles drift onto another's land, it obviously can interfere with the possessor's use and enjoyment of that land, thus giving rise to a claim for private nuisance as discussed, *supra*. However, the presence of the tiny particles that enter in the airspace immediately above the plaintiff's land also appears to be an actual physical invasion. If the court determines that the entry of these tiny particles constitutes a physical invasion, then the appropriate claim would be one for trespass to land. Likewise, if the tiny smoke particles begin to build up to such an extent that they leave a physical residue on the plaintiff's property then the court will almost certainly conclude that the appropriate claim is trespass to land. However, if the smoke appears to have been merely transitory and leaves no residue, then the claim is for private nuisance. Careful plaintiff's lawyers will probably plead such cases in the alternative, alleging both trespass to land and private nuisance.

There are times when the conduct of the defendant may give rise to both a private and a public nuisance claim. Imagine, for example, that the defendant has blocked a public road that leads to the plaintiff's land, thereby disrupting plaintiff's access to his or her property altogether. Although the defendant has created a public nuisance by interfering with the public's right to use the road, the plaintiff here may still bring the action for public nuisance as a private individual. This is because the plaintiff's injury is "different in kind" (i.e., interference with access to the plaintiff's private land) than the injury to the public (i.e., blocking a public road). Of course, the defendant's interference with access to the land also disrupts the plaintiff's use and enjoyment of the land. Because of that disruption, an action for private nuisance would also be appropriate. This is another example where careful plaintiffs' attorneys could plead in the alternative. Those attorneys would plead both the public nuisance with an injury different in kind and a private nuisance. Most cases of this type, however, seem to be litigated on a private nuisance theory.

As noted earlier, zoning laws and regulations have removed many problems from the area of law traditionally enforced by nuisance actions. A landowner cannot complain that the mere presence of a lawfully zoned business is interfering with the use and enjoyment of his or her property. Thus, a service station conducting business in a lawful manner within an area that has been zoned for such a purpose would not be a private nuisance merely by virtue of its location next to the plaintiff's private residence. However, if the service station conducts it business in a negligent or otherwise unpermitted manner, such as by creating excessive lighting, noise, odors, or trash, then the plaintiff may have a claim for private nuisance. The service station may conduct business in the area for which it was zoned, but it must do so in an appropriate manner.

The basic rules governing actions for private nuisance are fairly easy to state, and claims are generally allowed where there is an interference with the plaintiff's use and/or enjoyment of land. However, as the foregoing discussion illustrates, the facts and circumstances that give rise to such claims are quite varied. In the end, typically courts and juries must analyze the facts in each individual case to determine whether the claim for private nuisance is valid.

B. Bases of Liability

As with public nuisance, private nuisance is not a new and separate basis of liability. Instead, it is an area of the law that combines all three categories of tort liability: intent, negligence, and strict liability. Thus, a private nuisance action, just like public nuisance actions discussed previously (*see* section I.B, *supra*), may be grounded in any of those three bases of liability. And, much like public nuisance, the same conduct by the defendant may also involve all three bases in the period leading up to the litigation of the claim.

Thus, one defendant may be engaging in otherwise lawful blasting on his or her own property. Nevertheless, if the noise, soot, and vibrations are disrupting the use and enjoyment of the plaintiff's adjoining property, then there may be an action for private nuisance. Since blasting is one of the classic examples of strict liability (*see* Chapter 14, *supra*, Common Law Strict Liability), the plaintiff's basis of the private nuisance claim would be strict liability, and the plaintiff's nuisance claim could be brought without any proof of fault on the part of the defendant.

Another defendant may be allowing excessive smoke or odors to escape from his or her property due to the defendant's failure to use reasonable care to monitor such emissions, causing the odors and smoke to interfere with a neighbor's use and enjoyment of land. If this occurs the plaintiff neighbor may bring a claim for private nuisance, relying upon the defendant's negligence as the basis of the claim. The plaintiff would prove the failure to use reasonable care as part of the private nuisance claim. (*See* Chapter 4, *supra*, Negligence).

Finally, assume that for some reason the defendant gets angry at a neighbor, and as a result of that anger the defendant sets up floodlights that direct light into the neighbor's bedroom windows in the nighttime. Due to the strong light, the use and enjoyment of the plaintiff neighbor's land is disrupted. The plaintiff would have an action for private nuisance, and would utilize the defendant's intentional misconduct as the basis for proving the claim. (*See* Chapter 2, *supra*, Intentional Interference with Person or Property).

Just as with public nuisance claims (*see* section I.B., *supra*), there are times when a private nuisance claim may also be established by asserting more than one basis of liability. Suppose that the defendant neighbor allows odors and smoke to escape from his or her property due to the defendant's failure to use reasonable care. After enduring this for some period of time, the plaintiff goes to the defendant and complains about the odors and smoke, and informs the defendant that they are interfering with the plaintiff's use and enjoyment of land. If the defendant fails to remedy the situation after learning of the plaintiff's concerns, any further continuation of the odors and smoke by the defendant is now intentional, since (s)he knows that such continued action is creating the claimed tortious interference to a substantial certainty. Therefore, under these circumstances, the defendant's conduct that may have started merely as a negligent private nuisance was elevated to an intentional private nuisance by the defendant's knowledge of the consequences that it was causing.

C. Substantial Harm

Whether the plaintiff's claim is one for public or private nuisance, the harm suffered must be substantial. The concept of substantial harm is difficult and appears to involve something of a balancing test. Often comparing the extent of harm to a variety of different factors, courts have had different ways of expressing that balance.

Some cases have indicated that the claim for nuisance cannot be used to protect a hypersensitive use of one's land. If, for example, a particular plaintiff has excessively high expectations of quiet or is growing sensitive plants on his or her property, courts typically will not allow such an unusually hypersensitive plaintiff to control the actions of neighbors merely to satisfy the plaintiff's excessively high expectation. The action of nuisance is only designed to protect reasonable uses of land, and the concept of reasonableness, just as in the tort of negligence, is determined on the basis of an objective standard rather than a subjective one. (*See* Chapter 4, *supra*, Negligence).

Social custom or expectations may also be considered in determining when harm is substantial. If the community customs or expectations are consistent with the defendant's use of the land, then an action for nuisance is generally unavailable. For example, where defendants are otherwise lawfully operating a factory in an area that is already primarily being used for factories, then a single plaintiff will not be allowed to complain. The presence of factories in the community seems to fall within the accepted social custom or reasonable expectation of that community. If, however, the defendant is operating the same factory in the middle of a residential neighborhood, then an action for nuisance may be appropriate.

Another factor that is considered in nuisance actions is continuity of the conduct. In order for circumstances to give rise to a nuisance, many courts will look to the continuing nature of the activity. If, for example, a defendant causes a one-time escape of odors or smoke, then the court would probably rule that the escape was not a nuisance. If, however, the odors and smoke are released on a regular and continuing basis, the conduct more resembles that of a nuisance.

Continuity, however, is not a conclusive factor. Continuity must be considered together with other factors such as the magnitude of the harm. The greater the magnitude of the harm, the more likely the court will find the conduct to be a nuisance, even if it is not continuous in nature. If, for example, the defendant causes the release of smoke on only one occasion, but that smoke was so acidic as to peel the paint off surrounding homes, then the conduct looks like a nuisance.

The more typical cases of nuisance, of course, generally involve a combination of these factors, including both magnitude and continuity, all of which occur in a manner that exceeds social custom and expectation. Such actions usually result in a continuing as well as serious interference with the use and enjoyment of land in an area where such conduct is otherwise inappropriate.

D. Remedies

As with most torts, the reason for bringing a private nuisance claim is to seek compensation for the harm that has been done. However, nuisance claims are different from many torts. Whereas an automobile accident may be a one-time event with clearly contained damages, a nuisance may involve a long set of circumstances with repeated or recurring damages. Thus, a plaintiff in a nuisance action may want more than just a one-time payment of damages to remedy a past injury. A plaintiff in a nuisance claim may seek damages for the past injury, as well as damages for all future harm or reduction in the value of the property, and also an injunction to prevent the future occurrence of the nuisance. All of these remedies are potentially available in a nuisance action.

1. Damages

As with most tort claims, compensatory damages are available for the harm caused by a nuisance. (*See* Chapter 8, *supra*, Compensatory and Punitive

Damages). In the typical private nuisance case, there may have been some harm to the plaintiff's land due to the existence of the nuisance, and that harm is certainly compensable. The formula for determining the loss for harm to the land is to take the fair market value of the land as it existed just prior the injury and subtract the fair market value immediately after the nuisance. The resulting figure is the typical measure of damages to the land itself due to the nuisance.

Since a nuisance claim may be based on intent, there is also a possibility for the recovery of punitive damages. Thus, when the plaintiff can prove that the defendant's conduct was intentional, gross, willful, or wanton, the plaintiff may seek punitive damages as well.

Damages are usually the remedy most preferred by courts, if the amount of damages can be determined and a clear monetary judgment entered. However, injunctive relief is also usually available in private nuisance actions.

2. Injunctions

Injunctions are a form of equitable remedy. However, ordinarily equitable remedies are not available for most tort claims. This is because tort law is generally considered to be a "legal" matter, and as such the award of damages is considered to be an adequate remedy with respect to most tort actions. Therefore, the legal remedy of damages is typically preferred (as opposed to equitable remedies) in most tort actions.

Since private nuisance claims, however, are concerned with an interest in land, equitable remedies may also be available. A standard rule in equity is that such remedies are only available when the remedy at law (i.e., damages) is inadequate. Where land is concerned, every tract of land is considered unique. As a result, merely compensating the owner for harms by paying money damages would be inadequate. Therefore, in private nuisance cases courts generally also consider equitable remedies that may be available to protect the plaintiff's use and enjoyment of land. For a computer lesson on the topic, *see* Equitable Remedies—An Overview (CALI).

The equitable remedy that is most commonly available is the injunction. The plaintiff will typically ask the court to issue an injunction (i.e., a special court order) preventing the defendant from continuing the conduct that created the nuisance. In simple cases this is an easy remedy. Where, for example, one neighbor leaves floodlights on all night and those lights shine into the plaintiff's bedroom windows, the court might simply grant an injunction that forces the neighbor to turn off the floodlights after dark, or at some other appropriate later time prior to the plaintiff's bedtime.

However, many nuisance cases involve much more complex issues pertaining to injunctive relief. The more typical case arises when a plaintiff seeks to close down a business or factory because of noise, odors, smoke, and pollution. In this type of case, an injunction involves far more than simply requiring someone to turn off a few lights, as in the previous example, *supra*. If the court enters an injunction to prevent the defendant's factory from creating any noise, odors, smoke, and pollution, then the business or factory will probably have to close. To consider issuing such an injunction, the courts typically go through a process whereby they "balance the equities." In doing so, the court will weigh the value of the business against the needs of the individual plaintiff(s). The court may, for example, consider the capital investment, the number of jobs created, the extent of the payroll, and the amount of taxes paid by the defendant's business. By looking at those numbers, the court may determine that the size and value of the business is substantially more than the value of the plaintiff's claimed use and enjoyment of the land. The court may then refuse to grant the injunction, often choosing, instead, to compensate the plaintiff in damages for the permanent *future* loss of any use and enjoyment that would likely result from the defendant's continued operation of the factory.

Good examples of "balancing the equities" may be found in a series of older cases that involved an industry in the southeastern corner of Tennessee that was alleged to be polluting. When local residents sought injunctive relief to shut down the industry, the Supreme Court of Tennessee refused to grant the injunction, on the theory that closing the industry would have too great of an impact on too many people in the local community. *Madison v. Ducktown Sulphur, Copper & Iron Co.*, 113 Tenn. 331, 83 S.W. 658 (1904). When, however, the neighboring state of Georgia brought a similar action, claiming that pollution from this same industry was causing damage to a substantial part of that state, the United States Supreme Court was willing to grant the injunction, concluding that the interest of the whole state of Georgia was larger than the interests of the industry in just that small portion of the state of Tennessee. *Georgia v. Tennessee Copper Co.*, 206 U.S. 230 (1907).

Just because the injunctive relief is denied does not mean that the plaintiff cannot recover any remedy. The plaintiff may still be entitled to receive compensatory damages. However, as explained in the example, *supra*, the computation of such damages must reflect all of the plaintiff's loss, including compensation for reduction in the before and after market value of the plaintiff's use and enjoyment of the land with respect to all future harm as well as past harm. Therefore, the plaintiff would also recover compensation for the reduced market value of the property due to the defendant's continuation of the nuisance.

One of the objections often stated when injunctions are refused is that the courts are "licensing" the nuisance to continue. By allowing the business to continue to operate and only requiring the defendant to pay nuisance damages for any harm that it may cause, even future harm, courts are essentially permitting the business to pay for the right to pollute. In response, some courts have offered, as justification for denying injunctive relief, that in a crowded world certain businesses are needed, and if every injunction were granted, the loss of jobs, investments, and other financial gains would be huge.

E. Defenses Consistent with Basis of Claim

The defenses available in a nuisance action provide an interesting study in tort law. Since a nuisance may be based upon intent, negligence or strict liability, the defenses may vary significantly, depending upon the underlying basis for the nuisance claim. Generally, the defenses that may be used in nuisance are the very same as those that otherwise would be traditionally asserted in defense of each of these specific bases of liability. Thus, if the nuisance claim is based on intent, the appropriate defenses are the same as those for intentional torts. (*See* Chapter 3, *supra*, Defenses to Intentional Torts). For nuisance claims based on negligence, the defenses are those that are otherwise appropriate for negligent torts. (*See* Chapter 12, *supra*, Defenses to Negligence). Likewise, if the nuisance claim is based on strict liability, the defenses are those appropriate for strict liability torts.

1. Intent

When a nuisance is the result of intentional conduct, the defendant may be able to use the traditional common law defenses to intent as a defense to the claim. (*See* Chapter 3, *supra*, Defenses to Intentional Torts). The most commonly used defense to an intentional nuisance claim is that of consent. If the plaintiff has consented to the existence of the nuisance, that consent is a defense to a nuisance claim based upon intent. Consent could, of course, arise in several ways. For example, the plaintiff may have expressly consented to the nuisance when the defendant first checks with surrounding neighbors (including the plaintiff) and receives their prior approval to engage in certain activities that might otherwise be considered a nuisance. Such prior approval could qualify as an express consent. In the alternative, the plaintiff might have consented to the defendant's nuisance by implication. For example, when the defendant's nuisance-based conduct is apparent and the plaintiff offers no objection, the defendant might be able to assert that the plaintiff impliedly consented to the nuisance.

One significant difficulty with proving consent by implication involves the doctrine that deals with the concept of moving to an existing nuisance. Where the plaintiff moves into any area that already contains a known nuisance, such conduct by the plaintiff would appear to create an implied consent for that nuisance to continue. However, the courts have not treated moving to a nuisance as an absolute bar to recovery in every instance. *See* the discussion of "Moving to the Nuisance" in section II.E.4, *infra*.

2. Negligence

If a nuisance is created by negligence, the traditional common law defenses to negligence will apply. Today, such defenses also include comparative fault. (*See* Chapter 12, *supra*, Defenses to Negligence).

Suppose that a defendant is allowing smoke to escape and obstruct the view on a public road. That would, of course, create a public nuisance. If the plaintiff drove along the road and had an accident because of the obstructed view, the resulting harm would be an injury that is different in kind, for which the plaintiff could also bring a private action for that public nuisance. In defense of such a claim, the defendant might allege that the plaintiff failed to use reasonable care for his or her own safety, and that this failure was a substantial cause of the accident. For example, the defendant might claim that the plaintiff observed the smoke and negligently continued to drive into it. The courts would allow the defendant to use such a claim to help reduce or bar the plaintiff's recovery. The ultimate award would, of course, be a question of fact for the jury under either traditional contributory negligence or comparative negligence, depending upon the jurisdiction.

Since assumption of risk is also a traditional negligence defense that is now a part of comparative fault in most jurisdictions, that defense would also be available for most negligent nuisance claims. As noted previously, however, moving to the nuisance would not be an absolute bar to recovery. If the plaintiff knew there was a nuisance in the area and with that knowledge still bought land nearby (possibly even at a reduced price because of the presence of the nuisance), those facts would not be treated as assumption of risk. Instead, such facts would likely be treated as moving to the nuisance. *See* the discussion of "Moving to the Nuisance" that appears in section II.E.4, *infra*.

3. Strict Liability

The defenses that are generally available to strict liability claims are also available to defendants in a strict liability nuisance case. Today, those defenses are usually seen as part of most comparative fault regimens (even though strict liability is not based upon any fault by the defendant). The discussions that appear in the section on negligence defenses (*see* section II.E.2., *supra*) and moving to a nuisance (*see* section II.E.4., *infra*) are equally applicable to the strict liability nuisances as well.

4. Moving to the Nuisance

One of the most difficult issues with nuisance law and the appropriate defenses involves the issue of *moving to* the nuisance. Cases have arisen where the plaintiff knew that a nuisance existed in a particular place but nevertheless still chose to purchase property in that same area. Then, after moving into close proximity to the nuisance-causing activity, the plaintiff files suit alleging that the defendant's actions create a nuisance that interferes with the plaintiff's use and enjoyment of the land.

This type of conduct on the part of the plaintiff appears to fit within the facts and circumstances of several defenses. For example, if the plaintiff alleges an intentional nuisance, then the plaintiff's conduct in moving to the nuisance looks like implied consent. The plaintiff knew of the nuisance-causing activity, but still chose to purchase land in the same area. By doing so, it certainly would appear that the plaintiff was consenting to the nuisance activity, at least impliedly if not also expressly, depending upon the circumstances. (*See* section II.E.1., *supra*).

Likewise, if the plaintiff alleges a negligence or strict liability based nuisance, the fact that the plaintiff by moving to the nuisance appears to have either assumed the risk or been contributorily negligent would seem to be an appropriate defense, since the plaintiff knew about and understood the harmful nature of the nuisance-causing conduct and nevertheless voluntarily chose to encounter it. Under these facts the defendant might well assert the plaintiff's assumption of the risk or contributory negligence (or comparative fault, depending upon the jurisdiction) as a defense. (*See* section II.E.2., *supra*).

Despite the apparent availability of these potential defenses, however, there are certain economic reasons that may otherwise justify "moving to the nuisance" in certain situations. If the nuisance-causing activity was obvious and well known before the plaintiff purchased the neighboring land, then the purchase price of that land should have reflected its proximity to that nuisance. Presumably, prospective buyers would offer less for the land when its use and enjoyment is already disrupted by the known existence of a nuisance. To allow the plaintiff to purchase land for a reduced price, and then recover damages or injunctive relief because of the very nuisance that created the reduced price, would appear to grant the plaintiff a windfall recovery.

Thus, when the facts appear to satisfy these traditional defenses it would seem that "moving to a nuisance" should bar the plaintiff's recovery. However, that is generally not the rule, and "moving to a nuisance" is not, conclusively, a defense in and of itself. Instead, courts routinely say that "moving to the nuisance" is merely one factor to be taken into account in determining whether the plaintiff has experienced "substantial harm." (*See* section II.C., *supra*).

A few examples provide an illustration regarding how courts use "moving to the nuisance" as just one factor in determining whether the requisite "substantial harm" exists. In most cases, courts do not automatically permit a nuisance to continue to exist unabated merely because it may have pre-existed some current use of the land in question. Instead, most courts recognize that over time the land use in any given area may change. Something that may have once been appropriate in an area many years ago may no longer be in the best interests of the community today. New and developing uses may simply be more appropriate. Nevertheless, courts are generally unwilling to allow plaintiffs to use the mere presence of a nuisance as a reason to engage in purely speculative land purchases. Thus, a speculative land purchaser may knowingly seek land that is subject to a nuisance in order to acquire the land at a reduced price, but having acquired such land, most courts generally do not allow them then also to maintain subsequent litigation for purposes of seeking additional windfall profits because of the presence of that nuisance.

In reviewing "moving to the nuisance" cases, the courts frequently consider the changing nature of the area in question. For example, an area may have once been appropriate for farming and livestock, but as residential areas expand, the presence of large numbers of livestock may no longer be appropriate to that same area. Thus, a plaintiff that moves into a residential area where large numbers of livestock are still kept may be entitled to seek injunctive relief against the future use of the land for livestock purposes. Courts must review the individual circumstances under the factors discussed, *supra*, in the section on "substantial harm" (*see* section II.C., *supra*), and then "balance the equities" in order to achieve a fair result among all of the affected parties. (*See* section II.D.2., *supra*).

5. Self-Help to Abate a Nuisance

One additional issue needs to be addressed in the overall consideration of the law of nuisance, and it relates to the problem of self-help to abate a nuisance. This issue usually arises in the case of a private nuisance when a landowner believes there has been an interference with his or her rights to the use and enjoyment of land.

The issue typically arises when the landowner decides that relevant rights are being disrupted and that waiting for the legal process to grant an injunction and then seeking enforcement of that injunction will take too long. Instead, the landowner may simply decide to take matters into his or her own hands by going onto the offending nuisance property and dismantling the nuisance directly. Imagine, for example, that a landowner has grown tired of large floodlights shining from a neighbor's house directly into his or her bedroom every night. Rather than waiting for the legal process to run its course, the landowner simply enters onto the neighbor's property next door and breaks the lights. Under such circumstances, the landowner whose lights were broken will promptly sue for trespass to land, and seek damage for the trespass as well as damage to the broken lights. The party who broke the lights will defend by alleging self-help in order to abate a nuisance.

The defense of self-help to abate a nuisance is not one that is frequently litigated, however, because most attorneys would generally not advise a client to use force as a means of abating a nuisance. Instead, most attorneys would advise their clients to allow the legal process to work its way through to normal conclusion. Nevertheless, where the client does engage in self-help without first seeking legal advice, and then consults the attorney only after the action for trespass has been filed, the defense of self-help might be the only possible defense that may be available to the client.

Although somewhat similar to defense of property and the defense of necessity (*see* Chapter 3, sections III. and IV., *supra* Defenses to Intentional Torts), courts are generally not inclined to support the use of self-help. However, when courts do allow such a defense, it is usually limited only to those situations where the actual force used was otherwise reasonable in light of the threatened harm. In the example, *supra*, it would seem that breaking the neighbor's lights clearly would constitute excessive force in self help of the plaintiff's mere loss of sleep.

Checkpoints

- A nuisance may be a public or a private nuisance.
- A public nuisance is a substantial interference with the public's right to health, safety, comfort, and convenience.
- Ordinarily a public representative brings a public nuisance action.
- A private person can bring an action for public nuisance when that private individual suffers an injury that is different in kind.

- A private nuisance is the interference with an individual's use and/or enjoyment of land.

- Both public and private nuisances may be based on intent, negligence, or strict liability.

- Both public and private nuisances must show that the harm exceeds the value of the activity of the defendant.

- Plaintiffs may seek damages or injunctions to stop the nuisance.

- In order to grant an injunction, the courts typically will "balance the equities."

- The basis of the claim will determine the appropriate defense for an action in nuisance.

  - Intentional nuisances can be defended with the traditional defenses to intentional torts. Those include consent.

  - Negligent nuisances can be defended with the traditional defenses to negligent torts. In most jurisdictions those include comparative fault.

  - Strict liability nuisances can be defended with the traditional defenses to strict liability. In most jurisdictions, those now also include comparative fault.

- Moving to the nuisance is not an automatic defense to a nuisance action. It is merely a factor to consider in determining whether there was substantial harm.

- Using self-help to abate a nuisance is generally not favored by the courts.

Chapter 16

Products Liability

Roadmap

- Learn about the special problems associated with various harms caused by defective consumer products.

- Understand the historical background relating to the protection of consumers from product-related injuries.

- Appreciate the rules pertaining to the modern law of products liability by understanding how they have developed from both tort and warranty origins.

- Follow the development of the law of negligence as it adapted over the years to escape the limitations imposed by the requirement of "privity."

- Recognize the specific policy considerations involved in imposing strict liability in tort for harm caused by defective consumer products.

- Learn how to identify and distinguish the three categories of product defects: manufacturing defects, design defects, and marketing (or warning) defects.

- Learn how to recognize certain distinct categories of product defects such as "unavoidably dangerous" products.

- Understand the special rules that have developed with respect to prescription drug and medical device products.

- Recognize the potential categories of product sellers and other defendants who may be liable for damages caused by defective consumer products.

- Understand the types of damages that can be recovered as the result of injuries caused by defective consumer products, including the special limitations upon the recovery of damages for mere economic losses.

- Understand how the plaintiff's recovery for harms caused by defective consumer products is affected by the plaintiff's own misconduct in relation to the use of the product.

Products liability is an area of the law that governs the responsibility of sellers of products for injuries caused by product defects. Since its uncertain beginnings in the mid-19th century, this area of tort law has grown in importance to become one of the major sources of modern tort litigation. Much of this growth has occurred since the adoption of strict products liability in the 1960s, but to understand that development and the policy concerns that drove it, we must first examine the earlier experiments with imposing liability against the sellers of defective products based upon traditional negligence and warranty causes of action. It remains a feature of products liability that even today suits are brought on all of these theories of recovery.

Multiple theories are used in products liability litigation because this area of the law sits close to the intersection of tort and contract. Lurking somewhere in the background of most products liability actions is a contract for the sale of goods. The law of sales has highly developed rules governing the rights of purchasers and sellers of goods, and when the dispute about responsibility for injury caused by product defects involves the original buyer and seller, it is only natural to look to this body of law and to these parties' contract of sale to resolve it. The Uniform Commercial Code, for example, contains provisions for the operation and limitation of express and implied warranties. (*E.g.*, UCC sections 2-313–2-316.) When the parties have contracted with one another (i.e., when they are in "privity of contract") this law provided a good starting point for determining liability. Where the parties were strangers to one another, however, and if they lack privity of contract, then tort law was preferred since it governed accidental injuries inflicted between strangers. Nevertheless, in the nineteenth century courts were initially reluctant to extend negligence liability to this problem, for reasons that still resonate today.

I. Historical Background: Identifying the Policy Issues

Judges in the nineteenth century saw significant objections to extending liability in negligence. For example, consider the following type of situation:

> "If A. build[s] a wagon and sell[s] it to B., who sells it to C., and C. hires it to D., who in consequence of the gross negligence of A. in building the wagon is overturned and injured, D. cannot recover damages against A., the builder. A.'s obligation to build the wagon faithfully, arises solely out of his contract with B. The public have nothing to do with it." *Thomas v. Winchester*, 6 N.Y. 397, 408 (1852).

In the example, *supra*, the remoteness of the victim, D, from the negligence of the builder, A, injects considerable uncertainty into D's negligence claim. Questions arise whether the accident could be attributed to negligent maintenance by B or C, as well as whether D's use of the wagon was one that could have been anticipated by the builder. Furthermore, the parties in this case are connected by a daisy chain of contracts, and so it might be possible for D to sue C for renting him a defective wagon, and then C might try to pass the liability up the line until it reached the responsible party. On the other hand, if these various different contracts limited this responsibility, D might be out of luck. This possibility points up another concern, which is that this type of negligence action had the potential for imposing an unknown scope of liability on one of the parties to the original contract for the construction of the wagon. In an age that took a narrow view of even third party beneficiaries, this prospect threatened to disrupt the narrow world of private ordering by contract. No longer would the contract itself define the limit of a seller's responsibility; instead, tort law would impose additional duties of care to unknown third party users of the product. The courts feared that this could expose the parties to almost unlimited liability, an anathema to classical contract doctrine. It also made the manufacturer responsible for the conduct of unknown users of the product. A manufacturer might be able to estimate the needs and skills of the immediate purchaser, but would have no way of guessing whether remote users would be skilled and careful, or perhaps unskilled and in need of greater protection and safety.

The English case of *Winterbottom v. Wright,* 10 M. & W. 109, 152 Eng. Rep. 402 (Exch. 1842), is the classic exposition of this rule, as the court held that no negligence claim could arise where the parties were not in privity of contract. However, a number of exceptions soon modified the rule, of which the most important was the exception for products considered to be imminently dangerous to human life. This exception first appeared in *Thomas v. Winchester,* 6 N.Y. 397 (1852). There the defendant had mislabeled a bottle of poisonous belladonna as harmless extract of dandelion. The defendant sold the mislabeled bottle to a druggist, who resold it to a doctor, who in turn sold it to the victim's husband. The court viewed the danger of a bottle of mislabeled poison as a problem that very much involved the public, and not just the immediate purchaser (the druggist), who was more likely to resell it than to use it personally. In other words, the foreseeability of harm to remote third parties was clear, the danger was significant, and the contract did not draw the boundary of the defendant's duty. The expanded scope of liability also provided an additional incentive for safety on the part of those who traded in products that were so likely to cause harm to third parties. Finally, it should be noted that the intermediate parties were all reasonably acting in reliance on the defendant's label, so the case did not involve significant issues of intervening cause.

Courts recognized the *Thomas v. Winchester* exception to the traditional "privity" rule because the causal responsibility was clear and the risk to remote parties was both foreseeable and significant. Similar concerns led to the subsequent recognition of another exception in cases where the defendant in fact knew that the product contained a dangerous and latent defect when it was placed on the market. Liability was extended to anyone who might use the product, regardless of privity of contract, since once again the responsibility was clear and the risk to third parties was not only foreseeable, but also in fact known to the defendant. Indeed, the defendant's knowledge of the danger gives these cases an aspect of fraud that had long been a recognized ground for extra-contractual liability. Beyond these limited exceptions, however, the courts were long unwilling to go.

A. Negligence Escapes the Privity Limitation

The manufacturing and commercial developments of the industrial revolution began to strain the assumptions of the privity model. No longer did buyers deal directly with the manufacturer, and the manufacturer made a product tailored to a mass market rather than to an individual consumer. The "privity" rule protected manufacturers who dealt with consumers only through dealers and retailers, and therefore undermined important incentives for manufacturers to construct products carefully. Moreover, the use of the product by remote third parties could not plausibly be called unforeseeable; rather, it had become the norm.

MacPherson v. Buick Motor Co., 111 N.E. 1050 (N.Y. 1916), is the case credited with overturning the "privity" rule for negligence actions involving defective products. The plaintiff was injured while driving his Buick Model 10 when one of the wheels, which the plaintiff claimed was made of defective wood, collapsed while the car was in motion. Privity of contract did not exist because the plaintiff had purchased the car through a dealer. Likewise, the plaintiff could not invoke the second exception to the "privity" rule (discussed *supra*), because there was no evidence that Buick knew of the defect. Instead, the plaintiff argued that Buick was negligent in not discovering the defect through proper testing and inspection of the wheel, which Buick had obtained from an independent supplier. The "imminently dangerous" exception, *supra*, did not seem to apply either, because an automobile's purpose was not destructive like poison or explosives. Nevertheless, the New York court, in an opinion by Judge Cardozo, ruled that the lack of privity of contract would not bar the claim. In doing do, the court explained that: "If the nature of a thing is such that it is reasonably certain to place life and limb in peril when negligently made, it is then a thing of danger." *Id*. at 1053. In other words, the key became the foreseeability of harm to the remote user of the product, to whom a duty was owed by the manufacturer to use due care in the construction of the product.

Significant barriers to recovery in negligence remained, however, even after the removal of the "privity" rule. Most obviously, the plaintiff still had to prove that the seller was negligent in the preparation of the product, a task that could be difficult when the plaintiff had little knowledge about the manufacturing process, while the defendant could always introduce evidence of its quality control. In some cases, however, a plaintiff could overcome this difficulty by using the evidentiary doctrine of *res ipsa loquitur*, that allowed the jury to infer negligence just from the occurrence of the accident, which in practical terms meant from the mere existence of the defect itself. As a further limitation on the action, contributory negligence and assumption of the risk could be invoked as defenses that totally barred the plaintiff's recovery. The plaintiff simply could not recover anything if (s)he had failed to exercise due care in using the product, or if the plaintiff used the product in spite of being aware of the defect. As Judge Cardozo observed in *MacPherson*: "It is possible to use almost anything in a way that will make it dangerous if defective." *Id*. Thus, although negligence had escaped the limitations of the "privity" doctrine, recovery by plaintiffs in many cases was still far from assured.

B. The Policy Argument for Strict Liability in Tort: The *Escola* Concurrence

For a glimpse of the state of products liability litigation in the mid-20th century, consider the case of *Escola v. Coca-Cola Bottling Co.*, 150 P.2d 436 (Cal. 1944). There, the plaintiff waitress received severe cuts when a bottle of Coca-Cola exploded in her hand. The basis of her claim was negligence, but she was forced to rely on *res ipsa* because of the lack of any specific evidence of neglect on the part of the defendant. Even this approach was questionable, however, since the element of "exclusive control" was uncertain, given the number of parties besides the defendant bottling company that had handled the bottle, including the manufacturer of the bottle, the restaurant where the plaintiff was working when the accident occurred, as well as the plaintiff herself. The majority of the California Supreme Court, however, heroically helped the plaintiff over these hurdles, stretching the *res ipsa* doctrine to the breaking point along the way. The court affirmed a verdict in the plaintiff's favor, and broadly construed the "exclusive control" requirement of the *res ipsa* doctrine to apply to the time when the defendant had exercised exclusive control over the bottle back when it was inspected for defects and charged with gas at the defendant's bottling plant. *Id.* at 440. Although the plaintiff in *Escola* eventually did prevail in her negligence action, the case is mostly remembered today for the concurring opinion by Justice Traynor. That opinion laid out a policy rationale for the adoption of strict liability for injuries caused by defective products.

Justice Traynor argued that strict liability would accomplish at least four desirable policy goals. First, strict liability would encourage manufacturers to reduce the hazards created by defective products by providing a stronger incentive to eliminate defects. In Justice Traynor's view, the manufacturer is often in the best position to know about the potential dangers from defects and to take the necessary precautions against them. Second, strict liability would perform a loss shifting and loss spreading function. The losses from product-related injuries will be shifted to manufacturers, who can better anticipate these costs and spread them among the public through its pricing of the product. Strict liability in this way would perform an insurance function, pooling the risk from potential product defects by having each consumer pay a small portion of the expected accident costs as part of the price of the product. In this way, accident costs would not be allowed to crush a single injured victim, but instead would be shared relatively painlessly by all the consumers of the product. Third, strict products liability would simplify the trial of these actions by eliminating many difficult factual issues typically associated with proving the defendant's negligence. Finally, strict liability would help to rationalize developments in the law of implied warranty. Rather than requiring a purchaser to sue the retailer for breach of warranty, and then allow a series of actions to pass that liability back up the chain of supply, strict liability would allow more efficient litigation directly against the party responsible for the defect.

Many commentators have criticized Justice Traynor's arguments for strict liability. For example, modern law and economics analysis suggests that negligence and strict liability should lead to the same expenditures on accident avoidance, with the only difference being which party bears the cost of the accidents that are not prevented. If so, strict liability will not necessarily be the most effective way to "reduce the hazards to life and health" caused by defective products, despite Judge Traynor's suggestion to the contrary. *Id.* at 462. Furthermore, some accidents are easier for the public to avoid, by making proper and careful use of the product. This latter point suggests that the conduct of the product user must remain an important consideration no matter which liability regime is chosen. Finally, tort litigation is inevitably a cumbersome and expensive way to provide compensation, so that mechanisms such as workers compensation and private medical, accident, and life insurance are often better and more efficient means to protect individuals from the disastrous effects of an accident or illness.

Still, one important reason for preferring strict liability to negligence is the concern that negligence does not do an adequate job of controlling the risks of an activity. In the case of products liability, we have already mentioned the difficulty plaintiffs faced in proving negligent conduct. If this logistical problem resulted in defense verdicts simply because negligence could not be proved and not because such negligence did not exist, then the negligence approach would not send a strong enough liability signal to product manufacturers, and thereby, manufacturers would not have a sufficient economic incentive to take more appropriate safety precautions. Strict liability would solve this problem by eliminating the issue of the defendant's fault and forcing manufacturers to internalize all the costs of their defective products. Such an approach might promote both product safety and administrative efficiency by simplifying the case for the plaintiff.

Eventually, the arguments in favor of strict liability carried the day. However, before turning to that development we will briefly examine an alternative avenue of recovery in defective product cases utilizing a branch of law already mentioned, *supra*: the law of implied warranty.

C. Breach of Implied Warranty and the Limits of Contract

Traditionally, those persons injured by defective products also had another theory of recovery available to them in the law of warranty. Warranty, with its roots at least partially in contract law, originally shared the privity limitation that hampered the development of recovery in negligence. However, because warranty also played an important role in purely commercial disputes, warranty causes of action in defective product cases also came with certain additional requirements, such as reliance and prompt notice to the breaching party of any breach. These additional restrictions in warranty claims could be a hindrance in personal injury actions. Contract concepts also allowed warranties to be disclaimed or limited, or the remedies for their breach to be restricted. Warranty law did, however, have at least one advantage over negligence, in that liability was strict: the fault of the defendant was not the issue, but only the failure of the product to live up to the express and implied representations made about it.

Warranty liability developed along similar lines as negligence. The implied warranty of merchantability became, in effect, a tort duty imposed by law that the goods must be non-defective and suitable for their ordinary purposes, which included a requirement that the goods must also be reasonably safe. Courts then gradually loosened or eliminated the privity requirement in personal injury actions, did not require notice, and made the implied warranty impossible to disclaim. These developments received their fullest expression in *Henningsen v. Bloomfield Motors, Inc.*, 161 A.2d 69 (N.J. 1960), where the court allowed the purchaser of a new Plymouth automobile and his wife to sue Chrysler Corporation directly, in spite of their lack of privity and an express disclaimer of all implied warranties. The evidence before the court indicated that these waivers were the result of unfair bargaining power that the ordinary consumer could not overcome, and the court therefore determined that public policy required that the consumer be protected with a non-waivable implied warranty.

II. Modern Product Liability Begins

The modern era of product liability began with the decision of the California Supreme Court in *Greenman v. Yuba Power Products*, 377 P.2d 897 (Cal. 1963), and shortly thereafter the promulgation of section 402A of the Second Restatement of Torts in 1965. In the *Greenman* case, Justice Traynor, now with a majority of the court behind him, explicitly abandoned warranty law for tort and held that: "A manufacturer is strictly liable in tort when an article he places on the market, knowing it is to be used without inspection for defects, proves to have a defect that causes injury to a human being." *Id.* at 900. The American Law Institute then almost immediately afterwards incorporated this new rule of liability in section 402A, imposing strict liability on sellers of products that are in a "defective condition unreasonably dangerous to the user or consumer," if the seller was in the business of selling the product. In this form, the rule was quickly adopted by a majority of the states. Subsequent case law has led to a further refinement and amplification of these original rules, to the extent that products liability now has its own independent section of the Third Restatement of Torts. The remainder of this chapter will examine the rules that govern liability for defective products.

A. Defect: Manufacturing Defect

A product seller is not liable simply because its product caused an injury. Rather, liability is imposed when the product has a defect of some kind, and this defect in the product is the cause of the harm. A manufacturing defect is the most straightforward example. Here, in the words of the Third Restatement, "the product departs from its intended design even though all possible care was exercised in the preparation and marketing of the product." RESTATEMENT (THIRD) OF TORTS: PRODUCTS LIABILITY §2(a). Under this approach, the standard of comparison between a defective and a non-defective product is the manufacturer's own intended design, and the liability that is imposed is strict, since care in preparation does not matter. In this way, the basic policy concerns of strict liability are carried forward into the new Third Restatement: plaintiffs are not required to prove negligence, thereby simplifying their burden of proof, and manufacturers can set their level of quality control based on the expected number of accidents, whose costs can then be spread among product users as a component of the price. Manufacturing defects present the purest case of strict products liability.

Nevertheless, sometimes plaintiffs can still face significant burdens in proving a case of strict liability. For example, proving the existence of the defect may be difficult if the product was destroyed in the accident, or, if the tainted food was thrown out before it could be tested for defects or impurities. Furthermore, even if a product defect can be proven, the existence of that defect also must be traced back to the sale of the product by the target defendant. This means that a defect resulting from some later alteration of the product by the retailer would not result in liability against the manufacturer. As with most other tort claims, the plaintiff still must establish the requisite causation, proving that the product *defect* itself (not simply the product) in fact caused the injury that was otherwise foreseeable. Finally, the plaintiff can expect to face charges that the injury did not result from the product defect, but rather from the plaintiff's contributory negligence or misuse of the product. These issues, however, are mainly problems of proving the necessary facts to support the claim; the law itself is relatively clear.

B. Defect: Design Defect

Developing a workable rule for judging when a product is defectively designed has proved more challenging. In comparison to manufacturing defects, a defectively designed product has turned out just the way the manufacturer intended. For this reason, no obvious standard of comparison is available by which to judge whether the product as designed is more dangerous than it ought to be. Defective design cases have been around from the beginning of strict product liability (i.e., the *Greenman* case, *supra*, was a design defect case), but the proper standard for making the crucial judgment of defect was uncertain. The text and comments to section 402A did not even identify the special problems inherent in determining design defects. Instead, it merely imposed liability generally if the product was in a "defective condition unreasonably dangerous," and then in a comment simply defined "defective condition" as "a condition not contemplated by the ultimate consumer, which will be unreasonably dangerous to him." RESTATEMENT (SECOND) OF TORTS § 402A (1965) cmt. g. Additionally, the term "unreasonable danger" was described in another comment as "dangerous to an extent beyond that which would be contemplated by the ordinary consumer . . . with ordinary knowledge common to the community." *Id.,* comment *i.* This somewhat circular attempt to define what is defective, when applied to problems of design defect, became known as the "consumer expectations," or "consumer contemplation," test.

The "consumer expectations" test was based on the perception that consumers neither expected nor wanted products that were perfectly safe. The ordinary consumer understands, for example, that in order to perform their functions ovens must get hot, knives must be sharp, and that cars must travel at significant rates of speed, and that all of these are potentially dangerous. Because these dangers are well understood, these products are not defective in design under this view. What the ordinary consumer does not want, however, is a product that hides a latent or unknown danger, or one that includes a danger that otherwise cannot be anticipated and guarded against. So, for example, if an oven does not have sufficient insulation so that its exterior is dangerously hot to the touch or even causes a fire, that would not be a danger that the ordinary consumer would expect under a "consumer expectations" test. Similarly, Mr. Greenman's Shopsmith lathe was defective because an ordinary consumer would expect it to hold the wood being turned in place, rather than coming apart during ordinary operation and allowing the wood to fly out and strike the operator. The unexpected danger in the product in these cases is enough to categorize the design as defective, and any product with similar hidden and unexpected danger is probably also defective. But, design defect litigation did not stop there. Instead, the consumer contemplation test tended to act as a minimum standard of liability, and left open the question of what other types of designs might be "defective." What should the rule be, for example, if the expectations of consumers were not clear, or if the product could easily be made safer, and the manufacturer simply decided not to do so? Imposing liability in such cases would require a different approach to design defect liability.

Consider, for example, the problem of an obvious danger such as the lack of a safety guard on a machine tool, or the lack of a protective cage for the operator of a forklift. An ordinary consumer contemplating the product might conclude that it is extremely unsafe, which under the "consumer expectations" test would mean that the product is not defectively designed: the low expectation of safety means that the ordinary consumer of such a product would not be misled or surprised by these dangerous propensities. What the consumer might well not be able to judge, however, is whether the product could easily have been made safer by a design change in the product. Such a design change could significantly reduce injuries from the product, but it would also probably result in increased costs for the product, and perhaps even a potential loss of usefulness if the safety feature makes the product harder to use in some circumstances. These considerations, as noted, *supra*, are beyond the experience and expectations of the ordinary consumer. Nevertheless, such factors still might be assessed in a subsequent trial conducted after the fact of the plaintiff's injury, all in an attempt to consider whether the original design was defective because the manufacturer could have made it safer but did not.

The standard by which courts have attempted to perform this hindsight design analysis became known as the "risk-utility" test. This test was an explicit attempt to balance the benefits and risks of a particular design to determine if it was reasonably safe. In its most popular form the risk-utility test considered such factors as:

(1) the utility of the product;
(2) the seriousness of the dangers posed by the product;
(3) the availability of safer substitute products;
(4) the ability to design a safer product that would still be useable and affordable;
(5) the user's ability to avoid the danger by being careful;
(6) the user's awareness of the dangers of the product; and
(7) the manufacturer's ability to spread the loss through the price of the product or by means of insurance.

It should be noted that this collection of factors covers a wide and confusing array of considerations that go well beyond simply a comparison of the risks and utility of the product. Also included in the mix of considerations is the existence of substitutes or design changes, as well as the consumer's own knowledge of the risks and ability to use the product safely. With no guidance regarding exactly how all these factors are to be weighed, the test tends to give lawyers lots to talk about, but hardly creates a bright line test for determining whether a given design is defective.

Under this approach, the existence of a safer design or a safer substitute product is only one factor to consider in determining whether the product is defective. This also opens the possibility that a jury could find that a product was defective even though no alternative was available; in other words, that the product was so unsafe and had so little utility that it should not even be marketed at all. Although actual cases of such a finding are rare, perhaps the best known example is *O'Brien v. Muskin*, 463 A.2d 298 (N.J. 1983), involving a vinyl liner for an above-ground swimming pool. Nevertheless, lawyers have argued for such liability for products such as tobacco, alcohol, or handguns.

The new Restatement (Third) of Torts: Products Liability generally argues against such categorical liability, instead effectively making proof of an alternative safer design a requirement for recovery on a design defect theory: "A product . . . is defective in design when the foreseeable risks of harm posed by the product could have been reduced or avoided by the adoption of a reasonable alternative design . . . and the omission of the alternative design renders the product not reasonably safe. . . . " RESTATEMENT (THIRD) OF TORTS: PRODUCTS LIABILITY § 2(b). However, the Third Restatement does still recognize at least the possibility of a "manifestly unreasonable design," in which the very design feature that makes the product unreasonably dangerous is also the feature that makes it desirable, so that no alternative product is possible. The Third Restatement gives an exploding cigar as an example of this type of product design. Apart from such unusual products, however, proof of a reasonable safer design is generally required. This is the one of the more debated aspects of the new Third Restatement, and some courts that previously had adopted the "risk utility" test have refused to require proof of an alternative safer design. On the other hand, a number of state legislatures have passed tort reform statutes specifically requiring such proof. *See, e.g.,* Tex. Civ. Prac. & Rem. Code § 82.005.

So, what exactly is a "safer alternative design?" First, the design change must result in an increase in safety sufficient to have prevented or significantly reduced the harm to the plaintiff. This is a fundamental causation requirement. The new design also should not introduce significant new dangers as the cost of eliminating the risk that harmed the plaintiff. In addition, the alternative design must be one that the manufacturer could feasibly have adopted at the time the product was marketed. The "feasibility" of the new design involves a multi-pronged inquiry. Many safety features also reduce the utility of the product by making it harder or more inconvenient to use. The overall safety gain must be worth this loss of utility, so that the greater the gain in safety, the more loss of utility can be tolerated. The safety precaution must also use technology that was available to the manufacturer given the "state of the art" that existed in the industry at the time of manufacture. In other words, the design is judged at the time of manufacture, and generally subsequent technological advances do not retroactively make older products "defective."

Finally, the alternative design must be economically viable in the marketplace, so that a proposed safety feature that would render the product too expensive to market successfully would not be required. In sum, the alternative design must be one that is practicable in all these ways, while still likely to have prevented the harm.

The actual design of the product that harmed the plaintiff is then weighed against this theoretical alternative, in an attempt to decide whether its design renders it "not reasonably safe." In other words, the actual design might be less safe (at least in some respects) without being defective, when such factors as utility, consumer preference, the obviousness of the danger, and the seriousness of the risk are considered. For example, one could argue that a cloth-top convertible is certainly less safe than a car with a solid roof, and yet it would probably not, for that reason alone, be considered defective. The lack of protection is obvious, and consumers would choose it because the attractions of open-air motoring outweigh the potential obvious risks. The Third Restatement on Products Liability gives as another example a bulletproof vest that provides only front and back protection, and which is chosen because of considerations of cost, flexibility and comfort. Such a vest is not defective even though an alternative design that provides full wrap-around protection might be safer in some situations. The more protective vest is also more expensive and less comfortable, so it might inhibit a person's movement or not be worn at all because of how uncomfortable it is. RESTATEMENT (THIRD) OF TORTS: PRODUCTS LIABILITY § 2, cmt. *f* Illustration 10. In a similar fashion many products are designed and intended for use only by experienced and expert users. With respect to these products, the design need not be unnecessarily encumbered with safety features that the expert does not need or even want. However, when these types of products are marketed, such restrictions must be made clear to potential buyers. (*See* section II.C., *infra*).

Finally, the fact that a danger is obvious, or clearly warned against, does not necessarily preclude design defect liability. Under the approach taken by the Third Restatement and most courts today, the obviousness of the danger is not a safe harbor defense if the manufacturer could have designed out the risk at reasonable cost. In part, this position is a reaction to the problem of foreseeable user mistakes. Even though the danger of a power saw with an unguarded blade or a machine tool with a dangerous pinch point is obvious, it is also predictable that a user could encounter it due to a moment's inattention or carelessness. If the manufacturer could easily provide a guard that would protect against this risk, the design of such a product could still be found to be defective. It is therefore not always possible to warn one's way out of a design defect problem.

C. Defect: Failure to Warn

Sometimes the risks of a product are an inherent part of its utility. Ladders carry the user many feet above the ground, corrosive chemicals remove rust but they can also cause burns, and medications can give a good night's sleep or kill if taken in excess. In such cases, the law requires that the consumer be given adequate warnings so that the product can be used safely. When the lack of an adequate warning means that the product is not reasonably safe, the product is said to have a warning (or marketing) defect.

The duty to warn begins with the manufacturer of the product, who bears the primary responsibility to take reasonable steps to discover potential risks and then provide an adequate warning to the user. Because the duty is stated in terms of reasonableness, the manufacturer is not liable for failing to warn about dangers that could not have been discovered, nor about uses of the product that were not foreseeable. RESTATEMENT (THIRD) OF TORTS: PRODUCTS LIABILITY § 2(c), cmt. *m*. Within these limitations, however, the duty to warn can still be quite extensive. Part of the problem here is shared with design defect litigation: after the fact, it is often easy to imagine a better warning that would have prevented the accident in question. However, in contrast to design changes that often involve quite complex and expensive "risk-utility" considerations (*see* section II.B., *supra*,) product warnings can often appear to be simple and cheap, and therefore cost justified in a "risk-utility" balance. Thus, in warning defect cases it is often easy for the plaintiff to offer proof of a better warning that would have prevented the harm had it been given.

Warnings are most important when the danger is hidden or not known to the ordinary consumer, so that the product becomes, in effect, a trap. The manufacturer is in the best position to be aware of such dangers and should provide notice to the consumer. On the other hand, the manufacturer need not warn about dangers that are open and obvious. RESTATEMENT (THIRD) OF TORTS: PRODUCTS LIABILITY § 2, cmt. *j*. For example, the unguarded blade of a power saw is a danger that would be apparent at once, and nothing is gained by requiring a warning. Whether a design change to provide a blade guard is needed is a separate question, as discussed *supra*, but the failure to warn of this obvious danger does not lead to liability.

Substantively, the warning that the manufacturer gives must be adequate to inform the consumer of the risk, and in some cases instruct how to avoid it. The adequacy of a warning is a matter of infinite debate, and there are many cases that provide examples of warnings that appear to convey the necessary information that, nevertheless, somehow fails to get through to the consumer. The first requirement is that the warning itself must actually reach the ultimate (i.e., intended) user of the product. Thus, some products, such as ladders, are covered with warnings and instructions. Placing the warnings directly on these products assures that they are available at the point of use. Of course, for many products this is not possible, either because more extensive explanations are needed or because the product itself is too small in size to accommodate the warning label. In such cases an instruction and warning booklet sold with the product may be the best that can be done. In cases involving the sale of prescription drugs and medical devices, there are special rules addressing who must be warned, and how. (*See* section II.D., *infra*).

The warning that is provided also must be clear enough to alert the user to the danger, and conspicuous enough that the user will see it and be motivated to heed it. How a warning is heeded of course varies with the situation and the product. Many warnings consist of instructions for the product's safe use. The idea is that with proper instruction the consumer can use the product with reasonable safety. In other cases, however, the warning concerns a risk that cannot be eliminated, even by careful use. Warnings regarding the side effects of prescription drugs fall into this category, but so also do warnings about potential allergic reactions to food products and cosmetics. With respect to prescription drugs, providing warnings as to possible side effects satisfies the law's concerns for protecting the patient's personal autonomy by allowing informed consent. The case is somewhat different, of course, with allergies. If a consumer is allergic to peanuts, for example, it is not possible to consume a product containing peanuts safely, and avoidance is the only safe action. Here the law requires a warning if the manufacturer knows that the product contains a substance to which a substantial number of people are allergic, and the ordinary consumer would not anticipate its presence. RESTATEMENT (SECOND) OF TORTS § 402A, cmt. *j*. Thus, a jar of peanut butter need not carry any further warning about peanut allergies beyond the name of the product, since peanuts are clearly expected by the consumer and those with peanut allergies are already aware of the danger. However, at least one national fast food chain has on its menu a warning that its food is fried in peanut oil, because the ordinary consumer might not suspect that an order of french fries could contain peanut residue.

Finally, the duty to warn may require the manufacturer to anticipate foreseeable misuses of the product and warn against them as well. Just as a manufacturer may be required to design a product to anticipate and protect against foreseeable misuse, so a similar duty may require warnings about common but dangerous misuses of the product. This rule does not require that the manufacturer warn against unforeseeable and unreasonable uses of the product, but it does require that the manufacturer alert the consumer to the more common dangers associated with misuse.

D. Unavoidably Dangerous Products: Prescription Drugs and Medical Devices

Prescription drugs and medical devices could easily be treated under ordinary product liability rules governing product defects, but section § 402A itself, in comment *k*, recognized that these products might require special treatment. Comment *k* is devoted to the problem of "unavoidably unsafe products," and gives the Pasteur treatment for rabies as an example: the treatment can have dangerous side effects that cannot be prevented, but the alternative is inevitable death from rabies, so the risk is worth it. Although usually not so dramatic, many prescription drugs offer the consumer the same basic choice of significant benefits combined with a risk of potentially serious harm. Rather than leave the "risk-utility" question to be settled by litigation on a case-by-case basis, however, comment *k* indicates that such products, once approved for sale, are not defective nor are they unreasonably dangerous. Comment *k* then cautions, however, that the product must be properly prepared and accompanied by proper warnings. In practice, this means that harm from prescription drugs is basically a problem of proper warnings.

In *Brown v. Superior Court*, 751 P.2d 470 (Cal. 1988), the California Supreme Court approved the approach of comment *k*, and held that it would apply generally to all prescription drugs. The court also made it clear that the warning doctrine would apply here in the same way it would with respect to any other product, so that the manufacturer is required to warn only about risks and side effects about which it knew or should have known as the result of reasonable testing. Thus, a manufacturer would not be liable if a drug proved to have a dangerous side effect that testing did not and could not have discovered in advance of the product's marketing.

This view of prescription drugs as presenting a warnings problem is also carried forward in the Third Restatement. In § 6, the Third Restatement notes that drugs can be defective because of a "manufacturing" defect (i.e., comment *k*'s proviso that the drug must be properly prepared), a design defect or a warning defect. However, the definition of a defectively designed drug is one where the risks so outweigh the benefits that a reasonable health care provider would not prescribe it for any class of patients. Thus, unless the drug is so dangerous that it should never be prescribed to anyone at all, the Third Restatement also limits liability to cases of failure to warn (and manufacturing defects).

In the case of medical devices and prescription drugs, the manufacturer's sole duty is to warn the health care provider, generally the prescribing physician. Since it is the physician who makes the decision whether to prescribe the drug, it is the physician, therefore, who is in the best position to describe for the patient the risks and benefits of various drug therapies. Additionally, since the warnings that accompany many prescription drugs are extensive and very technical, drafted for the expert, and not readily understandable by the ordinary consumer, providing such complex and technical information in warnings given directly to the drug user would, in most cases, be completely useless. The user of a prescription drug product or medical device cannot even acquire these products without first obtaining a prescription from a health care provider. For this reason, the health care provider is typically referred to as a "learned intermediary" who is expected to translate the mass of information provided by the drug manufacturer into terms the patient can understand. The health care provider is also in a position to tailor the warning to the particular needs and circumstances of each patient. In most cases, therefore, the manufacturer satisfies its duty to warn once it provides adequate warnings and instructions to the physician or other "learned intermediary."

However, courts have recognized a few limited situations in which the manufacturer cannot rely on the "learned intermediary" and must provide warnings directly to the consumer. In some cases, for example those involving mass immunization programs, no "learned intermediary" is typically involved, and the patient seldom receives an individualized disclosure of the risks associated with the vaccine when it is distributed directly to the public. In such cases, the manufacturer is required to provide a warning directly to the patient if it is reasonably possible to do so. Similarly, the health care provider may not be actively involved in the decision to use drugs such as birth control pills, and so an adequate warning brochure must accompany the product. Some have argued for similar treatment of any drug that the manufacturers market directly to consumers via television and other public media advertising, on the grounds that here, too, the role of the "learned intermediary" is being intentionally by-passed. The law on this point is still developing, and the Third Restatement took no position on it.

III. The Cast of Potential Defendants: Who Is a Seller?

The rule of strict liability for defective products applies to all commercial sellers of the product. The list includes, first, the original manufacturer of the product, who in most cases is the party responsible for the product's design, manufacture, and accompanying warnings. The rule also extends to wholesalers and retailers, even if these parties have played no part in creating the defect in the product, and indeed even if they could not possibly have discovered or guarded against the defect. This is, remember, a rule of liability without fault. The extension of this liability even to parties who have no part in creating the defect is justified under the underlying policies in support of strict liability because these parties are responsible for putting the product into the hands of the consumer. (*See* section I., *supra*). Of course, each of these intermediate sellers would then generally have a right of indemnity from the manufacturer if the latter were the one solely responsible for the existence of the defect. (*See* Chapter 7, *supra*, section III.A., Indemnity). This rule also protects the consumer by providing another possible defendant in cases in which the manufacturer cannot be sued, for example, because the manufacturer is outside the jurisdiction of the local courts, or insolvent. *Vandermark v. Ford Motor Co.*, 391 P.2d 168 (Cal. 1964). Some jurisdictions by statute provide limited immunity for retailers and other distributors in cases in which the manufacturer is responsible for the defect and otherwise can be sued in the local jurisdiction, viewing the inclusion of the other sellers as redundant and wasteful. Of course, these protections would not apply in any case in which the plaintiff claims that the retailer was also responsible for the defect, as by improper preparation of the product or by an independent failure to warn of the danger.

Both the Second and Third Restatements limit the rule of strict liability to commercial sellers, that is, those who are in the business of selling the product. RESTATEMENT (SECOND) OF TORTS § 402A, cmt. *f*; RESTATEMENT (THIRD) OF TORTS: PRODUCTS LIABILITY § 1, cmt. *c*. This limitation excludes the casual seller of products, such as a business that only occasionally sells off some of its unneeded equipment. It is not necessary, however, that the sale of the product be the seller's main occupation, so long as it is part of the seller's regular business. So, for example, a gasoline station would be a commercial seller of food products from its mini-mart and auto parts from its service bay.

Although § 402A took no position on the subject, subsequent cases have imposed liability on manufacturers of component parts and suppliers of raw materials for injuries to the ultimate users of the finished product. However, for this liability to apply, the component part or raw material itself must be defective and cause the injury. Strict liability is not imposed against these defendants for defective installation or handling of the component part, since in that case, the defect would not have existed at the time the product left the component part maker's factory. The only exception here is the situation in which the component part manufacturer participates in the integration of the component with the finished product, and the defect arises from some problem with this connection. *See* Restatement (Third) of Torts: Products Liability § 5.

Courts have also extended strict products liability to some leases of products, provided that the lessor was in the business of commercial leases. Examples would include companies that rent automobiles and construction equipment. *Cintrone v. Hertz Truck Leasing*, 212 A.2d 769 (N.J. 1965). Even though no "sale" takes place and no ownership of any product is transferred, the commercial lessor is viewed, for policy reasons, as also being responsible for the mass distribution of products into the hands of consumers.

Furthermore, strict liability is applied in some cases where there is no transaction at all. This would include defective products given away as free samples by a party who was a commercial seller of such products, as well as defective products used as demonstrators, such as the defective fork lift truck in *Delaney v. Towmotor Corp.*, 339 F.2d 4 (2d Cir. 1964).

Special rules govern commercial sellers of used and refurbished products. Although sellers of used products put them into the stream of commerce, many argue that strict liability is inappropriate because the policy bases supporting it do not operate very well in the used product market. Sellers of used products may not be closely connected to manufacturers, and may therefore be less able to communicate with the manufacturer regarding problems with product defects. This means that such sellers are less able to assist in the discovery and elimination of problems with the product, and they cannot easily obtain contractual indemnity against the manufacturers. More importantly, perhaps, sellers of used products often do not create the same expectation of quality and safety that is found in the sale of new products. Used products are frequently sold "as-is" by resellers who act as middlemen. Hence, they often make no claims about the products, but simply help the transfer from the previous owner. Imposing strict liability could seriously disrupt the operation of this market.

Rather than strict liability, the majority rule imposes at most a negligence standard on the sellers of used products, at least when all the defendant does is resell the product without making any change(s) to it. Restatement (Third) of Torts: Products Liability § 8. Strict liability can reappear, however, if the reseller refurbishes or remanufactures the product and introduces a new defect into the product. In addition, the Third Restatement would impose strict liability for manufacturing defects if the marketing of the product would lead the consumer to expect no greater risk of defect than if the product were new. In other words, it treats the seller of products advertised as "like new" as if they were in fact sellers of new products. It should be noted, however, that this rule only applies to manufacturing defects; for design defects, the reseller is still in no position to affect the manufacturer and the negligence rule prevails.

One final potential defendant is the provider of services who makes use of a defective product in the course of the service, such as a house cleaner who uses a defective cleaning product that damages the customer's home, or the physician who uses a defective hypodermic needle to give an injection. The issue is whether to treat this party as a provider of services who would be liable only under a negligence standard, or as the seller of a product and, thus, liable under a strict liability standard. Two guideposts are significant in making this determination. First, if the product is consumed in the course of the service, it is treated generally as the sale of the product, as in the example of the defective cleaning product. On the other hand, if it is not consumed, as in the case of the hypodermic needle, it is more like a service transaction for which only negligence would apply. However, even if the product is consumed, many courts will still not treat it as a product sale if it was consumed in the course of a professional service, such as the provision of medical or hospital services. In that case the essence of the transaction is viewed as the provision of the professional service, and the professional standard of care in negligence is viewed as the proper rule to govern liability. (*See* Chapter 4, *supra*, section II.C., Negligence).

IV. The Economic Loss Limitation

The economic loss rule is one of the most significant limitations on the scope of recovery for product related injuries. This limitation prohibits the recovery of damages for pure economic loss based on strict products liability (a similar limitation also applies to negligence). As used here, pure economic loss means a loss resulting solely from the product's failure to perform properly, unaccompanied by personal injury or damage to other property. Such losses can only be recovered in an action for breach of an express or implied warranty. The case of *Seely v. White Motor Co.*, 403 P.2d 145 (Cal. 1965), will serve to illustrate the problem and explain the rationale for this rule.

In *Seely*, the plaintiff purchased a truck from defendant White Motor Co. The truck performed poorly, bouncing roughly while driving and eventually crashing and overturning when the brakes failed. However, the plaintiff sustained no personal injury in the crash, so that the damages were limited to the value of the truck and the plaintiff's lost profits because the truck was unavailable for business. Under these circumstances, the California Supreme Court, in an opinion written by Justice Traynor, allowed recovery on a warranty theory but not on the tort theory of strict products liability. This limitation, it will be noted, came only about two years after the same court's landmark adoption of strict liability in the *Greenman* case. (*See* section II., *supra*).

As the court explained, the reason for the distinction lies in the responsibility that the manufacturer can be said to have undertaken in selling the product:

> [A manufacturer] can appropriately be held liable for physical injuries caused by defects by requiring his goods to match a standard of safety defined in terms of conditions that create unreasonable risks of harm. He cannot be held for the level of performance of his products in the consumer's business unless he agrees that the product was designed to meet the consumer's demands. 403 P.2d at 151.

In other words, issues of personal injury and safety require the fixed and unavoidable standards of tort law, while issues of product performance may be left to the private ordering of the parties, especially when the claim arises between businesses. By extension, the economic loss rule covers damage to the product itself, such as the damage to the defective truck in *Seely, supra,* when it overturned. Damage to "other property," however, is covered by the tort rule. Thus, if the truck had been carrying merchandise that was also damaged when the truck overturned, the damaged merchandise would be considered "other property" for which the owner could recover in strict products liability.

V. The Plaintiff's Conduct

The final issue to consider is the extent to which the conduct of the plaintiff might bar or limit recovery. At the time of the original adoption of strict products liability, the prevailing rule in most jurisdictions was still that contributory negligence acted as a total bar to recovery for negligence. Comment *n* to § 402A therefore adopted the rule generally applicable to strict liability, which was that contributory negligence was not a defense but that assumption of the risk was a total bar to recovery. With the general move among most jurisdictions to comparative negligence, the distinction between these two defenses lost much of its force. On the other hand, it became apparent that a plaintiff's misconduct could encompass more than, as comment *n* put it, "failure to discover the defect in the product, or to guard against the possibility of its existence." For example, suppose the plaintiff drove while intoxicated and as a result lost control of the car and got into an accident. If the plaintiff's injuries in the accident were aggravated because the car was defectively designed, how should the courts take account of the plaintiff's responsibility for causing the accident in the first place? The plaintiff's misconduct (i.e., by driving while intoxicated) did not really relate to the product defect at all, being neither a failure to discover the defect nor to guard against the possibility of its existence; the conduct would be negligent even if the car had no defects at all.

The general response of the courts and legislatures has been to apply the apportionment rules of comparative negligence to products liability cases, in spite of the semantic and conceptual difficulty involved in comparing the contribution of the defective product, where the conduct of the defendant is theoretically irrelevant, with the contribution of the plaintiff's negligent conduct. This is the position adopted, for example, in § 17 of the Third Restatement. The justification for adoption of this rule lies in the need for incentives for the plaintiff to use the product with care. It is not true that the manufacturer is always in the best position to avoid or minimize the risk of harm; in at least some cases, the plaintiff is in the best position to do so, and a rule of comparative fault penalizes the product user who fails to use due care. (*See* Chapter 12, *supra*, section I.B., Comparative Negligence).

Another aspect of the plaintiff's conduct that can bar or limit recovery goes under the general heading of "misuse." As we have seen, manufacturers may have a responsibility when designing products and instructing purchasers about their safe use to anticipate various types of foreseeable misuse of the product. However, in some cases the use of the product is so far outside what can be anticipated that the manufacturer is not expected to take it into account. Such unforeseeable misuses do not lead to liability because the misuse eliminates one of the crucial elements of the plaintiff's *prima facie* case. For example, unforeseeable misuse may be an indication that the product is not defective at all. Likewise, misuse in some cases can also eliminate the causation element, because the misuse is deemed the proximate cause of the harm and not any defect in the product itself. In such situations, therefore, the misuse bars recovery by fatally undermining the plaintiff's *prima facie* case. Finally, in some jurisdictions, misuse is treated as an affirmative defense that must be pleaded and proven by the defendant. Not surprisingly, the Third Restatement has left the determination as to how courts should address the concept of misuse in strict liability cases to be decided according to local law. Restatement (Third) of Torts: Products Liability § 2, cmt. *p*.

Checkpoints

- Products liability deals with the problem of harm caused by defective products.

- Liability for harm caused by defective products was originally based on negligence or breach of warranty, but both of these actions were limited by the requirement of privity of contract.

- As both negligence and breach of warranty shed the privity limitation in cases involving personal injury, another theory came to the fore: strict liability in tort.

- The policy arguments for strict liability in tort in product cases included:
  - that it would provide a better incentive for manufacturers to take steps to reduce or eliminate product defects;
  - that it would provide a loss shifting and loss spreading function;
  - that it would be easier to administer because it would eliminate proof of fault; and
  - that it would be easier to administer because it would allow injured victims to sue the manufacturer directly.

- Strict liability in tort in products cases is based on the existence of a product defect.

- Products have a manufacturing defect when they depart from the manufacturer's intended design.

- Products have a design defect when the foreseeable risks posed by the product could have been eliminated by a feasible design change, and the failure to adopt the design change makes the product not reasonably safe.

- Products have a warning (or marketing) defect when the manufacturer fails to inform the user of known risks of the product, or fails to instruct the user on how to use the product safely.

- A different approach is taken with prescription drugs and medical devices, which are deemed to be unavoidably dangerous but potentially highly beneficial. Here, the most basic obligation is to warn of known risks.

- Strict liability in tort is imposed on those in the business of selling products. This includes the manufacturer and intermediate sellers such as wholesalers and retailers. It has also been extended to commercial lessors of products, but not to sellers of used products unless they remanufacture the product or create the impression that the product is as good as new.

- Strict liability in tort does not apply to product cases involving solely economic loss.

- The plaintiff's conduct is now an important consideration in products liability litigation, either as comparative responsibility or as misuse.

Chapter 17

Defamation

Roadmap

- Learn the basic definitions pertaining to common law actions for defamation.

- Understand the distinction between common law slander and common law libel.

- Understand the distinctions between common law slander *per se* and common law libel *per quod*.

- Understand the meaning of the "reference" requirement for actions for defamation.

- Understand the "publication" requirements in actions for defamation.

- Understand the application of "truth" as a defense to common law defamation, as well as other common law privileges to actions for defamation.

- Understand how the requirements for the common law tort of defamation have been modified to comply with the requirements of the U.S. Constitution in certain special situations.

The tort of defamation protects an individual's interest in reputation. It achieves that objective by providing compensation for statements that lower a plaintiff's standing in the community, affect the esteem, respect, goodwill or confidence in which the plaintiff is held, or that incite adverse, derogatory, or unpleasant feelings against the plaintiff.

I. Common Law Definitions

The common law tort of defamation finds its roots in "seditious libel." Seditious libel was a crime that allowed the government to criminally punish those who criticized governmental officials or government actions (and, at one point even the clergy). Under the crime of seditious libel, truth was not a defense. Indeed, if it were shown that a defendant's allegations were true, the defendant would be punished more severely on the theory that true criticisms are more likely to harm the government than false ones. Perhaps the most famous criminal libel case arose in 1735 when editor John Peter Zenger was prosecuted in New York for criticizing the Royal Governor. Among other things, Zenger satirically alleged that the Governor was a "spaniel" and a "monkey broke loose from his chains." During the prosecution, the Chief Justice of the Province of New York disbarred two lawyers who tried to represent Zenger. Nevertheless, in perhaps the first case of "jury nullification," the jury refused to convict Zenger even though there was overwhelming evidence against him. *Crown v. John Peter Zenger*, [1735], 17 How. St. Tr. 675.

Defamation was (and is) also a tort, and an important one in many other common law jurisdictions (*e.g.*, England and Australia) where there is a thriving torts defamation bar. The common law tort involves four separate and distinct elements:

(1) a defamatory statement;
(2) that is made of and regarding the plaintiff;
(3) that is published to others; and
(4) that (depending on the type of defamation involved) causes plaintiff injury.

As we shall see in section II, *infra*, however, recent constitutional decisions place a constitutional overlay on the tort in the United States.

Defamatory Statements. In general, defamation occurs when the defendant makes a statement of fact that tends to lower the plaintiff's reputation in the community, to lower the esteem in which (s)he is held, or that deters others from associating with the plaintiff. *See* Restatement (Second) of Torts, Section 559, Comment *e*. A variety of allegations might be regarded as defamatory. For example, if the defendant claims that the plaintiff is insane, that (s)he committed criminal acts, that (s)he suffers from a loathsome or venereal disease, or is dishonest or incompetent in his or her profession, a defamation action may lie. *See id.* However, each case must be evaluated on its own facts and circumstances. For example, an allegation that might not be regarded as defamatory as to most individuals might be regarded as highly defamatory if made regarding other individuals (*e.g.*, that a kosher butcher sells bacon). *See Braun v. Armour & Co.*, 254 N.Y. 514, 173 N.E. 845 (1939). Of course, if the allegation is true, it is not actionable.

Historically, the tort of defamation was divided into "slander" and "libel." Slander involved oral defamatory statements, while libel involved written statements (although the writing could also be a sign or a picture rather than a formal writing). As a general rule, libel was actionable without proof of any damage. In other words, once the plaintiff established that a communication was libelous, the defamatory statement was actionable without specific proof of loss. Damage to the plaintiff's reputation was presumed, because a libelous statement was regarded as more permanent than an oral one, and thus, more likely to be damaging long term.

In theory, it was relatively easy to distinguish libel from slander in earlier times. Defamatory statements that were made in writing (*e.g.*, in books, magazines or newspapers) were regarded as libel, whereas oral statements were treated as slander. However, in more recent times not all defamatory statements are so easily categorized. For example, although they could be regarded as oral, defamatory suggestions in motion pictures have sometimes been regarded as libel. *See Burton v. Crowell Publ'g Co.*, 82 F.2d 154 (2d Cir. 1936). Moreover, as new forms of communication have developed, it has become increasingly difficult to distinguish libel from slander. In general, the focus now is on whether the particular communication has the potentially harmful characteristics of writings (in particular, its greater permanence and breadth of distribution) rather than oral works.

Historically, the distinction between libel and slander was important because slander required proof of actual damage to the plaintiff's reputation. At common law, once the plaintiff's evidence had been submitted, the court would then determine (as a matter of law) whether the written or spoken words were defamatory as a matter of law. When there was uncertainty about whether words were defamatory, the matter would be submitted to the jury.

At common law different rules applied when an oral communication fit within one of the four categories of slander regarded as so-called "slander *per se*." Slander *per se* was actionable without proof of damage, and existed when the defendant suggested any of four things: that the plaintiff committed a criminal offense, suffered from a loathsome or venereal disease, engaged in conduct incompatible with his or her profession, or (in the case of women) had been unchaste. Slander that was not *per se* (i.e., because it required proof of extrinsic facts known by the recipient of the communication in order to be slanderous) was referred to as *per quod*. Since all libel was actionable without any proof of damages, the characterization of libel *per se* had a slightly different meaning. It referred to those statements whose meaning was defamatory on its face, as opposed to libelous *per quod* statements which required proof, as in slander *per quod*, of extrinsic facts.

Illustrative of the distinction between libel *per quod* and libel *per se* is the holding in *Lega Siciliana Social Club v. St. Germaine*, 77 Conn. App. 846, 825 A.2d 827 (2003). That case arose when the defendant objected to a liquor license issued to a social club (believing that the license would bring increased traffic, noise, and disruption to the area), and as a result sent a letter to a local alderman complaining about the license. In the letter, the defendant stated that the club had Mafia connections (since its membership was restricted to individuals of Sicilian ancestry), and, therefore, that the club had the political muscle to do whatever it wanted. Since the Mafia was known to be involved in various illegal activities (*e.g.*, bribery, illegal gambling, manufacturing and distribution of narcotics), many of which involved moral turpitude and were punishable by imprisonment, the libelous statement was regarded as *per se* defamatory. Moreover, the defamatory nature of the allegations were enhanced further by the fact that the defendant had also suggested that the club had used its Mafia connections to bring about violence designed to achieve its objectives. The court held that the defendant's statements constituted libel *per se*, noting that they were of a type that would tend to "diminish the esteem, respect, goodwill or confidence in which the plaintiff is held, or to excite adverse, derogatory, or unpleasant feelings or opinions against [it]." 825 A. 2d at 832.

When slander or libel is actionable, a variety of damages may be recovered. The most obvious type of recoverable damages is for injury to the plaintiff's reputation, including wounded feelings and humiliation. However, the defamer might also be held liable not only for his or her own statements, but also for the statements of others who repeat the original defamation, provided that the repetitions are regarded as reasonably foreseeable. However, when the defendant has not made an allegation of "fact," but has simply parodied or satirized the plaintiff, there may be no defamation. For example, if the defendant portrays the plaintiff in a satirical way (*e.g.*, suggesting that the first time that plaintiff had sex was in an outhouse with his mother), but the parody makes clear that the statement is not factual (because it contains a disclaimer stating that it is a parody and is not to be taken seriously), there can be no defamation. *See Hustler Magazine v. Falwell*, 485 U.S. 46 (1988). Likewise, if the defendant simply states his or her opinion of the plaintiff, in such a way as not to impute any fact, defamation will not lie. *See id.*

Scope of the Tort. At common law, the tort of defamation was regarded as "personal" so that any injury must be to the plaintiff himself or herself. This meant that third parties did not have standing to sue for such a personal, dignitary tort. As a result, a dead person could not be defamed, and neither could the decedent's heirs or estate sue on his or her behalf. *See Bello v. Random House, Inc.*, 422 S.W.2d 339 (Mo. 1967).

Reference to Plaintiff. In order to be actionable, the defamatory statement must refer to the plaintiff. The reference can be either explicit or implicit. However, depending on the size and nature of the group that has allegedly been defamed, the plaintiff may or may not be able to show that a publication refers to him or her individually. For example, if a company consists of A, B & C individuals, and a publication asserts, that: "A & B are the only honest members of the company," the publication could be regarded as referring to C and accusing her of dishonesty by implication, even though C was not specifically named.

Illustrative of the "reference" requirement is the holding in *Neiman-Marcus v. Lait*, 13 F.R.D. 311 (S.D.N.Y. 1952). In that case, the defendants published a book stating that some Neiman-Marcus models and sales girls were "call girls," "party girls," or "company girls." In other words, the defendants suggested that the models and sales girls were prostitutes. In the same book the defendants also suggested that many of the males who worked at the store were gay. When various Neiman-Marcus salespersons and models filed suit, defendants moved to dismiss on the basis that no particular person had been named in the book, and therefore that "no ascertainable person is identified by the words complained of." *Id.* at 313. The court rejected this notion stating that, when a libeled group is particularly small, *all* members of the class might be able to sue. The problem in *Neiman-Marcus* was that the publication did not libel all members of the two small groups of individuals who worked as salesmen and saleswomen. In other words, it did not suggest that all of the members of these two groups were prostitutes or gay, and the question was whether the individual plaintiffs in each group had been personally libeled. Relying on the Restatement of Torts § 564, the court suggested that each member of a small group could maintain a defamation action even though the defamatory publication referred to only some members of the group. As a result, the court held that the salesmen (a group of 15 out of a total of 25) could sue, but the court also held that the group of saleswomen was so large (382) that an action for group defamation could not be maintained by the 30 individual plaintiff saleswomen, unless they could establish circumstances suggesting that the publication referred to them individually. Ultimately, the court concluded that no "reasonable man would take the writers seriously and conclude from the publication a reference to any individual saleswoman." *Id.* at 316.

Publication requirement. In order to recover in defamation, the defamatory statements must be "published" to a third party. To satisfy this requirement, it is not enough that the defendant makes derogatory statements that are heard only by the plaintiff. No reputational injury can occur unless others (apart from the defamed individual) also hear the statements. However, the publication need not be published to the entire world. It is sufficient if the publication is made to any third party or group of individuals and causes the plaintiff reputational damage.

One of the interesting aspects of defamation is that one who repeats a defamatory statement can also be held separately liable for the defamation.

Thus, if a newspaper repeats a defamatory statement made by an individual, and merely adds that the allegations are simply "alleged," such a statement does not necessarily insulate the newspaper from potential defamation liability. *See Lundin v. Post Publ'g Co.*, 217 Mass. 213, 104 N.E. 480 (1914). Instead, just as with the initial defamer, the newspaper may also be held liable. Likewise, all others who participate in the publication process (e.g., editor, newspaper boy, carrier) are also potentially liable.

At one point in history, when a newspaper was published, each copy that was sold was regarded as a different publication for which a separate defamation action could be brought. However, most jurisdictions now apply the "single publication rule" under which a single edition of a newspaper is treated as just one publication, no matter how many copies are sold. Of course, if many copies are sold, the quantity of the distribution will still have a bearing on the amount of damages that may be recovered by the plaintiff. *See* RESTATEMENT (SECOND) OF TORTS, Section 577A.

II. Truth and Other Defenses

At common law, truth was a defense in a defamation action, but the defendant bore the burden of proof on the question of truth. *See* RUSSELL L. WEAVER, ANDREW T. KENYON, DAVID F. PARTLETT & CLIVE P. WALKER, THE RIGHT TO SPEAK ILL: DEFAMATION, REPUTATION AND FREE SPEECH 5–8 (2006). In other words, in the clash between individual and societal interests in speaking freely, versus an individual's interest in protecting his or her reputation, the common law cut the balance decisively in favor of the individual's reputation. *Id.* If the jury could not decisively resolve whether an allegedly defamatory statement was true or false, then the plaintiff was allowed to recover.

The common law also recognized various privileges in defamation actions. For example, judges were absolutely privileged for statements made during the course of judicial proceedings, as were attorneys and witnesses. However, some U.S. courts required that the statements must be relevant to the proceedings, and they did not protect statements made about the proceedings to the media. *See Adams v. Alabama Lime & Stone Corp.*, 225 Ala. 174, 142 So. 424 (1932). A similar privilege applied to statements made during legislative proceedings. In *Barr v. Matteo*, 360 U.S. 564 (1959), the privilege was further extended to included statements made by federal executive officials in the course of their duties. Where otherwise applicable, these absolute privileges could be asserted, regardless of the defendant's personal motive in making the statement. Relatedly, there was also a qualified privilege of "fair comment" for members of the press and others who reported on accurately stated facts from public proceedings and other matters of public concern.

Qualified privileges were only available in certain situations where the defendant's statement, even though otherwise defamatory, was made in good faith. For example, in *Toogood v. Spyring*, [1834] 149 Eng. Rep. 1044, it was explained that statements are privileged when they are "fairly made by a person in the discharge of some public or private duty, whether legal or moral, or in the conduct of his own affairs, in matters where his interest is concerned." *Id.* at 1050. This statement evolved into the notion of qualified privilege, which allowed individuals some leeway in making statements regarding matters affecting their own interests, the interests of others (where the statement is being made to the other to help protect the other's interests, when there is a common interest between the recipient and the speaker), or where the communication is to one who may act in the public interest. However, qualified privileges could be lost if they were abused (*e.g.*, if defendant acted maliciously).

There has been considerable controversy regarding whether defamation liability can be premised on mere statements of opinion, or whether it must be based solely on statements of fact. In *Gertz v. Robert Welch, Inc.*, 418 U.S. 323 (1974), the Court made its now famous statement that "there is no such thing as a false idea" under the First Amendment. *Id.* at 339. It further noted that society depends upon the marketplace of ideas rather than the judicial process to correct opinions that may be pernicious. However, in *Milkovich v. Lorain Journal*, 497 U.S. 1 (1990), the Court refused to hold that expressions of opinion are absolutely privileged. Insofar as some opinions may be understood as being based on assumptions of fact, they may be actionable as statements of facts. However, defendants are always free to argue that a particular fact should not be inferred from a given opinion, and in certain situations they may even retain the common law privilege of "fair comment," *supra*, as a defense.

III. The Constitutionalization of Defamation

Until the early 1960s, the common law definitions of defamation held sway in the United States. Prior to that, the U.S. Supreme Court treated libel as unprotected speech and allowed the individual states to define the tort in the manner they deemed appropriate. The Court did so because, as it stated in *Beauharnais v. Illinois*, 343 U.S. 250 (1952), "[l]ibellous utterances [are not] within the area of constitutionally protected speech" because they have "such slight social value as a step to truth that any benefit that may be derived from them is clearly outweighed by the social interest in order and morality." *Id.* at 257. As a result, the states were free to define the tort of defamation and to determine the scope of recovery.

The United States Supreme Court's approach to defamation dramatically changed with its holdings in *Garrison v. Louisiana*, 379 U.S. 64 (1964), and *New York Times Co. v. Sullivan*, 376 U.S. 254 (1964). In those cases, the Court decreed the end of the crime of seditious libel in the United States, and placed significant restrictions on a plaintiff's ability to recover damages in a civil defamation case. The Court's shift in approach was prompted by the turmoil of the 1960s civil rights movement. *See* HARRY KALVEN, JR., THE NEGRO AND THE FIRST AMENDMENT (1965). In the *New York Times* case, the Court reversed a state court verdict awarding defamation damages to the police commissioner of Montgomery, Alabama. The case began when an editorial advertisement published in the *New York Times* criticized police handling of civil rights demonstrations in Montgomery, and suggested that the police had responded with intimidation and violence. The advertisement did contain some factual inaccuracies, but most were generally minor and insignificant. Although not specifically named in the advertisement, the police commissioner argued that the advertisement created the false impression that his office had condoned the alleged intimidation and violence. A jury awarded him one-half million dollars in damages for libel based upon Alabama law that allowed the jury to "presume" damages (rather than requiring the jury to compute them on the basis of some demonstrated showing of loss), and the Alabama Supreme Court upheld the award.

In considering the case, the United States Supreme Court was concerned by the implications of the verdict. The *New York Times* had circulated only a small number of newspapers in Alabama, but nonetheless faced very substantial damage liability, as did each of the four black Alabama clergymen who had also been found jointly and severally liable along with the defendant newspaper. In deciding the case, the Court emphasized the "profound national commitment to the principle that debate on public issues should be uninhibited, robust, and wide-open," and that it may well include "vehement, caustic, and sometimes unpleasantly sharp attacks on government and public officials." *Id.* at 270. The facts and circumstances of the *New York Times* case provided ample indication that defamation law could be applied in a way that would chill such public debate. Although the tort included certain defenses (*e.g.*, truth), those defenses did not protect the plaintiff against a large damage judgment based on minor inaccuracies. And, although the newspaper might have been negligent in publishing the inaccuracies (because it did not check and confirm the facts by examining records available in its own archives), the damage award seemed disproportionate to the conduct.

In rendering its decision in the *New York Times* case, the Court decided to create more breathing space for First Amendment speech interests. In particular, the Court articulated higher liability standards for defamation actions brought by public officials. Since public officials make decisions and policy on behalf of the government, their actions and decisions must be monitored and evaluated by the electorate they represent, and subjected to public approval, criticism and debate. Moreover, just as public officials are immune from liability for defamatory statements they make in the course of their official duties, it naturally follows that critics of public officials should be able to speak more freely about governmental officials. As a result, the Court held that a public official could not recover for defamation without proving, by clear and convincing evidence that the statement was made with "actual malice." In effect, as discussed *infra*, this new "actual malice" requirement imposed upon the plaintiff the additional burden of proving that the defamatory statement was in fact false. What had formerly been a defense in common law defamation actions now became a part of the plaintiff's *prima facie* case in constitutional defamation cases brought by public officials. Moreover, by imposing this enhanced standard on the traditional requirements for proving defamation, the Court conferred constitutional protection upon a specific subcategory of defamation defendants: those who defame public officials. Defamation of non-public officials was not affected by the decision.

Under the *New York Times* decision, the term "actual malice" functions as a term of art. It does not require a showing of mean-spiritedness, hatred, or ill will as had formerly been required for proving traditional "common law malice." Instead, a public official plaintiff under this new standard was required to prove that the defendant published the defamatory statement with "knowledge that [the statement] was false [or in] reckless disregard of whether it was false or malicious." *Id.* at 280. In other words, for public official plaintiffs, defamation liability could not be premised on strict liability or even simple negligence. Subsequent Supreme Court cases have elaborated further on the "actual malice" requirement, explaining that it can be shown if the plaintiff establishes that the defendant exhibited a "high degree of awareness of probable falsity," [*see Garrison v. Louisiana*, 379 U.S. 64, 74 (1964)], or when the publisher "entertain[s] serious doubts as to the truth of his publication." *See St. Amant v. Thompson*, 390 U.S. 727, 731. Thus, when a person has the opportunity to check the truthfulness of the information, but simply fails to do so, although such conduct might be negligent, it does not satisfy the requisite state of mind required for *New York Times* "actual malice."

As a result of the *New York Times* case, and its progeny, "actual malice" has become a constitutional question that is reviewable independently on appeal. In most cases, trial court decisions in favor of defamation plaintiffs are overturned routinely on appeal. Thus, unlike many foreign countries that have thriving practices in plaintiffs' defamation litigation, there is no equivalent in the United States. Given the hurdles to recovery, few (if any) lawyers can make a living based on representing public officials in defamation actions in the United States. *See* Russell L. Weaver, Andrew T. Kenyon, David F. Partlett & Clive P. Walker, The Right to Speak Ill: Defamation, Reputation and Free Speech (2006).

For a plaintiff to determine whether the requisite *New York Times* "actual malice" exists, (s)he must be able to probe the editorial process. In recognition of this need, the Court has rejected arguments for an editorial privilege against discovery. However, in the vast majority of cases, such discovery (which would involve a detailed examination of the editorial process) is prohibitively expensive. *See id.*

Under the *New York Times* decision, the term "public official" included any governmental official with significant responsibility and discretion in managing public affairs. Subsequently, this term has been defined broadly enough to also include candidates for public office [*see Monitor Patriot Co. v. Roy*, 401 U.S. 265, 271 (1971)], as well as former office holders insofar as the allegedly defamatory statements relate to the performance of their official duties. *See Curtis Publ'g Co. v. Butts*, 388 U.S. 130, 164 (1967). Even to the extent that a defamatory statement may relate to some private aspect of a public official's life, the "actual malice" standard will nonetheless apply.

Public Figures. Although public officials may have significant impact on public discourse, their public status is sometimes exceeded by the influence of even certain private individuals. These individuals are often regarded as "public figures," who merely by virtue of their notoriety, fame, credibility, or personality, command public attention. In recognition of this, the Court in *Curtis Publishing Co. v. Butts*, 388 U.S. 130 (1967), subsequently extended the *New York Times* "actual malice" standard to include public figures. Providing increased protection for defamatory speech against these individuals reflected an understanding that, like public officials, public figures are "intimately involved in the resolution of important public questions or, by reason of their fame, shape events in areas of concern to society at large." *See Curtis Publishing Co. v. Butts*, 388 U.S. 130, 164 (1967), Warren. J. concurrence.

Public Interest Standard. A common denominator of the *New York Times* and *Butts* decisions is that public expression, even if defamatory, merits First

Amendment protection if it implicates public issues material to effective self-governance. This premise might suggest that First Amendment defamation standards should correlate to the nature of the speech rather than to the status of the defendant. And, indeed, in *Rosenbloom v. Metromedia, Inc.*, 403 U.S. 29 (1971), a plurality of the United States Supreme Court sought to move defamation jurisprudence in that direction. In *Rosenbloom*, three justices held that the *New York Times* "actual malice" standard should extend to defamatory statements concerning matters of general or public interest. However, the plurality's approach failed to command a majority of justices, and the *New York Times* "actual malice" standard has remained fixed over the past few decades upon the public status of the defamed individual. Nevertheless, as we shall see, public interest principles have still crept into the Court's analysis.

Private Individuals. In *Gertz v. Robert Welch, Inc.*, 418 U.S. 323 (1974), the Court held that the *New York Times* "actual malice" standard did not apply to defamation actions brought by solely private individuals. *Gertz* involved a defamation action by an attorney who represented a family in a wrongful death action against a police officer. The defendant's magazine described the lawyer as a "Communist fronter" and suggested that he was acting as part of a "Communist campaign against the police" and was involved in a "frame-up" of the particular officer. In addition to his role as an attorney, and thus an officer of the court, the plaintiff had also served on various government boards and commissions. Rejecting the notion that Gertz was a public official or a public figure, the Court held that he should be treated as a private individual. In doing so, the Court weighed the public interest in free communication, and its goal of promoting informed self-governance, with the individual interest in compensation for reputation. The Court concluded that when private individuals are defamed, the state has a greater interest in providing compensation for damaged reputations. In addition, the public interest in receiving the speech is diminished. Moreover, the Court concluded that the *New York Times* "actual malice" standard exacts too high a price when applied to defamation suits by private individuals. Unlike public officials or figures, they do not invite public attention to their actions and they have not voluntarily exposed themselves to a higher risk of reputational harm. Nor do they command access to the media so that they have the possibility to mitigate reputational injury through self-help. As a result, the Court held that private individuals could sue under a lower defamation standard. Thus, under the *Gertz* decision, so long as a state does not impose strict liability in defamation suits by a private individual, it may establish a standard for recovery that is less than that provided in the *New York Times* "actual malice" standard. Unfortunately, absent a uniform standard for defamation actions by private individuals, criteria vary among the states. Some have adopted the *New York Times* "actual malice" standard, while others use a negligence standard, or one based upon some other public interest criterion. *Gertz* did, however, mandate that a plaintiff's recovery should be based on actual damages when liability is premised on negligence, and that presumed and punitive damages may be awarded *only* when *New York Times* "actual malice" is established. Additionally, the *Gertz* Court expressed uncertainty about what standard (i.e., one based upon *New York Times* "actual malice" or on the public interest) would apply in the case where a solely private figure plaintiff sued a non-media defendant.

Gertz also provided further insight into the definition of the term "public figure." The Court noted that public figures are individuals who "have assumed roles of special prominence in the affairs of society." *Id.* at 345. The Court defined two types of public figures. First, there are those individuals who "occupy positions of such pervasive power and influence that they are deemed public figures for all purposes." *Id.* Second, there are individuals who "have thrust themselves to the forefront of particular public controversies in order to influence the resolution of the issues involved." *Id.* The common denominator of a public figure, in either category, is that (s)he has invited public attention or comment. The Court acknowledged, at least hypothetically, the possibility of an "involuntary public figure," but concluded that such individuals would arise only rarely. Applying these newly articulated standards to Gertz, the Court found that he did not have widespread fame in the community and thus he did not fit into the first category of public figures. To the extent that Gertz served as an attorney in a relatively high profile case, an argument could have been made that he had thrust himself into the controversy with an intent (and even obligation) to influence the outcome. The Court, however, refused to treat trial lawyers as necessarily within the category of public figures.

Gertz was followed by the decision in *Time, Inc. v. Firestone*, 424 U.S. 448 (1976), in which the Court held that a well-known socialite was also not a public figure. The case involved a divorce proceeding with lurid testimony that drew extensive public attention. Based on the testimony, a national news magazine stated that the husband was granted a divorce on the basis of his wife's adultery and extreme cruelty. The characterization of adultery as a basis for the divorce decree technically was inaccurate. In deciding that the plaintiff, Mrs. Firestone, was a private individual, rather than a public figure, the Court emphasized two things. First, although she was prominent in certain elite social circles, the Court did not regard this fact alone as sufficient to render her a public figure. The Court noted that Mrs. Firestone had not voluntarily injected herself into a public controversy in an effort to influence its outcome (even though she had conducted news conferences, retained a public relations expert to present her story to the public, and hired a newspaper clipping service to send her articles about herself). Second, the Court found that a divorce proceeding was not a matter of public concern. Although the public might have an interest in such matters, and a divorce trial implicated the process of self-governance (*e.g.*, the functioning of the courts), the Court concluded that the impact of such proceedings upon the public were relatively remote. Moreover, the Court explained that in order to obtain a divorce, individuals have no choice but to utilize the court system. As a result, the Court limited the concept of public figure status to situations when serious issues of public policy clearly are present.

The public figure concept was further delineated (and narrowed) in *Proxmire v. Hutchinson*, 443 U.S. 157 (1979), and *Wolston v. Reader's Digest Association, Inc.*, 443 U.S. 111 (1979). In the former case, William Proxmire, a United States Senator, labeled an individual's federally subsidized research as a waste of taxpayer money. Indeed, the Senator awarded the researcher his "Golden Fleece Award," which was given to public officials who had fleeced taxpayers of their money. Although the comments were well publicized, the Court concluded that the researcher was not a public figure because he did not possess pervasive fame or notoriety and had not pursued the limelight. Similarly, *Wolston* involved a book that identified the plaintiff as a Soviet agent. Although the plaintiff had been subpoenaed to testify in a prior (although distant) investigation, and had been held in contempt for refusing to comply, he denied any Soviet relationship. Again, the Court concluded that the plaintiff was not a public figure, since he had not sought public attention. The Court found that mere involvement in a criminal matter did not provide a sufficient basis for treating an individual as a public figure.

Even though *Rosenbloom's* progeny rejected the notion of a public interest standard (*see* discussion *supra*), questions of public interest nevertheless have crept into the Court's defamation analysis. In *Firestone*, the nature of the public controversy was obviously important to the outcome of the case. Likewise, in *Philadelphia Newspapers, Inc. v. Hepps*, 475 U.S. 767 (1986), the Court determined that a private figure plaintiff suing a media defendant need not prove actual falsehood if the statement does not touch a matter of public concern.

Although the *Gertz* Court left open the question of whether presumed and punitive damages could be recovered by a private figure defamation plaintiff from a non-media defendant, and whether different standards should apply to such a plaintiff who was not involved in a matter of public interest, those issues were resolved in *Dun & Bradstreet, Inc. v. Greenmoss Builders, Inc.,* 472 U.S. 749 (1985). That case involved a credit reporting agency's dissemination of an inaccurate credit report. Instead of focusing upon the status of the defendant (as a media defendant), a plurality focused on the question of whether the defamatory statement related to a matter of public interest, and held that the *New York Times* "actual malice" standard governs presumed or punitive damages only when the subject of the defamation relates to a matter of public concern. Thus, the analytical framework that had previously been rejected in *Gertz* for purposes of determining the reach of *New York Times* "actual malice," was embraced in *Dun & Bradstreet*. Nevertheless, the Court still continues to apply the *New York Times* "actual malice" standard (rather than the public interest standard) to suits brought by public officials and public figures.

Checkpoints

- Defamation includes statements that lower the plaintiff's reputation or esteem in the community.

- In order to be actionable, not only must a statement be defamatory, it also must refer to the plaintiff, must be published, and must cause injury (unless the defamatory statement involves libel or slander *per se*).

- In order to be actionable, an allegedly defamatory statement must be untrue.

- Defamatory statements may be protected by various privileges, including the judicial, executive or legislative privileges, the qualified privilege, or the privilege for "fair comment."

- Defamation was historically unprotected under the First Amendment.

- Defamatory expression may include speech that is facilitative of informed self-government and thus worthy of First Amendment protection.

- Today, public officials may not recover for defamation unless they establish *New York Times* "actual malice" (i.e., proof that defendant knew that the statement was false or acted in reckless disregard for its truth or falsity).

- Today, public figures also may not recover for defamation unless they establish *New York Times* "actual malice."

- A public figure is someone who occupies a position of such pervasive power and influence as to be a public figure for all purposes, or who has thrust himself or herself into the forefront of a particular public controversy in order to influence the resolution of the issues involved.

- The U.S. Supreme Court allows states to apply a lower standard to private individuals.

- Presumed or punitive damages generally may not be recovered in constitutional defamation cases absent a showing of New York Times "actual malice."

- If a defamatory statement does not implicate a matter of public concern, presumed or punitive damages may be recovered in constitutional defamation cases without a showing of New York Times "actual malice."

- The U.S. Supreme Court has not privileged statements of opinion from a defamation claim.

Chapter 18

Invasion of Privacy

Roadmap

- Understand the origins of the right of privacy.

- Learn about the requirements for the tort of "appropriation" and how to distinguish it from the requirements of the related tort of "publicity."

- Learn about the requirements for the tort of "intrusion" upon the plaintiff's right of seclusion.

- Learn about the requirements for the tort of "public disclosure of private embarrassing facts."

- Learn about the requirements for the tort of "false light" invasion of privacy.

- Understand the development of modern statutory and case law distinctions pertaining to the various categories of privacy actions.

- Understand how the requirements for certain individual common law privacy torts have been modified to comply with the requirements of the U.S. Constitution in certain special situations.

The "right to be let alone," although not specifically enumerated by the Constitution, was characterized by Justice Louis Brandeis as "the most comprehensive of rights and the right most valued by civilized men." *Olmstead v. United States*, 277 U.S 438, 479 (1928) (Brandeis J., dissenting). Modern privacy torts can be traced to a seminal law review article written by Samuel D. Warren and Louis D. Brandeis, who were worried about undue media probing into "the sacred precincts of private and domestic" editorial practices that overstepped the boundaries of decency and propriety, and the unauthorized circulation of private portraits. *See* Samuel Warren and Louis Brandeis, The Right to Privacy, 4 Harv. L. Rev. 193 (1890).

Partly in response to the Warren and Brandeis article, most states began to recognize some type(s) of tort action(s) for invasion of privacy during the twentieth century. Originally, these actions sought to protect the plaintiff's personal dignitary interest in being free from emotional distress and embarrassment that typically accompanied such invasions. While not all states have been uniform in their approach to privacy, over time many have defined the tort in such a way that it could be committed in any of the four following ways:

(1) **appropriation**, for the defendant's advantage, of the plaintiff's name or likeness;
(2) **intrusion** upon the plaintiff's seclusion or solitude, or into the plaintiff's private affairs;
(3) **public disclosure** of embarrassing private facts about the plaintiff; and
(4) publicity which places the plaintiff in a **false light** in the public eye.

William L. Prosser, *Privacy*, 48 CAL. L. REV. 383 (1960); *see also* RESTATEMENT (SECOND) OF TORTS §§ 652A-652E.

As a result of these original classifications, today most tort claims for invasion of privacy are brought as one of four specific tort causes of action: appropriation (or sometimes also "publicity"); intrusion; public disclosure of private embarrassing facts; and false light. Each of these individual privacy torts will be addressed in greater detail in its own separate subsection, *infra*.

I. Appropriation

This branch of the right of privacy allows recovery for appropriation of the plaintiff's name or identity for the defendant's commercial purposes. In other words, the focus of this tort is on the commercial loss inherent in the defendant's use of the plaintiff's name or identity for that person's own benefit. William L. Prosser, *Privacy*, 48 CAL. L. REV. 383 (1960); *see also* RESTATEMENT (SECOND) OF TORTS §§ 652A-652E. As a solely dignitary invasion, even where the plaintiff is a private person who had never sought to use his or her name or likeness for commercial gain, when the defendant does commercially appropriate that person's name or likeness, the plaintiff's personal autonomy in regard to making such decisions is harmed (i.e., the decision whether or not to commercially market his or her own name or likeness). Of course, in cases where the plaintiff is a celebrated person whose name or likeness already has recognizable economic value akin to a separate property right, the plaintiff typically focuses less upon the dignitary harm and more upon the actual value of the use of his or her own name. Because of this, a somewhat related action for the tort of "publicity" has also been recognized, at least in some jurisdictions. Since this so-called action for "publicity" protects an individual's economic interest in the use of his or her own name, image, or talent, actions based upon the concept of "publicity" are typically treated as a type of intellectual property. As such, actions for "publicity" are of special concern to athletes, entertainers, performers, and other celebrities who often actively market their names and likenesses for their own commercial benefit. For more discussion as to how the "publicity" tort differs from the tort of appropriation, *see* Chapter 22, *infra*, addressing Business Torts.

Although most cases relating to the appropriation of a plaintiff's name or likeness typically do involve actions brought by famous persons, even where the plaintiff is not known as a celebrity whose name or likeness already has an established economic value, non-celebrity plaintiffs have also been able to obtain recovery for proven losses caused by another's use of their name or identity by maintaining the tort of "appropriation." For example, in *Ainsworth v. Century Supply Co.*, 693 N.E.2d 510 (Ill. App. Ct. 1998), the court upheld the plaintiff's action for damages brought by a non-famous individual whose likeness was used in a television commercial promoting the sale of ceramic tile. The court sustained the plaintiff's claim that the defendant was paid to create a television commercial and thus had received a commercial benefit.

Ordinarily, in order to recover for either the tort of "publicity" or the tort of "appropriation," the defendant must appropriate the plaintiff's name or likeness for some commercial purpose or in some other manner that is inconsistent with the plaintiff's use. Nevertheless, not all commercial benefits fall within the scope of this tort. For example, when a newspaper mentions a famous person's name or publishes his or her likeness, clearly there has been a potential appropriation for commercial benefit. But, if the plaintiff is a newsworthy individual, this sort of publication is not considered to be an appropriation within the context of this tort. *See Colyer v. Richard K. Fox Publ'g Co.*, 162 App. Div. 297, 146 N.Y.S. 999 (1914). Instead, the tort is more likely to be applied when the defendant makes an unauthorized use of the plaintiff's name or likeness in a commercial advertisement (*e.g.*, suggesting that the plaintiff endorses or uses the product, as in *Ainsworth, supra*). *See* RESTATEMENT (SECOND) OF TORTS §§ 652A-652E.

In many situations (*e.g.*, when a newspaper or television station is reporting on a newsworthy event involving a famous person), First Amendment speech interests sometimes will trump an individual's privacy interest. However, in *Zacchini v. Scripps-Howard Broadcasting Co.*, 433 U.S. 562 (1977), the Court concluded that a news organization had overstepped its bounds. In that case, a television station broadcast the plaintiff's performance as the "human cannonball" from blast off to landing. Although there was debate over what constituted the entire act, the key moments were captured and broadcast to the television audience. The Court found that the right of publicity protected an entertainer's right to trade upon his or her talents to make a living, and also protected society's interest in the facilitation of creative energy. Although it recognized newsgathering as an important media function, the Court concluded that the news station should be required to pay damages. Persons interested in viewing the act had ready access to it, provided they were willing to pay the price for admission. Absent an opportunity to earn money for the spectacle, the performer's incentive to deliver the performance and the audience's opportunity to view it would diminish or vanish.

II. Intrusion on Plaintiff's Seclusion or Solitude

Ordinarily, this branch of the tort of privacy is actionable when there is a highly unreasonable interference with the plaintiff's seclusion or solitude. For example, the tort of "intrusion" occurs when the defendant intentionally intrudes into the plaintiff's home (*e.g.*, by peering through plaintiff's windows), or eavesdrops on the plaintiff's conversations through sophisticated microphones or wiretapping. *See McDaniel v. Atlanta Coca-Cola Bottling Co.*, 60 Ga. App. 92, 2 S.E.2d 810 (1939). For example, in *Dietemann v. Time, Inc.*, 284 F. Supp. 925 (C.D. Cal. 1968), magazine photographers misrepresented themselves in order to gain entrance to the plaintiff's home, and once inside they took pictures of the interior of the house. The court found that the case involved an actionable invasion of privacy, based upon the tort of intrusion.

For this tort to occur, the plaintiff is required to prove that the defendant intentionally intruded upon his or her solitude or seclusion. Typically, this means that the intrusion must invade some physical personal space in which the plaintiff is said to have a "reasonable expectation of privacy," such as a home, or apartment, or some other private area. As a result, this tort is not actionable when the defendant simply (and without interfering) observes the plaintiff's actions in public [*see Forster v. Manchester*, 410 Pa. 192, 189 A.2d 147 (1963)], or overhears comments spoken openly in a public place. However, when the defendant constantly shadows the plaintiff's actions with detectives in such a manner as to suggest improprieties on the plaintiff's part, the case may be actionable. *See Pinkerton Nat'l Detective Agency, Inc. v. Stevens*, 108 Ga. App. 159, 132 S.E.2d 119 (1963).

Unlike the intentional tort of trespass to land, not every simple invasion of the plaintiff's private space is necessarily actionable for the tort of intrusion. (*See* Chapter 2, section III.A., *supra*.) Instead, the intrusion must also be "highly offensive" to an ordinary person. A case that illustrates this requirement is *People for the Ethical Treatment of Animals v. Berosini*, 111 Nev. 615, 895 P.2d 1269 (1995). There, the plaintiff was a world renowned animal trainer who sued People for the Ethical Treatment of Animals and the Performing Animal Welfare Society for publishing a videotape that showed him shaking and punching his trained orangutans and hitting them with some kind of rod in the backstage area just prior to a live performance. At trial, there was testimony suggesting that the plaintiff had repeatedly mistreated various animals. The court concluded that the plaintiff could not maintain a defamation action against the defendants because the videotape was true (i.e., it showed true facts of what had occurred). The court also rejected the plaintiff's intrusion claim, noting that any claimed expectation of seclusion or solitude was not reasonable under these circumstances. The plaintiff had never expressed any concern about anyone (*e.g.*, backstage personnel) seeing him with the animals, and he had stated that his primary concern in punching the animals was merely to focus their attention. Indeed, the plaintiff saw nothing wrong with his backstage treatment of the animals in preparing them to perform. As a result, the court concluded that there was no intrusion into the plaintiff's seclusion. In addition, the court further observed that any intrusion that may have occurred was not "highly offensive" under these circumstances. In doing so, the court considered the degree of intrusion involved, as well as the context, the conduct and circumstances surrounding the intrusion (including the intruder's motives and objectives), the setting into which the intrusion occurred, and the plaintiff's own limited expectations of privacy. The court concluded that the videotaping was not intrusive, since it did not intrude upon the plaintiff's privacy in a way that would be highly offensive to a reasonable person.

A person can have a reasonable expectation of privacy even in places that the person does not actually "own" or possess. Therefore, the tort of intrusion may be available in some situations even when the person cannot otherwise sue for trespass. *See, e.g., Harkey v. Abate*, 131 Mich. App. 177, 346 N.W.2d 74 (1983) (public restroom); Annotation, "Retailer's Surveillance of Fitting or Dressing Rooms as Invasion of Privacy," 38 ALR4th 954 (1985). Conversely, as stated *supra*, not all cases of trespass give rise to an actionable tort of intrusion. Unlike trespass, which occurs when a defendant enters real property without permission or privilege, the tort of intrusion also requires the defendant's act to be highly offensive. A number of courts have found various intentional intrusions of personal space not to be offensive. *See, e.g., McLain v. Boise Cascade Corp.*, 533 P.2d 343 (Or. 1975); *Mark v. Seattle Times*, 635 P.2d 1081 (Wash. 1981), *cert. denied* 457 U.S. 1124 (1982).

As one might expect, there is a considerable range of opinion regarding which intrusions should be considered "offensive." The difference between the cases is more than a matter of degree. Although few cases discuss the issue directly, courts do not seem to agree on the way in which the intrusion must "offend." Some, like the court in *Berosini, supra,* focus on whether the defendant disrupted the plaintiff's solitude. However, another well-known case upheld the right of a photographer to take photos of Jacqueline Kennedy Onassis, as long as he acted in an unobtrusive manner. *Galella v. Onassis,* 487 F.2d 986 (2d Cir. 1973). Other courts focus less on the means of intrusion and more on the event or private activity that is observed. For example, in *Carter v. Innisfree Hotel, Inc.,* 661 So. 2d 1174 (Ala. 1995), hotel guests discovered a peephole in their room several hours after entering their room. Before they discovered the peephole, they had engaged in private acts. The court allowed the guests to recover against the hotel for intrusion even though they did not realize the intrusion was occurring, and even though they had no evidence that anyone had looked through the peephole during the activities in question. Apparently, the mere presence of the observation device was itself intrusive. *See also Hamberger v. Eastman,* 106 N.H. 107, 206 A.2d 239 (1964) (listening device); *Harkey v. Abate,* 131 Mich. App. 177, 346 N.W.2d 74 (1983).

In general, defendants have fared relatively well in intrusion cases. Most of the cases in which courts have imposed liability are those involving an actual trespass onto the plaintiff's property. Media defendants have a particularly good record in these cases. However, courts have imposed restrictions in especially outrageous cases (*e.g.,* when a photographer scares someone in order to take a particularly candid shot of his scared face).

III. Public Disclosure of Private Embarrassing Facts

An action for invasion of privacy may also be maintained on the basis of the defendant's disclosure of private facts in a way that would be highly offensive and objectionable to a reasonable person of ordinary sensibilities. *See* William L. Prosser, *Privacy,* 48 CAL. L. REV. 383 (1960); *see also* RESTATEMENT (SECOND) OF TORTS §§ 652A–652E. For this version of the privacy tort, the Restatement requires that the public must not have an otherwise legitimate interest in receiving the information. *Id.* Also, as with both the intrusion tort (*see* section II., *supra*) and the false light privacy tort (*see* section, IV., *infra*), the manner by which the defendant discloses private facts about the plaintiff must have been highly offensive to a reasonable person before any liability can be imposed. Thus, mere published disclosures of private facts, even if otherwise embarrassing, will not suffice.

Somewhat unique to the public disclosure tort is the additional requirement of publication. However, the concept of "publication" necessary to establish liability for this tort is more of a term of art. Unlike other torts such as defamation that also have a "publication" requirement (*see* Chapter 17, *supra*), for purposes of the tort of public disclosure of private facts, merely disclosing the information to others is not enough. The publication has to be more widespread so as to make it truly "public" in nature. Thus, in *Kuhn v. Account Control Technology, Inc.*, 865 F. Supp. 1443 (D. Nev. 1994), the court granted summary judgment to a defendant collection agency that merely revealed the plaintiff's credit problems to his co-workers.

Illustrative of the tort of public disclosure of private facts is the case of *Green v. Chicago Tribune Co.*, 675 N.E.2d 249 (Ill. App. Ct. 1996), in which a woman sued a newspaper's staff for photographing her son receiving emergency treatment for a bullet wound from which he later died, as well as for printing statements made by her as she grieved over her deceased son's body. The son's body was in a private hospital room, and the newspaper staff entered the room to photograph her son's dead body even after the plaintiff had refused to make a statement to them. Afterwards, the newspaper staff eavesdropped on her personal and private statements made to her son, and later included those statements and a photograph of the son in an article about the increasing homicide rate. The plaintiff claimed invasion of privacy because the newspaper staff had "trespassed" into the son's room, photographed her son's body without the plaintiff's consent, prevented the plaintiff from entering the son's room while the staff took photographs of his body, "eavesdropped" on the plaintiff's private statements to her just-deceased son, published an article containing quotes from the plaintiff's statements to her son along with a photograph of the son lying dead, and published a photograph of the son previously undergoing medical treatment prior to his death. The court concluded that the newspaper had disclosed private facts (i.e., a conversation in a private hospital room with the plaintiff's just-deceased son) after she had told the newspaper staff that she wanted to keep the matter private, and that a jury also could have found the publication of such facts under these circumstances to be highly offensive. The court further addressed the newspaper's potential First Amendment concerns by concluding that the publication did not involve a matter of legitimate concern to the public.

Nevertheless, application of the public disclosure privacy tort becomes more problematic when a media report does accurately disclose personal, embarrassing, or intimate details about an individual, and the question is whether truth should serve as a defense. In *Cox Broadcasting Corp. v. Cohn*, 420 U.S. 469 (1975), the Court reviewed a finding of liability for the tort of public disclosure of private facts based upon a state law that prohibited the publication of a rape victim's name. The Court determined that because the victim's identity had been obtained legally from a public record, the privacy claim and verdict could not stand. This outcome depended not just upon the truth of the report, but also upon the public nature of the record. Likewise, in *Landmark Communications, Inc. v. Virginia*, 435 U.S. 829 (1978), which involved a newspaper report of a confidential judicial disciplinary proceeding, the Court refused to impose damages for the public disclosure tort, finding that the information not only was truthful but had also been lawfully obtained. Finally, in *Smith v. Daily Mail Publishing Co.*, 443 U.S. 97 (1979), the Court was confronted by a newspaper's publication of a child murderer's name that had been obtained legally. Although the Court declined to establish an absolute privilege for the disclosure of truthful private information, it refused to impose liability for the publication of accurate information on an issue of "public significance," stating that public disclosure tort liability could not be established absent "a state interest of the highest order." However, the Court did not define the term "public significance."

The Florida Star v. B.J.F. 491 U.S. 524 (1989), was like *Cox Broadcasting Corp., supra,* in that it involved a newspaper's publication of a rape victim's identity in violation of state law. The facts differed, however, because law enforcement officials had inadvertently provided the victim's name to the newspaper, and the newspaper had published the story without realizing that publication violated its own internal policy against publishing the names of sex offense victims. The case was further complicated by the fact that the rape victim was still alive and received threatening calls from the perpetrator after the story was published. Nevertheless, because the information had been lawfully obtained, and the law did not distinguish between inadvertent and intentional publications, the Court found that the narrowly tailored requirement was not satisfied. In a dissenting opinion, Justice White maintained that the decision effectively eliminated the tort.

Although free speech principles frequently triumph in clashes with privacy principles, the Court has not held that truth is an absolute defense in a privacy case. Nevertheless, as the prior cases suggest, the truth of statements can have an important impact on whether the defendant is held liable (as will other factors such as whether the information was obtained in a lawful manner and whether it relates to the public interest). For example, in *Bartnicki v. Vopper,* 532 U.S. 514 (2002), a public disclosure of private facts privacy suit was brought when a cellular telephone conversation was illegally intercepted in violation of state and federal law, and was then aired publicly on a radio show. The conversation included threats of harm to management by a teacher's union president that were made to the union's chief negotiator during contract negotiations. Even though the Court recognized the importance of the privacy interest, and acknowledged that disclosure of such communications might chill private speech, the Court found the statutes unconstitutional as applied to a case where the defendants played no role in the illegal procural of the material and the conversation involved a matter of public interest. The Court refused to decide, however, whether protection would extend to the disclosure of trade secrets, domestic gossip, or other matters of purely private concern.

IV. False Light

A privacy action based on the portrayal of the plaintiff in a "false light" requires proof that, not only did the defendant cast the plaintiff in a false light in the public eye, but it was also done in a way that would be highly offensive to a reasonable person, and in reckless disregard for the truth or falsity of the publicized matter. *Russell v. Thomson Newspapers, Inc.*, 842 P.2d 896, 907 (Utah 1992) (*quoting* RESTATEMENT (SECOND) OF TORTS § 652E (1977)). Similar to the tort of defamation, a suit for false light privacy cannot be maintained unless there is evidence suggesting that the defendant made a misrepresentation of "fact" that created a false impression on the public's part regarding the plaintiff. In other words, if the defendant simply satirizes the plaintiff, or makes obviously false claims in jest, then this tort will not lie. *See Hustler Magazine v. Falwell*, 485 U.S. 46 (1988).

False light privacy bears some relation to the publication of private facts tort in that both of these torts require a "publication" and both torts also require the defendant's actions to be highly offensive to a reasonable person. (*See* discussion in section III, *supra*). However, although the publication of private facts tort involves the publication of *true* information about the plaintiff, the false light version involves a portrayal that is actually false or has the capacity to deceive. It might seem that because the publication of false information arguably has less value than the publication of true information, courts might be even more inclined to impose liability in false light cases. Nevertheless, in *Cain v. Hearst Corp.*, 878 S.W.2d 577 (Tex. 1994), the court rejected a claim by a prison inmate who sued a newspaper for referring to him as a burglar, thief, pimp, and killer, and for suggesting that he was a member of the "Dixie Mafia" who had killed as many as eight people. In finding against the plaintiff, the court noted that the false light privacy tort duplicated other existing causes of action, particularly defamation, while at the same time it lacked many of the procedural limitations that accompany actions for defamation. Texas is not alone in rejecting this false light branch of the privacy torts, and a significant number of other jurisdictions have reached similar results.

In those jurisdictions that do recognize this privacy tort, a defendant's use of the plaintiff's own words can sometimes give rise to a false light privacy claim. For example, where a paper publishes excerpts from a speech, but those excerpts grossly distort the plaintiff's message, the plaintiff may be able to recover under a false light theory. Similarly, if a third party has spoken about the plaintiff, the plaintiff may be able to recover against a defendant who reprints misleading excerpts of that statement. *See, e.g., Varnish v. Best Medium Publ'g*, 405 F.2d 608 (2d Cir. 1968), *cert. denied* 394 U.S. 987 (1969). In both of these cases, the courts have treated the defendant's publication of the other person's words as a statement by the defendant.

Since false light claims as well as many public disclosure privacy claims (*see* section III., *supra*) often involve suits against various media defendants that have published allegedly offending materials, these types of privacy torts typically raise a number of additional constitutional issues. The seminal application of First Amendment principles to the law of false light privacy was *Time, Inc. v. Hill*, 385 U.S. 374 (1967), which involved a magazine's misrepresentation of a family's hostage experience. The family sued under a state law that permitted false light privacy claims even if the subject was newsworthy. However, the Court rejected the claim, relying on the *New York Times* "actual malice" standard that it had previously applied in constitutional defamation cases. In other words, the court held that unless the plaintiff could establish that the media defendant had published the misstatement knowingly or in reckless disregard for the truth, the defendant could not be held liable for false light privacy. *See* Chapter 17, section III, *supra*, for a more detailed discussion of the *New York Time* "actual malice" standard.

A false light privacy claim also cannot be successfully maintained if the story, although false, is otherwise newsworthy. Such was the holding in *Cantrell v. Forest City Publishing Co.*, 419 U.S. 245 (1974), a case concerning a newspaper's mischaracterization of a family's living conditions, where the *New York Times* "actual malice" standard was also applied. However, the Court did suggest that proof of the defendant's "actual malice" might not be constitutionally required in cases involving private figure plaintiffs.

Checkpoints

- The tort of privacy protects an individual's dignitary interest in privacy against intrusion and publication.

- There are four distinct aspects of the right of privacy: appropriation of the plaintiff's name or likeness; intrusion into the plaintiff's seclusion or solitude; public disclosure of private embarrassing facts about the plaintiff; and portrayal of the plaintiff in a false light in the public eye.

- The tort of "appropriation" allows recovery for appropriation of the plaintiff's name or identity for commercial purposes.

- The tort of "publicity" protects something akin to a property right, and it can be violated when a performer's entire act is broadcast without permission.

- The tort of "intrusion" occurs when the defendant intentionally intrudes upon the plaintiff's seclusion or solitude in a manner that would be highly offensive and objectionable to a reasonable person.

- The tort of "public disclosure of private facts" occurs when the defendant discloses private true (but embarrassing) facts about the plaintiff in a manner that would be highly offensive and objectionable to a reasonable person.

- The tort of "false light" occurs when the defendant publishes false or misleading information that casts the plaintiff in a false or misleading light in the public eye, and does so in a manner that would be highly offensive to a reasonable person and also with *New York Times* "actual malice."

- False light privacy claims (except, perhaps, for claims by private figure plaintiffs) are governed by the *New York Times* "actual malice" standard and newsworthiness considerations.

- Newsworthiness will be a defense in cases concerning disclosure of private information, provided that the information was lawfully acquired and truthful.

- Information from public records concerning a matter of public significance may be published, barring a state interest of the "highest order."

- Truth has not been established as an absolute defense to a privacy action based upon publication of information taken from public records.

Chapter 19

Civil Rights

Roadmap

- Understand how the basic common law torts may be utilized in cases involving violations of civil rights.
- Understand the use of specific Constitutional provisions in seeking recovery for violations of civil rights.
- Understand the basic statutory scheme for establishing liability for violations of civil rights.
- Recognize the measure of damages applicable for violations of civil rights.

I. Tort Claims for Civil Rights Violations

Issues involving civil rights are usually thought to be solely a question for Constitutional Law. However, in many instances aggrieved individuals may also seek a private civil remedy when their civil rights have been violated. Such actions typically involve private tort claims. Tort law, of course, is the area of law that provides civil claims and remedies for harms to various different legally protected interests. It is tort law that shifts the loss, by way of compensation, from the injured party to the person who caused the injury. Therefore, a claim for an injury to anyone's civil rights, in its most basic sense, is a tort claim.

The interference with a person's civil rights may take many forms. It may be anything from a denial of the right to vote, to a personal injury due to the use of excessive force by law enforcement personnel. Although the remedies typically sought in civil rights torts will vary depending upon the type of claim asserted, most include at least some compensation in the form of money damages.

As with many injuries, civil rights claims often assert some of the basic intentional tort claims. Thus, under appropriate circumstances, the torts of assault, battery, false imprisonment, malicious prosecution, abuse of process, and intentional infliction of emotional distress are among the most commonly asserted intentional tort claims in civil rights actions. (*See* Chapter 2, *supra*, Intentional Interference with Person or Property, and Chapter 20, *infra*, Misuse of Legal Process).

The basic rights granted in the Constitution of the United States also provide the underlying law for many civil rights claims. In fact, violations of those rights may even give rise to claims based upon certain specific rights that are guaranteed by the Constitution itself.

Finally, legislation may also provide the basis for certain additional civil rights claims. In particular, federal legislation provides the primary source for many modern claims alleging violations of civil rights. Those statutes may protect individuals from violations of their basic Constitutional rights by state officials, as well as from violations of many other rights inferred from the language of the Constitution.

With all of these claims, determining the appropriate measure of damages can be problematic. Obviously, some of the interferences with civil rights will produce personal injury. For example, claims for the use of excessive force by law enforcement officers often involve personal injury damages. Some other claims, however, may not produce traditional personal injury and property damage losses. For example, the denial of a right to vote or the right to a hearing may not produce any tangible economic injury. In these types of cases, the determination of an appropriate measure of damages is more difficult.

This chapter provides an overview of all of these various types of civil rights claims. The basic intentional tort claims will be reviewed first, followed by claims based on direct violations of the Constitution, as well as federal statutes protecting civil rights. Also included is a discussion of the appropriate measure of damages that can be recovered in various civil rights actions.

II. Basic Common Law Claims

When government officials use excessive force, tort law supplies a remedy. The typical case arises when law enforcement officers attempt an arrest. During the course of the arrest, the law enforcement person may often need to use at least some degree of force. For example, it sometimes may be necessary for an arresting police officer to use force in order to place someone in hand cuffs and then position that person in the back seat of the police car. Usually, once arrested, the suspect is then taken to a holding facility and confined. Without appropriate authority for the arrest, or if the force used was excessive at any point of this process, a series of basic intentional torts may have been committed.

When the law enforcement officer chases and apprehends someone, an initial claim could be based upon the torts of assault and battery. The assault might occur during the chase, where the plaintiff would claim that the pursing officer had the necessary intent along with the other elements for this tort. The chase, an overt act, obviously produced an apprehension by the suspect of immediate bodily contact (if captured), and the pursuing law enforcement officer appears to have the present ability to carry out the threat. Subsequently, a battery might occur when the law enforcement officer catches the suspect and then hand cuffs him or her.

When the plaintiff is taken into custody and placed in the police car, the possibility of a false imprisonment arises. Clearly the defendant police officer had the intent to confine the plaintiff within the backseat of the locked police vehicle to prevent escape. In addition, there is an obvious physical confinement of the plaintiff's person within the automobile, of which the plaintiff is certainly aware. That confinement continues as the suspect is taken by the police officer to the jail and then placed in a locked cell or other detention facility.

Once the criminal process has begun, the possibility arises for the plaintiff accused to bring an action for the tort of malicious prosecution. The elements of such a claim may be easily stated as follows:

(1) a criminal action initiated by the defendant against the plaintiff;
(2) a lack of "probable cause" to begin that criminal action;
(3) common law malice by the defendant;
(4) a termination of the prosecution in favor of the accused plaintiff; and
(5) special damages suffered by the plaintiff.

If all of these elements were proven by the accused, then the plaintiff would have a claim under that intentional tort as well. For further details as to the torts of malicious prosecution and abuse of process, *see* the discussion in Chapter 20, *infra*.

As a result of the incidents described, *supra*, it is also possible that the plaintiff might even have a claim for intentional infliction of emotional distress. Potential threats intentionally made by the arresting police officer and/or other police personnel, as well as the subsequent confinement and prosecution of the accused might be so extreme and outrageous as to cause the plaintiff to experience severe emotional distress under these circumstances. Nevertheless, this particular intentional tort (i.e., intentional infliction of emotional distress) is rarely asserted as a standalone tort in these situations, since the numerous other intentional torts already present are usually sufficient to permit the plaintiff also to recover for such emotional distress damages.

Since the law enforcement officer in this scenario is working as an employee of a city, state or federal government, there is also the possibility that the plaintiff may wish to assert some form of vicarious liability against the employer. If the officer was acting in the scope of employment, then the employer might be held vicariously liable for the torts that were committed by the police officer against the plaintiff. As a part of such claim, plaintiffs may even bring a claim against the appropriate governmental entity asserting direct liability for negligent hiring or entrustment. In addition to these claims against the actual governmental entity that employed the police officer(s) who committed the initial tort(s) (as discussed, *supra*), the plaintiff might also add claims against supervisors, trainers, and other officers claiming that they individually were also directly liable for negligence in hiring, training, and supervising the original tortfeasing officer(s). (*See* Chapter 13, *supra*, Vicarious Liability).

Based upon all of the foregoing discussion, it should be obvious that an arrest that is not carried out properly can give rise to numerous tort claims to recover damages for the plaintiff. However, there are also special defensive arguments that can be asserted in the context of a law enforcement situation to avoid tort liability in many of these situations.

For example, the false imprisonment and the malicious prosecution torts require the plaintiff to prove that the action was initiated without legal authority. If the law enforcement officer had legal authority to make the confinement and begin the criminal process, there is no claim. Legal authority for an arrest and for a criminal prosecution frequently involves "probable cause." The concept of probable cause is studied in detail in courses such as Criminal Procedure. For basic torts, however, that phrase usually means that the officer had a reasonable belief that a crime had been committed and a reasonable belief that the person being apprehended committed that crime. If the facts show that level of reasonable belief, then there is no claim for false imprisonment or malicious prosecution.

Likewise, law enforcement officers may also be able to defeat claims for assault and battery by proving that they acted with legal authority and without excessive force. Of course, police officers are not allowed to use any and all available force. Instead, traditional common law rules indicate that an officer may only use reasonable force to make an arrest. Such a rule leaves questions of fact for the jury in many cases. Many states have passed legislation outlining the degrees of force that may be used in differing situations. Those statutes should be consulted in order to determine the specific rules in any particular jurisdiction.

For vicarious liability and negligent entrustment, there are also certain additional defenses. If it is shown that the law enforcement officer used reasonable force and had legal authority for the conduct, the officer is, of course, not liable. Defeating liability for the officer will also release the employer from vicarious liability. The claims based upon direct liability for negligent hiring or entrustment by the governmental entity that employed the police officer or by the other defendants who hired and or supervised that officer will turn on the specific conduct of each individual defendant. Therefore, it is necessary to prove that each individual defendant used reasonable care in hiring, training, and supervising the police officer whose initial actions gave rise to these claims. Even if the officer is held liable for some tort, the claim for negligent hiring or entrustment may fail if those defendants responsible for such decisions used reasonable care. Where the arresting officer is relieved of all liability by proving that (s)he used appropriate force and acted with proper legal authority, there is also no legal basis for any claim against any of these other potential defendants for negligent hiring or entrustment. Since no underlying tort has been committed, those defendants' conduct in hiring or training or supervising the police officer was not a cause of any harm to the plaintiff.

Although not actually a civil rights claim, other conduct by government officials may also give rise to tort claims. When law enforcement officers attempt to arrest a possible law violator, sometimes their conduct will create a new danger that risks injury to other, innocent, people as well. Automobile high-speed chases, for example, have been known to end in accidents that involve multiple cars. When innocent bystanders are injured, they may be able to pursue separate claims against the officer(s) individually, as well as the responsible government entity, based on negligence. (*See* Chapter 4, *supra*, Negligence). The injured plaintiff must prove that the officer-driver of the automobile failed to use reasonable care, just as in any negligence case. However, to aid in proving such negligence, most jurisdictions have statutes that indicate the nature of reasonable care that must be used by officers when they are involved in high-speed chases. These statutes allow officers to exceed posted speed limits and to run traffic control signals such as traffic lights and stop signs in appropriate situations, provided that the officers use flashing lights and sirens, and maintain reasonable care even under the circumstances of the high-speed chase.

When an officer finds it necessary to fire his or her gun during the course of an arrest, it is also possible that the bullets may hit innocent people or their property. When this occurs, the claim against the officer is again one of negligence and not intentional tort. Typically, the officer did not intend to hit the person who was injured (or their property), but the officer may have simply failed to use reasonable care in discharging a weapon. Again, those statutes that specify the nature of force that may be used by officers in making an arrest (discussed *supra*) may also help in determining whether the officer's use of force that injured the innocent bystander was reasonable.

All of the examples discussed to this point assume that the law enforcement action is occurring in a public area. However, there are times when law enforcement officers may find it necessary to enter private homes. For example, this need may arise when police officers seek to search the home or to arrest someone within it. In the absence of proper authority, this type of conduct can give rise to a claim for trespass to land. As with the traditional trespass tort claim, the elements are met just as soon as the officer enters the home. The officer intends to be where (s)he is, and clearly the officer has directly entered the land of another. Ordinarily, this is sufficient to support liability for trespass to land. (*See* Chapter 2, section III.A., *supra*, Trespass to Land). Of course, just as with the other intentional torts discussed *supra*, if the police officer has entered into the plaintiff's home with proper legal authority this will be a defense to any potential claim for trespass. In this circumstance, the easiest way to establish proper legal authority and thus avoid the possibility of such a claim is for the officer to obtain a proper warrant prior to the entry. Materials on search and arrest warrants are, of course, covered in a course on Criminal Procedure.

Even in the absence of a traditional common law intentional tort remedy, the law of torts is somewhat unique in that it can often be construed and even expanded to create a new remedy when an injury occurs. This is even true of injuries caused by an injury to a person's civil rights. The law of torts creates a remedy for situations when a person has been injured due to the conduct of another. For example, the right to vote is an important civil right for which there is no traditional common law tort remedy. Thus, when an individual has been inappropriately denied the right to vote, it was necessary for tort law to create an entirely new "civil rights" claim whereby the denied voter could recover damages resulting from the deprivation of this important legal right. Of course, determining the actual amount of those damages in civil rights cases can still be quite difficult. That topic is discussed further in section III.C., *infra*.

III. Constitutional and Statutory Claims

Despite the broad range of traditional tort claims that can be used when an individual is denied a civil right, the law in the United States does not rely solely on such claims in these circumstances. The Constitution of the United States and various statutes passed pursuant to it have created a range of duties owed to citizens that are even broader than those addressed by the traditional common law torts. By using the Constitution and these associated statutes, plaintiffs have additional claims and protections for civil rights violations. The protections provided by the Constitution are, of course, fully discussed in courses on Constitutional law. It is necessary, however, to briefly review some of that law in order to illustrate how tort law provides individual remedies when those rights have been infringed.

Even a brief overview of the Constitution of the United States reveals a few obvious structural features. Most of the rights guaranteed to individuals appear in the amendments to the Constitution. The first eight amendments provide a series of protections against federal infringement, while the 14th Amendment protects against state infringement. The 14th Amendment incorporates all of the rights found in the first eight amendments and through that incorporation, these rights also find protection against state action.

Because of that structural format, it is possible to look at civil rights litigation as two different types of actions. There are the actions brought against the federal government due to conduct by federal agents, and there are actions brought against state or local governments due to the conduct of state or local agents. Actions brought against federal agents and the federal government are based, primarily, on the first eight amendments to the U.S. Constitution. Actions brought against state or local agents and state or local governments are based, primarily, on the 14th Amendment to the U.S. Constitution, as well as various statutes passed pursuant to that amendment.

A. Constitutional Claims

When a plaintiff has been injured by conduct of federal agents in a way that violates certain civil rights, the plaintiff may seek to bring a claim for those injuries. The limitations on federal conduct appear, primarily, in the first eight amendments to the United States Constitution. However, when those provisions are considered, a significant deficiency is revealed. Although the first eight amendments to the Constitution prohibit or limit certain federal government conduct, those amendments do not specify what is to happen if agents of the federal government violate those amendments. There is no specific grant of a remedy in those amendments.

The Fourth Amendment to the Constitution, for example, guarantees that people have a right to be secure in their homes and that those homes will not be subject to "unreasonable search and seizure." This amendment, however, does not specify a remedy if such an "unreasonable search and seizure" does occur.

In *Bivens v. Six Unknown Named Agents of the Federal Bureau of Investigation*, 403 U.S. 388 (1971), the United States Supreme Court had the opportunity to analyze such a problem. In that case, a group of agents of the Federal Bureau of Investigation entered the home of a family without a warrant and without probable cause. After a search, the agents left. The family sued for the invasion of their home based on the prohibitions found in the Fourth Amendment. The problem with the claim in the *Bivens* case was that the Fourth Amendment did not specifically provide for a remedy. The amendment prohibited the conduct that occurred, but it did not appear to provide a method of redress for that conduct. The United States Supreme Court, however, used traditional tort theory to create a remedy. To understand the Court's decision, it is important also to understand that it is common in tort law for the law to create a remedy whenever a legal duty has been violated, and since the Fourth Amendment clearly created such a duty, it was appropriate for the Court to use the law of torts to create a new remedy.

The method the Court used in creating this new remedy from the Fourth Amendment is similar to the traditional rules concerning "negligence *per se*." (*See* Chapter 4, section III.C., *supra*, Negligence). In many cases, when a defendant violates a statute, that statute is used as the basis for imposing a specific duty. The violation of the statute is the breach, and if that breach causes injury, the court will allow recovery of damages for negligence. This is, in fact, what the United States Supreme Court did in the *Bivens* case. The federal agents violated the 4th Amendment to the Constitution. That amendment, much like a statute, created a duty. The violation of that amendment was the breach. The breach of the duty caused the injury for which the United States Supreme Court would provide a remedy.

Using an analysis similar to *Bivens*, it is easy to see how civil rights actions against federal agents and the federal government could develop. The first eight amendments to the United States Constitution provide a series of limitations on power and duties imposed upon the federal government and federal agents. Each of those amendments can be considered almost like a duty in a tort claim. A breach of any of those duties potentially could give rise to damages that could be recovered. The courts will allow the plaintiff to use those duties in the amendments as the bases of claims against federal agents and the federal government.

The First Amendment to the United States Constitution, for example, protects citizens' rights to freedom of religion, speech, the press, and assembly. The violation of any of those rights could represent a sufficient breach to give rise to a claim for damages.

The Fourth Amendment, noted in the *Bivens* example, *supra*, protects against unlawful search and seizure. These types of violations are more common in civil rights claims involving actions against federal law enforcement officials, as in *Bivens*, and when they occur a so-called *Bivens* action is used to provide relief for injured plaintiffs.

The Fifth Amendment protects against being forced to testify against oneself and it also guarantees certain procedural rights. Again, the violation of these rights can give rise to a tort claim similar to the one created in *Bivens*, *supra*.

It should be noted, however, that civil actions for conduct in violation of the Fourth and Fifth Amendment are not as common as it might seem. And, when such violations do occur, they typically arise during the course of a criminal trial. For example, the defendant in the trial will often seek to have evidence excluded that was obtained in violation of his or her Constitutional rights. Under Constitutional law and evidence law, evidence gained in violation of those rights may not be admissible. Although the evidentiary issue is one that is more frequently litigated, if the party is injured by the Constitutional violation, a tort claim could also be brought.

The Eighth Amendment to the United States Constitution also has been used to give rise to injury claims. That amendment protects against cruel and unusual punishment. Although those seeking to abolish the death penalty frequently discuss the amendment, it may also arise in certain civil actions. For example, where a prisoner is subject to abuse by guards or to inhuman prison conditions, the prisoner may assert a claim for relief as a civil tort action. The duties imposed by the Eighth Amendment will be treated as the duties to support the tort claim in order to seek redress for those injuries.

B. Statutory Claims

When a plaintiff is injured by conduct from a state agent, the nature of the plaintiff's claim is different from the *Bivens* action discussed, *supra*. After the Civil War, the United States Congress passed a series of statutes designed to protect civil rights. The statute is 42 U.S.C. 1983. Unlike the Constitutional amendments noted in the immediately proceeding section, *supra*, this statute specifically creates an entirely new remedy. It states that when any person is acting "under the color of state law" to deprive someone of a constitutional right, then the injured party shall have a claim for damages. Due to the nature of the statute, therefore, actions against state and local agents and state and local governments are usually brought under Section 42 U.S.C. 1983, where typically they are referred to as "Section 1983 actions," or "1983 civil rights actions."

When an injured plaintiff seeks to bring a claim under Section 42 U.S.C. 1983, the statute speaks of violations of constitutional rights. The plaintiff, therefore, must first show the violation of a constitutional right in order to maintain the claim. The first eight amendments, standing alone, protect against conduct by the federal government. They are not directly applicable against state action. However, the 14th Amendment does impose limits on state action. It protects individuals from deprivations of life, liberty, and property without due process of law. Therefore, by virtue of the 14th Amendment, states and state agents cannot deprive individuals of life, liberty or property without due process, just as federal agents are prohibited from doing so under the first eight amendments of the Constitution, as discussed, *supra*. (*See* section III.A., *supra*).

The due process clause guarantees appropriate procedural regularity. This means that if a state agency is seeking to deny a person some rights or privileges otherwise guaranteed by the Constitution, that person is entitled to certain "due" process. There may be some disputes regarding the degree of process that is due, but state action cannot be arbitrary. If, for example, someone is about to lose state subsidies, that person is probably entitled to some opportunity to be heard. If the state denies that person any right to be heard, the person could bring an action for damages. The plaintiff's claim would assert that Section 42 U.S.C. 1983 guarantees the protection of the plaintiff's Constitutional rights from state infringement. Since the state, acting "under color of state law" has denied the plaintiff's right to be heard, (s)he would be entitled to damages for the state action in denying that right.

The 14th Amendment to the Constitution has been interpreted to incorporate all of the rights guaranteed in the first eight amendments. By operation of the 14th Amendment, therefore, citizens are protected from violations by state authorities of those same rights that the first eight amendments protect from federal infringement. Since plaintiffs can sue federal agents and the federal government for violations of those rights by bringing a *Bivens* action, a plaintiff can also sue state agents and state governments for violations of those same rights by using Section 42 U.S.C. 1983, the 14th Amendment and the doctrine of incorporation.

Since the first eight amendments can be used through the doctrine of incorporation, excessive force cases by state law enforcement officers can be brought as "civil rights" actions under Section 42 U.S.C. 1983. Examples are easy to imagine. If a state or local law enforcement officer enters a person's home without a warrant and causes personal injury and property damage, that officer can be sued under Section 42 U.S.C 1983 which allows recovery for violations of the plaintiff's constitutional rights. By entering into the house "under color of state law" and causing personal injury and property damage, the state officer has deprived the plaintiff of property without due process of law. In addition, since the first eight amendments are incorporated into the Fourteenth Amendment, the protections of the Fourth Amendment would also apply. The state officer engaged in an unlawful search and seizure while acting "under color of state law" and, as a result, all of those claims would be a part of the plaintiff's action.

However, it also should be remembered that, in addition to a Section 1983 "civil rights" claim, several common law tort claims could also provide additional bases for an action. (*See* section II., *supra*). Thus, in the state officer example discussed *supra*, the plaintiff's attorney could also add intentional tort claims for assault, battery, false imprisonment, trespass to land, and trespass to chattels. Addressing each of these claims individually, the officer committed a trespass to land simply by directly entering the house without proper authority. By detaining the person, the officer may have committed a false imprisonment. If the plaintiff sustained any personal injury as a result of this incident, the officer may also be sued for battery, and possibly also an assault. Finally, if damage occurred to any of the personal property inside the plaintiff's house, this would give rise to an additional action for the tort of trespass to chattels.

In a typical civil rights case, the plaintiff's attorney will likely assert all of the federal civil rights claims, as well as claims based upon any applicable common law torts. Since a Section 42 U.S.C. 1983 action is a federal claim, that claim can be brought in federal court. The additional state common law tort claims can also be joined with the Section 1983 action in the same federal court case.

In the initial discussion of the possible common law tort claims, it was mentioned that some civil rights claims might also be brought for the tort of negligence. For example, claims arising out of automobile accidents involving the alleged negligence of state and or federal officials must be distinguished from the federal *Bivens* actions and Section 42 U.S.C. 1983 claims. In order to recover under either of these claims, however, the plaintiff must be able to prove that the conduct by the governmental agent was done intentionally, or at least with knowledge that the circumstances were substantially certain to occur.

Most of the previous discussion has dealt with the violation of constitutional rights that occur during various attempts by governmental agents to enforce the criminal laws. Such claims are common and are frequently seen and litigated in the courts. Those claims, however, are not the only types of civil rights claims that allow recovery for violations of constitutional rights. Congress and various states have passed legislation to protect other types of constitutional rights as well. The most common claims found outside the criminal law enforcement area are those for employment discrimination such as Title VII of the Civil Rights Act of 1964. Although subsequently amended on several occasions, this statute provides the basic framework for protecting employees from discrimination due to sex, race, religion, and national origin. Additional legislation in this area protects workers from age discrimination, disability discrimination, and unequal pay based on gender.

Allegations of employment discrimination involve a completely different type of process. These types of civil rights violations typically provide options for administrative hearings, with the ultimate determinations usually made by the federal courts. The law in this area continues to expand and grow with judicial interpretations of these statutes. Sex discrimination, for example, has grown from simple cases of job differences based on gender to actions to protect employees from sexual harassment. Although these cases involve federal actions based on federal statutes, they sometimes appear to be in the nature of tort claims. Nevertheless, they still can be used to provide additional remedies for people who have been injured by the breaches of various duties owed to citizens in some of these other areas.

C. Damages

There are times when a plaintiff may bring a tort claim merely to confirm the existence of some legal right or liberty that had been infringed. However, that is not the most common reason why such actions are filed. Instead, tort claims are designed to compensate an injured party for actual damages that have been suffered. Civil rights claims, as with most other tort claims, are usually brought to recover similar compensation for injuries caused due to the violation of the plaintiff's civil rights.

However, civil rights claims have presented certain difficulties regarding the determination of the appropriate measure of damages that can be recovered. For example, some plaintiffs have brought civil rights claims seeking to recover damages merely for the value of the right that was lost. These claims assert that the infringement of *the right itself has value*. The difficulty with such a claim should be obvious. When an individual is denied the right to vote, clearly that person's civil rights have been harmed. However, how is the value of that harm to be measured? If, for example, the candidate for whom the plaintiff would have voted wins the election anyway, then there is no ultimate harm for the loss of the plaintiff's single vote. Likewise, if that same candidate had lost by a large number of votes, the addition of the plaintiff's one vote would not have changed the outcome and, again, there is no harm. There would only be harm if the candidate lost by just one vote, and then the plaintiff's single vote could in fact have made a difference in the outcome of the election. Although technically accurate, such an analysis completely overlooks the *value* of that individual plaintiff's right to vote. If officials could avoid paying damages for intentionally denying people or certain groups of citizens their right to vote simply by claiming that those votes would not have changed the ultimate outcome of the election, then the voting rights of all citizens would be in great danger. It is for this reason that the law must seek to determine a monetary value of the plaintiff's individual *right to vote*.

Similar problems have arisen in cases involving the denial of a "due process" hearing before the removal of some right or privilege. If the plaintiff would have lost that right or privilege even after receiving a hearing, then there does not appear to be any real harm done. However, once again the importance of procedural due process requires that every citizen must be given at least some *right to be heard*, and, once again, the monetary value of this right must also be determined.

Just as it may be difficult at times to see any actual harm resulting from the loss of a particular civil right in any given situation, it is also hard to imagine a precise figure that would adequately compensate a person for the value of one of those civil rights. How is it even possible to prove that a right to vote is worth a certain amount of dollars, or that the right to a "due process" hearing is worth a different amount? And, is one citizen's right to vote, or to have "due process" valued the same as that of another citizen?

Once again, to address these problems in calculating a specific dollar amount of damages needed to adequately compensate for civil rights claims, the courts have relied on basic tort law. Thus, the usual measure of damages in civil rights claims is determined in the same way as similar losses that are routinely awarded for other tort claims. Typically, those damages may include property damage or personal injury. For example, property damage might arise when government agents harm real or personal property during their actions. Likewise, personal injury may result from the excessive use of force or as the result of some other personally directed misconduct, and such damages typically include individual components such as lost wages, medical bills, disability, "pain and suffering," and emotional distress. (*See* Chapter 8, *supra*, Compensatory and Punitive Damages). As for determining damages to compensate for the infringement of a plaintiff's more intangible "due process" or voting "rights," courts typically allow juries to make these types of awards in much the same manner as they assess other nonpecuniary losses such as emotional distress or "pain and suffering."

One additional form of compensation is available under some civil rights claims. Section 42 U.S.C. 1983 has a special provision for the award of attorneys' fees to the prevailing plaintiff. Specifically, under Section 42 U.S.C. 1987, successful litigants may recover their own reasonable attorney's fees in addition to other damages. This can be a substantial benefit to plaintiffs who ordinarily must pay their own attorneys fees out of the proceeds of any final judgment that they may recover. That fee typically may range between 30 percent and 40 percent of the final award. Thus, the federal civil rights statute effectively allows the plaintiff to keep the entire award, by requiring the defendant to pay the plaintiff's attorney a reasonable fee, in addition to any other damages awarded.

Checkpoints

- Traditional common law torts are frequently used to recover damages when a person's civil rights are violated. These common law torts include:
  - assault;
  - battery;
  - false imprisonment;
  - trespass to land;
  - malicious prosecution; and
  - negligence.
- For actions against federal officers, courts use the duties imposed by the Constitution and create a tort remedy for the harm that was done.
- For actions against state officers, courts use the duties imposed by the Constitution and the action created by the federal statutes under Section 42 U.S.C 1983.
- In order to recover damages for a civil rights violation, the plaintiff must prove the actual harm suffered.
- Actions brought under Section 42 U.S.C. 1983 also allow recovery of the plaintiff's attorney's fees under Section 42 U.S.C. 1987.

Chapter 20

Misuse of Legal Process

Roadmap

- Understand the distinction between the torts of "malicious prosecution" and "abuse of process," as well as what special interests are protected by each.

- Distinguish the circumstances in which the tort of "malicious prosecution" can be asserted and the circumstances when the tort of "abuse of process" can be asserted.

- Learn the specific legal requirements for the tort of "malicious prosecution of a criminal action."

- Learn the specific legal requirements for the tort of "malicious prosecution of a civil action."

- Learn the specific legal requirements for the tort of "abuse of process."

This chapter addresses a special category of tort claims that have been created primarily for the purpose of protecting individuals against harms inflicted upon them as the result of certain types of abuses of the legal system. Injuries for these torts typically range from emotional distress and embarrassment to actual economic losses incurred by persons who have been forced to defend themselves against various types of unjustified legal actions, both civil as well as criminal. These torts are classified as "intentional," because they each require some type of specific wrongful intent by the defendant.

There are essentially two basic types of torts involving the intentional abuse of legal process. These torts are similar in that both involve some improper purpose or motive by the defendant with respect to using the legal system in a way that causes tortious injury to the plaintiff. However, they are distinguished from one another in that the tort of "malicious prosecution" focuses upon the defendant's motive in *wrongfully initiating* a legal action against the plaintiff that was inappropriate from the very beginning, whereas the tort of "abuse of process" involves the use of various types of legal process which, although *properly initiated* against the plaintiff, nevertheless should not have been brought at all because of the defendant's improper motive in doing so.

Sometimes the distinction between these two torts can become somewhat blurred, although each tort has its own unique requirements for imposing liability against the defendant.

The common law has long recognized the tort of "malicious prosecution" as a remedy for persons wrongfully subjected to criminal prosecution. *See generally* Note, *Groundless Litigation and the Malicious Prosecution Debate: A Historical Analysis*, 88 YALE L.J. 1218 (1979). By contrast, the tort of "abuse of process" is much more recent in origin. Nevertheless, throughout the history of American jurisprudence, the courts generally have disfavored both of these torts. This is partly due to the strong tradition in American constitutional law that favors the "open access" to courts by all citizens for the resolution of their conflicts, even if some of those conflicts may turn out to have been based upon somewhat questionable or even improper legal grounds. Recognizing subsequent civil tort claims against litigants from prior civil or criminal cases who have been unsuccessful with their claims can have a definite "chilling effect" upon the assertion of many valid, although perhaps unpopular or uncertain, legal claims. Such concerns have led many courts in the United States to take a very strict view in regard to the interpretation and application of both of these tort causes of action.

I. Malicious Prosecution (of a Criminal Action)

Historically, the tort of "malicious prosecution" was recognized as a remedy *only* with respect to injuries resulting from the wrongful initiation of *criminal* prosecutions against the plaintiff. Over time, however, this tort has been expanded in many jurisdictions to include wrongfully initiated *civil* actions as well. (*See* section II., *infra*). As a result, depending upon the particular jurisdiction involved, the specific legal requirements for the tort(s) of "malicious prosecution" tend to vary somewhat in response to these various differences.

In most jurisdictions, the common law tort of "malicious prosecution" of a criminal action consists of some variation of the following specific requirements:

(1) a criminal prosecution initiated by the defendant;
(2) a lack of "probable cause" to begin that criminal prosecution;
(3) common law malice by the defendant;
(4) a termination of the prosecution in favor of the accused plaintiff; and
(5) special damages suffered by the plaintiff.

To understand exactly how this tort was designed to function, it is necessary to examine each of these requirements just a bit more closely.

A. Criminal Prosecution Initiated by the Defendant

In the majority of situations, it is usually quite obvious whenever any criminal prosecution has been initiated against someone. Typically, as soon as formal charges are brought against an accused person, that person will be arrested by law enforcement officers, advised of those charges, and taken to jail. Clearly, in such instances, a criminal prosecution has begun.

However, depending upon the jurisdiction, there are actually several ways in which a criminal prosecution can be initiated. Formal criminal charges can be brought by the actual filing of a criminal warrant against the accused by the person initiating such charges. This can be done either by the state through a law enforcement officer or other representative, or by a private individual. In addition, the state can also initiate a criminal proceeding against an accused by obtaining an "indictment" (or by a variation called an "information" in some jurisdictions). This is a formal criminal charge issued by a grand jury composed of citizens who have listened to evidence of the alleged crime presented *ex parte* by the state before deciding whether to initiate the criminal charges. The issuance of any of these formal documents is sufficient to "commence" a criminal "prosecution" of the accused.

With respect to this element of a malicious prosecution case, the defendant must have taken an active role in actually initiating the charge that typically extends beyond merely causing a formal criminal charge to be brought against the accused. Thus, the mere report by the defendant of a suspected criminal offense to law enforcement officials will not, without something more, satisfy this requirement. Instead, this initiation requirement contemplates that the defendant has actively instigated the prosecution. For example, where the defendant, a store security guard, personally witnesses the plaintiff engage in suspicious conduct that reasonably appears to be shoplifting, the defendant could certainly report such conduct to law enforcement authorities without incurring any liability for this tort. However, where the same security guard persists in demanding that the accused be arrested and charged with shoplifting even after an investigation by law enforcement authorities failed to reveal evidence of any crime, the defendant would likely be considered as having "initiated" the criminal prosecution.

Apart from actually initiating a criminal prosecution, the defendant in a malicious prosecution action can sometimes satisfy this requirement merely by procuring the continuation of criminal proceedings that were previously initiated against the accused by the defendant or even by another. Specifically, Restatement (Second) of Torts, § 655 (1977) explains that:

> "A private person who takes an active part in continuing or procuring the continuation of criminal proceedings initiated by himself or by another is subject to the same liability for malicious prosecution as if he had then initiated the proceedings."

This section has been construed to encompass other types of conduct besides merely actively seeking to continue criminal proceedings beyond the point when such charges should have been discontinued against an accused. For example, it has also been applied in situations where the defendant simply fails to take appropriate action to have criminal charges dismissed against an accused, once it becomes obvious that such charges are without merit. *See Banks v. Nordstrom*, 787 P.2d 953 (Wash. App. 1990).

B. Lack of "Probable Cause" for the Criminal Prosecution

"Probable cause" is a special legal term that means, in essence, that there is no *reasonable basis* in fact to believe that a crime has been committed and that the accused is the person most likely responsible for having committed it. Where the facts pertaining to the accused's alleged involvement in a crime are in dispute, the requirement of probable cause does not require a factual determination that the accused is actually guilty. Instead, probable cause merely requires that at least some reasonable basis must exist for believing that the accused has committed the crime charged.

This means that in order to satisfy the legal requirements of probable cause, the person who initiates the criminal proceedings must make a good faith effort to investigate all of the facts surrounding the alleged criminal activity. However, it is not that person's responsibility to actually resolve any factual disputes that may arise as to the accused's ultimate guilt or innocence. That is why, in the previous section, *supra*, the grand jury is allowed to initiate formal criminal charges against accused persons who are not even present in court (or even permitted at this stage of the proceedings to present opposing evidence), based solely upon *ex parte* evidence presented on behalf of the state that criminal conduct has occurred and that the person accused is the one most likely responsible for it. If there is at least probable cause for the grand jury to believe that a crime has been committed by the accused, the final resolution of those facts, as well as the ultimate determination of the accused's guilt or innocence with respect to the charges, will be left for an entirely different jury (i.e., the trial jury) to resolve, if the criminal case progresses to that point.

In a malicious prosecution action, the determination as to whether probable cause existed for the initiation of a criminal prosecution is ultimately a legal question for the court to determine. In making that determination, a court will typically consider numerous factors, including the reliability of all witnesses and other evidence implicating the accused, the effort expended in gathering that evidence, as well as in investigating the charges, the prior background of the accused, and any evidence that might exonerate the accused. Although some courts have concluded that probable cause involves a "mixed question" of law and fact requiring a jury to determine the existence of certain facts before they can be applied by the court in determining probable cause, in the final analysis the question is usually one that must be determined by the court as a legal matter. In the case of a formal criminal indictment presented directly to a grand jury, a lack of probable cause usually results in the failure of that body to initiate formal charges against the accused even from the very beginning. However, when the defendant acts individually to initiate criminal charges directly against the accused, the individual accuser still must have the requisite probable cause, and the subsequent dismissal of such charges against the accused will usually constitute at least *prima facie* evidence of the lack of probable cause. *See* the discussion in section D, *infra*.

C. Common Law Malice by the Defendant

Even where the plaintiff otherwise is able to establish the lack of probable cause for the criminal charges initiated against him or her, an action for "malicious prosecution" (of a criminal action) still cannot be sustained unless, as the very name of this tort suggests, the defendant has acted with *malice*. Unfortunately, the precise meaning of this concept is not altogether certain.

"Common law malice" in the law of torts is actually a very confusing term, since it can refer to any one of several completely different (yet still closely related) legal concepts. To help in distinguishing among these different common law concepts, consider the following specific terms typically used by courts when attempting to define common law malice.

Actual malice. This type of common law malice refers specifically to an actual feeling by the defendant of hatred, spite, animosity, or ill will toward the plaintiff. *See Williams v. Kuppenheimer Mfg. Co.*, 412 S.E. 2d 897 (N.C. 1992). Specific proof of the defendant's actual, subjective state of mind is generally required in order to establish this type of "actual malice."

Legal malice. This type of common law malice is somewhat broader than "actual malice," *supra*, and can also include actions that are motivated by *any* improper or wrongful motive. *See Owens v. Kroger Co.*, 430 So. 2d 843 (Miss. 1984). Once again, the defendant's subjective state of mind is determinative, but "legal malice" can be established even if the defendant is motivated by something other than actual hatred, ill will or spite toward the plaintiff, so long as that motive is otherwise improper or wrongful.

Malice in law. Unlike either actual or legal malice, *supra*, "malice in law" does not require any proof of the defendant's subjective state of mind. Rather, it refers simply to any intentionally tortious action that is done without any just cause or excuse. *See Sanders v. Daniel International Corp.*, 682 S.W. 2d 803, 808 (1984). Malice in law is the broadest of these three definitions of common law malice. It simply imputes malice from any intentionally wrongful misconduct that injures another person without justification or other legal excuse.

As if all this were not already confusing enough, the United States Supreme Court in its majority opinion in *New York Times Co. v. Sullivan*, 376 U.S. 254 (1964), recognized yet another type of malice used exclusively within the context of certain constitutional defamation (and extended later to some privacy) cases which it also referred to by the unfortunate use of the same term, "actual malice." This very unique type of malice was defined as any statement about the plaintiff made "with knowledge that it was false or with *reckless disregard* of whether it was false or not." *Id.* at 280. (*See* Chapter 17, section III., *supra*, Defamation). Although also referred to as "actual malice," this concept should not be confused with the common law term known identically as "actual malice" (discussed, *supra*) which requires actual proof of the defendant's subjective state of mind as to a feeling of hatred, ill-will or spite directed against the plaintiff. *New York Times* "actual malice" is generally not used at all when determining the existence of common law "actual malice" for purposes of the tort of malicious prosecution.

For purposes of construing and applying the common law malice requirement for the tort of "malicious prosecution," most courts consider proof of the defendant's "actual malice," "legal malice," or even "malice in law" to be sufficient. However, some courts have even found the defendant's "reckless disregard" of the plaintiff's legal rights sufficient to satisfy the "malice" requirement for this tort. *See Peasley v. Puget Sound Tug & Barge Co.*, 125 P. 2d 681 (1942). The important point to remember here is that the specific type of proof necessary to establish each of these different variations of "common law malice" may differ significantly from one jurisdiction to another, depending upon the specific type of malice involved. Thus, while some courts have inferred the requisite common law malice for this tort from the mere absence of probable cause for the original criminal charge asserted against the accused (i.e., malice in law), other courts might actually require the plaintiff to prove some type of subjectively bad or improper motive by the defendant (e.g., common law "actual malice," or at least "legal malice").

D. Termination of the Prosecution in Favor of the Accused

An outright dismissal of the original criminal charges against the accused will obviously satisfy this requirement, as will a trial and verdict of acquittal in favor of the accused. For this reason, a civil action for the tort of "malicious prosecution" cannot be maintained while the underlying criminal charges are still pending against the accused, or while they remain otherwise unresolved. There must be an actual "termination" of the underlying criminal proceeding before this element of the "malicious prosecution" (of a criminal action) tort can be established, and that termination must be in favor of the accused.

However, what about situations where the accused pleads "guilty" to some reduced criminal charge, or where the accused is ultimately convicted of a lesser, but included, offense than the one for which the prosecution was originally initiated? In these latter instances, even though the accused has definitely fared significantly better than the outcome of a completely successful criminal prosecution, a conviction (or plea) of any kind is generally not regarded as a termination of the prosecution *in favor of* the accused. Likewise, even if the state agrees not to prosecute the accused on existing criminal charges (for whatever reasons other than those pertaining solely to the merits of the charges, such as by granting a *nolle prosequi*), such a termination is ordinarily not considered to be *in favor of* the accused for purposes of this tort.

E. Special Damages

The final requirement for the tort of "malicious prosecution" (of a criminal action) is that of "damages." Sometimes referred to as the "special injury" rule, in most jurisdictions the plaintiff must demonstrate that (s)he has sustained some type of actual loss or harm as the result of the defendant's "malicious prosecution." Typically, there will be obvious damages such as out of pocket expenses incurred by the accused in hiring an attorney or in otherwise maintaining a defense against the wrongful criminal charges. However, there may be other economic losses as well, such as the loss of employment while the accused was wrongfully incarcerated in connection with the criminal prosecution, or getting fired from a job because of adverse publicity created merely by virtue of the criminal accusation.

In addition to actual economic losses, most courts also recognize any number of emotional harms that typically result from being wrongfully accused of criminal misconduct. Such harm may range from embarrassment at being arrested, detained, fingerprinted, photographed, and incarcerated, to the psychological stigma often attached to persons who have even been accused of criminal wrongdoing, regardless of the eventual outcome. These types of emotional distress damages are similar to those dignitary injuries typically asserted in claims for the intentional tort of false imprisonment or for the tort of defamation. Thus, in most jurisdictions, the plaintiff in a "malicious prosecution" action is permitted to recover whatever damages are shown to be causally connected to the defendant's tortious behavior in maliciously instituting the unfounded criminal charges.

F. Special Defenses to the Tort of Malicious Prosecution

Traditionally, the courts have recognized a number of special situations in which the defendant may be able to avoid liability for the tort of "malicious prosecution." One of these involves the so-called defense of "guilt in fact." Even in situations where the accused prevails in the underlying *criminal* prosecution, the accuser may still be able to prove in the subsequent *civil* "malicious prosecution" action that in fact the accused was "guilty" of the crime charged. This is because of the differences between the burdens of proof applicable to these two different types of actions. In the original criminal action against the accused, the state may simply have been unable to prove that the defendant was "guilty" "*beyond a reasonable doubt*" so as to obtain a criminal conviction of the accused. As such, the criminal proceedings will have been terminated "in favor of the accused" (*see* discussion in section I.D., *supra*). Nevertheless, if the accuser (i.e., the defendant in the subsequent civil "malicious prosecution" action) can prove merely "*to a preponderance of the evidence*" (a lower standard of proof) that the accused in the original criminal prosecution was in fact guilty of the crime accused, then the defendant can still prevail in the civil "malicious prosecution" action. Since the *preponderance* burden of proof is significantly less in the civil "malicious prosecution" action, this defense is at least potentially applicable in many situations, even where the accused was acquitted in the underlying criminal prosecution.

Additionally, where the accuser, before initiating the underlying criminal prosecution, first sought and then in good faith relied upon the advice of legal counsel, some courts have concluded that such proof will also negate any "malice" by the defendant that is necessary for the action to succeed. *See Birwood Paper Co. v. Damsky*, 229 So. 2d 514 (Ala. 1969). While perhaps not technically a true "defense," since the legal effect of such proof is to negate one of the requirements for the *prima facie* tort itself, a defendant who proves good faith reliance on the advice of legal counsel may still be able to avoid liability for "malicious prosecution."

Likewise, for reasons of public policy, certain participants in the original prosecution of an accused person are simply immune from potential tort liability altogether with respect to any tort claims arising out of the performance of their official duties in the criminal prosecution. Thus, the state prosecutor and the trial judge are both absolutely immune from civil liability for the tort of "malicious prosecution," so long as they have acted solely within their respective prosecutorial and judicial capacities in the underlying criminal prosecution. Of course, a prosecutor motivated by malice, who assumes additional roles solely for the purpose of instigating or perpetuating an unfounded criminal prosecution, may risk losing this immunity. *See* RESTATEMENT (SECOND) OF TORTS § 656 (1977), comment *b*.

II. Malicious Prosecution (of a Civil Action)

As an adaptation of the traditional common law tort of "malicious prosecution" (of a criminal action), some jurisdictions recognize a separate tort cause of action in situations where the defendant has maliciously and unsuccessfully asserted a *civil* action against the plaintiff. Often referred to as "malicious prosecution" (of a *civil* action), this tort is quite similar to the traditional tort of "malicious prosecution" (of a criminal action) discussed in the preceding section, *supra*, except that it can be maintained against a defendant who has maliciously (and unsuccessfully) initiated a *civil* claim against the plaintiff. Although the basic requirements of both actions are very similar in most respects, there are still certain important distinctions between these two separate torts.

Among the most obvious distinction is the fact that this tort is based upon the defendant's malicious filing of a *civil* claim against the plaintiff. While generally this requires an actual civil "complaint" to be filed, as well as the issuance of a summons against the plaintiff, considerable debate has arisen even among those jurisdictions that recognize this cause of action as to exactly what type of "probable cause" is necessary for the filing of such a civil complaint. In criminal prosecutions, the law in most jurisdictions is fairly well settled as to the legal meaning and requirements for "probable cause." *See* the discussion in section I.B., *supra*. However, how should this same requirement be applied with respect to the filing of a *civil* complaint?

Arguably, a separate tort cause of action is not necessary at all, since adequate legal sanctions are already in place against both litigants, as well as their attorneys, to prevent the filing of purely frivolous civil complaints by either group of individuals. *See* Fed. R. Civ. Proc., Rule 11(b). However, are such sanctions alone sufficient to deter these types of completely unmeritorious claims? And, given these existing rules that prohibit the filing of "frivolous" legal claims, does it necessarily follow that as long as there is at least some potential merit to a civil claim (i.e., that the claim is not totally "frivolous"), then there is also sufficient "probable cause" for asserting it against the plaintiff, regardless of the likelihood of a favorable potential outcome and regardless of the claimant's motive for bringing it? Construing "probable cause" in such a broad sense, the "lack of probable cause" requirement necessary for sustaining a civil malicious prosecution claim would be completely absent in all but the most frivolous of cases. Thus, the potential applicability of this tort would be greatly restricted, and this may be one reason why this tort has not been as widely recognized as malicious prosecution of a criminal action. By contrast, however, other courts have continued to apply the traditional definition of "probable cause" by simply adapting it and applying it within the setting of a civil litigation (i.e., reasonable grounds to believe that a viable civil claim can be sustained against the plaintiff). Under such an interpretation, if the underlying civil claim turns out to be unsuccessful (i.e., it is rejected by either the court or a jury), then, at least arguably, that would provide a sufficient basis for pursuing a "malicious prosecution" (of a civil action) claim, provided that all of the other requirements for the action are also present. *See Nelson v. Miller*, 607 P. 2d 438 (Kan. 1980).

Some courts have managed to avoid this issue altogether by continuing to require the plaintiff in a malicious prosecution (of a civil action) claim to prove some type of special injury as a result of having successfully defended the underlying civil claim. However, unlike claims involving its criminal counterpart, when applied to a malicious prosecution (of a civil action) claim in which there has been no actual arrest, no loss of freedom, and in many cases (e.g., where the costs of the underlying civil litigation have been awarded by the court to the successful defendant in the underlying civil litigation), the plaintiff is often unable to offer proof of any special damages otherwise sufficient to sustain the action. *See Friedman v. Dozorc*, 312 N.W. 2d 585 (Mich. 1981). Finally, because of concerns over these and other related issues, some courts have simply declined to recognize this tort altogether.

III. Abuse of Process

The tort of "abuse of process" developed, at least in part, because of certain procedural inadequacies in the "malicious prosecution" tort(s) that prevented its application in some situations, even though the plaintiff sustained harm directly as a result of the defendant's malicious use of an otherwise proper legal process. Unlike the tort of "malicious prosecution" which focuses upon the defendant's motive in *wrongfully initiating* either criminal or civil proceedings against an accused, in the tort of "abuse of process" the legal process is being used for precisely the very purpose for which it was designed. Nevertheless, such *use* (even though otherwise lawful) is still considered tortious because of the defendant's wrongful motive.

Although the defendant's improper motive is key to both of these two different tort claims, that motive is assessed from different perspectives. In the malicious prosecution cause of action, there was never a legal justification for the underlying claim to be brought in the first place, and the defendant's improper motive is what caused the claim even to be initiated. However, in an abuse of process cause of action, the underlying legal process or claim does have legal merit. It has not been unjustifiably issued or initiated. Nevertheless, because of the defendant's improper motive, that process or claim has been *abused* to accomplish some ulterior purpose for which it was never intended. Thus, as its name implies, the tortious conduct for this tort arises from the *abuse* of an otherwise properly issued legal process.

A simple example might serve to illustrate this distinction. Suppose that the defendant is the minority shareholder in a corporation in which the plaintiff holds a majority of the stock, and that the company's annual meeting has been scheduled at which a vote will be taken over a controversial issue about which the two parties disagree. In order to prevent the plaintiff from attending the shareholders' meeting and casting a majority vote in opposition to the defendant's position, the defendant causes a subpoena to be issued that requires the plaintiff to attend a deposition involving a completely different legal matter that is currently pending between these same two parties in a distant city. The defendant intentionally schedules the deposition for the very same time as the shareholders' annual meeting. In order to comply with the subpoena, the plaintiff must travel to the distant city and is forced to miss the stockholders' meeting and vote, thereby allowing the defendant's minority vote to prevail. The subpoena is a valid legal process that was lawfully issued by the court for the very purpose of ensuring the plaintiff's attendance at the deposition in the distant city. Nevertheless, even though this process was issued and used for its intended purpose, the defendant had an entirely improper motive for doing so. That motive really was to prevent the plaintiff from attending the shareholders' annual meeting and voting in opposition to the defendant's position.

To determine whether the defendant in this scenario may be liable for the tort of abuse of process, it is necessary to examine each of the individual requirements for this tort. As with the "malicious prosecution" torts (*see* sections I. and II., *supra*), the specific requirements for "abuse of process" vary significantly from one jurisdiction to another. Generally, however, there are three basic requirements for this tort:

(1) issuance of some type of valid legal process;
(2) an ulterior purpose by the defendant; and
(3) special damages.

Once again, to understand how this tort was designed to operate, as well as how it differs from the somewhat similar tort(s) of "malicious prosecution," we need to examine each of these specific requirements.

A. Issuance of Some Type of Legal Process

This requirement is for *any* type of formal legal process that has been lawfully issued by or on behalf of a court "to bring a party or property within its jurisdiction." *See Silvia v. Building Inspector of W. Bridgewater*, 621 N.E. 2d 686 (Mass. App. 1993). Thus, not only does the filing of an actual criminal (or civil) complaint satisfy this requirement, but the mere issuance of a summons, or even a subpoena (as in the example, *supra*) may be considered as a "legal process" for purposes of this tort action. This requirement is satisfied by the mere *issuance* of the legal process itself, and, unlike the separate tort of "malicious prosecution" (*see* section I., *supra*), this element of the tort is only satisfied where the process has been properly and lawfully issued.

B. An Ulterior Purpose by the Defendant

Since "abuse of process" is an intentional tort, the defendant's subjective motivation for causing the process to issue must be related to some "ulterior purpose" to satisfy this requirement. An ulterior purpose refers to the defendant's true (i.e., subjective) motivation for causing the lawful process to be issued, and that purpose must be for something *other than* that for which the process was actually designed to be used. *See generally* RESTATEMENT (SECOND) OF TORTS § 682 (1977). In trying to explain this concept of "ulterior purpose," some courts have compared it to extortion or coercion, whereby the defendant intends to "force" the plaintiff to give up some legal right in order to gain some inappropriate or unjustified advantage over the plaintiff. In the example, *supra*, the defendant's true (i.e., "ulterior") purpose in causing the subpoena to issue was not to take the plaintiff's deposition; it was to prevent the plaintiff from attending the shareholders' meeting and casting a majority vote against the interests of the defendant. The existence of an "ulterior purpose" sometimes can be proven directly, as where the defendant makes a demand for some collateral advantage over the plaintiff. However, as in the example, *supra*, it may also be implied merely from the defendant's use and disposition of the process once an unfair advantage over the plaintiff has been obtained. *See Ladd v. Polidoro*, 675 N.E. 2d 382 (Mass. 1997).

Consider another example. Suppose that the plaintiff purchases merchandise from the defendant, and then pays for it with a "bad check." Clearly, the defendant would have "probable cause" to initiate a criminal proceeding against the plaintiff (for the crime of writing a bad check), and certainly by doing this, the plaintiff would likely not be able to prove the "absence of probable cause" requirement for the tort of "malicious prosecution" against the defendant merchant. However, suppose further that after bringing the criminal charges against the plaintiff, the defendant then approaches the plaintiff and offers "to have the criminal charges dismissed" if the plaintiff will pay off the original "bad check," together with an additional 25 percent charge for "all of my time and trouble in pursuing this matter." The intended purpose of the criminal charges that were brought against the plaintiff was to enforce the criminal law prohibition against the writing of "bad checks." The filing of criminal charges has initiated a lawful criminal prosecution that does not cease merely because the accused may ultimately offer to repay the debt. While this may certainly mitigate any punishment that ultimately may be imposed against the accused in the criminal prosecution, the plaintiff's mere repayment of the "bad check" charges does not terminate the prosecution, because the recovery of the defendant's money is only collateral to the true purpose for which criminal charges were brought against the accused. However, in this scenario, the defendant has acted with an "ulterior purpose" of simply trying to collect a debt from the plaintiff, together with possibly making a bit more than the original debt would have allowed, by misusing the criminal prosecution as a means to collect that debt. Here, the defendant's "ulterior purpose" can be even more easily proven by the defendant's statement about dismissing the criminal charges.

C. Damages

As with the tort of "malicious prosecution" (*see* section I., *supra*), the plaintiff must also prove some type of special harm or damage resulting from the defendant's "abuse of process." However, often these damages are much more difficult to prove. For example, in the scenario just discussed, *supra*, the plaintiff might not be able to claim as damages in an "abuse of process" action against the defendant the additional costs of hiring an attorney to provide legal representation in the criminal "bad check" prosecution (which typically would be recoverable in a "malicious prosecution" action), since the criminal prosecution was lawful and ultimately likely to succeed (since the plaintiff did in fact write a "bad check.") Likewise, even the cost of re-paying the original amount of that "bad check" might not be recoverable in the plaintiff's "abuse of process" claim, since that too was a lawful debt that was owed to the defendant. Nevertheless, the additional 25 percent charge paid to the defendant for gaining the defendant's dismissal of the criminal charges might still qualify as "special damages" for this tort. Moreover, since this is an intentional tort, and depending upon the level of egregiousness of the defendant's behavior in abusing the legal process, the plaintiff might also be permitted to recover punitive damages against the defendant in appropriate situations. (*See* Chapter 8, *supra*, Compensatory and Punitive Damages).

Likewise, in the initial "abuse of process" example discussed *supra*, the plaintiff might wish to assert damages for the cost of travel to the distant city as well as other expenses associated with the taking of the deposition that (s)he was compelled by the subpoena to attend. However, in all likelihood those costs would still have been incurred anyway, just at a different time or in a different amount, since the plaintiff's deposition was undoubtedly necessary at some point in the other litigation. However, by missing the crucial shareholder's meeting and subsequently losing out to the defendant's minority vote, the plaintiff might also be able to claim the loss of any economic damages that may have resulted from losing the shareholder vote. Unfortunately, even if the plaintiff is able to prove that the defendant's "abuse of process" changed the ultimate outcome of the vote, the actual dollar amount of such losses might be extremely difficult to prove because they simply may be too speculative or uncertain in amount.

IV. Misuse of Legal Process

Despite the differences between "malicious prosecution" and "abuse of process," these two individual tort causes of action often are still confused. As a result, some courts have simply decided to combine the requirements of each tort by merging them into a single intentional tort cause of action, often referred to as "misuse of legal process." Of course, the specific requirements of this "combined" new tort will vary significantly, depending upon the particular version that has been adopted. Likewise, a few jurisdictions have even modified the original common law actions of "malicious prosecution" and "abuse of process" by enacting statutes that broaden the scope of these actions.

Checkpoints

- The tort of "malicious prosecution" focuses upon the defendant's motive in *wrongfully initiating* some type of legal action against the plaintiff that was inappropriate from the very beginning.

- The tort of "abuse of process" involves the use of various types of legal process that, although *properly initiated* against the plaintiff, nevertheless should not have been utilized at all because of the defendant's improper motive in doing so.

- In most jurisdictions, the tort of "malicious prosecution" of a criminal action consists of some variation of the following specific requirements:

  - a criminal prosecution initiated by the defendant;

  - a lack of "probable cause" to begin that criminal prosecution;

  - common law malice by the defendant;

  - a termination of the prosecution in favor of the accused plaintiff; and

  - special damages suffered by the plaintiff.

- "Common law malice" in the law of torts can refer to any one of several completely different (yet closely related) legal concepts, including:

  - *Actual malice* (i.e., an actual feeling of hatred, spite, animosity, or ill will toward the plaintiff);

  - *Legal malice* (i.e., somewhat broader than "actual malice," also including actions that are motivated by *any* improper or wrongful motive);

  - *Malice in law* (i.e., any intentionally tortious action done without any just cause or excuse, regardless of the defendant's subjective state of mind) or possibly even recklessness.

- Both "malicious prosecution" and "abuse of process" generally require proof of some type of "special injury."

- The "guilt in fact" of the accused is a defense to the "malicious prosecution" of a *criminal* action, since the accuser may still be able to prove the accused's guilt under the lesser civil burden of proof based upon the mere preponderance of the evidence.

- The intentional tort of "abuse of process" generally consists of three basic requirements:
  - issuance of some type of legal process;
  - an ulterior purpose by the defendant; and
  - special damages.

Chapter 21

Misrepresentation

Roadmap

- Learn the basic elements of each of the three different misrepresentation torts: intentional misrepresentation (i.e., fraud); negligent misrepresentation; and strict liability for misrepresentation.

- Understand what is meant by a misrepresentation.

- Learn how to distinguish between statements of facts and statements of opinions for purposes of establishing liability for misrepresentation.

- Recognize and be able to apply the appropriate bases of liability for misrepresentation.

- Learn how to distinguish the different tests for determining the proper plaintiff when that plaintiff is the recipient of the misrepresentation versus when that plaintiff is a third party.

- Recognize the appropriate damages that may be recovered for a misrepresentation.

- Learn how to determine the actual measures of loss for economic harm caused by misrepresentation.

As with many other types of tort claims, the common law tort of misrepresentation covers a broad range of claims that can utilize any of the three bases of liability: intent, negligence or strict liability. However, regardless of the particular basis, tort liability for a misrepresentation basically involves a claim that allows the plaintiff to recover for losses caused by reliance on the false statements of others. For purposes of discussion, in this chapter we will focus primarily upon the *intentional* version of misrepresentation that is typically referred to as fraud or deceit. Where appropriate certain distinctions between intentional misrepresentations (i.e., fraud) and each of the other two bases for imposing liability for misrepresentation will also be addressed.

I. Basic Elements

The basic elements of an intentional misrepresentation (i.e., fraud) are:

(1) false representation of a material fact;
(2) scienter;
(3) intent to induce reliance;
(4) justifiable reliance; and
(5) damages.

Although it is necessary to discuss each of these elements in detail, a few preliminary comments may be helpful. The false representation element for all misrepresentation torts requires that there must be some active presentation of the falsehood. Mere silence is rarely sufficient, except in negligent misrepresentation where sometimes an affirmative duty to provide factually correct information to the plaintiff may arise The element of scienter is unique to intentional misrepresentations, whereas scienter is replaced in the tort of negligent misrepresentation with the breach of a legally recognized duty owed by the defendant to the plaintiff. In the strict liability version of misrepresentation, the plaintiff is not required to prove either scienter or negligence, since liability is not based upon any notion of fault whatsoever. The requirement of justifiable (i.e., reasonable) reliance is common to all three types of misrepresentations (i.e., intentional, negligent, and strict liability). In some ways, the reliance element is what supplies the necessary causation. Finally, all types of misrepresentation require the plaintiff to prove at least some type of harm, although the manner by which damages are determined may vary somewhat, depending upon the specific type of misrepresentation involved.

A. False Representation

Since all versions of the tort of misrepresentation are only available to persons who have been injured by false representation, the necessary first element is a false representation. It is commonly stated that misrepresentation is based on a false *statement,* but the term false *representation* is a better way to describe this element. Although a false statement will give rise to a misrepresentation, there are other ways to falsify a fact than by merely making a statement. For example, suppose that the prospective buyer of a home asks the seller if the home has termites or has been treated for termites, and the seller responds, "This home has no termites. It has been inspected for termites and none were found." Now, assume that neither of these statements is true. In fact, the home was inspected for termites, and termite damage was found. Clearly, that would be a false representation, since this was obviously a false statement of fact (actually, in this example there are two false statements of fact: the home *does have* termites, and termites *were found* in the inspection).

In fraudulent misrepresentation cases, however, few cases arise that are as easy as the one described, *supra*. Instead, parties more frequently engage in a discussion that leads to confusion as to precisely what facts were stated by the defendant. Imagine, for example, that the prospective buyer of a home asks the seller the very same question as in the previous example, *supra*: does the home have termites or has it been treated for termites? This time the seller responds that: "This house has been inspected for termites, and received the full termite treatment." Now, assume that in fact the house was once treated for termites many years ago. However, a recent inspection revealed a return of termites, as well as termite damage. The house now really needs a new termite treatment and substantial repairs. Compare the seller's statement to these true facts. Is it a "false" representation? The seller did state the truth. The house (truthfully) had been inspected for termites and (again truthfully) it had been treated for termites. Unfortunately for the buyer, the way the seller stated these facts would lead a reasonable buyer to believe that everything is fine when, in fact, there are substantial termite problems. This type of circumstance creates a half-truth in the mind of the buyer. The buyer believes one thing while another thing is actually true. It is also obvious that this is exactly the condition that the seller was intending to create. The seller has carefully crafted a technically accurate response to the buyer's question that was still not entirely truthful, since revealing the whole truth would likely have caused the buyer to back out of the sale (or at least to offer less money to purchase the home). In this situation the courts would probably determine that the seller has made a false representation. The seller has created a false impression in the buyer's mind and having done so the seller now has an obligation to clear up the misunderstanding or the result will be a false representation.

The false representation element does require, however, at least some representation by the seller. For example, if the defendant in this scenario involving the buyer's request about termites or termite treatment says nothing at all and merely remains silent after the buyer specifically asks about termites, there is no claim. Likewise, if the buyer never even asks the buyer about termites, then the seller is under no obligation to disclose the fact that termites were found in the house, even though the seller has knowledge of this fact (and even if the seller is also aware that the buyer does not have such knowledge). Once again, assume that the seller allows the buyer to inspect the home before the purchase, but that inspection failed to disclose the presence of termites in the home. If the buyer sues for misrepresentation, the traditional rules suggest that there would be no claim, since most courts would likely find that the seller never made any representation, false or otherwise.

The idea that there is no affirmative duty to speak is generally consistent with the traditional rules of tort law. Although there are some circumstances that do require an affirmative duty for the defendant to act, such as when the defendant has voluntarily undertaken to assist someone, there is generally no duty to come to someone's aid or to supply information when none has been requested. This idea is reflected in the distinction between misfeasance and non-feasance. Contract law is ordinarily concerned with non-feasance, so that if someone agrees to do something and then does not do it, there may be a contract action. However, tort law is primarily concerned with misfeasance such as when someone begins to do something and does it poorly. (*See* Chapter 9, *supra*, Limited Duty). Thus, tort law is generally not concerned with non-feasance, and this distinction is seen quite clearly in the area of false representations. A false representation exists when someone begins to make some kind of a representation, but does it poorly. However, a false representation does not exist as an actionable tort claim when someone merely remains silent, unless (as in the case of negligent misrepresentation) there was some affirmative duty to speak correctly.

Nevertheless, the examples, *supra*, still leave many confusing circumstances as questions of fact for the jury, and a few additional examples will illustrate just how complex this issue can be. Continuing with our same scenario, imagine that the seller of the home knows there are termites in the home, as well as the presence of substantial termite damage. However, the seller does only minimal repair work that is merely sufficient to hide the most obvious structural damage to the home, but not sufficient to properly repair the damage. The seller subsequently paints over the repair work so that it will not be noticed. The seller then allows the buyer to inspect the home before purchase, but the buyer fails to discover the concealed termite damage. A court will likely treat the seller's actions as making a false representation. Although the seller did not say anything, nevertheless, the seller was still engaged in providing false information by actively concealing the true condition of the termite damage in the home. The seller's active concealment will likely justify a finding that the seller has made a false representation.

It should be noted that many jurisdictions provide an exception to the rule that there is no duty to speak in situations where the fact in question goes to the very heart or core of the entire transaction. In other words, where the issue at hand is one that is so important that one party would realize that the other party would consider the information critical, courts may recognize an exception to the traditional common law rule of *caveat emptor* (i.e., let the buyer beware). Indeed, situations such as those involving the disclosure of termites (or termite damage) in home sales, is one of the very circumstances that led to this exception. Some courts have recognized that the issue of termites is so important in the purchase of a home that the disclosure of such information is essential to the transaction. Those courts would require a seller to speak on the issue. It should be noted that in modern real estate transactions, most home sale contracts have express provisions requiring termite inspections so that the issue is now handled in the contract.

For an additional example involving active concealments, consider a typical used car transaction. Many car owners, wishing to sell or trade their car in order to purchase a new one will wash, wax, clean up the interior, and generally make the car more presentable for sale. Such actions do not create a false representation, since by doing so the owner is merely putting the vehicle in its most presentable condition. Even if the owner goes a step further and takes the car to a well-lighted lot in the evening so that the car really sparkles under the bright lights, there is still no false representation. However, suppose that the owner, knowing that the car burns oil badly (because of a serious engine problem), drains the oil from the car and puts in much heavier weight oil and then allows the engine time to cool down before showing it to a prospective buyer. Only after the engine is cool does the owner permit the buyer to take the car for a test drive. When the buyer first starts the cold engine, there will not be any smoke emitted from the tail pipe due to the combination of heavy oil and the cool engine. The apparent absence of oil smoke from the engine during the brief test drive would reasonably suggest to the prospective buyer that the engine was in good condition. In this scenario, however, the car owner has gone well beyond merely cleaning up the car. (S)he has actually attempted to mislead the prospective buyer by making an active concealment. Such a situation would likely create a question for the jury to decide whether the seller had made a false representation.

B. Material Fact

The discussion of a false representation naturally leads to the next prong of the misrepresentation requirement: the false representation also must be one of a *material fact*. A "material" fact is one that the parties knew to be important and one that the plaintiff would have relied upon when entering into the transaction. Collateral matters or unimportant facts will not give rise to a claim for misrepresentation.

The false representation must also relate to a fact, as opposed to a mere opinion. Facts usually involve concepts or ideas that are capable of being proven right or wrong. Only such ideas or concepts can be the subject of a misrepresentation case. Many of the statements made in the previous section, *supra*, were examples of statements that involved facts. For example, the discussion of termites shows that the home either had or did not have termites. The seller's statement as to the existence or non-existence of termites was a fact. Not only are these statements of fact, they are obviously material facts in relation to the purchase of a home. Nevertheless, in misrepresentation cases there are many other types of representations that can create a question as to whether they pertain to facts or opinions. Since it is often difficult to distinguish these concepts with any degree of certainty, a jury may be asked to decide whether a particular statement was a fact or an opinion. As a result, the courts have had to develop specific rules to aid in determining what actually constitutes a fact and what constitutes an opinion.

Statements that appear to be speculation or conjectures are typically regarded as nothing more than opinions. Since truth or falsity of facts can usually be verified by objective evidence, whenever a defendant's statement indicates uncertainty or ambiguity, the plaintiff should be put on notice that the matter to which it pertains is one that should not be relied upon. Such statements may be easily identified. For example, in dealing with the sale of land or chattels, a seller's statements of value are usually seen as opinions rather than statements of fact. The true value of the property is typically something that can be objectively established, apart from the seller's often-biased statement of value. Likewise, statements about condition, future use, or quality would rarely be considered facts. Imagine that the seller of a parcel of land tells a buyer that:

> "This is a great tract of land. It is one of the best row crop farms in the county. You should be able to make a good living growing corn on this land. In addition, if the state ever extends the interstate out this way, this land would sell for a fortune as a gas station site."

Clearly, all of this information is an opinion. These statements are not the type that should be relied upon as facts.

Likewise, statements of approximation are rarely regarded as statements of facts. In buying large tracts of land, the seller will typically say something like: "This tract has about 100 acres." Determining the exact acreage of a tract is difficult for anyone to know with certainty, without the aid of a survey. However, if the tract was subsequently surveyed and determined to have only 95 acres, there would not be a claim for misrepresentation. Instead, most courts would likely hold that the seller's statement was merely a statement of opinion.

The example of the seller of land talking about the quality or value of land falls under the general heading of sales talk, or "puffing." It is recognized that during sales transactions, the seller will frequently make extreme or exaggerated statements about the value or quality of the thing to be sold. Sellers of used cars are traditionally thought to engage in serious sales puffing when seeking to close the deal. For example, the seller might say: "This is a great little used car. It should last a long time. It will get great gas mileage. You can't do any better than this one." Those statements would likely be considered just puffing and as opinions. As such they are generally not actionable.

However, there are some statements of quality or value that may be actionable. When a speaker holds himself or herself out as having special knowledge as to the quality or value of an item being sold, then the speaker will be held liable when the statements are not accurate. For example, it is the job of real estate and property appraisal experts to provide accurate estimates regarding the value of land or chattels. These experts often provide appraisals of the value of land, antiques, or other property, and they frequently charge for their services. When they give an opinion, that opinion is actionable, because it represents a true fact (i.e., the fair market value of the item being appraised, based upon their training and experience as an expert appraiser).

Similarly, opinion statements of law offered by legal experts are treated as facts for purposes of misrepresentation. Thus, when a lawyer gives an opinion on an issue of law, that opinion may be actionable as a statement of fact if it is incorrect, because lawyers hold themselves out as having special knowledge of the law. When they are factually mistaken, they can be liable. However, when a non-lawyer gives an opinion on the law that opinion is not actionable. Oddly, many non-lawyers sometimes believe that they know the law. Thus, when a traffic accident occurs, ordinary bystanders are often very willing to state who they believe was "at fault." Nevertheless, such statements of opinion involve a legal issue, and as such they are not actionable when given by non-lawyers.

There are times, however, when a statement of law even if given by a non-lawyer may be actionable as a statement of fact. When the statement is not only a statement of law, but it is also an implied statement of underlying facts, the statement might be actionable. Imagine that a homebuyer is looking at a house owned by a plumber. The plumber, seeking to sell the house, makes certain factual statements about the plumbing. If the plumber says: "The state building code requires an 8-inch sewer pipe," that would be a statement of law, and the buyer would have no action based upon it. If, however, the plumber said: "This house meets the state building code," that statement would be actionable, even though it too may seem to be a statement of law. This latter statement also implies a statement of fact (i.e., that the seller/plumber knows the facts about the construction of the home and is factually affirming that it meets the state code).

Another issue that arises with opinions is when someone makes a prediction about the future. Predictions of the future are generally considered to be opinions, since it is assumed that no one can accurately predict the future. Thus, a seller of land, a home, or a chattel who says: "This will rise in value at the rate of 10 percent a year," is obviously making a statement of opinion based upon what the seller is predicting to occur in the future. Nevertheless, there are situations when even statements involving future predictions are actionable. An example is when the future prediction implies the current existence of a fact. The future prediction becomes actionable because the plaintiff believes that the defendant knows of current facts that support the prediction. For example, suppose that the seller of a parcel of land says: "The value of this land will increase when the county paves the road." Although a close case, this statement would likely be regarded as a question for the jury, since it could reasonably be construed as stating either a present fact or a future prediction. That portion of the statement *supra*, asserting that the value of the land will increase is clearly a future prediction. However the other portion stating, "when the county paves the road" might lead the buyer to believe that the county has already decided to pave the road.

Another example of future predictions that may create a false statement of present material fact occurs when the speaker's prediction implies a current intent to act in the future. Many contracts, for example, involve promises to act in the future. Ordinarily, when someone fails to act in the future, the claim is based on the contract. However, occasionally the plaintiff may seek to turn the breached contract into a tort. For example, if a defendant promised to repay a loan in two years, and then failed to repay it, the normal action would be in contract. The plaintiff might try, however, to sue for the tort of fraud (an intentional misrepresentation). In that case, the plaintiff would allege that the defendant had no intent to repay the loan at the time when the agreement was made. Such intentions, of course, are hard to prove, since the plaintiff would have to prove the defendant's actual state of mind by showing that, at the time of the contract, the defendant had no intent to perform. If successful, however, this would be a false present material fact that could support the plaintiff's action for the tort of fraud.

C. Scienter

Scienter is a requirement that is uniquely applicable only to the intentional tort of misrepresentation (sometimes also called fraud or deceit). Specifically, the element of scienter requires the plaintiff to prove that the defendant knew that the statement was false, or made the statement without belief in its truth, or in reckless disregard of the truth. In addition, scienter also requires the plaintiff to prove that the defendant actually intended to induce the plaintiff's reliance by making the false representation. (*See* section II.F., *infra*). It is this very concept of scienter that supplies the necessary degree of legal fault that otherwise justifies imposing liability for an *intentional* misrepresentation. By contrast, in order for the plaintiff to prove an action based on negligent misrepresentation, (s)he need only establish that the defendant made the false representation without using reasonable care to determine whether the statement was true or false. As discussed, *supra*, before liability for a negligent misrepresentation can be proved the plaintiff must first establish that the defendant owed a duty to make a truthful representation to the plaintiff. (*See* sections I.A. and I.B., *supra*). Requiring proof of negligence instead of scienter, is what distinguishes the intentional version of misrepresentation (i.e., fraud) from the negligent version of misrepresentation. Finally, where the misrepresentation is based on strict liability, no fault element is required at all to establish liability. Instead, simply proving that the statement is false is sufficient to establish strict liability for the misrepresentation, even if the defendant exercised all due care in trying to determine the truth or falsity of the statement.

D. Proper Party Plaintiff When Plaintiff Was Recipient of Statement

In addition to limitations on the allowable damages that may be recovered in a misrepresentation action (*see* section II., *infra*), there are also limitations on the allowable plaintiffs who can bring these different types of misrepresentation claims. The issue of the proper party plaintiff is not complex in situations when the defendant made the representation directly to the plaintiff. Under those circumstances, it is clear that the defendant knew the identity of the plaintiff, knew the circumstances surrounding the plaintiff's intended use of the information, and had at least some direct contact in dealing with the plaintiff. If the other elements of misrepresentation are met, the plaintiff/recipient of the statement can recover for personal injury, property damage, and economic losses. Ordinarily, that recovery is allowed, regardless whether the basis of the plaintiff's claim is intent (i.e., fraud) or negligence (i.e., negligent misrepresentation). However, as discussed, *supra*, when the basis of the misrepresentation claim is strict liability, it is subject to the limitations noted in the immediately preceding subsection. (*See* section II.C., *supra*).

E. Proper Party Plaintiff When Plaintiff Was a Third Party

When the plaintiff was not the immediate recipient of the statement, but was someone who subsequently relied on it instead, additional issues arise. This type of situation commonly occurs when accountants provide audits for large companies. Once the audit is completed, the company for whom the audit was made may subsequently use that audit report in order to get loans, make purchases, or engage in other business transactions with third parties. As a result, many people doing business with the company ultimately may rely on the audit report in order to extend credit or to transact business with the company.

The classic case that addresses this issue is *Ultramares Corp. v. Touche,* 255 N.Y. 170, 174 N.E. 441 (1931). In that case, a major accounting firm did an audit for a company. The audit showed the company to be solvent, and subsequently other companies extended credit based on the audit. However, the audited company turned out not to be solvent, and those who lost money in reliance on the audit sued the accounting firm. The *Ultramares* court divided the issue according to whether the basis of the claim was intent or negligence. The greater the level of fault, the further the duty would extend. If the defendants made intentional falsehoods in the audit, then any plaintiff that was among a small group or class of possible plaintiffs that the defendant could foresee as relying on the report could recover. Although the defendant accountants in *Ultramares* did not know the statement was false, it was still possible that those defendants had acted in reckless disregard of the truth, so as to justify a finding of liability for the tort of fraud. However, if the claim was based on negligence, the group of possible plaintiffs was much narrower. The court limited the possible plaintiffs to only those individuals whose identities the defendants knew, whom the defendants knew would use the representation, and with whom the defendant had some contact. Thus, the court explained, if the defendant had known the specific identity of the plaintiff, and knew that the plaintiff was going to extend credit based on the audit, and the defendant had mailed copies of the audit to that plaintiff, then the plaintiff could recover under a negligent misrepresentation theory. However, if those facts did not exist the plaintiff would lose under negligent misrepresentation.

The *Ultramares* decision has not been universally accepted. Some jurisdictions have expanded the group of possible plaintiffs when the basis of the misrepresentation claim was negligence. Additionally, however, there are two other possible rules. Some jurisdictions use the same rule that is used for intentional misrepresentations. That rule would allow a plaintiff to recover even for a negligent misrepresentation when the plaintiff was a member of a small group or class that the defendant could foresee to rely upon the statement. The Restatement of Torts has suggested this rule. Another approach would extend liability to the full extent of most tort cases. Those jurisdictions would allow recovery by *any* foreseeable plaintiff.

F. Intent to Cause Reliance

Depending upon the basis of the claim, the scienter requirement for an intentional misrepresentation can be somewhat problematic. For example, in fraud cases the plaintiff must prove that the defendant actually intended to induce reliance by the plaintiff. (*See* section I.C., *supra*). However, in complex litigation involving reliance by third parties, the defendant's actual intent to induce reliance is seldom directly addressed. Instead, in those cases it is usually sufficient if the plaintiff merely proves that the defendant made the representation knowing that the third party plaintiff could rely upon it. Thus, the issue in these types of cases is frequently addressed in terms of identifying the proper plaintiff. (*See* section I.E., *supra*). For example, the defendant may have made a statement intending to induce reliance by party A, but party B subsequently claims reliance and sues. Although the courts in these types of cases could easily assume that the defendant intended to induce reliance by someone, the issue is usually discussed only in terms of whether the plaintiff is a proper party to bring the suit.

G. Justifiable Reliance

The reliance requirement is applicable to all of the misrepresentation torts, and it typically involves two different determinations. First, the plaintiff must prove that (s)he in fact relied upon the statement at issue. If the plaintiff ignored the statement or relied upon something other than the misrepresentation, there is no claim.

Even this type of reliance is not always a simple mater to determine. For example, there are times when a defendant may make a series of statements about a transaction. The plaintiff may find some of the statements important and rely upon them, while ignoring others altogether. If the parties' transaction subsequently leads to litigation, the plaintiff typically will point to a few false statements made by the defendant and claim that they were the statements that induced the plaintiff's reliance to enter into the transaction. The question of fact for the jury will be to determine whether the plaintiff did, in fact, rely upon the statements in question.

There are other times when, despite any statements made by the defendant, the plaintiff will conduct his or her own research prior to entering into a transaction. If that transaction subsequently leads to litigation, the plaintiff will likely also claim that it was the defendant's false statements that induced the plaintiff's reliance to enter into the transaction. In these cases, the jury typically must decide whether the plaintiff relied upon the claimed false representations made by the defendant, or upon his or her own investigation. If it is determined that the plaintiff relied upon his or her own investigation rather than the defendant's statements, then there is no claim for misrepresentation.

Addressing the second aspect of reliance in misrepresentation cases, courts routinely add that the required reliance must have been justifiable (i.e., reasonable under the circumstances). Although construing the reliance requirement in this way certainly seems appropriate in most cases, it can lead to confusion in that courts sometimes appear to be making two inconsistent statements. For example, courts typically will say that plaintiffs are under no duty to investigate a statement made by the defendant to determine whether it was true or false. However, applying the justifiable reliance rule they will also say that a plaintiff cannot rely on an obvious falsehood. On their face, these two statements appear to be inconsistent. Since plaintiffs are under no duty to investigate a statement by a defendant, it could be said that the plaintiff's simple contributory negligence is not a defense. Thus, if the plaintiff fails to use reasonable care to determine whether the statement is true or false, the plaintiff may still recover for the falsehood. However, if the statement is so obviously wrong that a reasonable person would have seen the falsehood, the plaintiff cannot rely upon such a statement, since the obviousness of the falsehood would make the reliance similar to assumption of risk. The plaintiff knew that the statement was false and accepted it anyway.

Although courts usually do not discuss the issue in terms of contributory negligence and assumption of risk, this analysis may help to illustrate the distinctions. The plaintiff may accept as true whatever statement the defendant has made. However, where that statement is obviously false there is no *justifiable* (or reasonable) reliance.

II. Damages

Although the tort of misrepresentation may be based on intent, negligence, or occasionally even strict liability, some type of actual harm still must be proven in order to recover damages under any version of this tort. Depending upon the type of misrepresentation involved, the plaintiff may have suffered personal injury, property damage, or economic loss. Misrepresentation is one of the few torts that will allow recovery for all three of these types of damages in appropriate cases, although the most common type of damages recoverable in most misrepresentation claims are those based upon the plaintiff's economic loss. For example, in the majority of intentional or negligent misrepresentation actions, the plaintiff will seek economic damages for lost funds after relying on audits and extending credit, or when purchasing items that proved not to be as represented.

Thus, when considering the combination of bases of claims and types of damages that can be asserted in a misrepresentation action, the plaintiff potentially might recover for personal injury, property damage, and economic losses when the claim is based upon the intentional misrepresentation tort of fraud or upon negligent misrepresentation. However, when the action for misrepresentation is based on strict liability, there is a substantial limitation on what damages the plaintiff can recover. The only permissible recovery for strict liability misrepresentations is found in RESTATEMENT (SECOND) OF TORTS § 402B. In that section, when a defendant makes a public misrepresentation about a product that leads to personal injury or property damage for the plaintiff, the plaintiff can recover without proof of fault. It should be noted, however, that this provision is not widely used in most misrepresentation claims, since it requires a public misrepresentation concerning a product, and the damages are limited to personal injury or property damage only. Therefore, the strict liability misrepresentation tort is typically asserted only in certain defective product cases. (*See* Chapter 16, *supra*, Products Liability).

It should be remembered that most of the original common law intentional torts did not require proof of actual harm. The mere existence of intent by the defendant and the resulting consequences of the defendant's misconduct are usually sufficient to sustain liability for such torts. (*See* Chapter 2, *supra*, Intentional Interference with Person or Property). However, the tort of intentional misrepresentation (i.e., fraud) did not arise from the same origins as these early common law intentional torts. Therefore, to establish liability for the tort of intentional misrepresentation (i.e., fraud), the plaintiff must also prove some type of actual damage, even though the defendant has acted with the requisite scienter for such an action. Likewise, just as the plaintiff has always been required to prove actual harm to establish a *prima facie* case of liability for the tort of common law negligence, the negligent misrepresentation tort also requires proof of some type of actual harm.

For personal injury claims arising out of a defendant's misrepresentation, the measure of loss is ordinarily the same as for any other tort. Some of the more common measures of such loss would be lost wages, medical bills, and "pain and suffering." (*See* Chapter 8, *supra*, Compensatory and Punitive Damages).

For property damage in misrepresentation torts, the measure of loss is determined just the same as for any other property damage tort. Thus, if the property is damaged for less than the full amount, the measure is determined by a simple formula whereby the court subtracts the "fair market value" of the property (i.e., what the property would cost in an exchange occurring in a free and open market) determined immediately *after* the injury from its "fair market value" just *before* the injury. The resulting amount (known as the property's "diminution in value") would represent the measure of loss. Ordinarily, to establish the "fair market value" of any property the parties are required to offer evidence from expert witnesses qualified to testify as to what those values are. Then it is a question for the trier of fact (i.e., usually the jury) to determine damages.

Consider a simple example where the "fair market value" of the property immediately before the injury was $5,000, as compared with only $2,000 after the injury. Damages for the diminution in value of the property would be the difference of $3,000. As an alternative measure of damages, some jurisdictions may allow repair costs as evidence of the amount of damage to the property. In addition, some jurisdictions may also allow recovery for the plaintiff's "loss of use" of the property while it is being repaired. Nevertheless, if the property has been totally destroyed, the measure of loss is simply determined on the basis of its "fair market value" at the time of its destruction.

Economic losses arise when the transaction, as measured by the value of either the services or the property involved, turns out to be less valuable than what it should have been had the representations been true. Those losses may be determined using one of two possible measures. It may be possible to recover economic losses based upon loss of the bargain itself. This approach is typically referred to as the "benefit of the bargain" rule. In situations where the value of the bargain may be determined under this rule, the court will subtract the actual value of the property (or services) received in the transaction from the value of the property (or services) as represented. The resulting difference reflects the "benefit of the bargain" damage. If, for example, the property was represented to be worth $5,000 but its actual value was only $2,000, then the damages would be $3,000. Awarding plaintiff the "benefit of the bargain" damages calculated in this manner places the plaintiff in exactly the same position that (s)he expected to be in had the property in fact been worth what the defendant represented.

A second measure of economic loss is often referred to as the "out of pocket damages" rule. With this measure, the court is seeking to put the plaintiff in the position that (s)he started in *before* the transaction even took place. To determine this measure, the court will subtract the actual value of the property (or services) received by the plaintiff from the amount paid by the plaintiff. The resulting difference represents the plaintiff's "out of pocket" damages to be awarded. For example, if the actual value of property (or services) received by the plaintiff was $2,000, but the price paid by the plaintiff was $4,000, then the damages would be $2,000. Returning the plaintiff's $2,000 (i.e., the amount of money originally paid out of pocket by the plaintiff) would put the plaintiff back in the position (s)he was in immediately prior to entering into the transaction. The plaintiff started with $4,000. That plaintiff now has property worth $2,000 and will receive another $2,000 in cash in "out of pocket" damages.

Checkpoints

- The basic elements of intentional misrepresentation (i.e., fraud) are:
  - a false representation of a material fact;
  - scienter;
  - intent to induce reliance;
  - justifiable reliance; and
  - damages.
- A representation requires some statement or act to convey an idea. Under most circumstances, silence will not be a representation.
- In order to recover, there must be a false statement of a material fact. Opinions and predictions of the future are generally not actionable.
- Personal injury, property damage and economic losses can be recovered when the claim is based on intentional misrepresentation (i.e., fraud) or negligent misrepresentation.
- Strict liability misrepresentation is typically only available for public misrepresentations concerning the sale of a product. Solely economic losses are generally not recoverable in strict liability misrepresentation.
- The recipient who relies upon a false statement can recover for an intentional tort (i.e., fraud) when the statement was made with scienter (i.e., an intentionally false statement made for the purpose of inducing the plaintiff's reliance).
- When the plaintiff is a third party who heard the false statement and relied, that plaintiff can still recover for intentional falsehoods when the plaintiff is a member of a foreseeable group.

- When the plaintiff is a third party who heard the false statement and relied, that plaintiff can recover for a negligent falsehood depending on the rule in the applicable jurisdiction. The possible rules are:

  - The *Ultramares* rule: The defendant must have known the purpose, the person, and had some linking contact with the plaintiff.

  - The Restatement Rule (the group rule): The defendant must have foreseen the general group or class of which the plaintiff was a member.

  - The foreseeable plaintiff rule: The defendant is liable if the plaintiff was a foreseeable plaintiff.

- The measure of loss when the plaintiff seeks the "benefit of bargain" (loss of bargain) recovery is the value as represented less the actual value received.

- The measure of loss when the plaintiff seeks the "out of pocket" recovery is the amount paid less the actual value received.

Chapter 22

Business Torts

Roadmap

- Learn the elements of the tort of intentional interference with a contract.
- Learn the elements of the tort of interference with a prospective economic advantage.
- Understand the nature of the tort recovery based upon an insurer's bad faith refusal to pay an insurance claim.
- Recognize various common law theories for interference with intellectual property rights.

As we have seen throughout this text, tort law is a broad area of the law that seeks to provide a remedy for harms done to others. Although the typical tort case may involve a claim for personal injury that arises out of incidents like automobile accidents or medical malpractice, tort law provides remedies for almost all injuries.

The area of business torts draws upon this same common law rationale of providing a remedy for injuries that have occurred. However, in the business torts area, the claims are rarely for personal injury. In fact, the claims are rarely even for injury to real or personal property. Instead, business tort claims are somewhat unique in that they typically seek only economic damages, such as those for interference with a business relationship or for harm to some intellectual property.

Actions based upon business torts are frequently available along with contract claims or statutory claims. Some of the cases in this area, for example, discuss the damages that are available for each of these different types of claims. The contract claim will usually allow recovery for economic loss under a contract. Such a claim may even allow for recovery of expectation damages. Statutory claims often provide for specific remedies authorized by statute. The business tort claims typically involve traditional common law damages in which the recovery of foreseeable losses is usually the appropriate test.

Since many business tort claims involve intentional conduct, those claims may also involve a request for punitive damages.

I. Intentional Interference with a Contract

A. General Nature of the Tort

Tort claims for interference with a contract are different from many other tort actions. Most other tort claims seek to recover for some personal injury or property damage. However, claims asserting interference with contract seek recovery for purely economic harm. The plaintiff will allege that the interference created economic losses that cannot be otherwise recovered.

The interference with contract claim also has another special feature: usually, three separate parties are involved in the action. Since the plaintiff is already in a contractual relationship with another person, ordinarily those two parties are bound to perform their original agreement under the traditional rules of contract law. And, if the other person breaches that contract, then the plaintiff would sue that person just as in any claim for breach of contract. However, in this tort action, the defendant, a third party, has interfered between the plaintiff and the other contracting party and induces the breach of that contract. Although the plaintiff still has an ordinary breach of contract claim against the breaching party to the contract, the plaintiff may also bring this claim against the third party for the tort of interference with the contract.

The basic format of the claim helps illustrate the elements of the tort of intentional interference with a contract. Most jurisdictions require:

(1) the existence of a validly enforceable contract;
(2) the defendant's knowledge of the existence of that contract;
(3) malicious, improper, or intentional interference with that contract;
(4) a breach of that contract; and
(5) damages on the part of the plaintiff.

Each of these elements, *supra*, must usually be pleaded and proven by the plaintiff. However, a brief comment on each will help to illuminate some of the issues that can arise with this tort.

Initially, there must be a validly enforceable contract between the plaintiff and another party in order for this tort claim to arise. (There is also a separate tort for an interference with a *prospective economic advantage* that will be discussed in section III., *infra*.) Once the contract is breached, the plaintiff can sue the other party to the contract for breach of contract, just as in any contract action. However, it is not possible for the plaintiff to also sue the breaching party for the tort of interference with the contract. Instead, that tort must be brought solely against the third party who interfered with the parties' original contract.

The defendant in the tort claim of interference with contract must have known of the contract. Thus, in most jurisdictions this tort requires intentional conduct by the defendant, since the claim seeks a remedy for purely economic loss. Although a few jurisdictions may extend this tort to include the defendant's negligent interference with contract, intent is the most common basis for this claim. By knowing of the existence of the contract and yet continuing to interfere in the relationship, the plaintiff is acting with knowledge that some type of interference is at least substantially certain to occur. Some jurisdictions even refer to this intent element as one of "scienter," but that actual term is more typically associated with tort claims for fraud. (*See* Chapter 21, *supra*, Misrepresentation).

The third element requires that the defendant's conduct must be malicious, improper, or intentional. As noted, *supra*, this tort is generally based upon the defendant's intentional misconduct and not negligence. This is because the only damages available for this tort are those involving purely economic loss, and most jurisdictions simply do not permit such damages in ordinary negligence claims. Another rationale for requiring some type of wrongful intent for this tort is based upon the very nature of the United States economy as a free market that anticipates substantial competition among different businesses. In fact, our antitrust laws actually require free and open competition, and the courts help to ensure that those markets remain free and open. Thus, one party to a contract is not allowed to intentionally prevent other businesses and people from engaging in advertising, negotiations and other conduct that is protected in a free market. As such, any interference with contracts between other parties that will give rise to a tort claim must be "wrongful" or "improper." Many jurisdictions often treat this as a separate element of the plaintiff's case by requiring proof of intent or wrongfulness. In addition, the defendant to the tort claim may raise the absence of any wrongful intent as a defense in justification for the interference. *See* section I.B., *infra*, for a further discussion of this concept.

There must be a breach of contract caused by the defendant. In some ways, this simply represents the causation element of the tort. Merely intending to cause a breach in the plaintiff's contractual relations is not a tort. Instead, the defendant actually must bring about the breach or there is no claim.

Finally, the plaintiff must prove that (s)he suffered some harm as a result of the breach of contract with the other party. This means that the interference with the contract not only must cause a breach in the plaintiff's contractual relation with another party, but the plaintiff must also prove some actual economic harm as a result of that breach. To further illustrate how some of these requirements operate in a typical interference with contract case, consider the following examples, *infra*.

The landmark case in the interference with contract area is *Lumley v. Gye*, 2 El. & Bl. 216, 118 Eng. Rep. 749 (1853). In that case, a noted performer had agreed to appear at a music hall owned by the plaintiff. Once the contract was entered into, the defendant induced the performer to leave the other music hall and appear at his music hall instead. The plaintiff sued the defendant for interference with contract. Notice how the facts and circumstances of this case fit the elements discussed above. There was a valid and enforceable contract between the plaintiff and the performer. The defendant knew of this contract, and intentionally encouraged the performer to leave the first music hall and to perform at the defendant's music hall. This caused the performer to breach the original contract with the plaintiff and to perform for the defendant instead. The plaintiff suffered an economic loss due to the performer's breach of contract.

This example may cause many to wonder how modern sport coaches manage to sign long term contracts only to leave prematurely and go to other employers. The simple answer is that many of these types of contracts specifically address the issue of what will happen if the coach leaves the place of employment prior to the expiration of the contract and goes to a competing coaching position. Such contractual provisions may range from merely allowing the coach to leave to requiring a specific payment by the competing employer. This point is important in the overall management of such cases. Once a contract is signed, the breach of that contract may lead to an action based on contract law between the parties to the original agreement. It may also lead to the tort claim if there is a third party intervener. In some areas, the movement of people among jobs is so common, that drafters of contracts have learned to take care of that contingency in the language of the employment agreements.

The case of *Lumley v. Gye, supra,* is an example of where the third party intervener has actually enticed one of the parties to the contract to breach the contract. However, it is also possible in some situations that both parties to the contract may still want to perform it, but the defendant third party intentionally creates some barrier or burden to its performance. If that should occur, then either or both parties to the contract may have a claim for the interference with the contract. This type of case is not as common, nor is it as well received as those where there is a direct enticement for just one of the parties to the contract to breach it. In order to aid in understanding how these claims operate, each of the requisite elements for this tort will be discussed individually within the context of these special issues.

B. Justification

As stated, *supra*, the claim for intentional interference with a contract requires that the defendant's actions must be "wrongful." Nevertheless, the law will not support a claim when there was some justification for such actions. This issue may be raised in one of two ways. Since the plaintiff has the burden of proving that the conduct of the defendant was intentional and wrongful, the defendant may offer proof in opposition to the plaintiff's assertion that the defendant intended to interfere with the contract. If the trier of fact is more persuaded by the defendant's evidence, then the plaintiff would simply fail in establishing a *prima facie* claim altogether. However, the defendant may also try to assert some public policy reason in support of the interfering behavior. If so, then such a justification would be a defense. Some examples will help to illustrate this distinction.

Suppose that the plaintiff has contracted to perform work at a variety of different locations, and that the defendant contacts each of those places and convinces the employers not to allow the plaintiff to perform. Initially, this certainly appears to be a clear interference with the plaintiff's contracts. However, in justification for this action the defendant may claim any number of different public policy reasons for the interference. For example, the defendant may offer proof that the plaintiff was not properly licensed to do the work, or that the plaintiff was not properly trained to do the work, or that completion of the work would cause some other harm to one or both of the contracting parties or to some other persons. There are no clear rules for what will be recognized as a justification. Instead, the issue is whether the conduct of the defendant appears to be protecting some clear interest of the public, the employer, or even the plaintiff.

Another interesting issue of justification involves the use of strikes or boycotts. Clearly a strike or boycott usually constitutes an interference with an existing contract. When a labor organization goes on strike, the striking employees are refusing to meet the terms of a current contract between the employer and their labor union. In addition, by picketing the work locations, the union members are also seeking to prevent other workers from honoring their contracts with that same employer. In the labor field, of course, federal law protects such interference, recognizing the employees' right to strike and picket. Under the same federal law, however, the existence of secondary boycotts is usually not allowed. Thus, if the union decides to strike and to picket another firm, not because of an actual labor dispute with that firm, but because the second firm is continuing to do business with the firm that the union is having a dispute with, this would constitute a secondary boycott and as such it would not be protected.

The problem with strikes and boycotts, however, is that they may also be protected by the Constitution of the United States, the First Amendment of which protects the right to free speech. There are times when members of a group may be permitted to maintain a secondary boycott and to enforce that boycott through picketing. For example, from the 1960's and on, labor groups have frequently boycotted and picketed food suppliers over the issue of farm wages. In many ways, these boycotts may be viewed as secondary boycotts. Thus, a group may picket a restaurant chain because the suppliers of food to that chain do not pay their farm workers what is viewed as a reasonable wage. Such picketing may result in the inability of suppliers to be able to sell and deliver goods to the restaurant chain, or for its own non-striking employees to go to work. Since the United States Supreme Court has recognized a protection for commercial speech, these examples appear to be protected free speech demonstrations that otherwise might have been disallowed as secondary boycotts. Courts have continued to expand the protection for such activities.

C. Interference with Own Contract

Once a contract has been breached, the injured party will typically sue the other (i.e., breaching) party to the contract for breach of contract. Ordinarily, this contract action is the only claim that the injured party will have against the other party that has breached the contract. Of course, as explained *supra*, the injured party may also sue the intervening party for the tort of interference with contract, but with very few exceptions the injured party to a contract cannot also sue the other (breaching) party to a contract for this same tort. Nevertheless, there is one exception that does allow recovery in tort by one party to a contract from another party to the same contract and that arises in cases involving the bad faith failure to pay an insurance claim. That example is discussed in section VI., *infra*. Another somewhat related issue involves an employee's "wrongful discharge" from an employment contract. Litigation based on "wrongful discharge" appears to have some elements of contract and some of tort. That issue is discussed next.

II. Wrongful Discharge

As previously discussed, *supra*, ordinarily one party to a contract cannot sue another party to a contract in tort when the contract is breached. The non-breaching party's only claim is in contract. However, where an employee claims to have been "wrongfully discharged" from an employment contract, some interesting problems may arise.

When an employee has a clear, long-term contract, that employee may not be discharged unless the terms of the contract are met. For example, the contract may permit discharge for disciplinary reasons, for reduced financial conditions of the company, or for other stated reasons. Typically, if an employee is discharged under such a contract, the employee will simply sue in contract, claiming that the terms and condition of the contract were violated.

However, not all employees have long-term contracts. Many employees are hired under "at will" contracts. This means that such employees serve "at the will" of their employers. The employee may be fired for any reason, or for no reason at all. The employee may, for example, simply come into work one morning and be told that (s)he is fired. There may be no reason for the firing, and no reason needs to be stated. Many jurisdictions still recognize the right of employers to fire "at will" employees without offering a reason.

Courts and legislatures, however, have created a series of exceptions to the "at will" contract. When an employee brings a claim after having been fired from an "at will" contract, the claim cannot be based on the employment contract itself, since there typically is not one. Instead, the claim is often based on some other statute or public policy. Such claims, therefore, appear to be more in the nature of a tort claim rather than a typical contract claim. These claims are frequently referred to as claims for "wrongful discharge."

The first obvious exception to the right to fire an employee pursuant to an "at will" contract is that the termination must not have been for discriminatory reasons. Modern federal and state statutes protect employees from discrimination on the basis of race, religion, age, gender, and national origin. If the employee can prove that the firing was based on such discrimination, then the employee would have a claim under the applicable federal or state law. Imagine, for example, that a 60-year-old man is fired from his job in a music store. The man notices that all of the older "at will" employees have been fired and replaced with younger employees. The man may have a claim alleging that the music store decided to present a younger image and fired all of the older employees to move in that direction. If the proof shows this to be true, the fired "at will" employee would receive a recovery.

Many federal and state statutes also provide protection for employees who assert their rights under these statutes. If, for example, an employee is fired for bringing a statutory discrimination claim or for filing for workers' compensation benefits as allowed by law, then the employee would have a "wrongful discharge" claim. Those statutes are intended to make sure that an employee may invoke the remedy provided by the legislation without fear of losing a job in the process.

Another exception to the rule pertaining to "at will" employment is that the employment may not actually be "at will." Although the employment contract might state that the employment is "at will," that same contract may also contain other language establishing that it is not. A typical method of adding language to an "at will" contract is through work rules or an employment manual. Courts frequently construe these documents as a part of the employment contract. Thus, if an apparent "at will" employee is fired, but finds that the method of termination was inconsistent with work rules or other published employment documents, the fired employee may have a breach of contract claim.

There is also a general public policy exception to the "at will" employment rule. If the fired employee can show that the termination is against public policy, then the employee may have a "wrongful discharge" claim. A typical public policy example exists when an employee is fired for refusing to perform an illegal act as a part of the job. In addition, firing for being a "whistle blower" of other wrongful or illegal acts by the employer is usually a basis for bringing an action for "wrongful discharge."

These "wrongful discharge" claims appear to be in the nature of tort claims because they are rarely based on the contract language itself. Instead, they are usually based on statutes or general public policy. Nevertheless, they tend to include elements of both contract and tort damages. Thus, although the basic recovery in a "wrongful discharge" claim is for loss of wages from the job based upon the wage rate as the basic measure, if the employer's misconduct in firing the employee is extreme, other damages (sometimes even including punitive damages) may be recoverable as well.

III. Intentional Interference with a Prospective Economic Advantage

A. General Nature of the Claim

Interference with a prospective economic advantage is similar to intentional interference with contract discussed in section I., *supra*. However, it is also very different in other ways. The similarities are clear. Like intentional interference with contract, this tort arises in a business setting where the plaintiff seeks to recover purely economic damages for the loss of a business opportunity. And, as a tort seeking purely economic loss as damages, most jurisdictions will require a showing of intent. Thus, just as with the intentional interference with contract tort, negligence claims ordinarily will not be allowed in actions based upon interference with a prospective economic advantage. In addition, the plaintiff also has to prove that the conduct of the defendant was the cause of the loss, and the plaintiff's mere failure to gain a prospective economic advantage is not sufficient to blame the loss on just anyone. The plaintiff must be able to prove the connection between the defendant's misconduct and the economic injury.

The major difference between these two claims is also what creates the real difficulty with this tort. The intentional interference with a contract requires the existence of a presently enforceable contract. By contrast, interference with prospective economic advantage is a claim that is brought when there is no current contract. Instead, the plaintiff alleges that (s)he had the probability of a future economic gain with which the defendant interfered.

The absence of a presently enforceable contract raises a potential conflict between protecting the interests of the plaintiff and assuring a free and open market. Free and open markets assume and encourage vigorous competition among all people. No one person has the right to set aside a certain type of business or activity and claim it for him or herself. In fact, antitrust laws prohibit such conduct. Because of this, much of the defendant's conduct that a plaintiff might want to allege in support of the interference with prospective economic advantage case simply involves the type of thing that the defendant might claim as nothing more than aggressive competition in the market. Because of this conflict between the tort claim and a free market, this claim is not generally as favored as the one for interference with contract.

Free competition will not, therefore, lead to liability. Parties are free to advertise and to seek new business. Even when that new business leaves a party with whom the plaintiff has done business for years, that alone does not give rise to a claim. Free competition is protected in the market. Therefore, successful prosecution of a claim for interference with economic advantage requires something more than merely losing business. Courts have reviewed numerous cases where this claim has been raised. Some of the easier cases that favor plaintiffs are where the defendant is in a special relationship with the plaintiff, such as where the defendant is in a fiduciary relationship with the plaintiff and the defendant takes advantage for him or herself. A fiduciary owes the principal all advantages that come to the fiduciary while acting in that capacity. Thus, if the fiduciary takes an advantage away from the principal, the principal may sue to recover it.

There have also been successful claims when the plaintiff alleges a bad motive for the interference. For example, suppose that the defendant goes into competition with the plaintiff merely for the purpose of causing economic harm to the plaintiff. For example, defendants who engage in substantial price-cutting by reducing prices even below their own cost may be subject to a claim of merely seeking business for the purpose of harming the plaintiff (i.e., by forcing them out of business altogether). Such claims, however, are not always successful, since sometimes defendants do offer goods and services below cost merely to clear inventory or to increase market share by attracting new customers. Such activities are permitted in a competitive market. Retail establishments, for example, typically offer "lost leaders." Those are items priced below costs and are advertised for the purpose of bringing customers into the store. Such activities are not actionable, even though they certainly may result in the loss of business by competitors.

There are times when a plaintiff may also allege that the defendant has engaged in an improper or illegal method of obtaining future business. Such activities may include allegations of fraud or deception. In these types of cases the plaintiff is more likely to recover for loss of prospective business. The law will protect an open market, but it must be a fair and legal open market. When the defendant engages in illegal activity, such conduct is not protected.

The antitrust laws of the United States are designed to protect open markets. Defendants who go so far as to reduce competition by their activities often will find that those activities are not protected. Although antitrust claims are similar to the tort of interference with the prospective economic advantage, they are usually brought under the appropriate statutory authority instead of as a separate tort cause of action.

In short, the absence of an enforceable contract makes a claim for interference with prospective economic advantage much more difficult for the plaintiff. The courts are just as likely to protect open market competition, as they are to protect the plaintiff's claim of loss. Therefore, in order to prevail in these types of claims the plaintiff will clearly have to prove intent, and typically even more, such as bad motive, fraud, deception, or some other illegal or wrongful conduct by the defendant.

B. Gifts or Inheritance

There are a few additional expectancies that plaintiffs sometimes seek to recover when asserting claims for intentional interference with a prospective economic advantage. Occasionally, plaintiffs will allege that they had the expectation of receiving gifts, devises from wills, or some inheritance that has been defeated by the defendant's misconduct. However, such claims are usually difficult for plaintiffs to prove.

In most instances these types of expectancies have little protection under the law. Donors of gifts may change their minds at any time up to the actual delivery of the gift. Those who expect to transfer property at their own death may also change their mind and change the will right up until the time of death. Although the donor or decedent may have even made multiple promises to transfer property by gift or devise, the law normally will not enforce those promises, and, at most, it provides only a limited protection to the promisee. However, if the plaintiff can show that the defendant prevented the transfer of the property by gift or devise by proving conduct such as undue influence, threats, or duress, then the plaintiff may be able to recover the property or its value. In addition, if the plaintiff can show that the transfer was prevented by some other tort (such as theft of the property or even the murder of the donor), then the property can be recovered.

C. "At Will" Contracts

As discussed previously in section II., *supra*, "at will" contracts create a special problem in the area of interference with business relationships. Some "at will" contracts involve the interference with a presently enforceable contract. Many such "at will" contracts, however, involve future expectations, and when they do, potential actions for interference with prospective economic advantage may arise. For example, parties may have contracts that are set to expire at a date certain, but which the plaintiff employee may expect will be renewed. However, the defendant may cause the other party to the contract to fail to renew it. Such contracts typically involve employment contracts or leases. In order to recover for the failure to renew such contracts, the plaintiff must prove some of the same elements that are discussed in section II., *supra*, pertaining to "at will" contracts. Ordinarily, this will involve proof of some legislatively protected interest or some other public policy requiring the contract to be extended.

D. Justification

In the previous discussion on intentional interference with contract (*see* section I.B., *supra*), it was stated that justification for the interference is a defense to such a claim. Clearly, all of those same justifications would also be a defense to any claim for interference with prospective economic advantage.

In addition, simply engaging in open competition in a free market is also another important justification for this type of interference.

IV. Interference with Evidence

A relatively new tort is gaining acceptance in the United States. However, it is still not recognized by all jurisdictions. This tort may be called "spoliation" of evidence, and it is asserted when a party to litigation has intentionally destroyed evidence that would be important to that litigation (and that is usually adverse to the party that destroyed it). When this tort has been recognized, the claim is normally based on intent, since courts are less likely to allow recovery for mere negligent spoliation.

However, even when this "spoliation" tort is not recognized, the plaintiff is still not without some remedy. The civil rules of procedure in most jurisdictions provide for sanctions to be imposed by the court against parties who intentionally destroy evidence. In addition, individual court rules usually allow for jury instructions that permit the jury to infer the damaging nature of the evidence from the fact that a party has intentionally destroyed it. Some jurisdictions find that these rules alone are adequate for any harm to a litigant caused by the loss of the evidence.

V. Negligent Interference with Business Relationship

Thus far in this chapter our discussion of liability for interference with contract and interference with prospective economic advantage has involved claims that are based upon intentional torts. In order for the plaintiff to succeed, the plaintiff must prove that the defendant knew about the relationship and then acted intentionally for the purpose of bringing it to an end. Merely negligent interferences with these types of business relationships provide no basis for recovery. The reason is that the damages typically available in these torts are based upon purely economic losses, and courts ordinarily do not allow recovery in negligence for purely economic losses.

However, there are a few times when the recovery of solely economic losses may be permitted, even where the defendant has only acted negligently. Some tort actions specifically provide for such recovery. For example, malpractice by attorneys or accountants frequently results in just economic losses to their clients, and when they do, claims for negligence for such losses are typically allowed. Likewise, as discussed in the previous chapter, misrepresentation claims may also result in purely economic losses. (*See* Chapter 21, *supra*, Misrepresentation). For most other types of negligence claims, the traditional rule does not allow recovery for the plaintiff's purely economic loss. As such, tort claims based upon the *negligent* interference with a contract or the *negligent* interference with a prospective advantage are usually not sustained.

Of course, as with any other negligence action, where the plaintiff sustains economic loss that is otherwise directly connected to a personal injury or property damage, courts may allow recovery of such loss, since the plaintiff is *not* seeking recovery of *solely* economic losses. Instead, the economic loss is connected directly to some additional personal or proprietary interest for which other types of damages are recoverable. (*See* Chapter 8, *supra*, Compensatory and Punitive Damages). These types of economic loss damages are sometimes referred to as "parasitic" damages, since no independent cause of action exists solely for their recovery, but they can still be recovered when they are combined with other types of allowable damages. Under this concept, a plaintiff might be able to recover economic loss for a negligent interference with a business relationship if (s)he can prove that such losses are otherwise connected with personal injury or property damage arising from the same negligence.

Presently, only a very few cases have allowed recovery for solely economic loss in negligence (apart from the exceptions discussed, *supra*). Although those cases have not yet set a trend for the future, they certainly bear watching.

VI. Bad Faith in Insurance Contracts

As explained in the discussion, *supra*, the general rule is that one party to a contract usually cannot sue for the tort of interference with the contract against another party to that same contract. Instead, if a breach occurs, the proper action between the parties to the contract is one for breach of contract, and not tort. However, there is one clear exception to this rule.

When a party purchases insurance, that party becomes the owner of the policy. Depending on the nature of the policy, the purchasing party may also have an additional status. For example, the owner of a life insurance contract may also be the insured under that same policy. When the insured dies, the insurance company has a contractual duty to pay the named beneficiary of the contract. If the insurance company that issued the life insurance contract refuses or delays in paying the claim, the appropriate remedy would appear to be one based upon a breach of contract action for the amount of the policy.

However, sometimes treating this type of claim as one for breach of contract often works an extreme injustice on the beneficiary of the insurance policy. Consider the normal progression of events that typically occurs in these types of situations, from the insurance company's failure to pay through the subsequent breach of contract litigation to recover the insurance amount. Assume that the life insurance policy amount is $1 million. Upon the death of the insured, the beneficiary is required to provide the insurance company with proper notice of the decedent's death, along with appropriate information establishing the beneficiary's identity. Under the terms of the insurance contract, the beneficiary is then entitled to receive the $1 million. However, if the insurance company refuses to pay or delays it's payment for an extended period, the insurance company can invest the insurance proceeds and continue to earn income on that investment. At this point, in order to recover the insurance funds, the beneficiary would have to hire a lawyer, and bring a breach of contract action against the insurance company. Even if the beneficiary ultimately does win the contract claim, all that would be recoverable would be the $1 million. However, the beneficiary, by being forced to file a lawsuit to collect the insurance proceeds, has actually incurred greater losses, such as the additional attorney's fees to pursue the litigation, as well as the loss of investment earnings of the proceeds during the period of the parties' contract litigation. (In some cases, the prevailing plaintiff in this breach of contract action might also be awarded his or her attorney's fees at the discretion of the trial court, but (s)he would certainly never be entitled to the lost investment earnings.) Courts have recognized that this type of situation can create an economic incentive for insurance companies to delay their payment of insurance claims for longer than otherwise reasonable periods. Indeed, it might even be possible in some situations for the insurance company to delay the payment long enough so that the company's investment earnings during the period of the delay could generate enough money to pay the beneficiary's claim (and without ever having to pay out the contractual policy amount).

In order to counter the potential injustice that can arise in these types of situations involving the payment of life insurance claims, the courts have allowed a tort action for the insurance company's "bad faith failure to pay" an insurance claim. In the example discussed, *supra*, the insurance company would be required to pay the life insurance claim promptly upon the filing of the death notice and receipt of the beneficiary's appropriate identification materials. Failure to promptly pay this claim would allow the beneficiary to recover not only the contract damages for the face amount of the policy, but also punitive damages. It is the addition of the punitive damages that makes the claim one for tort, since punitive damages cannot be recovered in ordinary breach of contract actions. And, it is the potential for this additional tort recovery that provides the financial incentive for the insurance company to pay the claim promptly.

Courts have also provided additional remedies for the failure to pay various other types of insurance claims as well. For example, consider a typical automobile liability insurance policy with a maximum amount of $100,000 that the insurance company is obligated to pay for any claim against its insured. This means that when the insured person is sued following an automobile accident, the insurance company has agreed to pay the claim, but only up to the maximum amount determined by the $100,000 policy limits. If the judgment against the insured is greater than the policy limit of $100,000, the insurance company will only pay the first $100,000 of that judgment (i.e., up to the amount of the policy limit), and the insured party will remain personally responsible for paying the remainder of the judgment amount. But what happens when the insured does not have the funds to pay the additional amount of any judgment? When insured parties are faced with the possibly of incurring a liability judgment that exceeds the amount of their insurance policy limits, plaintiffs in such litigations frequently try to settle for the maximum amount of the insurance coverage (i.e., the full policy limits). Imagine that an insured defendant has been sued for $1 million dollars. Also assume that the maximum amount of that defendant's liability insurance coverage is $100,000. Suppose also that the plaintiff in the litigation against the insured has offered to settle the claim for the full $100,000. The insured will likely demand that the insurance company accept the plaintiff's settlement offer, since doing so would relieve the insured from any potential excess liability should the case go to trial and result in a judgment in excess of the insured's $100,000 policy amount. Now, assume that the insurance company that represents the defendant refuses to settle for the maximum, and only offers $25,000 to settle the claim. Assume also that the plaintiff refuses the insurance company's low settlement offer, and the case eventually goes to trial where the judgment is greater than the maximum amount of the policy. In such situations the courts may still make the insurance company pay the full amount of the judgment (even though it exceeds the insurance policy amount) if the insured can prove that the insurance company's failure to settle the claim was not in good faith. Doing so provides an additional incentive that forces the insurance company to pay if it fails to act in good faith when attempting to settle legitimate claims against the insured.

VII. Common Law Intellectual Property

In the modern legal world, intellectual property is seen, primarily, as a statutory issue. Law students, lawyers, and judges tend to think first of the statutes that control copyright, trademarks, patents, and trade secrets. It is important to understand, however, that many of those areas of the law had their beginnings in tort law. Because of this, many of the claims and remedies that originated in tort law still exist in some form in the modern world. Thus, actions to protect these forms of intellectual property may also include those common law claims.

The phrase "intellectual property" offers some insight into the theories that underlie it. Copyrights, trademarks, and patents are designed to protect creations. When an imaginative mind comes up with a new creative application, (s)he will want to protect that concept from unpermitted use by others. The law assumes that these different types of intellectual property are all forms of property that need protecting. In a manner similar to the way that real property and chattels are protected from trespasses, intellectual property may also be protected. Tort law provides the initial claims and remedies when someone has sought to use, without consent, the intellectual property of another.

However, the protection of intellectual property typically does not speak in terms of trespass. This is because the term trespass had its origins in early common law where the ancient writ of "trespass" was used for the protection of tangible real property and chattels against actual physical invasions of one kind or another. When speaking of intellectual property, the law speaks, instead, of infringement. The infringement of intellectual property is the *use* of that concept or property, by another, *without consent* of the creator.

In reviewing the different types of intellectual property that may be protected, there seems to be a fairly common thread. The usual method of infringement by a tortfeasor is to use the intellectual property of another in the market and, in doing so, confuse the consumer into thinking that (s)he is getting the original or real creation. By doing this, the tortfeasor is taking business away from the creator of the intellectual property. In addition, the public consumer may be getting (often unknowingly) a creation that is not as high a quality as the original. Therefore, an underlying theme in many of the intellectual property cases is that the tortfeasor has created confusion in the mind of the public. This theme is, in fact, one of the elements of many of these claims.

Another common theme in intellectual property cases focuses on what can be protected. The intellectual property needs to be a new creation in order to receive protection. This theme has several issues that follow naturally.

First, the person seeking to protect his or her creation cannot be seeking protection for an old and well-known concept. To use an absurd example, if a plaintiff tried to claim intellectual property protection for the wheel, the courts would decline the claim, since the creation and invention of the wheel is obviously old technology that has been well established.

In addition, the courts frequently say that generic terms cannot be protected. For example, a plaintiff cannot claim rights in terms that are mere descriptions of generic items. However, the concern over the use of generic terms has led to numerous other issues. A good example can be found in the sale of soft drinks. The term "soft drink" is a generic term, as are the terms "soda" and "soda pop." No plaintiff can use those terms and then try to prevent others from using them. They are generic terms that describe a particular kind of drink, as opposed to a specific drink or drink producer. In contrast, the terms "Pepsi-Cola" and "Coca-Cola" are protected terms. No one can use those terms for a new drink product without getting permission from the companies that own the rights to those names, and those companies aggressively protect their rights in those names. One of the major fears of companies that own well-known names is that the names will become generic over time. Xerox, for example, is a company that makes photocopy machines. However, the term "Xerox" is a proper name, and the word itself is a noun that is used to uniquely identify those particular copy machines made only by the Xerox company. For obvious reasons, the company does not want individuals to refer to copies that come out of various other different copy machines as "Xerox copies." If that were to occur, the term "Xerox" eventually could become a generic term through its casual use by the public, and the legal protections for the term itself would be lost. To prevent this from happening, the copies should not be referred to as "Xerox copies," unless in fact they were made on a Xerox machine. Otherwise, they are simply photocopies, which is a proper generic term.

Finally, since only new creations can be protected, mere ideas and concepts alone cannot be protected. Electricity, for example, is a natural fact that has been discovered. A person could not prevent others from using electricity. However, particular types of light bulbs, the distribution of electricity, and various other appliances that use electricity are new creations that can be protected.

Thus, the basic concept of protecting intellectual property is one that is very appropriate for tort law. Since new creations are treated as a form of property (i.e., intellectual property), tort law provides protection in the form of various specific claims, as well as appropriate relief, against the interference with such creations, just as it does various other more tangible form(s) of property. Some of these actions are discussed in the following section, *infra*.

VIII. Unfair Trade and Competition

By engaging in different forms of unfair trade practices, the defendant is interfering in the plaintiff's creations in a way that is similar to the claim for interference with a contract. (*See* section I., *supra*). The plaintiff in both situations has rights that have been interfered with to the plaintiff's detriment. In addition, the defendant for personal gain has caused that interference. The law, therefore, supplies a remedy for the plaintiff's harm. For purposes of this discussion, there are several different types of interferences that may fall generally under the heading of unfair trade.

A form of unfair trade that is similar to defamation is known as product disparagement. Although the U. S. Supreme Court has extended free speech protection to include many forms of commercial speech, thereby bringing the concepts of advertising and commercial discussion into the realm of constitutional law, commercial speech still has not received quite the same level of protection that has been afforded to the more traditional types of free speech. Nevertheless, there are still substantial free speech rights associated with commercial speech and product disparagement cases similar to those that also arise in the defamation cases. (*See* Chapter 17, *supra*, Defamation). For example, when a defendant makes false and disparaging comments about a plaintiff's product, the plaintiff may have a product disparagement claim (as compared with a constitutional defamation claim). In the context of constitutional law, most producers of products would be seen as public figures, since they actively advertise and make claims to the public about their own products. Likewise, if the defendant says something negative about the product, the plaintiff may have to prove *New York Times* "actual malice," requiring the plaintiff to show that the defendant knew the statement was false or spoke in reckless disregard of the truth. (*See* Chapter 17, section III., *supra*, Defamation).

In a similar vein, general false advertising may also give rise to a tort claim. Where a seller of goods or services makes false statements about those goods or services, the statements may be actionable. Today, an action for false advertising may be brought by one of two different groups of plaintiffs: consumers who purchase goods or services based upon false claims and are subsequently harmed in the use of those goods or services; and competing sellers of goods or services.

Trade secrets are another commonly protected creation in the commercial world. A company may create anything from a new industrial process to a secret formula for a fast food product, and those inventions are protected as trade secrets. If a defendant steals or obtains such a trade secret by fraud, then the conduct is actionable.

Trademarks are also commonly used in the commercial world. Companies frequently create special names, marks or logos to help the consumer identify their products in the market, and to distinguish their products from those of competitors, and consumers regularly ask for products using specific company trademarks. In addition, consumers select products from store displays based upon the names and logos appearing on the labels. If a defendant uses another company's trademark without consent, the use is actionable.

A somewhat related issue involves "trade dress." In addition to creating special names and logos, companies sometimes also create special packaging, colors, and forms of products that distinguish their products from others. Many consumers pick products from store shelves based upon the shape or color of a bottle, and they rely on their distinctive shapes or colors to allow them to find a particular product quickly. If a competing seller tries to make a product that appears too similar in color or shape, a possible claim for infringement of trade dress may arise.

A. "Passing Off"

Many of the issues discussed in the immediately proceeding section, *supra*, have a common element: the use of a competitor's name, logo, marks, form, color, or packaging to attempt to create confusion in the market. It is this confusion in the market that is the very basis for providing relief in a "passing off" claim. The "passing off," or creation of confusion in the market, may occur in several different ways. A customer may enter a retail establishment and ask for a product by name. That would, in fact, be asking for the product by its "trade mark." If the seller knowingly supplies the customer with a competing product, that would be "passing off." Imagine, for example, that a customer enters a restaurant and asks for a "grape Nehi." The waiter, however, intentionally supplies another brand of grape soda. That would be "passing off."

Many sellers are less likely merely to substitute one product for another. More commonly, a seller might offer its own product as a substitute, and try to make it appear as close to the well-known product as possible while not actually representing it to be that product. Not infrequently, sellers will use names, logos, color or packaging that is close, but not exactly like a well-known product to create this type of confusion in the market. Nevertheless, this conduct is still regarded as "passing off," and it would be treated as trademark or trade dress infringement. The concept of "passing off" is quite common throughout many areas of intellectual property. As the following sections, *infra*, indicate, there are several other specific types of intellectual property infringements that usually result in some form of "passing off."

B. Copyright

Copyrights may be one of the better-known forms of intellectual property. A person who creates writing, music, photography, or other artistic works has the right to the exclusive use of that work for a certain period of time. Although the copyright attaches immediately upon creation of the work, if the plaintiff wishes to receive extended protection under the law, as well as certain special remedies, along with an easing in the requirements of proving a claim for infringement, it is important initially to formally register the work.

However, not every infringing use will necessarily result in a copyright violation. Instead, there are certain uses that are permitted, even for copyrighted materials. For example, quotation, comments, descriptions, and other forms of "fair use" are typically allowed. However, copying lengthy passages of copyrighted materials without citation would clearly constitute an infringement.

Modern technology has given rise to a series of difficult copyright issues. The modern photocopy machine, VCR, DVD-recorder, smartphones, and the Internet have made it possible for people to easily copy many works that are otherwise protected by law. Rather than paying for an original copy of the work, people often find it convenient simply to copy works using some of these modern technologies. The concern over mass copying, sharing, and pirating of artistic creations has raised serious issues regarding how future creators of such works will receive compensation for their efforts. Undoubtedly, there will be much future litigation regarding some of these conflicts between modern technology and the protections created by copyright laws and the need to provide financial incentives to create new artistic works.

C. Patent

Patents are much like copyrights (*see* the discussion, *supra*). Whereas copyrights protect the creation of artistic works, patents protect the creation of new inventions. Creators of new inventions may seek to retain the exclusive rights to those inventions for a term of years by having the invention patented. In order to do so, it is necessary to have the new invention registered in the U.S. Patent Office. The patented item must, in fact, be a new invention. A person may not patent old science. Once patented, others cannot use it without consent from the patent owner. The elements for a patent infringement claim are simple to state. The plaintiff must prove a valid patent and also that it is being infringed. Due to the complexity of new inventions, however, the proof of the cases is difficult.

The law of patents is so complex that it has become its own specialty in the practice of law. Attorneys who wish to practice patent law must take a special patent law exam.

D. Right of Publicity

One of the more interesting areas of intellectual property protection involves the so-called right of "publicity." This area is similar to claims relating to the right to privacy and is, in fact, an outgrowth of that area. Therefore, when studying the right of publicity, it is important to understand its relationship with the separate privacy claim of commercial appropriation. *See* Chapter 18, section I, *supra*, for a more thorough discussion of the closely related tort of commercial appropriation.

Commercial appropriation is one of the older privacy tort claims that traditionally was asserted whenever a defendant used the name or likeness of another without consent, for commercial reasons. The damages would be based upon the economic value of the name or likeness in question. Since traditionally this tort was considered to be a dignitary tort, it was personal to each individual plaintiff. That meant that this action did not survive the death of the plaintiff, nor could it even be assigned to a third person during the plaintiff's lifetime. Originally, this did not create much of a problem for courts in situations where the plaintiff was a private person who had never previously traded upon his or her own name or likeness. For those plaintiffs, the commercial appropriation claim certainly was adequate to protect them from the embarrassment and emotional distress that typically accompanied merely personal dignitary invasions by persons who used their names or likenesses for their own commercial gain.

Nevertheless, the commercial appropriation claim traditionally has also been asserted to recover for harm arising from the use of celebrity plaintiffs' names or likenesses without their consent. While far less common in many older appropriation cases, today celebrities commonly rely on endorsements for substantial income. Because of this, many courts today now regard these plaintiffs' interests in their "celebrity" as a form of intellectual property, instead of focusing upon harm to the plaintiffs' personal dignitary interests through use of the traditional privacy torts. (*See* Chapter 18, *supra*, Invasion of Privacy).

Whether such celebrities are from the sports or entertainment world, companies often pay large fees to use their names and likenesses in various product advertisements and promotions. If a defendant uses such a name without consent, and without the usual payment of these substantial fees, the commercial appropriation claim, although still used in some jurisdictions, is simply not as well suited to protect the plaintiff's legal interest that is most at issue, namely the plaintiff's property interest in the use of his or her own name or likeness. For that reason, the tort of "publicity" has been recognized in many jurisdictions, as a separate and distinct tort from the traditional commercial appropriation privacy tort.

A claim based upon the right of publicity receives protection beyond the mere use of the plaintiff's name or likeness. Many celebrities also have distinctive voices, characteristics or other features. When a defendant uses such features for his or her own commercial purposes, the celebrity may have a claim for the value of that use as well. One of the earlier cases in this area is instructive. *Midler v. Ford Motor Co.*, 849 F.2d 460 (9th Cir. 1988). A company sought to use the well-known singer, Bette Midler in an advertisement. When she declined, the company got another singer to perform a voice recording. The other singer performed the song so that it sounded exactly like Bette Midler. Ms. Midler brought suit for the value of her distinctive voice and recovered.

It is interesting to note just how similar these cases are to some of the other forms of confusion in the marketplace. In many publicity tort cases, the defendant is trying to use the distinctive features of the celebrity to confuse the public into believing that the celebrity is actually the person who is performing, just as in the *Midler* case, *supra*. Viewed in that light, it is obvious that recovery will be allowed. This is, in fact, just another form of "passing off." Other examples of the right of publicity have arisen whereby celebrities ranging from Elvis Presley to Vanna White have had their distinctive features used by others. Such uses often lead to liability.

The use of the distinctive features of Elvis Presley raises yet another one of the difficulties associated with the right of publicity, as well as one of its most distinctive differences. As discussed, *supra*, the right of publicity is a relatively new tort. As such, it does not have a long history of use among the various courts that have applied it. For example, most jurisdictions that have adopted it have treated it just like the other right of privacy torts. However, as explained previously, the difficulty with these other privacy torts is that they typically do not survive the death of the individual. Thus, when a defendant has used the distinctive features of a *deceased celebrity* the issue arises as to whether representatives of the deceased's estate can bring a claim for harm to the decedent's "publicity." The courts have taken several approaches. Some courts have concluded that if the celebrity had reduced the use of his or her own name, likeness, or distinctive characteristics to a tangible property right during life, then the estate continues to own that as a property right. In those jurisdictions, the estate is merely protecting the decedent's property right and is not seeking recovery for a separate personal dignitary privacy right. These jurisdictions typically recognize this as the separate tort of "publicity." Some jurisdictions have recognized exclusively only one tort claim (e.g., commercial appropriation), or the other (e.g., publicity) for the commercial use of a person's name or likeness, whereas some jurisdictions apparently recognize both claims as entirely separate torts. *See, e.g., People for the Ethical Treatment of Animals, v. Berosini*, 895 P. 2d 1269 (Nev. 1995). Other jurisdictions have passed legislation protecting the right of publicity beyond death.

Since this area of the law is still fairly new, it remains in a state of change. Future legislation and decisions will have to be reviewed to follow the development of the law.

Checkpoints

- The elements of intentional interference with a contract are:
  - present existence of an enforceable contract;
  - knowledge on the part of the defendant of that contract;
  - malicious, improper, or illegal interference with that contract;
  - a breach of that contract; and,
  - famages to the plaintiff caused by the breach of the contract.
- The elements of intentional interference with a prospective economic advantage are:
  - probable economic advantage to be gained in the future;
  - knowledge on the part of the defendant of that relationship;
  - malicious, improper, or illegal interference with that relationship;
  - a termination of that relationship; and,
  - damages to the plaintiff caused by the termination of that relationship.
- Justifications for interference with contracts or future advantages include:
  - fair competition;
  - protection of the public;
  - protection of the defendant;

- protection of the plaintiff; and,
- public policy.
- Bad faith failure to pay an insurance claim allows recovery as if in tort, and that may include punitive damages.
- Intellectual property is protected by tort claims in a manner similar to real property and chattels.
- Claims for the interference with an intellectual property right usually result in damages for the economic value of that right.
- The infringement of an intellectual property right usually results in the defendant seeking to cause some confusion in the mind of the public.

Mastering Tort Law Checklist

Chapter 2 • Intentional Interference with Person or Property

❏ Intent, negligence and strict liability are the three bases of liability.

❏ Intent is proven by showing that the defendant acted for the purpose of bringing about the consequences or acted with knowledge that the consequences were substantially certain to occur.

❏ Children and others of diminished capacity are not automatically exempt from intentional torts. The only question is whether such defendants had sufficient mental capacity to form the requisite intent.

❏ Transferred intent operates where a defendant intended one of the five intentional torts in the original writ of trespass and accomplishes one of the five intentional torts in the original writ of trespass.

❏ The law will allow the intent to transfer from the tort intended to the tort accomplished.

❏ Those five original writ of trespass torts are assault, battery, false imprisonment, trespass to land and trespass to chattels.

❏ The elements of assault are:
  - Intent to bring about a harmful or offensive touching or the apprehension of that touching;
  - Apprehension of immediate bodily contact;
  - Some overt act on the part of the defendant; and
  - The present ability of the defendant to carry out that immediate bodily contact.

❏ The elements of battery are:
  - Intent to bring about a harmful or offensive touching or the apprehension of that touching; and
  - A harmful or offensive touching.

❏ The elements of false imprisonment are:
  - Intent to bring about a confinement;
  - Confinement within boundaries;
  - Physical confinement;

- Knowledge on the part of the plaintiff of the confinement or harm to the plaintiff by the confinement; and
- No legal authority for the confinement.

❏ The elements of intentional infliction of emotional distress are:
- Intent or reckless conduct;
- Extreme and outrageous behavior by the defendant; and
- Severe emotional distress.

❏ The elements of trespass to land are:
- Intent to be on the land; and
- Being on the land of another.

❏ The elements of trespass to chattels are:
- Intent to interfere with a chattel; and
- Harm to the chattel that causes less than full market value.

❏ The elements of conversion are:
- Intent to interfere with a chattel; and
- Harm or interference that is total destruction or an exercise of dominion over the chattel to the exclusion of the rights of the true owner.

Chapter 3 • Defenses to Intentional Torts

❏ Consent may be express or implied.

❏ Implied consent may be implied by:
- Circumstances; or
- Conduct; or
- Custom

❏ Consent in medical malpractice (i.e., negligence) cases saves a doctor from a cause of action for battery, where the doctor's treatment would otherwise be an intention harmful touching.

❏ The elements of self-defense are:
- Reasonable belief that the individual is being threatened with immediate harm; and
- Extent of force is reasonable in light of the circumstances.

❏ The elements of defense of others are:
- Depending on the jurisdiction, either:
- Reasonable belief that some other individual is being threatened with immediate harm, or accurate belief that some other individual is being threatened with immediate harm;
- Extent of force is reasonable in light of the circumstances.

❏ The elements of defense of property are:

- Reasonable belief that property is being threatened with immediate harm; and
- Extent of force is reasonable in light of the circumstances.

❏ The elements of necessity:
- For public necessity, there is an imminent and serious threat to the public.
- For private necessity, there is an imminent threat to an individual or his or her property.

Chapter 4 • Negligence

❏ In negligence cases, duty is a question of law. The judge decides whether the defendant owes a duty of care to the plaintiff. In most cases involving physical damage, we owe a duty to the world at large.

❏ In most negligence cases, actors must behave as a reasonably prudent person under the same or similar circumstances.
- This is an objective standard, and courts do not take account of an individual's mental deficiencies.
- However, courts do consider some subjective characteristics. In particular, physical disabilities are considered in setting the reasonably prudent person duty standard.
- Similarly, courts take account of an individual's exceptional knowledge and skills.

❏ Children are judged by a special duty standard.
- In most jurisdictions today, courts compare children to a reasonably prudent person of like age, intelligence, and experience.
- However, when children engage in a "dangerous activity that is characteristically undertaken by adults," they are judged by the objective reasonably prudent person standard.

❏ Professionals are judged by a special duty standard — a standard that is set by the profession itself.
- In most cases, professionals must act as an ordinary member of their profession under the same or similar circumstances.
- The professional standard normally must be established by expert testimony.

❏ In determining whether an actor has breached the reasonably prudent person standard, most courts use a balancing test, weighing the advantages and disadvantages of the actor's conduct. The most famous articulation of the balancing test is Learned Hand's formula from the *Carroll Towing* case — whether $B<PL$.

❏ Custom evidence is not dispositive on the issue of breach. It is admissible, and might be powerful evidence that a party has behaved reasonably (or not). But in the end, it is for a judge or jury to determine whether an actor has acted as a reasonably prudent person.

❏ Courts sometimes treat violations of a criminal statute or a regulation as negligence per se, even if the statute or regulation is silent on the question of civil liability. Courts do so only when the statute meets a two-part test.

• First, the statute must be designed to protect a class of persons within which the plaintiff falls.

• Second, the statute must be designed to protect against a type of risk that matches the harm suffered by the plaintiff in the case at hand.

❏ There are several well-known exceptions to negligence per se:

• One example is where the actor's violation of a statute is deemed reasonable, for example where adhering to the statute would be more dangerous than violating its terms.

• Another example is where an actor does not, or should not, know about facts that make the statute applicable.

❏ Negligence per se does not mean automatic liability. A plaintiff still needs to prove the remaining elements of the claim, including causation and damages.

❏ When evidence of a defendant's breach of duty is unavailable, a plaintiff can sometimes proceed by using the doctrine of *res ipsa loquitur*. In these cases, courts allow juries to infer negligence if the plaintiff is hurt in an accident that does not normally occur in the absence of negligence by someone in a class of actors within which the defendant falls.

Chapter 5 • Cause in Fact

❏ Causation is established under the "but-for" test.

❏ Do not assume that multiple causes or multiple parties means that the "but-for" cause test will not work:

• If the "but-for" cause test does not work because causes cancel one another out, use the substantial factor test;

• If separate harms can be allocated to separate causes, do so.

❏ In medical and toxic tort cases, statistical proofs are often important in demonstrating that the harm was caused by the defendant's conduct, but the inference must either be strong in itself or supported by other circumstantial evidence.

Chapter 6 • Proximate Cause

❏ Proximate cause deals with the issue of the proper scope of the defendant's liability.

❏ An older test for proximate cause, the direct cause test, based its analysis on the presence or absence of intervening causal factors. It is no longer much used, but the issue of intervening causes remains important.

❏ Foreseeability of the resulting harm is the more modern test. One application of this rule is that the plaintiff must be a foreseeable victim of the defendant's negligence.

❏ The general type of harm that the plaintiff suffered must also be foreseeable as a result of the negligence. We say that the harm must be "within the risk"; hence this test is called the risk rule.

❏ An important limitation on the risk rule is the "thin-skulled plaintiff" doctrine: liability is not limited because the extent of harm was greater than what was foreseeable.

❏ Intervening causes do not automatically cut off liability. If the intervening cause was foreseeable, the harm will likely still be within the risk.

❏ Efforts by the victim to cope with or avoid the risk created by the defendant are considered foreseeable, at least if they are reasonable and foreseeable responses to the danger.

❏ Intervening causes that cut off liability are called "superseding" causes. Superseding causes are defined as extraordinary and unforeseeable intervening events.

❏ A cause will not be superseding if the defendant had a duty to protect the plaintiff from it.

Chapter 7 • Multiple Tortfeasors

❏ Joint and several liability means that a defendant is responsible for the whole amount of a plaintiff's harm, even if the conduct of another actor contributed to the loss.

• The rule traditionally applied in cases where a plaintiff suffered an indivisible loss at the hands of more than one actor.

• Today, the all-or-nothing nature of tort law has changed, and courts frequently assess liability based on each party's level of fault. No consensus has emerged about how this change affects joint and several liability.

- • Some jurisdictions continue to apply the traditional rule. Other jurisdictions apply it only under certain circumstances. Yet others have abolished joint and several liability completely.
- ❑ Cases involving multiple tortfeasors often raise causation issues when the plaintiff cannot identify the individual defendant who caused the harm.
  - • In limited circumstances, courts have created special rules to avoid unfair outcomes. For example, multiple defendants can be liable under a theory of enterprise liability if they jointly controlled a risk.
  - • Similarly, defendants might bear the burden of establishing that they did *not* cause the plaintiff's harm under alternative liability, a theory that applies where defendants simultaneously create an identical risk of harm.
  - • Several courts have extended alternative liability in cases involving certain types of products. In these "market share liability" cases, each defendant's liability is limited by the amount of product that it sold in the relevant market at the relevant time.
- ❑ Indemnity means complete reimbursement.
  - • It often applies in situations where one party contractually agrees to indemnify another for liabilities.
  - • Indemnity also applies in limited circumstances where parties are not in a contractual relationship.
  - • One example is where an actor is only vicariously liable and seeks reimbursement from the active tortfeasor. (*See* Chapter 13.)
  - • Another example is where a retailer is liable under a products liability theory and seeks reimbursement from the manufacturer after demonstrating that it could not have discovered the product's defect through reasonable inspection. (*See* Chapter 16.)
- ❑ Contribution is partial reimbursement.
  - • Traditionally, it permitted a defendant who had paid a judgment to recover pro rata shares from other culpable tortfeasors.
  - • With the advent of comparative fault, however, most states have moved to a system of comparative contribution where each defendant's reimbursement is proportional to the share of fault that a factfinder has assigned to each tortfeasor.

Chapter 8 • Compensatory and Punitive Damages

- ❑ A tort award for physical injury can include pecuniary losses, such as recovery for past and future medical expenses.

❑ A tort award for personal injury can include an award for past and future lost income.

❑ In some jurisdictions, awards of damages for future losses (e.g., future medical expenses or lost income) must be discounted to present value.

❑ A tort award for physical injury may also include damages for so-called "pain and suffering."

❑ A tort award for physical injury can include an award for loss of consortium to the injured person's spouse (and, sometimes, children).

❑ In appropriate situations, courts may award damages for "wrongful death."

❑ Some states place legislative caps on certain types of damages, particularly pain and suffering.

❑ Damage awards may be limited by the collateral source rule.

❑ In an appropriate case, punitive damages may be awarded in a torts case, but the U.S. Supreme Court has placed constitutional limits on punitive damage awards.

Chapter 9 · Limited Duty

❑ "Non-feasance" refers to situations in which the law of negligence does not impose any affirmative duty upon the defendant to act whatsoever.

❑ By contrast, the doctrine of "misfeasance" refers to situations where the defendant has acted, but in some manner that the law regards as negligent.

❑ Under the "rescue rule," if the defendant negligently places any person in a position of peril, the defendant will be found to owe an affirmative duty to anyone else who may be injured while attempting to rescue that victim (even though no duty otherwise may have been owed to the rescuer).

❑ The "voluntarily assumed duty rule" states that when a defendant, although under no legal duty to act whatsoever, nevertheless voluntarily takes any action with respect to the plaintiff, the defendant voluntarily assumes a legal duty to non-negligently complete that action.

❑ Even in situations where a defendant ordinarily owes no affirmative duty to act, courts can still impose such a duty based upon the existence of certain "special relationships" between the defendant and the plaintiff.

  • In imposing this duty, courts have recognized a wide variety of different types of "special relationships," including that of "common carrier-passenger," "employer-employee," "parent-minor child," "doctor-patient," "teacher-student," "jailer-inmate," "landlord-tenant," "business invitor-invitee," as well as a myriad of other types of special legal relationships.

❏ Under the "public duty" rule, an affirmative duty to act will not be imposed upon a public entity for the benefit or protection of any individual citizen merely by virtue of the existence of the public entity-citizen relationship.

  • The economic burden of sustaining such a duty would simply be too great for most public entities to bear.

  • Instead, before any such affirmative duty will be imposed upon a public entity there must be some uniquely-identified relationship found to exist between the public entity and the specific victim involved that will otherwise justify requiring the entity to act in some specific manner with respect to that particular victim rather then merely the public at large.

❏ Even in the absence of a common law duty on the part of the defendant to act in a given set of circumstances, a court might still impose such a duty where the defendant has contracted with the plaintiff, expressly agreeing to assume such a duty.

❏ As long as the contract is not contrary to public policy, contractual duties will generally be enforced by the courts.

❏ The recovery of emotional distress damages in negligence actions are controlled by different rules, depending upon the type of emotional distress damages involved.

  • Defendants owe only a limited duty with respect to damages based upon the negligent infliction of *purely* emotional injuries, whereas plaintiffs are not so limited in their recovery of "parasitic" emotional distress damages in an ordinary negligence action.

❏ A variety of different approaches have been applied with respect to the recovery by bystanders of damages for their *purely* emotional distress injuries sustained as a result of injuries negligently inflicted by the defendant on a third person.

  • These approaches, known as the "impact rule," the "zone of impact rule," and the *"Dillon* rule," all seek to impose certain restrictions on the scope of the defendant's duty that is owed to these bystanders with respect to their recovery of such purely emotional distress injuries.

Chapter 10 • Premises Liability

❏ The concept of "premises liability" simply refers to the tort liability of various owners and occupiers of real property with respect to persons who are injured on the premises.

❏ Unlike most other areas of the law where the defendant's liability for the tort of negligence is generally based upon traditional common law rules that define the defendant's duty in relation to the exercise of reasonable care under the circumstances, in premises liability cases the defendant's duty of care is determined according to the legal classification of the injured plaintiff.

❏ The special premises liability rules pertaining to the landowner's duties owed to entrants who are injured on the premises are applicable only with respect to *dangerous conditions* on the premises as distinguished from injuries that are caused by various *activities* conducted on the premises and for which the landowners and occupants must always exercise reasonable care under the circumstances.

❏ A "trespasser" is someone who enters or remains on the land of another without any permission or an invitation to do so.
  • A landowner or occupant owes NO DUTY to a trespasser, except to avoid inflicting a willful or wanton injury.

❏ A "licensee" is a person who enters or remains on the land with the permission or consent of the landowner (either express or implied), but not under such circumstances as would justify treating the entrant as a true "invitee" for purposes of the landowner's duty of care.
  • In general, the landowner has no duty to prepare the land for entry by a licensee. Instead, licensees generally are required to accept the premises as they find them.
  • A landowner or occupant ONLY OWES a DUTY TO WARN licensees of KNOWN, HIDDEN DANGEROUS CONDITIONS that exist on the premises.

❏ An "invitee" is any person who enters or remains on the premises (either at the express or implied invitation of the landowner or occupant), for some purpose that is associated with the owner's business (either directly or indirectly), or for some other purpose for which the premises are held open for entry by members of the general public.
  • A landowner or occupant owes a DUTY to EXERCISE REASONABLE CARE IN MAINTAINING the premises in a condition that is REASONABLY SAFE for entry by invitees.

- In most instances, such a duty requires the landowner or occupant to (1) make a reasonable inspection of the premises, and then to (2) either warn (if appropriate) or remove or repair the hazard.

❏ Under the so-called "attractive nuisance" doctrine a young child's status as a "trespasser" does not conclusively determine the duty that is owed by the landowner. A duty of *reasonable care* may still be imposed upon any landowner or occupant who has reason to anticipate the presence of trespassing young children on the premises who may, by virtue of their young age and inexperience, be unable to appreciate its highly dangerous condition.

❏ Once an adult trespasser's physical presence on the premises has been discovered by the landowner or occupant (either actually or, at least, indirectly), the entrant's status may be changed from that of a mere "trespasser" to that of a "discovered trespasser" to whom the landowner or occupant owes a higher duty, such as that normally reserved for "licensees" or in some cases, even "invitees."

❏ Firefighters, police officers and other public safety individuals who enter onto the premises in the performance of their official responsibilities, for reasons of public policy, are treated as mere "licensees" upon the premises to whom the landowners and occupants only have a duty to warn of known hidden dangerous conditions existing on the premises.

❏ Social guests are persons who have been expressly invited onto the premises by the landowner or occupant.
- Most courts have declined to classify them as "invitees," since they are present on the premises purely for social purposes and not for any business or other purpose for which the premises are otherwise held open to the general public.
- Instead, they are ordinarily treated as mere "licensees," to whom the landowner or occupant must only warn of known hidden dangerous conditions that exist on the property.

❏ By statutes in most jurisdictions typically referred to as "recreational use" statutes, persons who gratuitously enter onto rural lands with the permission of the landowners and sustain injury while engaged in some recreational pursuit on those premises are treated as mere "trespassers" for purposes of defining the scope of the landowner's duty of care.

❏ The only duty owed by landowners and occupants with respect to injuries sustained by recreational entrants on their property is to refrain from willfully or wantonly inflicting any injury, provided the entrant was engaged in an approved recreational activity, and that the landowner or occupant has not charged a fee for the entry or otherwise received some valuable consideration from the entrant.

❏ A minority of courts have made significant modifications in the traditional common law classification scheme by either abolishing one or more of the traditional entrant categories altogether, or by combining the two categories of "licensee" and "invitee" into just one category (i.e., that of the "invitee" category).

❏ A few jurisdictions have simply abolished the traditional category-based system of determining duty altogether and replaced all of the entrant categories with just a single duty of care based upon the exercise of "reasonable care under the circumstances."

❏ Traditionally, the common law refused to impose any duty whatsoever upon landlords with respect to their tenants, or even an injured guest of the tenant, where an injury occurred on leased premises. This rule was known simply as the doctrine of "*caveat lessee.*" Over time, however, courts gradually began to create special "exceptions" to this no-duty rule whereby a duty of "reasonable care under the circumstances" was imposed upon landlords and lessors of real property in a variety of special situations such as:

  • Where the injury occurs in a "common area" of the leased premises over which the landlord has retained exclusive control;

  • Where the landlord voluntarily undertakes to make some repairs to the leased premises, and performs those repairs in a negligent manner;

  • Where the leased premises contained a latent (i.e., hidden) defect which existed at the time of the leasing; and

  • Where the premises were leased for use by the public.

❏ More recently, a few courts have abandoned the traditional "no duty" rule (and its attendant "exceptions") altogether, replacing it with a single duty, as in other negligence cases, based entirely upon the landlord's exercise of "reasonable care under the circumstances."

Chapter 11 • Wrongful Death and Survival

❏ Wrongful death and survival claims are usually matters of state statutory law.

❏ Survival claims allow recovery for damages suffered by the injured party for the period of time between the injury and death of that person.

❏ Wrongful death claims allow recovery of damages that are suffered due to the death of the person. They are usually figured based upon the date of death and run to the normal life expectancy.

❏ The usual proper party plaintiffs are the representatives of the estate of the deceased.

❏ Wrongful death damages usually include the loss of future income that the deceased would have earned. It may also include such things as funeral expenses and administration of the estate.

❏ Survival damages include all of those damages that the deceased could have recovered had the deceased lived. They include the ordinary medical bills, pain and suffering, and lost wages from the time of injury to the time of death. Those damages may also include loss of consortium of any spouse.

❏ The wrongful death and survival statutes will usually specify who will receive the award. It usually includes spouses and children first.

Chapter 12 • Defenses to Negligence

❏ At common law, contributory negligence on the part of the plaintiff barred the plaintiff's recovery.

❏ Only Alabama, Maryland, North Carolina, Virginia, and Washington, D.C., still bar recovery if the plaintiff was contributorily negligent.

❏ Even in a state where contributory negligence is no longer a bar, these elements still form the basis for comparing plaintiff's behavior with the defendant.

❏ If the plaintiff violated no duty, acted reasonably, or was not the cause in fact or proximate cause of his or her own injury, then the jury will have nothing to compare when it compares negligence of the parties.

❏ In common law jurisdictions, to avoid the harsh consequences of the contributory negligence bar, the courts developed the doctrine of last clear chance, (LCC).

❏ As the LCC doctrine has evolved, the jury was asked to distinguish between an inattentive plaintiff and a helpless plaintiff, and the inattentive plaintiff is given less protection from the defendant's negligence than the helpless plaintiff.

❏ At common law, the defense of assumption of risk (AR) by a plaintiff also operated as a complete bar.

❏ AR could be expressed or implied. If implied it could be primary or secondary.

❏ While most comparative negligence jurisdictions have done away with AR as a complete defense, if plaintiff's conduct is expressed, or if it is implied, and "primary," or knowing, it may bar the plaintiff's recovery altogether, because the defendant is then held not to have a duty that runs to the plaintiff.

❏ In sports injury cases, for example, if the plaintiff impliedly consented to the risk of injuries that ordinarily can occur in that sport, the plaintiff's recovery will be barred.

❏ Statutes of limitation run from the time of the tort, including the reasonable discovery of injury, while statutes of repose run from some other fixed point, like the signing of a contract or the completion of the construction of a building.

❏ While charitable immunity has receded with the prevalence of insurance, family immunity can yet raise its head where children seek to sue their parents for negligence, often barring the suit.

❏ In cases where a child plaintiff and his parents sue a third party, and the parents are also negligent, the court may not allow the parents' negligence to be imputed to the child, especially where the parents are immune from suit from the child.

❏ Governmental immunity was expanding when municipal bankruptcies started to occur, but with tort reform, and the doing away with joint and several liability, governmental immunity has returned to its roots; and, again, turns on the nature of the government's actions: whether an act involves governmental discretion, or a proprietary function.

Chapter 13 • Vicarious Liability

❏ "Vicarious liability" refers to situations in which the tort liability of one person (i.e., the "active" tortfeasor) will be imputed to another person (i.e., the "responsible" tortfeasor) even though the "responsible" tortfeasor is otherwise not at fault in actually causing the plaintiff's injury.

❏ "Vicarious liability" is indirect (as opposed to direct liability) whereby the liability of one tortfeasor is imputed (or transferred) to another for reasons of public policy based solely upon the nature of the relationship that exists between the two tortfeasors rather than on the basis of any legal "fault" of the defendant.

❏ Although plaintiffs will often assert claims based upon both "direct" and "indirect" liability against the defendant, it is usually preferable in most situations to establish direct liability, since such claims are generally more "culpable" and, as such, typically result in greater damage awards.

❏ The doctrine of *respondeat superior* refers to a special category of cases in which vicarious liability is imputed against an employer for injuries to the plaintiff that have been tortiously inflicted by an employee while acting within the "scope of employment."

❏ In determining whether an employee is acting within the "scope of employment," various special situations must be taken into account.

❏ Under the "going and coming rule," some courts have declined to impute "vicarious liability" against the employer in situations involving injuries inflicted upon third parties by employees who are merely en route to (or from) their regular places of employment.

❏ However, courts have recognized a number of special exceptions. Among the most common of these exceptions, are situations
   • Where the employee while traveling to or from the place of employment is (either expressly or impliedly) rendering a "*special service*" to which the employer has consented; or
   • Where the employee while traveling to or from the place of employment is rendering some "*incidental benefit*" to the employer that is not otherwise common to ordinary commuting; or
   • Where the employee while traveling to or from the place of employment is actually subjected to some "*special hazard*" not common to ordinary commutes.

❏ A "detour" refers to a minor deviation from the employee's regular employment duties that still sufficiently relates to the employer's business to justify imputing "vicarious liability" to the employer for injuries inflicted upon the plaintiff by the employee, whereas a "frolic" is generally classified as a departure from the employee's "scope of employment" that is completely unrelated to the employment and is of a purely personal nature, for which the employer will not be vicariously liable.

❏ Ordinarily, where an employee commits intentionally tortious acts that cause injury to the plaintiff, such actions are usually considered to be outside the "scope of employment."

❏ Under the "dual purpose" doctrine vicarious liability may still be imputed to the employer even for an employee's intentionally tortious acts if at least part of the employee's actions were intended to further the employer's business.

❏ Although vicarious liability has generally been permitted in regard to the recovery of ordinary *compensatory* damages by a plaintiff who sustains an injury due to the misconduct of the defendant's employee while acting within the "scope of employment," many courts have declined to apply the doctrine of *respondeat superior* to justify vicariously imposing liability for separate punitive damages against the employer.

❏ Under the "complicity theory," punitive damages have been vicariously imputed against an employer for the aggravated tortious misconduct of an employee arising when the employer has become directly involved in authorizing or subsequently ratifying certain types of aggravated misconduct by employees.

❏ By definition, an independent contractor is someone who performs work for hire for the defendant, but who is not considered to be an employee.

❏ Traditionally, any person who hired an "independent contractor" could not be held vicariously liable for injuries that were tortiously inflicted onto the plaintiff by the independent contractor.

❏ This rule, however, is subject to numerous exceptions whereby vicarious liability can still be imputed against the employer of an independent contractor for injuries sustained by the plaintiff. Among these exceptions are situations where:

 • The work to be performed is "intrinsically dangerous"; or
 • The work subjects the worker to a "peculiar risk" that is different from the ordinary risks associated with the activity in question; or
 • The employer has a legally non-delegable duty to perform the work in question.

❏ A joint venture involves a special relationship among two or more persons with respect to a single business activity (that is usually undertaken for profit), whereas a joint enterprise involves a similar relationship among two or more persons with respect to a non-business related activity.

❏ While each individual participant in both a joint venture as well as a joint enterprise can be vicariously liable for injuries tortiously inflicted onto third persons by any other members, in a joint venture each member *also* owes a duty of care *directly* to each other member of the joint venture (whereas no similar duty is owed to one another among individual members of a joint enterprise).

❏ Both joint ventures as well as joint enterprises basically share at least the following minimum requirements:

 • Some type of agreement (either express or implied) among all of the participants in the activity in question;

- A common purpose; and
- An equal "right of control" over the activity involved.

❏ As distinguished from a joint venture, a partnership generally involves an ongoing, long-term business relationship between two or more persons, whereas a joint venture is typically based only upon a single, one-time business transaction.

  - In the case of potential liability incurred by individual members of a partnership for injuries that have been tortiously inflicted onto the plaintiff by any one of the partners, any subsequent tort claims are usually not directed at the partnership itself, since most partnerships are not recognized as separate legal entities that can be sued directly.
  - Instead, any recovery would normally come directly from the assets of the individual partners themselves.

Chapter 14 • Common Law Strict Liability

❏ Strict liability at common law had its birth in the law regarding the keeping of wild animals.

❏ Strict liability attaches both to wild animals and to animals known to be dangerous.

❏ *Rylands v. Fletcher* applied strict liability principles to damage done from the non-negligent escape of water kept artificially on his land by a land owner, and doing harm to a neighbor's land.

❏ Principles announced in *Rylands v. Fletcher* provided the impetus for *Restatement (Second) Torts*, Sections 519 and 520, regarding strict liability for abnormally dangerous activities.

❏ Judge Posner used comment (f) of RESTATEMENT (SECOND) TORTS, Section 520, to place new emphasis upon an examination of whether the exercise of due care would have avoided the accident. Where the exercise of due care would have prevented the accident, strict liability principles are unnecessary and wasteful because they over-deter the actors.

❏ *Res ipsa loquitur* is not the same as strict liability, as it only provides a mechanism for getting past the defendant's motion to dismiss the plaintiff's case, and, depending on the jurisdiction my shift the burden of production.

Chapter 15 • Nuisance

❏ A nuisance may be a public or a private nuisance

❏ A public nuisance is a substantial interference with the public's right to health, safety, comfort and convenience.

❏ Ordinarily a public nuisance action is brought by a public representative.

❏ A private person can bring an action for public nuisance when that private individual suffers an injury that is different in kind.

❏ A private nuisance is the interference with an individual's use and/or enjoyment of land.

❏ Both public and private nuisances may be based on intent, negligence, or strict liability.

❏ Both public and private nuisances must show that the harm exceeds the value of the activity of the defendant.

❏ Plaintiffs may seek damages or injunctions to stop the nuisance.

❏ In order to seek an injunction, the courts will "balance the equities."

❏ The basis of the claim will determine the appropriate defense for an action in nuisance.

  • Intentional nuisances can be defended with the traditional defenses to intentional torts. Those include consent.

  • Negligent nuisances can be defended with the traditional defenses to negligent torts. Those include comparative fault.

  • Strict liability nuisances can be defended with the traditional defenses to strict liability. Those now also include comparative fault.

❏ Moving to the nuisance is not an automatic defense to a nuisance action. It is merely a factor to consider in determining whether there was substantial harm.

Chapter 16 • Products Liability

❏ Products liability deals with the problem of harm caused by defective products.

❏ Liability for harm caused by defective products was originally based on negligence or breach of warranty, but both of these actions were limited by the requirement of privity of contract.

❏ As both negligence and breach of warranty shed the privity limitation in cases involving personal injury, another theory came to the fore: strict products liability.

❏ The policy arguments for strict products liability included:

  • That it would provide a better incentive for manufacturers to take steps to reduce or eliminate product defects;

  • That it would provide a loss shifting and loss spreading function;

- That it would be easier to administer because it would eliminate proof of fault; and
- That it would be easier to administer because it would allow injured victims to sue the manufacturer directly.

❑ Strict products liability is based on the existence of a product defect.

❑ Products have a manufacturing defect when they depart from the manufacturer's intended design.

❑ Products have a design defect when the foreseeable risks posed by the product could have been eliminated by a feasible design change, and the failure to adopt the design change makes the product not reasonably safe.

❑ Products have a warning defect when the manufacturer fails to inform the user of known risks of the product, or fails to instruct the user on how to use the product safely.

❑ A different approach is taken with prescription drugs and medical devices, which are deemed to be unavoidably dangerous but potentially highly beneficial. Here, the most basic obligation is to warn of known risks.

❑ Strict liability is imposed on those in the business of selling products.

- This includes the manufacturer and intermediate sellers such as wholesalers and retailers.
- It has been extended to commercial lessors of products, but not to sellers of used products unless they remanufacture the product or create the impression that the product is as good as new.

❑ Providers of services, especially professionals, are not "sellers" of products incidentally used in performing the service.

❑ Strict products liability does not apply to cases of pure economic loss.

❑ The plaintiff's conduct is now an important consideration in products liability litigation, either as comparative responsibility or as misuse.

Chapter 17 • Defamation

❑ Defamation includes statements that lower the plaintiff's reputation or esteem in the community.

❑ In order to be actionable, not only must a statement be defamatory, it must refer to the plaintiff, must be published, and must cause injury (unless the defamatory statement involves libel or slander *per se*).

❑ In order to be actionable, an allegedly defamatory statement must be untrue.

❏ Defamatory statements may be protected by various privileges, including the judicial, executive, or legislative privileges, or the qualified privilege, or the privilege for fair comment.

❏ Defamation was historically unprotected under the First Amendment.

❏ Defamatory expression may include speech that is facilitative of informed self-government and thus worthy of First Amendment protection.

❏ Today, public officials may not recover for defamation unless they establish actual malice (proof that defendant knew that the statement was false or acted in reckless disregard for truth or falsity).

❏ Today, public figures also may not recover for defamation unless they establish "actual malice."

❏ A public figure is someone who occupies a position of such pervasive power and influence as to be a public figure for all purposes, or who has thrust himself or herself into the forefront of a particular public controversy in order to influence the resolution of the issues involved.

❏ The U.S. Supreme Court allows states to apply a lower standard to private individuals.

❏ Presumed or punitive damages generally may not be recovered absent a showing of "actual malice."

❏ If a defamatory statement does not implicate a matter of public concern, presumed or punitive damages may be recovered without a showing of "actual malice."

❏ The U.S. Supreme Court has not privileged statements of opinion from a defamation claim.

Chapter 18 • Invasion of Privacy

❏ The tort of privacy protects an individual's interest in privacy against intrusion and publication.

❏ There are four distinct aspects of the right of privacy: appropriation of the plaintiff's name or likeness; intrusion into the plaintiff's seclusion or solitude; public disclosure of private embarassing facts; and portrayal of the plaintiff in a false light in the public eye.

❏ Information from public records concerning a matter of public significance may be published, barring a state interest of the "highest order."

❏ Truth has not been established as an absolute defense to a privacy action based upon publication of information taken from public records.

❏ Newsworthiness will be a defense in cases concerning disclosure of private information, provided that the information was lawfully acquired and truthful.

❏ False light privacy claims (except, perhaps, for claims by private individuals) are governed by the "actual malice" standard and newsworthiness considerations.

❏ The right of publicity is violated when a performer's entire act is broadcast without permission.

Chapter 19 • Civil Rights

❏ Traditional common law torts are frequently used when a person's civil rights are violated. These common law torts include assault, battery, false Imprisonment, malicious Prosecution, negligence, vicarious liability, negligent entrustment, and trespass to land.

❏ For actions against federal officers, courts use the duties imposed by the Constitution and create a remedy for the harm that was done.

❏ For actions against state officers, courts use the duties imposed by the Constitution and the action created by the federal statutes under 42 U.S.C 1983.

❏ In order to recover damages for a civil rights violation, the plaintiff must prove the actual harm suffered.

❏ Actions brought under 42 U.S.C. 1983 also allow recovery of attorney's fees under 42 U.S.C. 1987.

Chapter 20 • Misuse of Legal Process

❏ The tort of "malicious prosecution" focuses upon the defendant's motive in *wrongfully initiating* some type of legal action against the plaintiff that was inappropriate from the very beginning, whereas the tort of "abuse of process" involves various types of legal process which, although *properly initiated* against the plaintiff, nevertheless should not have been utilized at all because of the defendant's improper motive in doing so.

❏ In most jurisdictions, the tort of "malicious prosecution" of a criminal action consists of some variations of the following specific requirements:

 • A criminal prosecution initiated by the defendant;
 • A lack of "probable cause" for the criminal prosecution;
 • Common law malice by the defendant;

- A termination of the prosecution in favor of the accused; and
- Damages.

❏ "Common law malice" in the law of torts can refer to any one of several completely different (yet still closely related) legal concepts, including any of the following:
- *Actual malice.* This type of common law malice refers specifically to an actual feeling of hatred, spite, animosity, or ill-will toward the plaintiff;
- *Legal malice.* This type of common law malice is somewhat broader than common law "actual malice," and can also include actions that are motivated by *any* improper or wrongful motive;
- *Malice in law.* Unlike either actual or legal malice, "malice in law" does not require any proof of the defendant's subjective state of mind. Rather, it refers simply to any intentionally tortious action done without any just cause or excuse; or even recklessness.

❏ In most jurisdictions, both "malicious prosecution" and also "abuse of process" require proof of some type of "special injury."

❏ Under this rule the plaintiff must demonstrate that (s)he has sustained some type of actual loss or harm as the result of the defendant's "malicious prosecution" or "abuse of process."

❏ The "guilt in fact" of the accused is a defense to the "malicious prosecution" of a *criminal* action, since the accuser may still be able to prove the accused's guilt under the lesser civil burden of proof based upon the mere preponderance of the evidence.

❏ The intentional tort of "abuse of process" generally consists of three basic requirements:
- Issuance of some type of legal process;
- An ulterior purpose by the defendant; and
- Special damages.

Chapter 21 • Misrepresentation

❏ The basic elements of misrepresentation are:
- A false representation of a material fact;
- Scienter;
- Intent to induce reliance;
- Justifiable reliance;
- Damages.

❏ A representation requires some statement or act to convey an idea. Under most circumstances, silence will not be a representation.

❏ In order to recover, there must be a statement of fact. Opinions and predictions of the future are not recoverable.

❏ Personal injury, property damage and economic losses can be recovered when the claim is based on intent or negligence.

❏ Strict liability misrepresentation is only available for public misrepresentations concerning a product.

❏ The recipient of the statement can recover when there was intent to induce reliance on that party.

❏ When the plaintiff is a third party who heard the statement and relied, that plaintiff can recover for intentional falsehoods when the plaintiff is a member of a foreseeable group.

❏ When the plaintiff is a third party who heard the statement and relied, that plaintiff can recover for a negligent falsehood depending on the rule in the applicable jurisdiction. The possible rules are:

• The *Ultramares* rule: The defendant must have known the purpose, the person and had some linking contact with the plaintiff.

• The Restatement Rule (the group rule): The defendant must have foreseen the general group or class of which the plaintiff was a member.

• The foreseeable plaintiff rule: The defendant is liable if the plaintiff was a foreseeable plaintiff.

❏ The measure of loss when the plaintiff seeks the benefit of bargain (loss of bargain) recovery is the value as represented less the actual value.

❏ The measure of loss when the plaintiff seeks the out of pocket recovery is the amount paid less the actual value.

Chapter 22 • Business Torts

❏ The elements of intentional interference with a contract are:
• Present existence of an enforceable contract;
• Knowledge on the part of the defendant of that contract;
• Malicious, improper, or illegal interference with that contract;
• A breach of that contract;
• Damages to the plaintiff caused by the breach of the contract.

❏ The elements of intentional interference with a prospective economic advantage are:
• Probable economic advantage to be gained in the future;
• Knowledge on the part of the defendant of that relationship;
• Malicious, improper, or illegal interference with that relationship;
• A termination of that relationship;

- Damages to the plaintiff caused by the termination of that relationship.
❑ Justifications for interference with contracts or future advantages include:
  - Fair competition;
  - Protection of the public;
  - Protection of the defendant;
  - Protection of the plaintiff;
  - Public policy.
❑ Bad faith failure to pay an insurance claim allows recovery as if in tort, and that may include punitive damages.
❑ Intellectual property is protected by tort claims in a manner similar to real property and chattels.
❑ Claims for the interference with an intellectual property right usually result in damages for the value of that right.
❑ The infringement of an intellectual property right usually results in the defendant seeking to cause some confusion in the mind of the public.

Index